Practical Blockchains and Cryptocurrencies

Speed Up Your Application Development Process and Develop Distributed Applications with Confidence

Karan Singh Garewal

Apress®

Practical Blockchains and Cryptocurrencies: Speed Up Your Application Development Process and Develop Distributed Applications with Confidence

Karan Singh Garewal
Toronto, ON, Canada

ISBN-13 (pbk): 978-1-4842-5892-7   ISBN-13 (electronic): 978-1-4842-5893-4
https://doi.org/10.1007/978-1-4842-5893-4

Managing Director, Apress Media LLC: Welmoed Spahr
Acquisitions Editor: Spandana Chatterjee
Development Editors: Matthew Moodie, James Markham, and Laura Berendson
Coordinating Editor: Divya Modi

Cover designed by eStudioCalamar

Cover image designed by Pixabay

Distributed to the book trade worldwide by Springer Science+Business Media New York, 233 Spring Street, 6th Floor, New York, NY 10013. Phone 1-800-SPRINGER, fax (201) 348-4505, e-mail orders-ny@springer-sbm.com, or visit www.springeronline.com. Apress Media, LLC is a California LLC and the sole member (owner) is Springer Science + Business Media Finance Inc (SSBM Finance Inc). SSBM Finance Inc is a **Delaware** corporation.

For information on translations, please e-mail booktranslations@springernature.com; for reprint, paperback, or audio rights, please e-mail bookpermissions@springernature.com.

Apress titles may be purchased in bulk for academic, corporate, or promotional use. eBook versions and licenses are also available for most titles. For more information, reference our Print and eBook Bulk Sales web page at http://www.apress.com/bulk-sales.

Any source code or other supplementary material referenced by the author in this book is available to readers on GitHub via the book's product page, located at www.apress.com/9781484258927. For more detailed information, please visit http://www.apress.com/source-code.

Printed on acid-free paper

Dedicated to Sardar Hari Singh Nalwa, the illustrious Khalsa General, and his valiant servitors who kept on crossing this terrifying world ocean, again and again and again. Fluttering like moths ever nearer to the fire. Caring not. Marrying the Messenger of Death. Again and again and again. So that the dream of the Lord of the Falcons may come to pass.

Table of Contents

About the Author

Karan Singh Garewal is an attorney at law in Canada. He has over 20 years of software development experience in C, C++, Go, JavaScript, Node, Ruby/Rails, Python/Django, Vue, PostgreSQL, Cassandra, and MySQL. Aside from being a novice farmer, the author's current interests are in real-time algorithmic trading systems. He is developing a neural network cryptocurrency trading platform on a C++, Cassandra, and Vue stack.

About the Technical Reviewer

 **Prasanth Sahoo** is a thought leader, an adjunct professor, a technical speaker, and a full-time practitioner in Blockchain, Cloud, and Scrum working for Tata Consultancy Services. He has worked on various cloud platforms, including Azure and Google Cloud, and also led the cross-functional teams to achieve the goals using Agile methodologies. He is passionate about driving digital technology initiatives such as Blockchain, Enterprise Architecture, and Agile by handling various community initiatives through coaching, mentoring, and grooming techniques.

He is a working group member in the Blockchain Council, CryptoCurrency Certification Consortium, Scrum Alliance, Scrum Organization, and International Institute of Business Analysis.

Acknowledgments

The publication of this book would not have been possible without the valuable contributions of the Apress team. Thanks guys. I would like to thank Jannat Kaur (*kauress.me*), neurobiologist, who was able to reluctantly emerge from her virtual reality world to do a code review of the Helium source code. Thank you Prasanth Sahoo for your expert technical review of this book. I am particularly grateful to Spandana Chatterjee who guided this book from inception to publication. Nothing would have come to fruition without Spandana's expert guidance. And, of course, thank you Divya Modi. Finally, I would like to thank Baljinder Singh for his selfless assistance, far above and beyond the call of duty.

Introduction

Let me cut to the chase. In this book, we will build a cryptocurrency called Helium from scratch in the Python language. You will learn the key algorithms that are used in blockchain and cryptocurrency applications, and this will help you develop your own applications with confidence in any language.

The *lingua franca* for Helium is Python. It is my impression that many of the developers who are interested in cryptocurrency and blockchain applications have expertise in languages other than Python. In order to make this book accessible to these developers, I have kept the Python language barrier as low as possible. For example, the Helium source code does not use Python classes. In addition, there are eight appendixes to this book which fill in various prerequisites. I have not attempted to follow Python best practices. This is deliberately so by design. The emphasis is on simplicity. The purpose of this book is to equip you with knowledge about the key algorithms that underlie cryptocurrency and blockchain applications.

If you are completely new to Python, you can download my book *Python Rocket Science* (`https://leanpub.com/python_rocket_science`); this book has been used in bootcamps to equip students with Python language expertise in a minimum amount of time. About 70 pages of this book is all that you need to read *Practical Blockchains and Cryptocurrencies*.

The first chapter of this book surveys the history of money and places Bitcoin within this historical context. There are many cryptocurrencies other than Bitcoin that are in circulation. The second chapter discusses some of the more prominent coins in the cryptocurrency ecosystem.

In Chapters 3–5, we will discuss the cryptography that is required for blockchain and cryptocurrency applications. We will take a deep dive into symmetric encryption, cryptographic hashes, and public key cryptography. You do not need any Calculus or Number Theory to go through these three chapters.

Chapter 6 contains a detailed discussion on the theory of blockchains. We will look at the essential characteristics of blockchains and how they are constructed.

In Chapter 7, we start making the Helium cryptocurrency. Helium is modeled after Bitcoin. This chapter specifies the configuration constants for Helium. Chapter 8 implements a blockchain for Helium. In a pattern that will repeat itself to the end of this book, we will validate our Helium source code with unit tests using the *Pytest* unit testing framework. Appendix 3 to this book provides all of the know-how that is required to utilize Pytest effectively. Chapter 9 is a theory chapter that discusses transaction processing in cryptocurrency networks. This chapter contains a detailed discussion of transaction data structures and transaction validation in Bitcoin-like cryptocurrency networks. The next chapter (Chapter 10) discusses Merkle trees, a particularly useful binary tree data structure that can be used to order and validate the transactions in a block. In Chapter 11, we implement all of the source code for transaction processing in Helium.

Helium uses two key-value stores (databases), the *chainstate* key-value store and the *blk_index* store. Both of these stores are *LevelDB* databases. Appendix 2 to this book equips you with the necessary *LevelDB* expertise. Chapter 12 discusses the purpose of these databases in a cryptocurrency application and provides a Python implementation for them in Helium.

Mining is a central feature of cryptocurrency networks that are modeled after Bitcoin. Mining is the process by which new currency units are created and transactions are added to the blockchain. Chapter 13 goes into an extensive discussion on the theory of mining. Mining involves the addition of blocks to a blockchain. The critical insight of Satoshi Nakamoto, the inventor of Bitcoin, was that a consensus as to the order in which blocks should be added to the blockchain could be achieved without the necessity of some central arbitrating body. This is the distributed consensus algorithm. A significant feature of this algorithm is that the validity of transactions does not depend on ordering and prioritizing transactions by time or in any other fashion. In this chapter, we will discuss in minute detail how a cryptocurrency like Helium achieves distributed consensus. In Chapter 14, we implement Python code for Helium mining, and this includes an implementation of the distributed consensus algorithm.

Cryptocurrency applications typically operate on peer-to-peer networks. Transactions and blocks are received from the network and nodes broadcast transactions and blocks onto the network. Chapter 15 of this book shows you how to implement a network interface for a cryptocurrency application. In this chapter, we will implement Python code that lets Helium operate on the localhost network (*127.0.0.x*). This is very useful for developers since we have a fully functioning cryptocurrency ecosystem on a single machine. The generalization to routable Internet addresses is a trivial exercise. This chapter utilizes concurrent mining operations. Appendixes 4 and 6 contain all of the concurrent Python background that you need to understand concurrency in Helium.

Financial applications such as cryptocurrencies need extreme resiliency. Cryptocurrency and blockchain applications must be as simple as possible. The English idiom is *simplicity is the hallmark of truth* (also called *Occam's razor*). Bitcoin and Helium implement this resiliency by using only one essential data structure which is a simple encoded text file which is managed by the host operating system. This file is a block file, and a blockchain is simply the collection of these files. Everything in Helium, including databases, can be rebuilt from these block files. In Chapter 16, we discuss resiliency in cryptocurrency networks and provide an implementation of resiliency for Helium.

Chapter 17 discusses wallet implementations for cryptocurrencies. In this chapter, we provide a simple command-line wallet for Helium. Wallet construction is not particularly difficult from the software developer's viewpoint. The complexity lies in the implementation of a wallet GUI.

Chapter 18 discusses the implementation of a testnet for Helium. A Helium testnet is essentially an implementation of the Helium network discussed in Chapter 15 over a certain IP address space (an overlay network in P2P terminology). The primary distinguishing feature of a testnet is the implementation of a faucet which permits nodes on the network to acquire coins that can then be utilized in transactions.

Finally, Appendix 10 of this book consolidates all of the source code for Helium in one spot. Appendix 9 contains all of the Pytest unit test files for Helium. Appendix 8 consolidates all the data structures used in Helium along with brief descriptions thereof.

Lastly, I would be amiss if I were to neglect in directing your attention to Appendix 7 which contains all of the Python code for constructing a simulated Helium blockchain of arbitrary, user-specified, height. Such a synthetic blockchain is immensely valuable for integration testing as well as examining the evolution of a blockchain when the cryptocurrency has certain characteristics.

CHAPTER 1

A Short History of Money

We are going to embark upon a deep dive into cryptocurrencies and blockchain applications. The canonical blockchain application is bitcoin, the world's first cryptocurrency. It would thus be fitting to survey the history of money and see how bitcoin has radically changed the paradigm for currency creation and distribution. In this chapter, I will present an opinionated history of money from the Neolithic age to the present time and, in particular, I will highlight landmark events in the evolution of money. This chapter will conclude with a brief overview of bitcoin and how it differs from traditional money.

The Neolithic Age

One of the earliest forms of human interaction was the exchange of goods. For example, a transaction could involve exchanging 100 eggs for a blanket or a stone ax for 35 hens. These types of transactions are called barter, and they involve the exchange of commodities between two transacting parties. An object or a commodity acquires value when it has utility (usefulness) and scarcity. Ornaments acquire value because of their beauty and the considerable effort that a skilled artisan has to expend to create them. The expenditure of considerable skill and effort makes ornaments scarce.

There is a fundamental problem with barter; it is an inefficient way to exchange value. For example, if you have an ax that you want to trade for some hens, then you will have to find a person who has some hens available for trade and who wants an ax. Conceivably, there could be no one who satisfies this criterion, in which case an exchange of value cannot be consummated. Furthermore, even if such a person exists, there is the issue of establishing an exchange rate, that is, how many hens should be traded for the ax. This depends on the size and quality of the ax as well as the quality of the hens. Finally, there is a divisibility problem. For example, there could be a person who wants an ax but only has 12 hens to trade. Finally, there is problem that bartered

© Karan Singh Garewal 2020
K. S. Garewal, *Practical Blockchains and Cryptocurrencies*, https://doi.org/10.1007/978-1-4842-5893-4_1

goods are not typically fungible. A thing is fungible if it is indistinguishable from any other thing of the same type. As these examples demonstrate, barter is a very inefficient technique for trade.

Necessity is the mother of invention, and consequently, the inefficiencies of barter produced the requirement of creating an efficient medium of exchange. Money or currency in the form of coins made its first appearance in China during the Neolithic age about 3000–4000 years ago. Money can be thought of as an object which represents a certain amount of value. For example, a metal coin with an ax inscribed on it could symbolically represent the exchange value of an ax. The efficacy of money in any form depends upon its acceptance as symbolically representing value. Such acceptance requires money to be a store of value. That is, if the coin with an ax inscribed on it is exchangeable for 35 hens today, then it should also be exchangeable for 35 hens 90 days hence. By 700 BC, the use of coin money had spread from China into the Indian subcontinent.

Around 210 BC the first Chinese emperor Qin Shi Huang introduced a standardized coin based on copper as the official currency of the first Chinese Empire and abolished other forms of money that were being used locally. It was a brilliant policy because it unified the empire by increasing trade across the breadth of the Empire. This, in turn, led to accelerated economic growth and prosperity in the empire. It was a golden age in China. Since copper was relatively abundant, these copper coins had low value. The acceptance of these coins was cemented by the fact that the treasury of the empire guaranteed the convertibility of the coins into utilitarian objects of value at a fixed rate. The introduction of this coinage had all of the characteristics that we now typically associate with money; they were accepted as a medium of exchange and a store of value, and finally the coins were fungible.

The Emergence of Banks and Banknotes

By the seventh century AD, bearer promissory notes had appeared in China, and they gained rapid adoption. A bearer promissory note is a document wherein the maker of the note promises to pay the bearer of the note a certain amount of money or commodity, either upon demand or at a certain fixed date in the future. Since the promissory note embodied a promise to pay a bearer, the holders of these notes would frequently sign them over to other recipients. Consequently, these notes started to circulate like a modern paper currency. Clearly, the acceptance and negotiability of bearer promissory notes depended upon the reputation of the maker. There must have been very wealthy merchants with stellar reputations whose promissory notes were accepted by the public as money. The rapid expansion in the use of promissory notes led the Tang dynasty to create a treasury that printed promissory notes which were backed by the wealth and prestige of the Empire. This was the first appearance of paper currency in the ancient world. At about the same time, bearer promissory notes made an appearance in India.

Hawala

The appearance of demand promissory notes on the Indian subcontinent led to a significant innovation. Previously, the exchange of value required the participants of a transaction to both be present at the time the transaction was consummated. Hawala (called Hundi in India) eliminated the need for participants to be present to consummate a transaction. In other words, value could be exchanged between parties far removed from each other. Hawala is believed to have been instrumental in the development of the ancient Silk Road from China to Venice.

The manner in which Hawala works is as follows. A transactor gives a person called a *hawaladar* value (say, some coins or a demand promissory note) and orders him to pay this value to a person in some remote city. The hawaladar contacts a hawaladar in the remote city and orders him to pay the intended recipient. At the end of the month or some other agreed-upon settlement date, the two hawaladars settle accounts among themselves. Notice that the order given to the second hawaladar is not accompanied by the transfer of value to him. Indeed, if the two hawaladars have equal amounts owing to each other on the settlement date, no value will be transferred by them when they settle their accounts *interse*.

If the recipient lived in a city very far away, several hawaladars could be involved in the transaction and the hawaladars would settle accounts between themselves periodically.

There are several aspects of Hawala which should be noticed. Firstly, it is based on a chain of trust. Secondly, value can be transferred between traders in remote locations without any money being transferred between the participating hawaladars themselves. For example, if traders in Peking used a hawaladar to order goods worth one million *Ban Liang* from traders in Shanghai during a settlement period and traders in Shanghai used a hawaladar to order goods worth 900,000 *Ban Liang* from traders in Peking, then the hawaladar in Peking would only need to transfer 100,000 *Ban Liang* to the hawaladar in Shanghai on the settlement date. The last aspect of Hawala worth noting is that it largely bypasses the modern commercial banking system.

The Roman Empire and the Origins of Inflation

There is one singular lesson to be learned from the history of currency in the Roman Empire. That lesson is how the debasement of coinage causes hyperinflation. There is also a secondary lesson: how an over-extended empire is forced to debase its currency and thus becomes the instrument of its own destruction.

Roman coins were made from a variety of metals, including silver, lead, iron, and copper. The standard coin of the empire was the *denarius*. The *denarius* was a 4.5-gram coin composed almost entirely of silver, meaning that it was a coin with at least 95% purity in silver. Silver was a relatively scarce metal in the Roman Empire, and considerable effort was required to mine it. The denarius cemented trade through the breadth of the vast Roman Empire and was widely accepted and circulated primarily due to the purity of the coin and the power and prestige of the Roman Empire. Not only was the denarius a stellar coin for facilitating trade but it was perceived as an excellent store of value.

However, the maintenance of the ever-expanding Roman Empire was a very expensive proposition. There were numerous cost impositions on the Roman treasury. For example, nearly 50,000 miles of roads were constructed to bind the empire, numerous aqueducts and public works were built, the Roman legions had to be well paid, the city of Rome had a population in excess of one million people, and the maintenance of the city was a considerable drain on the Roman treasury. Finally, trade accounts with distant countries such as India had to be settled. The trade between Rome and India was estimated to involve approximately 200 ships a year.

The problem confronting the Roman treasury was that the costs of the Roman Empire could not be sustained by taxation and the plunder of conquered territories alone. Rome did not have financial institutions or mechanisms for financing government deficits and debt. Thus, there were only three ways to finance government expenditures: increase the taxation level, increase the supply of silver, or debase the denarius. The Roman Empire itself contained only a few silver mines, so the production of silver could not be easily increased. Increased taxation was infeasible, so the Roman emperors started to debase the denarius. The drain of silver from Rome to India through trade deficits is believed to have been one of the major causes for the debasement of the denarius. At the time of Julius Caesar, the denarius was only 75% pure silver, and by the advent of the third century, its purity had declined to about 5%. This debasement had disastrous consequences and caused hyperinflation in the Empire. Trade collapsed as traders lost faith in the denarius. Traders and foreign mercenaries in the employ of Rome demanded payment in gold only. The Roman legions became weak and demoralized as the denarius became a worthless currency. The debasement of the denarius is proof that Rome could not bear the costs of maintaining its empire. The end of Rome is well known; Germanic and Hunnish barbarians from Asia repeatedly attacked the empire itself, and the last emperor to sit on the throne of Rome was a barbarian. The debasement of the denarius can be construed to be one of the major causes of the collapse of the empire.

Gold and the Plunder of the New World

The art, literature, and intellectual grandeur of Rome did not survive its collapse. Europe was plunged into a dark age lasting a thousand years as religious fanaticism and Christian superstition gripped the continent. By the early sixteenth century, Spain had colonized portions of the new world and was mining gold and silver using the aboriginal inhabitants as slave labor.

The prevailing economic theory at this time was called mercantilism. The foundational principle of mercantilism was that the wealth of a nation was measured by the amount of gold, silver, and other precious metals that were held in its treasury. In addition to spurring the search for gold and silver, this theory also led to the imposition of customs duties and other barriers that restricted the flow of trade between nations.

The Spanish incursion into the new world led to the mining and transportation of large quantities of gold and silver from the new world into Europe. About 10–20% of this gold and silver is presumed to have been looted by privateers acting under charters granted by the English Crown and buccaneers operating under pirate flags.

Spain used this influx of precious metals to build magnificent cathedrals, execute vanity projects, and most importantly finance wars for the benefit of the Church of Rome. The influx of gold and silver from the new world permitted Spain to maintain the largest army in Europe, build a large navy, and finance wars against England, France, The Netherlands, the German principalities, the Ottoman Empire, as well as non-Catholics who were viewed as heretics.

One of the immediate effects of the influx of gold and silver into Spain was to cause widespread inflation in Europe. In Spain, prices are believed to have increased by 300% over the sixteenth century. Spain had a primitive agrarian economy that did not benefit in large from the plunder of gold and silver from the new world. Spain had a disdain for commerce as a human endeavor and viewed it as having limited religious and ethical merit. Consequently, Spain became increasingly dependent upon the influx of precious metals to finance the extravagant imperial and religious misadventures of the King. The Spanish Exchequer being primarily reliant on the looting of gold and silver from the new world went into bankruptcy four times in the sixteenth century in the years 1557, 1560, 1576, and 1596. These sovereign bankruptcies were a clear indication that there was no taxation base of significance in Spain. Eventually, Spain lost its apex position in Europe, and by 1750, it was a backwater.

The Gold Standard

As Spain receded from the stage of world history, Britain began to emerge as the predominant power in Europe. Britain was a trading nation with a large and sophisticated merchant class and also valued the benefit of trade between nations. In addition, England had been at the forefront of the Protestant reformation and adhered to the Calvinist doctrine that the performance of everyday work had substantial religious value. In 1776, Adam Smith wrote *The Wealth of Nations* which demonstrated the fallacy of mercantilism and showed that free trade could be a nonzero-sum game in which each participant in trade could benefit due to the theory of comparative advantage. Adam Smith also introduced the concept of the division of labor and its benefits. *The Wealth of Nations* espouses the benefits of free markets and free trade and marks the starting point of modern economic theory. At this time, England also started to develop a sophisticated law of contract and the stellar innovation of joint-stock companies which allowed large amounts of risk capital to be raised efficiently. The invention of the joint-stock company kick-started the industrial revolution. Starting at the end of the eighteenth century, Britain embarked upon a century of colonial expansion.

In 1844, the British Parliament passed the *Bank Charter Act*, wherein the Bank of England promised to redeem its banknotes at a fixed rate into gold specie. This established a gold standard across the British Empire as well as in the United States, Canada, Australia, and other countries which had extensive trade relations with Britain. It also established the pound sterling as the world's reserve currency. Trading nations were content to use the pound sterling in trade and hold reserves thereof since they had the assurance that their currency holdings could be converted into gold. Gold is a precious metal in scarce supply, and the promise of redeem ability of banknotes issued by the Bank of England into gold at a fixed rate effectively constrained the ability of England or any other country adhering to the gold standard to print paper currency at will. A country printing its currency in excess of its gold and sterling reserves faced the possibility of a run on its currency as speculators converted their holdings of the currency into pound sterling or gold.

The enormous costs of World War I on the English Exchequer led Britain to impose exchange controls; this effectively suspended the convertibility of its currency into gold. Many European countries followed in lockstep and abandoned the convertibility of their currencies into gold. The effect of this was to cause massive inflation as the costs of World War I were financed by simply printing large quantities of paper currency to pay off the debt. In other words, the cost of World War I was passed on to the population by increasing the money supply. This meant that the costs of World War I were borne by the population of Europe through inflation. It is well known that inflation causes fixed income assets, such as bonds, to decrease in value. In 1925, Britain returned to the gold standard in order to preserve the status of the pound sterling as the reserve currency of the world. It would prove to be a short-lived effort.

The Great Depression and Keynesian Economics

On September 4, 1929, the stock market on Wall Street faltered and dropped significantly. Over the next month and a half, the stock market oscillated wildly indicating significant uncertainty among investors and speculators. Then on October 29, 1929 (Black Tuesday), the Dow Jones Industrial Average on the New York Stock Exchange plummeted by 20%. It was the beginning of the great depression, and it plunged the world into an unprecedented economic depression that lasted a decade. Industrial output in the United States declined by nearly 40%, trade collapsed by some 70%, and unemployment climbed to 25% of the population.

The impact on Britain and Europe was similar. Britain abandoned the gold standard fearing a run on the pound sterling. The foremost economic problem of the day was how to climb out of the great depression and get the world economy moving. There were two diametrically opposed points of view, the American Hooverites advocated fiscal conservatism and the need for governments to scale back their expenditures in order to prevent any further increases in the public debt. Opposing them was the great English economist, John Maynard Keynes, who argued in his book *The General Theory of Employment, Interest and Money* that increased public expenditures on public works should be undertaken to provide employment and increase production in the economy. The basic premise of Keynesian economics was that the increase in public debt would be paid for by the increase in tax revenue once the economy climbed out of the depression. This is the basic principle of Keynesian economics; public expenditures should be increased during recessions and depressions, and the public debt so incurred will be paid off when the economy recovers due to the increase in tax revenue. President Roosevelt's economic plan to bootstrap the American economy out of the depression was an exercise in Keynesian economics.

Implicit in Keynesian economics is the idea that the supply of money should not be tied to a standard guaranteeing the convertibility of the currency into gold or any other precious specie, that is, the government should be free to print money or incur public debt as required to maintain full employment. It's a neat theory, but as history has repeatedly demonstrated, the power to print money at will is like a dangerous and highly addictive drug that ultimately destroys the patient.

The Petrodollar System

The conclusion of World War II saw Europe shattered and the United States emerged as the sole economic powerhouse in the world. In 1944, the United States and European signatories assented to the Bretton Woods Agreement wherein the signatory countries agreed to peg their currencies to the US dollar at a fixed rate and the United States agreed to redeem the US currency holdings of any foreign central bank at the rate of 35 dollars for an ounce of gold. At this juncture in history, the United States held most of the world's gold. This agreement replaced the pound sterling with the US dollar as the reserve currency of the world. Bretton Woods also effectively established a gold standard across the world with the United States as the guarantor of the standard. The promise of convertibility at the rate of 35 dollars for an ounce of gold as well as the rapidly expanding American military and industrial power established the US dollar as the primary instrument to facilitate international trade.

Problems started to appear 18 years later as the United States got embroiled in the Vietnam War. The United States started to have persistent balance of payment deficits with its trading partners. In addition, the treasury had to grapple with the extensive war expenditures incurred by the Vietnam War and inflation. In 1971, Britain losing faith in the stability of the US dollar redeemed most of its US dollar holdings into gold. Fearing a run of the dollar triggered by Britain's actions and in order to protect US gold reserves from depletion, President Nixon suspended the convertibility of the US dollar into gold. This action converted the US dollar into a fiat currency. A fiat currency is a currency that is not convertible into gold or any other precious asset, and the value derives solely from the willingness of users to utilize it as a medium of exchange and a store of value.

The Treasury of the United States realized that with the US dollar off the gold standard, there was in principle no compelling reason for nations to use it in trade or as an international reserve currency. It was thus important to compel the use of the dollar as an international reserve currency rather than relying on the good faith of nations to continue using a fiat US dollar. This is the problem that the Petrodollar system solved.

Starting in 1974, the United States and oil-producing countries came to agreements to sell oil on international markets in US dollars only. The immediate effect of this was to require countries that wanted to purchase oil to maintain an adequate amount of dollar reserves. Such a country could obtain these reserves in two ways, either by selling goods to the United States and receiving dollars on its foreign exchange account, or by doing the same with a third country. There was an implicit supposition in the Petrodollar system that most US dollars circulating abroad would never return home – a supposition which was largely true if the world economy kept on expanding. Since these dollars would not return home, this effectively meant that the United States could purchase goods and services from countries for free (i.e., by simply printing dollars or dollar-denominated debt). Furthermore, since the dollar was not on a gold standard, the US Federal Reserve System was not constrained in its ability to print dollars at will. At present, the federal debt of the United States is in the range of 26 trillion dollars. This is a consequence of imperial overreach, unconstrained government spending, primarily on the military; a weak tax base that cannot sustain the recurring government expenses, the non-convertibility of the dollar, and the Petrodollar system.

Prior to the Petrodollar system, a currency acquired status as an international reserve currency through the guarantee of the maker to convert it into gold specie at some fixed rate. A country not wishing to hold the reserve currency could simply convert its currency holdings into gold. The Petrodollar system has replaced this with a compulsion. A country wanting to buy oil has to have fiat US dollars on hand to make such a purchase.

Making Money in a Fractional Banking System

Throughout the course of history, the power to create money has been viewed as a sovereign prerogative. For example, only the Roman emperor had the right to create denarius coins. So it might come as a surprise to you that in the modern world most of a nation's money is not created by the treasury but by banks. This is a consequence of the fractional reserve banking system.

In fractional reserve banking, a bank is required by law to hold a certain percentage of its deposits on hand to cover withdrawal requests. This is called the reserve requirement. Let's look at how a hypothetical bank can create money *ex nihilo* (out of nothing). Suppose we have a bank called Bank of Ontario which has initially no deposits or liabilities and has a statutory reserve requirement of 10%. A customer comes in and deposits one million dollars. The position of the Bank of Ontario is now as shown in Table 1-1.

Table 1-1. *Bank Position*

Total Deposits	$1,000,000	Loans Made	$0
Reserve Requirement	$ 100,000	Available to Lend	$900,000

The Bank of Ontario lends $900,000 to a borrower, and this borrower deposits the loan amount with the Bank of Ontario. The financial position of the Bank of Ontario is now as shown in Table 1-2.

Table 1-2. *Bank Position*

Total Deposits	$1,900,00	Loans Made	$900,000
Reserve Requirement	$190,000	Available to Lend	$810,000

Notice that the amount of funds that the bank can lend is

```
Amount Available for Loans = Total Deposits - Reserve Requirement - Loans Made
```

The Bank of Ontario now lends $810,000 to a customer who again deposits it with the bank. The financial position of the bank is now as shown in Table 1-3.

Table 1-3. *Bank Position*

Total Deposits	$2,710,000	Loans Made	$1,710,000
Reserve Requirement	$271,000	Available to Lend	$729,000

Notice that at this stage the bank has created an extra $1,710,000 of money (deposits with the bank) from the initial $1,000,000 deposit.

And if we continue in this manner, the Bank of Ontario can keep on making loans (money) up to a theoretical maximum amount dictated by the money multiplier:

```
Initial Deposit/Reserve Requirement
```

What this means is that if the bank receives a deposit of one million dollars, it can create up to ten million dollars in deposits (money) and derive the interest income from these loans.

If the bank charges an interest rate of 6% per annum on its loans to customers, it will derive a maximum interest income of $600,000 per annum. As you can appreciate, the ownership of a bank in a fractional reserve banking system is a very profitable proposition.

The adherents of the Austrian School of Economics (Friedrich Hayek, Ludwig von Mises, Ron Paul, etc.) posit that fractional reserve banking is inherently unstable and gives rise to boom-bust cycles, and furthermore, it is a form of legalized theft since it gives a preferential class the power to create purchasing power (money) out of nothing.

In monetary theory, M1 is defined as coins, paper currency, as well as other financial instruments that are as liquid as money; these include demand deposits at banks, travelers' checks, and so forth. M2 includes instruments that cannot be readily converted into money, such as bank savings deposits, 30-day treasury bills, money market funds, and so forth. M2 is comprised of instruments that take a short, fixed amount of time to convert into M1 specie.

It should thus not surprise you that most of M1 is composed of bank demand deposits.

Essential Monetary Economics

Let's take a brief look at the *Equation of Exchange*, which is a basic equation in monetary economics. This equation is represented as follows:

$$MV = PT$$

The Equation of Exchange is computed by reference to a fixed period of time, say, a year. M is the supply of money or M1. V is the velocity of money or the average number of times a unit of the currency circulates during the fixed period of time. Except in regimes of hyperinflation, we expect V to vary only slightly. The reason for this is that individual spending and savings habits are relatively stable over time. P is the price level in the economy, and T is the amount of transactions in the economy in the fixed time period. T is not the monetary value of the transactions in the economy but an independent index measure of the physical or real output in the economy.

The first thing to understand is that the Equation of Exchange is a tautology; it is always true. Secondly, this equation shows the relationship between the supply of money, the price level, and real output in the economy. For example, if the supply of money is increased but physical output does not increase at all, then the increased supply of money will be reflected entirely by price inflation. Similarly, if the money supply is held constant but physical production increases, there will be price deflation, that is, holdings of M1 will become more valuable.

Bitcoin Comes onto the Scene

By 2008, a multi-polar international system was emerging. The American economy was saddled with nearly ten trillion dollars of debt, and the convertibility of the dollar into gold had been relegated to a footnote in history. The position of the dollar as an international reserve currency was premised not upon a promise of convertibility and the prestige and soft power of the United States but by the compulsion of the Petrodollar system and military power.

In 2008, Satoshi Nakamoto published the white paper *Bitcoin: A Peer-to-Peer Electronic Cash System* on the cryptography mailing list *Metzdowd*. This paper laid out the theoretical foundations for a completely decentralized currency on the Internet. On January 3, 2009, Nakamoto released the first version of Bitcoin and mined the first block of bitcoins called the genesis block. Shortly thereafter, Satoshi Nakamoto, who is in all likelihood a pseudonym for one or several authors, disappeared from public view. In the remainder of this book, I shall use the word Bitcoin in the proper case to refer to the Bitcoin ecosystem and bitcoin in the lowercase to refer to the cryptocurrency itself.

Bitcoin has several critical features that distinguish it from traditional fiat currencies. Firstly, it is a purely decentralized digital currency that operates on the Internet. By digital, I mean that bitcoin does not have a tangible physical form such as a coin or a paper currency. The decentralized nature of bitcoin is a very important feature; bitcoin does not rely upon any centralized servers or points of control. Thus, it is theoretically immune to attempts to shut it down. Bitcoin is also a peer-to-peer network, and transactions on the Bitcoin network are consummated directly by the transacting parties without the necessity of an intermediary third party. This second factor removes banking institutions as players in the bitcoin ecosystem.

In conventional fiat money systems, banks play a critical role in recording and validating transactions. Bitcoin records transactions in a distributed ledger which no entity can control. Furthermore, this ledger can be examined by anyone to verify transactions. Time plays an important role in validating transactions in a conventional fiat money banking system. Transaction validity depends in part on the sequence in which transactions occur over time. Bitcoin does not have a concept of time, and in particular, transaction validity does not depend on the sequence in which transactions occur over time. This is a critical innovation; Bitcoin can reach a distributed consensus on transaction validity without relying on a clock or transactions occurring in a specific order over time or by using any central supernode.

In the Bitcoin ecosystem, transactions are validated only by cryptographic algorithms and through distributed consensus. In his white paper, Satoshi Nakamoto solved an important theoretical problem: how can one form consensus in a distributed system? We will spend quite a bit of time looking at distributed consensus algorithms since they are a critical component of cryptocurrencies as well as many blockchain applications.

In a conventional banking system, trust is an important element in the operation of the system. You deposit money in a bank or utilize its services because you trust the integrity of the bank. Bitcoin is based on a trustless model. The validation of transactions in the system does not require any entity to be trusted.

Transactions in a conventional fiat banking system are not anonymous. The details of any transaction are available to the transacting banks and any concerned authorities. In contrast, bitcoin is a pseudo-anonymous system. The level of pseudo-anonymity can be increased using mixers and other devices. In the alternative, we can use a truly anonymous currency such as Monero. Monero is a bitcoin-like currency with strong guarantees of anonymity.

In contrast to conventional banking systems, transactions in the bitcoin system are immutable and cannot be reversed. The public ledger in which bitcoin transactions are recorded is an immutable ledger which anyone can examine. The severity of immutable transactions can be mitigated by using escrow mechanisms that are available in Bitcoin. Bitcoin escrow permits values to be held conditionally pending transaction completion.

The last factor distinguishing Bitcoin from fiat money systems is that transaction costs are much lower and transactions can be consummated in a matter of minutes.

Any currency on the Internet whose transactions are not consummated peer to peer or those currency creation mechanisms are under the control of a centralized entity is not properly a cryptocurrency.

If we apply the Equation of Exchange to a world economy where only bitcoins are present and physical output is increasing over time, then the price level will be decreasing if the velocity of bitcoins remains more or less constant, that is, the value of a bitcoin must increase over time. To rephrase this, the Bitcoin monetary system is inherently deflationary; it protects and enhances the value of bitcoin holdings over time. Contrast this with the US dollar. Since December 23, 1913 (the date on which the US Federal Reserve Bank was created), the US dollar has experienced a cumulative inflation of nearly 2500% as of 2020. In other words, the current value of one US dollar is only 1/2500th of its value in 1913.

Fiat currencies can be printed at will, and in consequence, any notion of the scarcity of a fiat currency is an artificial contrivance. In contrast, bitcoin and similar cryptocurrencies build in scarcity by limiting the total number of cryptocurrency units that can be created. As indicated previously, this also has the effect of making the currency deflationary.

Bitcoin has already achieved status as a medium of exchange. But it is being used primarily for two purposes: firstly as a store of value or more properly as a long-term hedge against the US dollar and secondly to speculate against the stability of the dollar. The conservative consensus is that the Petrodollar system will eventually collapse in the emerging multi-polar world, and as the military power of the United States is equalized, the massive debt overload of the United States (some 26 trillion dollars as of the time of writing) will severely diminish international confidence in the dollar. Furthermore, the price inflation of 2500% over the period from 1913 to 2020 demonstrates that the increase in the US money supply has far exceeded the increase in the real output of the

United States. The weakening dollar will have two long-term consequences: firstly a flight from the dollar into scarce real resources such as land and secondly a flight into liquid hedges such as gold, silver, precious objects, and cryptocurrencies. These factors have led many speculators to the conclusion that bitcoin is a good long-term hedge against the US dollar.

The reader can note that bitcoin is attempting to play the same role as gold in a gold standard regime. In such a regime, an entity holding a currency is free to convert it into gold if his or her confidence in the currency weakens. Bitcoin provides speculators with the same option; they can divest themselves of their fiat currency holdings and hold bitcoin as a hedge against the instability of the fiat currency.

The characteristics of bitcoin constitute a threat to the stability and presumed legitimacy of conventional fiat currencies, and in consequence, there is a concerted effort by governments across the world to control or criminalize the propagation of bitcoin. Aside from the fact that bitcoin impinges upon the presumed sole sovereign prerogative of a government to create money, what concerns authorities is the constraints imposed upon their fiat currencies by their convertibility into bitcoin. One of the main avenues to control the diffusion of bitcoin into the fiat money system is the control or prohibition of the conversion of fiat currencies into bitcoin.

Table 1-4 summarizes the difference between bitcoin and fiat currencies.

Table 1-4. *Differences between Bitcoin and fiat currency systems*

	Bitcoin	**Fiat Currency System**
Centralized	No	Yes
Currency is scarce	Yes	No
Currency creation	Mathematical algorithm (mining)	Central bank
Trust is required	No	Yes
Transactions require financial institutions	No (peer to peer)	Yes
Transactions are irrevocable	Yes (escrow available)	No
Transactions are anonymous	Pseudo-anonymous	No
Transaction completion time	Very fast	Slow
Transaction costs	Low	High

The Darknet

The emergence of Bitcoin as a near money has also expanded the scope of the Darknet. The Darknet can be described as an overlay of encrypted nodes on the Internet which requires a specific protocol to access it. The largest component of the Darknet are peer-to-peer file sharing systems that distribute copyrighted material (principally movies). This segment of the Darknet relies primarily upon the BitTorrent protocol. Pirate Bay nodes are a significant player in this segment of the Darknet. The second important component of the Darknet is its role as a virtual marketplace for contraband. This aspect of the Darknet relies upon two facets: firstly bypassing the conventional banking system by transacting only in bitcoin or some other cryptocurrency and secondly the utilization of the TOR (The Onion Router) network to encrypt and hide the activities of transacting parties. TOR relies upon public key encryption, which we will study in detail in a subsequent chapter.

Conclusion

In this chapter, we have surveyed the history of money from the Neolithic age to the emergence of bitcoin. In the course of our historical excursion, we have studied coinage in the Roman Empire, the gold standard, and the Petrodollar system. We have also explained how the fractional reserve banking system works and the equation of money. We concluded our survey by looking at the emergence of Bitcoin and the main characteristics which differentiate it from money.

In the next chapter, we will look at the cryptocurrency ecosystem in greater detail.

References

Duncan-Jones, R., Money and Government in the Roman Empire, Cambridge University Press, 1998

Federal Reserve Bank of Chicago, Modern Money Mechanics: A Workbook on the Bank Reserves and Deposit Expansion, CreateSpace Independent Publishing Platform, 2015

Kemmerer E., Gold and the Gold Standard, Mises Institute, Creative Commons, 2009

Skinner, C., The Future of Banking in a Globalized World, John Wiley & Sons, Ltd., 2007

Spiro, David E., The Hidden Hand of American Hegemony Petrodollar Recycling and American Markets, 1st ed., Cornell University Press, 1999

Beatson, J., Burrows A., Cartwright J., Anson's Law of Contract, 29th ed., Oxford University Press, 2010

Nakamoto, S., Bitcoin: A Peer-to-Peer Electronic Cash System, last accessed on December 5, 2019, http://satoshinakamoto.me/bitcoin.pdf

CHAPTER 2

The Cryptocurrency Ecosystem

In the previous chapter, we surveyed the history of money and discussed how bitcoin changes the paradigm for currency creation and distribution. We also saw how bitcoin transactions differ from transactions in a conventional fiat money system. The advent of Bitcoin has spawned a large number of cryptocurrencies which are similar in varying degrees to it. They differ from Bitcoin in their characteristics, such as the total number of coins that can be produced, the speed and manner in which transactions are consummated, as well as the manner in which the cryptocurrency reaches consensus as to which transactions are valid. Furthermore, as we will see subsequently in this chapter, many cryptocurrencies are designed to handle domain-specific use cases.

In this chapter, we will review the characteristics of some of the more prominent alternate cryptocurrencies (called altcoins), such as Ethereum, Bitcoin Cash, Litecoin, Ripple, Binance Coin, Basic Attention Token, TRON, Monero, and Tether. If you are completely new to the cryptocurrency ecosystem, you may not understand some of the terminology used in this chapter. Do not let this detract you; you can come back to this chapter after reading some of the subsequent chapters.

Before we proceed further, recall that in order for a currency to be properly classified as a cryptocurrency, it must have the following two essential characteristics: firstly, the process by which the currency is created and distributed must be decentralized, and, secondly, the determination of transaction validity (consensus) must also be decentralized.

© Karan Singh Garewal 2020
K. S. Garewal, *Practical Blockchains and Cryptocurrencies*, https://doi.org/10.1007/978-1-4842-5893-4_2

Ethereum

In terms of capitalization, Ethereum (ETH[1]) is the second most popular cryptocurrency after Bitcoin. Ethereum differs substantially from Bitcoin.

Bitcoin is a value transfer network. The Bitcoin network transfers value (bitcoins) between transacting parties and keeps an accounting of the total value owned by all parties in a distributed ledger called a blockchain. The contract on which the transfer of value is premised is outside the Bitcoin ecosystem. Ethereum is a bit different. Like Bitcoin, Ethereum transfers value between transacting parties; however, the contract which transfers value between entities can be specified on the Ethereum blockchain. Thus, the Ethereum blockchain provides an accounting of the Ether (the Ethereum coin) held by entities and can also encode contracts which transfer value (*ether*) between entities. These contracts are called smart contracts.

Ethereum came on the scene with Vitalik Buterin's white paper in 2014.[2] In this paper, Buterin describes a cryptocurrency ecosystem which permits users to write contracts that can transfer value conditionally at some point in the future. These contracts are coded in a Turing complete language called Solidity. Solidity is a simple language containing control flow and loop constructs. Ethereum uses Solidity to specify conditions under which value is transferred between entities.

A language is called Turing complete if it can simulate all of the operations of a Turing machine. A Turing machine is an abstract machine with the following components. Firstly, there is an infinitely long tape which is divided into a sequence of cells. The machine has an alphabet consisting of a finite number of symbols and a special alphabetic character called a blank symbol. The machine also has a finite number of states. Each state describes a rule to write to a cell, optionally move to another adjacent cell, and migrate to another state. The machine starts at a certain cell on the tape ("we can say that the tape head is on the cell") and has a certain state. The tape head can read the symbol under the tape head and depending

---

[1]In this chapter, I will denote the exchange symbol for a cryptocurrency that is publicly traded on an exchange by its three-letter ticker symbol.

[2]GitHub, "Ethereum White Paper," https://github.com/ethereum/wiki/wiki/White-Paper, 2014

on the current state write a new symbol to the cell and then move the tape head one cell to the left or the right and go to a new state. For example, state 1 of the machine may have the rule "if the symbol read is 0, then write 1 to the cell and move the head one cell to the left and then go to
state 3." The essential characteristic of a Turing machine is that any computer algorithm can be represented by such a machine. Most computer languages are Turing complete, meaning their syntax can represent any computer algorithm.

Aside from smart contracts, Ethereum provides a platform for developing distributed applications (called DApp(s)). DApp(s) can issue their own cryptocurrencies called tokens. For example, if you want to interact with or use a particular dapp, you may need to buy tokens issued by the dapp. The rules for issuing these tokens are set out in an Ethereum standard called ERC-20.

Finally, note that smart contracts and DApp(s) are executed by the Ethereum Virtual Machine (EVM). A smart contract encoded in Solidity is transpiled to bytecode for execution by the EVM. Note that since Ethereum is a distributed peer-to-peer network, each node in the network maintains its own copy of the EVM.

Bitcoin Cash

We are going to examine the bitcoin mining process in great detail in a subsequent chapter, but for the time being, bear the following description in mind. A block consists of a number of transactions. Miners who mine a block can append this block to the Bitcoin blockchain. The incentive for a miner is that if he successfully mines a block, he will receive a predetermined reward (in bitcoins) for mining the block as well as all of the transaction fees for the transactions included in this block. The mathematical algorithms underlying bitcoin ensure that a block is mined approximately every ten minutes. A block also has a maximum size of 1 MB. This implicitly sets an approximate upper bound on the number of transactions that can be included in a block. This constraint means that Bitcoin is particularly poor at high-volume transaction processing. A transaction is approximately 500 bytes in size, and thus a block can contain approximately 2000 transactions.[3] Thus, the bitcoin network can process about 12,000 transactions in an hour or about 3.3 transactions per second. This is particularly poor

---

[3]A miner has the ability to select the transactions in constructing the block he will mine.

performance. For example, VISA can process about 10,000 transactions in a second. This constraint also indicates that bitcoin cannot efficiently process transactions at scale for a bitcoin-based economy.

Bitcoin Cash is a hard fork of bitcoin that attempts to increase the performance of Bitcoin by increasing the maximum size of a block to 7 MB. Other than this change, Bitcoin Cash is virtually identical to Bitcoin.

A hard fork takes an existing corpus of source code and makes a copy of it. Source code changes are then made to the forked copy which diverge from the source which was forked, and thus we have a body of common code up to the hard fork and divergent code bases thereafter.

Ripple

The main motivation for Ripple (XRP) is to create a cryptocurrency network for high-volume and very fast transaction processing. Ripple's aim is to supplant the SWIFT[4] network for international transactions. SWIFT is a messaging network used by participating banks and financial institutions. The messages in this network are instructions to a participating financial institution to pay value to some other participating entity in the SWIFT network. Ripple's target are the big payment processors in the SWIFT universe.

International transfer of value is terribly slow. A transfer can take anywhere from 24 hours to 5 days. Furthermore, transaction fees are very high. Ripple aims to implement a blockchain-based solution called RippleNet, which promises also instantaneous transfer of value, low transaction fees, transaction encryption, and strong protection against fraudulent transactions. As a concise summation,

---

[4]Society for Worldwide Interbank Financial Telecommunications, https://ripplecoinnews.com/ripple-vs-swift

Ripple intends to replace the antiquated SWIFT network with its mix of manual and automated processing with a decentralized blockchain application.[5]

Monero

Monero (XMR) is a bitcoin-like cryptocurrency that implements strong protocols to ensure the privacy of financial transactions. In Bitcoin, anyone can examine the distributed public ledger to determine the parties (bitcoin addresses) involved in a financial transaction as well as the amount of value transferred by the transaction. Furthermore, anyone can examine the public ledger to determine the amount of bitcoins owned by a public address as well as all of the transactions connected with this address.

Monero precludes such an examination by implementing an obfuscated public ledger. The Monero ledger hides the identity (public address) of the sender and the receiver of monero in a transaction as well as the amount of the transaction. Due to this, the monero transactions are not traceable and a transaction cannot be linked to any particular public address.

You will recall that a dollar bill is fungible, meaning that a one dollar bill is the same as any other dollar bill. Furthermore, if we look at a dollar bill in our wallet, we cannot determine the past transactions involving this particular dollar bill. In contrast, bitcoin is not strictly fungible in this sense. Since we anyone can examine the distributed bitcoin ledger, we can determine the complete history of transactions associated with a particular bitcoin. So, for example, if a bitcoin was involved in an illegal transaction in the past and this bitcoin is in your wallet, we can easily ascertain that this bitcoin participated in an illegal transaction in the past. Because of this, bitcoin is not a truly fungible cryptocurrency. In contrast, monero is fungible since we can never determine the past transaction history of a monero unit in your wallet.

---

[5]There is trenchant criticism on the Internet that Ripple is a failed project. For example, see www.fool.com/investing/2018/02/21/the-single-biggest-problem-facing-ripple-xrp.aspx, last accessed on February 8, 2020, and www.reddit.com/r/CryptoCurrency/comments/69voi5/ripple_is_a_scam/, last accessed on February 8, 2020. A prime objective of Bitcoin is to do away with middlemen and effect peer-to-peer transfer of value. Aside from having a centralized consensus, Ripple in effect adds an additional middleman to the fiat banking value transfer system.

Litecoin

Litecoin (LTC) was forked from Bitcoin in 2011. Litecoin differs from bitcoin in two principal ways. Firstly, the maximum number of litecoins that can be mined is 84 million compared to 21 million for Bitcoin. Secondly, Litecoin blocks are mined every 2.5 minutes approximately compared to 10 minutes for bitcoin.

Basic Attention Token

Digital advertising is the bane of the Internet. We are inundated with advertising, and many of us have trained our brains to ignore digital ads. The Basic Attention Token (BAT) presents an ingenious and entirely new paradigm for digital advertising. BAT is designed to improve the effectiveness of digital advertising, enhance privacy, and also reduce the amount of advertising that Internet users are exposed to. The BAT distributed app consists of the Brave browser as well as the BAT token, which is an Ethereum ERC-20 token. BAT has impeccable credentials. This specialized token as well as the browser is the brainchild of Brendan Eich, the inventor of the first Internet browser, Netscape Navigator, and the JavaScript language.

The way that it works is as follows. An entity wanting to advertise creates an Ethereum smart contract and includes some BAT tokens with the contract. When a person views this advertisement (in the Brave browser), he or she receives a portion of the tokens attached to the advertisement. Furthermore, the publisher of the page on which the advertisement appears also receives some tokens, and lastly, the Brave browser also receives some tokens. Notice that if a person views an advertisement, he or she is compensated for the attention given to the advertisement.

In the present digital advertising *milieu*, a user's preferences and viewing habits are tracked pervasively and communicated to centralized entities that store and analyze this data in order to feed targeted advertisements to the subject as well as categorize him or her for other purposes – all without the target's consent. The Brave browser only stores the user's viewing habits and preferences locally and does not transmit any of this information to centralized entities. Thus, BAT and the Brave browser present a fairly radical implementation of privacy protection.

Binance Coin

Binance is one of the world's foremost cryptocurrency exchanges. Binance provides a platform for trading cryptocurrencies. Binance Coin (BNB) is an Ethereum-hosted ERC-20 token. Its primary use case is the payment of trading fees and listing fees on the exchange. Traders receive a discount if they use BNB to pay trading fees.

TRON

TRON is a blockchain platform for decentralized applications; its primary use case is for the storage and distribution of censorship-resistant content in the digital entertainment space. Thus, it seeks to compete with centralized content providers such as Facebook, Netflix, image and audio repositories, blogging platforms, and so forth. TRON is quite an ambitious project.

One of the unique features of TRON is its integration with the BitTorrent protocol for the incentivized storage and retrieval of content. Users who provide storage space to store files or portions thereof receive some TRX coins when users download files using TRON's BitTorrent protocol.

TRON's architecture consists of three layers: a storage layer which is accessible through the BitTorrent protocol, a core layer which implements the TRON functionality including the TRON (TRX) cryptocurrency, and an application layer where distributed applications are implemented.[6]

---

[6]TRON is controversial for a number of reasons. Vitalik Buterin, the inventor of Ethereum, has claimed that TRON is not a genuine cryptocurrency since the consensus mechanism is centralized. This means that the TRON network can be shut down by sanctioning the entities that form consensus. There are a small number of consensus formers who are periodically voted into their positions. Their identities are always known. The other controversial aspect of TRON is that it has a supply 100 billion TRON units (TRX) that can be put into circulation, but there is no upper limit on this supply. The consensus formers can evidently just increase the supply on TRX by voting. In Bitcoin, not only is the number of bitcoins that can be issued fixed, but the issuance of new bitcoins is controlled by a mathematical algorithm that has nothing to do with voting. Bitcoin was designed with one overriding design objective: nobody should be able to shut the network down.

BitTorrent is a peer-to-peer file sharing protocol that is widely used to transfer files. A BitTorrent network consists of a collection of nodes sitting on top of a TCP/IP network, which each implements the BitTorrent file transfer protocol. This protocol enables a peer on the network to discover which peers have a file or a portion of it and then enables this peer to download the file from these peers. Though accurate estimates are not available, anecdotal evidence suggests that at any given time anywhere from 15 million to 30 million users are downloading files using BitTorrent.

Tether

Tether (USDT) is a stablecoin. Stablecoins are designed to maintain a stable value with respect to a fiat currency, typically the US dollar. Tether ensures this stability by evidently maintaining a US dollar for each Tether in circulation. These dollar reserves are supposed to be under the control of the entity issuing the Tethers, in this case iFinex. iFinex which controls Tether is currently facing lawsuits pertaining to transparency, inadequate auditing of reserves, and market manipulation.

The Gross Anatomy of Cryptocurrencies

The language used to implement a cryptocurrency has a direct bearing on its performance and maintainability. Let's take a look at the implementation languages as well as the gross characteristics of some of the leading cryptocurrencies in Tables 2-1 and 2-2.

Table 2-1. *Implementation Details*

Cryptocurrency	Language	Consensus Formation	Supply (Coins)
Bitcoin (BTC)	C++	Proof of work	21 million
Ethereum (ETH)	C++, Go, Rust	Proof of stake	Not fixed
Ripple (XRP)	C++	Distributed proof of stake	Not fixed
Litecoin (LTC)	C++	Proof of work	84 million

(continued)

Table 2-1. (*continued*)

Cryptocurrency	Language	Consensus Formation	Supply (Coins)
Bitcoin Cash (BCH)	C++	Proof of work	21 million
Monero (XMR)	C++	Proof of work	18.4 million
TRON (TRX)	Java	Distributed proof of stake	100 billion
Basic Attention Token (BAT)	C++	Delegated proof of stake	1.5 billion
Binance Coin (BNB)	ERC-20 token		200 million
Tether (USDT)	ERC-20 token		Not fixed

Table 2-2. *Transactions per Minute*

Cryptocurrency	TPS	Primary Use Case
Bitcoin (BTC)	3	Store of value, hedge against US dollar
Ethereum (ETH)	8	Smart contracts, distributed apps
Ripple (XRP)	1500	Supplant SWIFT network
Litecoin (LTC)	26	Store of value
Bitcoin Cash (BCH)	60	More TPS than Bitcoin
Monero (XMR)	4	Privacy of transactions
TRON (TRX)	2000	Distributed digital media and games
Basic Attention Token (BAT)	?	Alternate model for advertising
Binance Coin (BNB)	?	Transaction fees on the Binance exchange
Tether (USDT)		Convertibility into the US dollar

Conclusion

In this chapter, we have looked at the characteristics of some of the leading cryptocurrencies and their use cases. In the next chapter, we commence our examination of the core mathematical concepts that underlie cryptocurrencies and blockchains.

CHAPTER 3

Symmetric Encryption

The mathematical foundations of blockchains and cryptocurrencies are rooted in an area of Mathematics called cryptography (or cryptology). In this chapter and the three chapters that follow, we will examine these mathematical foundations. Even though I am not going to present the mathematical theory in a rigorous lemma-theorem-corollary style, I am going to present the theory in a lucid and understandable manner. The goal is to provide you with a clear understanding of the underlying mathematical concepts and theory. This deep exposure will be more than sufficient to enable you to develop blockchain and cryptocurrency applications with confidence.

Alright, let's begin our deep dive into cryptography.

How Symmetric Encryption Works

Symmetric or single-key encryption has been around for thousands of years. Symmetric encryption works as follows: a message (called plaintext) is encrypted with a secret key. The encryption process converts the plaintext into a garbled message called a ciphertext. The secret key is simply some sequence of characters or symbols. Only a person who has the secret key can decode the ciphertext and recover the origin plaintext. Mathematically, we can represent the encryption process as

```
c = E(k,p)
```

Here, E is the encryption algorithm (function), k is the secret key, and p is the plaintext. c is the ciphertext produced by the encryption algorithm. The decryption process can be represented as

```
p = D(k,c)
```

where D is the decryption algorithm. Note that the same key is used for encryption and decryption. Hence the term symmetric encryption key.

29

K. S. Garewal, *Practical Blockchains and Cryptocurrencies*, https://doi.org/10.1007/978-1-4842-5893-4_3

Figure 3-1 illustrates the encryption and decryption process.

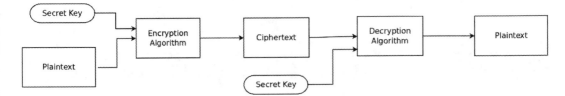

Figure 3-1. *Symmetric Encryption and Decryption*

A classic example of symmetric encryption is the Caesar cipher presumably used by Julius Caesar's Roman legions. In this encryption algorithm, every alphabetic character in the plaintext is replaced by a character which is three positions to the right (rotating to the beginning of the alphabet, if necessary) and spaces between words are ignored. For example, the letter p is replaced by the letter s and the letter z is replaced by the letter c. Thus, the plaintext *the legion has arrived* is encrypted as follows:

```
plaintext:  the legion has arrived
ciphertext: xkhohjlrqkdvduulzhg
```

In order to decrypt this ciphertext, we simply replace each character in the ciphertext with the character which is three characters to its left.

Design of Symmetric Encryption Algorithms

As we have seen, an encryption algorithm takes plaintext and a secret key as inputs and produces a ciphertext as its output. The encryption algorithm must be independent of both the plaintext and the secret key. Typically, an encryption algorithm consists of a finite number of rounds where each round is a finite sequence of substitution and transposition operations. A substitution operation substitutes some other character for an input character in the text, and a transposition operation rearranges or permutes a portion of the input text. Each round of the encryption algorithm garbles the plaintext to some extent, and this garbled output becomes the input for the next round of the encryption algorithm. In order to recover the plaintext from the ciphertext, the operations of the encryption algorithm must be reversible. Therefore, the decryption algorithm simply executes the rounds and operations of the encryption algorithm in reverse. The Caesar cipher that we discussed previously is a simple substitution cipher, and there are no transposition operations.

Symmetric encryption algorithms come in two flavors. Block ciphers partition the plaintext into blocks of fixed length and encrypt the plaintext one block at a time. Stream ciphers encrypt plaintext one byte at a time and are meant to encrypt data streaming over a network.

Devising a strong symmetric encryption algorithm that can withstand cryptanalysis is a non-trivial endeavor.[1] There are two main ways to attack an encryption algorithm and thus obtain the ability to decipher messages encoded by the algorithm. The first technique relies on a brute-force attack on the algorithm. This technique tries all possible secret keys until we obtain intelligible plaintext. The technique is not feasible if the keyspace is very large. Table 3-1 shows the relationship between the size of the encryption key and the time required to decrypt a message with a brute-force attack.

Table 3-1. *The Relationship Between Key Size and Decryption Time*

Key Size	Number of Keys in Keyspace	Average Time to Recover Plaintext (10^{16} Decryptions per Second)
8 bits	256	< 1 second
64 bits	2^{64}	0.25 hours
128 bits	2^{128}	$53.9*10^{12}$ years
256 bits	2^{256}	$18.3*10^{51}$ years

This table shows that larger keys offer greater protection against brute-force attacks than smaller keys.

The second avenue of attack relies upon the statistical analysis of the ciphertext. In the English language, certain letters of the alphabet appear with greater frequency than other letters and certain words appear with greater frequency than other words. For example, in a paragraph of text, the word "*the*" will ordinarily appear with greater frequency than the word "*aardvark*." Similarly, certain two-letter combinations (digraphs) appear with greater frequency than other combinations; and certain

---

[1]Cryptanalysis is the branch of cryptography which is concerned with discovering weaknesses in encryption algorithms and decrypting ciphertext when the secret key is unknown.

three-letter combinations (trigraphs) appear with greater frequency than other combinations. Table 3-2 taken from an analysis of 40,000 words categorizes the frequency with which letters appear in a large sample of text.[2]

Table 3-2. *Frequency Distribution of English Characters*

a	8.12	b	1.49	c	2.71	d	4.32
e	12.02	f	2.30	g	2.03	h	5.92
i	7.31	j	0.10	k	0.69	l	3.98
m	2.61	n	6.95	o	7.68	p	1.82
q	0.11	r	6.02	s	6.28	t	9.10
u	2.88	v	1.11	w	2.09	x	9.17
y	2.11	z	0.07				

An analysis of 40,000 words from the English language also indicates the frequency distribution of the 12 most common digraphs, as shown in Table 3-3.[3]

Table 3-3. *Frequency Distribution of the 12 Most Common Diagraphs*

th	1.52	he	1.28	in	0.94	er	0.94
an	0.82	re	0.68	nd	0.63	at	0.59
on	0.57	nt	0.56	ha	0.56	es	0.56

Cryptanalysis takes advantage of these structural language characteristics to decipher ciphertext. This analysis shows that a good encryption algorithm implements several substitution and transposition steps that alter or mask these language characteristics. In the ideal encryption algorithm, all digraphs, trigraphs, and n-word

---

[2]http://pi.math.cornell.edu/~mec/2003-2004/cryptography/subs/frequencies.html, retrieved January 4, 2020

[3]http://pi.math.cornell.edu/~mec/2003-2004/cryptography/subs/digraphs.html, retrieved January 5, 2020

combinations should have an equal probability of appearing in the ciphertext. Other cryptanalysis techniques take advantage of word order and the rules of grammar.

Another desirable property of an encryption algorithm is that a small change in the plaintext should cause a large change in the ciphertext; this is called an avalanche effect. The avalanche effect thwarts differential cryptanalysis which attempts to decode ciphertext by examining how different messages encrypted by the same algorithm differ from each other.

Aside from cryptanalysis, language analysis is important in the field of natural language processing (NLP). NLP has important applications in the design of chatbots, spam filters, language translators, as well as sentiment analysis, behavior prediction, and classification.

Advanced Encryption Standard

The Advanced Encryption Standard (AES) is the US National Institute of Standards' recommended symmetric encryption algorithm. In 1997, NIST announced a competition to replace the aging Data Encryption Standard. Four years later in 2001, AES was chosen as the winner among several competing encryption designs. AES is widely used by governments and financial institutions across the world. It is a very fast encryptor. Due to its small size, AES finds usage in devices ranging from microcontrollers to supercomputers. AES processes plaintext blocks of 128 bits and supports encryption key lengths of 128, 192, and 256 bits. It uses 10 encryption rounds if the selected key is 128 bits long, 12 rounds if the key is 192 bits, and 14 rounds if the key is 256 bits.

Table 3-4 enumerates some of the prominent symmetric encryption algorithms as well as their characteristics.

Table 3-4. *Symmetric Encryption Algorithms*

Name	Introduced In	Block Size (Bits)	Key Length (Bits)	Rounds
AES	2001	128	128, 192, 256	10, 12, 14
Serpent[4]	2001	128	128, 192, 256	32
RC2	1987	64	8–1024	18
Twofish[5]	2001	128	128, 192, 256	18

The Key Distribution Problem

For a party to decipher a ciphertext, he or she must possess the secret key. The problem arises when a secret key has to be distributed to a large number of recipients. In such a case, there is a significant danger that an adverse party will be able to intercept and appropriate the key. Symmetric key encryption is not a suitable technique when an encryption key has to be distributed to a large number of users. The solution to this key distribution problem lies in a cryptographic technique called public key encryption, which we will examine in a subsequent chapter.

Pseudo-Random Number Generators

Many cryptographic algorithms require the use of one or more random numbers, typically to initialize a process with a seed, generate keys, set a nonce, specify a salt, or randomize a variable. Instead of obtaining a random number by sampling some process in nature or on our computer, it is common practice to use a mathematical function to generate a sequence of pseudo-random numbers. A function that generates such a sequence is called a pseudo-random number generator (PRNG). A PRNG works as follows. The PRNG is seeded with some random number which is called a seed, and it then recursively generates a deterministic sequence of numbers. Note that, given the certain seed, the PRNG will always generate the same sequence of numbers.

---

[4]Serpent was the runner up in the NIST competition.

[5]Twofish was one of the top five finalists in the NIST competition. Twofish is optimized for 32-bit processors, and thus, it is significantly slower than AES.

A good pseudo-random number generator has statistical properties that make it very difficult to distinguish from a sequence of random numbers. In particular, in a high-quality PRNG, successive numbers are not correlated and the PRNG has a very large period before the numbers start to repeat.

The linear congruential generator (LCG) is a commonly used PRNG. It has a simple definition:[6]

$$X_{n+1} = (m*x_n + a) \bmod P$$

```
P >= 2 is an integer. P is the period of the PRNG.
The integer coefficient m is called the multiplier; m > 0 and m < P.
a is an additive integer constant where a > 0 and a < P.
The initial value of the generator x₀ is the seed.
```
x_n is the nth pseudo-random number generated by the function.

Note that LCG is a recursive function. It is very easy to implement and has the advantage of being a fast pseudo-random number generator. The statistical randomness of LCG is sensitive to the modulus value P and the seed which is selected. The GNU C library, glibc, uses a period of 2^{45}, a multiplier value of 25214903917, and a seed value of 11, in the specification of its LCG.

The following code implements the linear congruential generator in Python:[7]

```
class LCG:
    def __init__(self,mult,addr,prd,seed):
        self.multiplier = mult
        self.addr = addr
        self.period = prd
        self.lastValue = seed

    def generator(self):
        self.lastValue = (self.multiplier*self.lastValue + self.addr) %
        self.period
        return self.lastValue
```

---

[6]mod is the modulus operator; it returns the integer remainder for a division operation involving integers only, for example, 20 mod 7 = 6 and 5 mod 7 = 5.

[7]All Python examples use Python 3.8 or later.

```
lcg = LCG(11, 37, 1000, 0)
ctr = 0

while ctr < 10:
  ret = lcg.generator()
  print(ret)
  ctr += 1
```

The Mersenne Twister[8] is another high-quality PRNG of interest. In its most common derivation, it is seeded with the Mersenne prime number $2^{19937} - 1$ and it has a period of $2^{19937} - 1$.

Conclusion

In this chapter, we have examined the design of symmetric encryption algorithms and the cryptanalysis of these algorithms. We have also taken a look at the Advanced Encryption Standard, which is a widely used encryption algorithm. The distribution of encryption keys to a large number of users is a serious issue since it raises the possibility that a key may be stolen during the distribution process. In a subsequent chapter, we will show how public key encryption solves the key distribution dilemma. Finally, we have elucidated upon pseudo-random number generators.

In the next chapter, we will study cryptographic hash functions. These functions are particularly important in blockchain design.

References

Schneier, Bruce. Applied Cryptography: Protocols, Algorithms and Source Code in C, 1st ed., John Wiley & Sons, Inc., 1995

Ferguson Neils, Schneier, Bruce et al. Cryptography Engineering, 1st ed., Wiley, 2010

---

[8]`www.math.sci.hiroshima-u.ac.jp/~m-mat/MT/emt.html`, retrieved January 4, 2020

CHAPTER 4

Cryptographic Hash Functions

Don't get intimidated by the title of this chapter. The theory of cryptographic hash functions is not particularly abstruse. What is difficult is the construction of these functions from scratch. However, we need not concern ourselves with this aspect of the mathematical theory since most programming language libraries provide us with a good selection of functions to choose from.

Cryptographic hash functions are concerned with the very practical problem of determining whether a document or text string has been altered by some malicious actor. These functions play a very important role in the development of blockchain and cryptocurrency applications, so it is important that you have a good understanding of the mathematical theory of these functions.

An Introduction to Cryptographic Hashes

Consider this scenario. Suppose that you and I are on opposite ends of the Milky Way and I send you a message. Now upon receiving the message, you want to satisfy yourself that the message has not been changed by some unfriendly alien while it was in transit. Secondly, you want to satisfy yourself that the message was actually sent by me and not by some impostor. Suppose further that you are unable to securely communicate with me to ascertain these two issues. Cryptographic hashes (or cryptographic hash functions, if you will) address the issue of whether the message was tampered with while in transit. In this chapter, we examine these functions. In the subsequent chapter on digital signatures, we will examine the matter of authenticity; has the document or message really been authored by the person who purports to be its author?

One way that I can utilize to assure you that the message has not been tampered with while in transit would be if I sent you a string of characters called a message digest that is somehow related to the message. Suppose that you could then input the message into

© Karan Singh Garewal 2020
K. S. Garewal, *Practical Blockchains and Cryptocurrencies*, https://doi.org/10.1007/978-1-4842-5893-4_4

a machine and if this machine produced a message digest that matched the message digest that I have sent you, then you could conclude that the message has not been altered. If this machine produced a string output that did not match the message digest that I sent you, then you would conclude that the message was changed while in transit. Such a machine would be called a cryptographic hash function (or cryptographic hash algorithm) if it satisfied some constraints to be discussed shortly.

The string output produced by such a machine or cryptographic hash function is called a cryptographic hash or a message digest. Frequently, the output is simply, but incorrectly, called a hash.

The machine that we want to construct is a mathematical function or mathematical algorithm. So how do we construct such a function?

Cryptographic Hash Functions

A hash function is a function that takes a string of any length as input and produces a string as its output. As a simple example, consider the function $y = F(x)$ that takes a string x as an input and produces an output string where each character in the input string emits the next character as its output:

```
F('crypto') = 'dszqup'
```

This is a very simple hash function, but it is not a cryptographic hash function because it does not satisfy some required conditions.

A cryptographic hash function is a hash function which has four essential properties:

- The function produces an output string of fixed length.

- The function is collision-free.

- The function is irreversible.

- The function can be efficiently computed.

Note   We can construct hash functions that produce numbers instead of strings. However, we typically specify hash functions that emit strings. Blockchain and cryptocurrency applications invariably use cryptographic hash functions that produce hexadecimal string outputs.

Now let us look at the required properties of cryptographic hash functions.

The Fixed Length Output Property

This is a simple requirement. We want our cryptographic hash function to produce message digests that have a fixed length. Ideally, we want message digests that are small in size since this bears upon the efficiency of transmitting data over a network. The smaller the size of a message digest, the lower the probability that it will be inadvertently corrupted in the course of its transmission. Cryptographic functions that produce message digests that are 128 bits, 256 bits, and 512 bits in length are common.

The Collision-Free Property

It should be clear that if we have two different messages, then we want our cryptographic hash function to produce two different message digests, that is, if x and y are two different messages and $q = H(p)$ is our cryptographic hash function, then we require that

```
x != y implies that H(x) != H(y)
```

A collision would occur when x != y but H(x) = H(y). A hash function is said to be collision-free if the probability of a collision is infinitesimally small. A good cryptographic hash function may have collisions, but it is virtually impossible to find these collisions.

Typical cryptographic hash functions are not neat mathematical expressions in the classical sense, such as y = e^xln2x. They are a finite and sequential series of substitutions and transformations of the input text. Because the function specification is made in such a manner, we can never be absolutely certain that the function does not contain any collisions.[1]

The Irreversible Property

This is a commonsense requirement; we should not be able to derive a message from its message digest. A good cryptographic hash function is not reversible. This means that given an output y of a hash function $y = H(x)$, it is computationally infeasible to derive the input x from the message digest y.

---

[1]In the last chapter on symmetric encryption, we discussed substitutions and permutations on text input; you may want to review this portion of the chapter again.

Our previously discussed hash function

```
F('crypto') = 'dszqup'
```

is not a cryptographic hash function because it is reversible.

The Property of Efficient Computation

This is a desirable but not an essential quality of a good cryptographic hash function. We want our function to be able to compute message digests quickly. This property bears upon the scalability of applications that need to compute message digests. Consider, for example, a banking application that must process thousands of transactions per second, and each transaction requires the computation of one or more message digests. In order for this application to scale, it is essential that it be able to compute message digests very quickly.

Proving That a File Has Been Tampered With

Let us apply what we have learned so far to prove that a file has not been tampered with.

Suppose that we have a text file and a cryptographic hash function. We can compute the message digest of this file if we view the contents of this file as a long stream of characters. Then, if subsequently a new file is presented to us and it has the same message digest as the previous file, we can then conclude that these two files are identical since the message digests (cryptographic hashes) of both files are identical. Furthermore, if the message digests differ, we can conclude that the two files are not identical.

The Secure Hash Algorithm 256 (SHA-256)

Cryptographic hash functions are surprisingly difficult to discover. SHA-256, SHA-512, and RIPEMD-160 are three cryptographic hash functions that are in common use. Let us take a look at the SHA-256 and RIPEMD-160 hash functions which are used extensively in blockchain applications.

SHA-256 is an acronym for secure hash algorithm 256. The 256 indicates that the message digest (or cryptographic hash) that is emitted by this function is 256 bits in length.

Figure 4-1 shows how an SHA-256 message digest is generated for a message or a file.

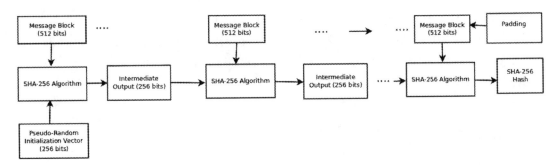

Figure 4-1. *SHA-256 Message Digest Generation*

The file or message is broken into consecutive blocks which are 512 bits in size. If the message or file is not exactly mod 512 (divisible by 512), then padding is added to the end of the message or the file (a 1 bit followed by zero bits) so that 512 divides the bit length of the message or file without a remainder.

Next, we construct a 256-bit random IV (initialization vector) using a pseudo-random number generator. This is just a 256-bit long pseudo-random sequence of 1 and 0 bits. The purpose of the IV is to increase the randomness of the hash generation process. We concatenate this IV with the first 512-bit block of the message or file. The resulting 768-bit block is input into the secure hash algorithm. This algorithm is a scrambling and compression function that outputs a 256-bit string. The algorithm is a series of substitutions and permutations of the 768-bit block.

We next take the second 512-bit message block and concatenate it with the previous 256-bit output. This 768-bit string is input into the same scrambling and compression function and a 256-bit output is produced. We proceed in this way, consuming the message blocks. The final 256-bit output is the message digest (or cryptographic hash) produced by the SHA-256 algorithm.

The heart of SHA-256 is the scrambling and compression function that is applied to each 768-bit block. For SHA-256, this function consists of 64 rounds. Each round takes a 768-bit block which is scrambled with bit shift and logical bit operations (OR, XOR, AND) and then fed into the next round. The last round produces a 256-bit output which is concatenated with the next 512-bit block of the message, and then the 64 rounds are again applied to this 768-bit block. This process repeats itself until the last block of the message has been processed.

The SHA-512 algorithm is conceptually similar except that the message block size is 1024 bits in length and the scrambling function consists of 80 rounds. Theoretically, the larger the number of steps involved in the scrambling process, the greater the cryptographic security of the function.

A Python Example for SHA-256

Python provides an implementation for SHA-256 as well as other cryptographic hashing algorithms in its *hashlib* module. The following Python code sample demonstrates the generation of SHA-256 hexadecimal-encoded message digests for strings:

```
import hashlib

def getSHA256MD(inputStr):
    m = hashlib.sha256()
    # convert the input string into a sequence of bytes
    strAsBytes = str.encode(inputStr)
    m.update(strAsBytes)
    # return the message digest as a hexadecimal string
    return m.hexdigest()

ret = getSHA256MD('the lazy brown fox jumped over the sleeping dog')
print(ret)
```

The result of executing this program is the SHA-256 hash:
1845c1824b7710df04f1307ea1618857c16e891278eb9dc7edba809915581283

RIPEMD-160

RIPEMD is an acronym for RACE Integrity Primitives Evaluation Message Digest. This cryptographic hash algorithm can emit message digests which are 128, 160, 256, and 320 bits in length. RIPEMD entered the public domain in 1996. RIPEMD-160 finds usage in the Bitcoin cryptocurrency as well as numerous other blockchain applications.

The algorithm to generate a RIPEMD-160 hash is conceptually similar to the process that generates a SHA-256 hash. RIPEMD-160 divides the input message into a consecutive sequence of 512-bit blocks. The message is padded with a 1 bit and a sequence of 0 bits to ensure that it is completely divisible by 512. Then a 64-bit string, encoding the length of the message, is appended to the message. The algorithm uses five 32-bit registers which hold the intermediate results as well as the final message digest. In order to start the hash generation process, these five 32-bit registers are initialized with some fixed values. The first 512-bit block is then mutated by a sequence of ten rounds where each round consists of a 16-step sequence of permutations and substitutions that act on the message block and the register values. The output of these ten rounds is a 160-bit value populating the five 32-bit registers. These register values are then input with the next block, and the process repeats itself until the last block of the message has been processed.[2] The final 160-bit value in the five registers is the message digest.

The following Python code generates a RIPEMD-160 hash value for a string. The output is encoded as a hexadecimal string:

```python
import hashlib

def getRIPEMD160(inputStr):
    r = hashlib.new('ripemd160')
    strAsBytes = str.encode(inputStr)
    r.update(strAsBytes)
    return r.hexdigest()

ret = getRIPEMD160('the lazy brown fox jumped over the sleeping dog')
print(ret)
```

Message Authentication Codes

In the previous sections, we have discussed how cryptographic hashes can be used to determine the integrity of a message, that is, to prove whether a message has been tampered with. Cryptographic hashes cannot be used to prove authenticity. Authenticity is concerned with proving that the sender of a message is whom she or he purports to be. Message authentication codes (MAC) provide assurances of message integrity and, in addition, provides limited assurances of authenticity. Message authentication code algorithms rely upon shared symmetric encryption keys.

---

[2]Basic Operations of Modern Hashing Algorithms, http://ena.lp.edu.ua:8080/bitstream/ntb/23749/1/7-26-29.pdf, last accessed on January 8, 2020

This is how message authentication codes work. A group of two or more individuals share a secret symmetric encryption key. A person who wants to send a message uses a MAC algorithm to compute a MAC value for this message. She then sends the message along with the MAC value to a recipient. The recipient computes the MAC value of the message using the MAC algorithm and the secret key. If this computed MAC value is equal to the MAC value delivered by the originator, then we conclude that the message has not been tampered with. Furthermore, the recipient can be assured that the message was sent by someone who has the secret key.

Figure 4-2 explains how message authentication codes are used.

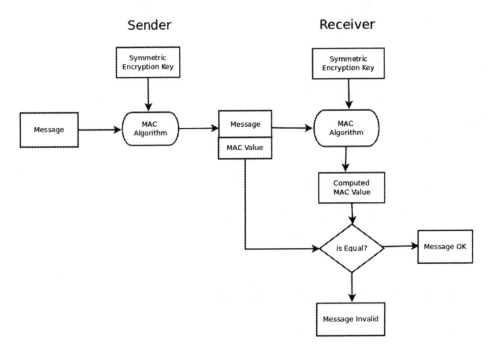

Figure 4-2. *Message Authentication Code Process*

You should note that the message does not have to be encrypted. There are many use cases where a MAC code is used along with plaintext. For example, operating system files are not encrypted but may have MAC values attached therewith in order to prove the integrity of the files. Another prominent use case pertains to the transmission of files over a network when we want assurance that the file was not compromised during transmission.

MAC codes provide only a limited assurance of authentication. Where a message along with a MAC code is received, we can only conclude that the message was sent by a person who has the symmetric encryption key. In particular, a person can purport to send a message as some other person who has the secret key, and the impersonated individual will not be able to repudiate this claim. As we will see in a subsequent chapter, digital signatures solve the integrity and authentication puzzle.

You may note an essential difference between cryptographic hash algorithms such as SHA-256 and MAC algorithms. Anyone can compute the SHA-512 message digest of a message. In contrast, a shared secret key is required in order to compute the MAC value of a message.

Conclusion

Cryptographic hash functions are foundational to blockchain applications. In this chapter, we have discussed the properties of cryptographic hash functions. We have also examined two prominent cryptographic hash algorithms: the secure hash algorithm and RIPEMD-160.

Cryptographic hash algorithms can prove the integrity of messages but cannot prove authenticity (who authored the message). We concluded this chapter with a discussion of message authentication code algorithms, which can not only prove the integrity of messages but also provide a limited form of authentication.

In the next chapter, we will delve into the foundations of public key cryptosystems.

References

Schneier, Bruce. Applied Cryptography: Protocols, Algorithms and Source Code in C, 1st ed., John Wiley & Sons, Inc., 1995

Ferguson Neils, Schneier, Bruce et al. Cryptography Engineering, 1st ed., Wiley, 2010

Basic Operations of Modern Hashing Algorithms, `http://ena.lp.edu.ua:8080/bitstream/ntb/23749/1/7-26-29.pdf`, last accessed on January 8, 2020

CHAPTER 5

The Alchemy of Public Key Cryptosystems

This chapter is concerned with what can be termed modern cryptography or asymmetric cryptography. In Chapter 3, we studied symmetric encryption and surmised that it has a significant scalability problem when the encryption key has to be distributed to a large number of recipients. For example, consider the scenario where an encryption key has to be distributed to thousands of recipients. Each transmission of the key to a recipient carries with it, a certain probability that the key will be intercepted by a malevolent actor. The aim of public key cryptosystems, *inter alia*, is to solve this scalability problem and also render moot the issue of the interception of the secret key by adversaries. The *piece de resistance* of the theory of public key cryptosystems are digital signature algorithms; these solve three problems simultaneously: (i) assuring the integrity of messages, (ii) assuring the authenticity of messages, and (iii) solving the scalability problem.

Public key cryptosystems find usage in a myriad of modern applications. For example, they are used in secure HTTP communications, virtual private networks, credit cards, ecommerce systems, smart cards, electronic identity cards, and international payment systems such as SWIFT and now in cryptocurrencies and blockchain applications.

In this chapter, I am going to start by summarizing the problem of distributing symmetric encryption keys and then provide a brief description of the canonical digital signature algorithm. After this, I will provide you with some of the mathematical theory underlying public key cryptosystems and finally proceed to discuss digital signature algorithms in greater depth. I will also provide code examples in Python as we proceed.

© Karan Singh Garewal 2020
K. S. Garewal, *Practical Blockchains and Cryptocurrencies*, https://doi.org/10.1007/978-1-4842-5893-4_5

The Key Distribution Problem Revisited

Once again, suppose that you and I are at the opposite ends of the Milky Way and that I want to send you a secret message. Firstly, you must possess the symmetric encryption key so that you can decrypt the message. Thus, if you do not have this key, I must transmit it to you. After I provide you with the key, I can then send encrypted messages to you and you will be able to decrypt them using the secret key. In order to detect whether the message has been altered while in transit, I can also transmit the SHA-256 hash of either the plaintext or encrypted message to you. This cryptographic hash can be appended to the message.

In the previous scenario, there are two outstanding issues which have to be addressed. Firstly, you do not know whether the message has actually been sent by me or by some hostile actor who is impersonating me. The message could have been crafted by anyone who has the encryption key. This is the authenticity problem. How do we prove that a message has been sent by the person who purports to be its author? The second issue is that the encryption key could have been intercepted by a hostile entity while in transit. There is no deterministic way to prove that the secret key has not been intercepted while in transit. This problem is compounded when the key has to be distributed to a large number of recipients. Consider, for example, an intelligence-gathering network where each node in the network must be supplied with the encryption key.

Heuristics of Digital Signature Algorithms

In public key cryptography, an asymmetric key generation algorithm is used to generate a public key and a private key pair. Each of these keys is a very long string. The person generating this key pair keeps the private key securely with him- or herself and distributes the public key to his intended recipients. For example, the public key can be distributed to the world at large by posting it on the Internet. The essential aspect of the distribution of the public key is that we do not care that a hostile entity has possession of this key. Since the entity that generates the key pair must keep the private key securely with himself, it is important that the asymmetric key generation algorithm makes it computationally infeasible to recover the private key from the public key.

A person can now encrypt a message with the public key and transmit it to the holder of the private key or simply post the encrypted message on the Internet. The asymmetric key generation algorithm guarantees that this message can only be decrypted with the private key, that is, it is computationally infeasible to decrypt the message without the private key. By computational infeasibility, we mean that it would take an enormous amount of time (perhaps eons) to decrypt the message in the absence of the private key.

Similarly, a message encrypted with the private key can only be decrypted by the public key corresponding to the private key. It is computationally infeasible for an adversary to recover the original message from the ciphertext without the public key. The public and private keys are inverses of each other in the sense that encryption operations performed by either key can be reversed by the other key. This is the essence of public key cryptosystems. Figure 5-1 shows this process.

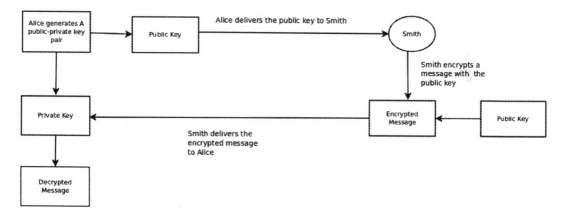

Figure 5-1. *Public Key Cryptosystem*

In the preceding process, Alice generates a public-private key pair and delivers the public key to Smith while keeping the private key securely with herself. Smith then encrypts a message with this public key and delivers the ciphertext to Alice. Alice then decrypts the ciphertext with her private key.

Alice knows that the message has been encrypted by a person who has the public key, but typically Alice will not know the identity of the person who actually encrypted this message (unless Alice knows with certainty that only Smith has the public key). The determination of this identity issue requires a public key infrastructure (PKI). We will discuss public key infrastructures shortly.

The other scenario is when Alice encrypts a message with her private key. Such a message can be decrypted by any person who holds the corresponding public key. The essential feature here is that the recipient of the message can conclude that the message was generated by the entity holding the private key. Furthermore, Alice cannot repudiate the assertion that the message was generated with the private key held by her. Note that in the absence of exogenous information, the recipient cannot associate the private key with Alice. One way of establishing such associations is through the use of certificate authorities (PKI).

Alice and Smith can engage in secure bidirectional communications if each party sends messages using the other party's public key.

Digital signature algorithms address two issues: firstly that a message has not been tampered with and secondly that the signature has been generated by a certain private key and hence by the holder of this key. The second aspect of the algorithm solves the authentication problem.

These algorithms consist of two stages: a signature generation stage and a signature verification stage. Figure 5-2 shows the steps involved in the signature generation stage.

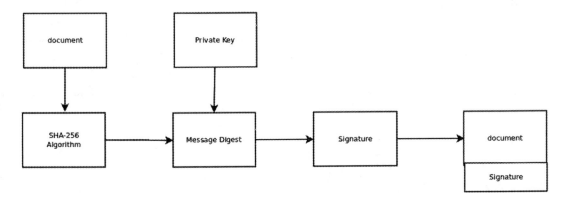

Figure 5-2. *Producing the Digital Signature of a Document*

Alice has generated a public private key pair and has a document that she wants to digitally sign.[1] In the first step, Alice generates a cryptographic hash of the document, say, the SHA-256 message digest of the document. Alice then encrypts the message digest with her private key. The result of this encryption is the digital signature of the document. In the second step, Alice concatenates the document and the digital signature and transmits this concatenated document to the recipient.

As we have noted previously, high-quality cryptographic algorithms such as SHA-256 have an avalanche effect. If a document is changed very slightly, even by a single bit, this will produce a message digest which changes dramatically. This same avalanche effect

---

[1]A document can be viewed as a sequence of characters and punctuation marks or equivalently as a sequence of bytes.

occurs when the private key is applied to the message digest. Lastly, note that the document itself need not be encrypted. In many important applications, we do not care that the document is transmitted in plaintext since our only concern is with detecting alteration of the document and with the authentication of the document. Of course, Alice can also choose to encrypt the document with her private key and then encrypt the SHA-256 message digest of the encrypted document with her private key.

The second stage of digital signature algorithms is the verification of the document by a recipient of the document. Figure 5-3 shows this process.

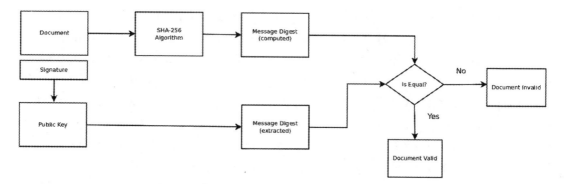

Figure 5-3. *Verifying the Digital Signature of a Document*

In the verification stage, the recipient of the concatenated document (say Smith) separates the document and the signature. In the first step, Smith computes the SHA-256 message digest of the document that has been received. In the second step, the signature that was concatenated with the document is decrypted by applying Alice's public key to the signature. This yields the message digest which was computed by the sender of the document. The two message digests are then compared. If the message digests are equal, then Smith can conclude that the document has not been tampered with while in transit and that Alice has signed and delivered this document since her private key matches the public key that Smith has used. If the message digests do not match, then there are three possibilities. Firstly, the document has been altered while in transit; secondly, Alice is not the author of the document; and lastly Smith does not possess the public key corresponding to Alice's private key.

Public Key Infrastructure

As you will recall, when Smith receives a message (or document) encrypted with a private key, all that he can infer about the identity of the sender is that this entity is in possession of the private key that encrypted the message. Smith must possess exogenous information in order to associate the identity of Alice with the private key. Similarly, when Alice receives a message that has been encrypted with her public key, then in the absence of exogenous information, she can only conclude that the message has been encrypted by someone holding her public key.

One way to associate an identity with a public key (and implicitly its private key) is through a certificate authority (CA). The following is the manner in which certificate authorities work. Firstly, the certificate authority obtains information on the identity of the applicant who claims to own a private-public key pair. The applicant provides the CA with his public key. The CA then asks the applicant to digitally sign a document provided by the CA. After the applicant has signed the document, the CA proceeds to verify the signature of the document. If the verification succeeds, it is proof that the applicant is in possession of the private key pertaining to the public key that he has supplied to the CA. The CA then issues an X.509 certificate to the applicant. This certificate is signed by the CA with its private key to prove the identity of the certificate issuer and to assure that it has not been altered. The issued certificate typically contains information identifying the applicant, such as the name, address, and other distinguishing particulars, the public key generated by the applicant, the expiry date of the certificate, and so forth.

Alice can provide proof of the authorship of a document in the following manner. Firstly, Alice will encrypt her certificate with her private key and concatenate it with the document she wants to deliver. Alice will digitally sign this concatenated document and attach the signature to the concatenated document. This will enable the recipient to securely verify the identity of the person who has signed the document by decrypting the certificate.

In a similar manner, when Smith encrypts a document with Alice's public key, he can also encrypt his certificate with his private key and concatenate the encrypted certificate with the document. Alice will now know the identity of the person who has sent her the document encrypted with her public key by decrypting the certificate with Smith's public key.

The RSA Algorithm

Several public-private key generation algorithms exist in the public domain. The two leading algorithms are *RSA* and the Elliptic Curve Digital Signature Algorithm (*ECDSA*). The RSA algorithm is the most widely used public key algorithm.[2] These algorithms rely upon computationally intractable problems in Mathematical Number Theory. For example, *RSA* relies on the fact that it is computationally infeasible to factor an extremely large number into a product of primes. ECDSA relies upon the difficulty of finding the discrete logarithms of extremely large numbers. The bitcoin code uses public-private key pairs that are generated using the Elliptic Curve Digital Signature Algorithm.

In this optional section, we are going to derive the RSA algorithm. Before we do this, we need a few pieces from Number Theory:

Definition (prime number): A positive integer n greater than 1 is called a prime number if it is only divisible by +1, -1, -n and n.

Theorem (the fundamental theorem of arithmetic): Any integer $m > 1$ can be factored into a product of prime numbers

$$m = p_1^{t1} p_2^{t2} p_3^{t3} \cdots p_n^{tn}$$

where $p_1 < p_2 < \ldots < p_n$ are prime numbers and t1, t2, … tn are natural numbers greater than 0.

Definition (relatively prime numbers): Two positive integers j > 1 and k > 1 are said to be relatively prime if their only common factor is 1.

For example, 6 and 9 are not relatively prime since 3 is a common divisor. 8 and 15 are relatively prime.

Definition (Euler's totient function, Q(n)): For any integer n > 1, Q(n) is the number of positive integers less than n that are relatively prime to n.

For example, Q(15) = 7 since the set of relatively prime numbers is { 2,4,7,8,11,13,14 }.

Theorem (Euler's theorem): For any integers a,n > 1 where a and n are relatively prime, $a^{Q(n)} \% n = 1$.[3]

---

[2]Rivest, R., Shamir L., Adelman, A., A Method for Obtaining Digital Signatures and Public-Key Cryptosystems, `https://people.csail.mit.edu/rivest/Rsapaper.pdf`, last accessed on January 13, 2020

[3]% is the modulus operator. For positive integers a and b, a%b is the integer remainder when a is divided by b.

For example, let a = 15 and n = 8, Q(n) = 4, and then

```
15⁴ % 8 = 50625 % 8 = 1
```

It should be clear that for a natural number m > 1, the prime factorization $p_1^{t1}p_2^{t2}p_3^{t3}$ ... p_n^{tn} is unique. The RSA algorithm relies upon the fact that it is computationally infeasible to obtain the prime factorization of very large numbers.

We can now derive an RSA public-private key pair as follows:

```
Step 1: Choose two large random prime numbers p and q where p does not
        equal to q.
```

```
Step 2: Calculate the product: n = pq.
```

```
Step 3: Because p and q are prime numbers, Euler's totient function value
        for n is Q(n) = (p-1)(q-1).
```

```
Step 4: Choose an integer 1 < e < Q(n) such that e and Q(n) are relatively prime.
```

```
Step 5: Get a positive integer d so that de % Q(n) = 1.
```

The public key is the tuple (n, e). The private key is the tuple (p, q, d). The public key tuple can be distributed freely; the private key tuple is kept secret.

Let us now look at the application of the RSA algorithm. Consider a document or message D. D can be viewed as a very long sequence of bits or equivalently as a massively large positive integer. Henceforth, we will consider D as such an integer. We make sure that our prime numbers p and q have been selected so that $D < pq$.

Smith, who has received the public key tuple (n, e), creates the encrypted message C as follows:

```
C = Dᵉ % n
```

C is a positive integer or equivalently is a very long sequence of bits.

Alice can now use her private key tuple (p, q, d) to decrypt the ciphertext:

```
D = Cᵈ % n
```

As a concrete example, let p = 7 and q = 5.

```
n = pq = 35
Then Q(35) = 24 and we select e = 17.
e and Q(n) are relatively prime.
```

```
We select d such that de % Q(n) = 17d % 24 = 1
d = 17

Now consider a document T = 12
```
Then the ciphertext is 12^{17} % 35 = 17
We decrypt the ciphertext with 17^{17} % 35 = 12

RSA public-private key encryption is the most widely used private-public key encryption system. It is just as secure as keys generated using elliptic curve cryptography (ECDSA). Following Bitcoin, we will use ECDSA key pairs. The logic of such keys is conceptually similar to RSA keys, and I will omit discussing their generation since a rigorous discussion of the underlying Mathematics will take us into a long digression. Our Blockchain code will contain the necessary library functions to generate ECDSA public-private key pairs.

Python Code Example

In the following Python example, we will use the *pycryptodome* package to lead Alice and Smith through a sequence of encryption, decryption, signature generation, and signature verification steps using RSA.[4] You should walk through this code carefully to see the mechanics of using public and private key pairs to encrypt and decrypt messages.

If you have not already done so, install this package:[5]

```
pip3 install pycryptodome

#========================================
# RSA Public-key cryptography example
#========================================
from Crypto.PublicKey import RSA
from Crypto.Cipher import PKCS1_OAEP
from Crypto.Hash import SHA256
from Crypto import Random
```

---

[4]https://pycryptodome.readthedocs.io/en/latest/, last accessed on January 14, 2020
[5]You should have installed Python 3.58 or later to use this package.

```python
from hashlib import sha256
import binascii

#====================================
# generate a RSA key-pair
#====================================
def RSAKeyPair(keylength):
    keyPair = RSA.generate(keylength)
    return keyPair

# Alice generates a RSA key-pair
AliceKeyPair = RSAKeyPair(1024)

# Alice's public-key
pubKey = AliceKeyPair.publickey()
print(f"public-key:  (n={hex(pubKey.n)}, e={hex(pubKey.e)})")

# Alice's public-key in PEM format
# PEM format Base64 encodes the key
pubKeyPEM = AliceKeyPair.publickey().exportKey()
print("PubKey PEM Format: " +pubKeyPEM.decode('ascii'))

# Alice's private key
print(f"Private key: (n={hex(pubKey.n)}, d={hex(AliceKeyPair.d)})")

# Alice's private key in PEM format
privKeyPEM = AliceKeyPair.exportKey()
print("PRIVATE KEY PEM FORMAT; " + privKeyPEM.decode('ascii'))

#=========================================================
# Smith encrypts a message using Alice's public-key
# message must be a binary string
#=========================================================
message = b"The quick brown fox jumped over the farmer's hedge"
cipher = PKCS1_OAEP.new(pubKey)
cipherText = cipher.encrypt(message)
print("CipherText: ", binascii.hexlify(cipherText))
```

```
#===========================================================
# Alice decrypts Smith's message using her private key
#===========================================================
decipher = PKCS1_OAEP.new(AliceKeyPair)
plainText = decipher.decrypt(cipherText)
print('Decrypted Text: ', plainText)

#===========================================================
# Alice signs a message by first generating the SHA-256
# digest of the message and then encrypting it with her
# private key.
# the string message is converted to a binary string
#===========================================================
message = b'let sleeping dogs lie, said the farmer'

hash = int.from_bytes(sha256(message).digest(), byteorder='big')
signature = pow(hash, AliceKeyPair.d, AliceKeyPair.n)
print("Alice's Signature:", hex(signature))

#============================================================
# Smith Verifies the signature by comparing the SHA-256 hash
# generated from the received message with the hash obtained
# by decrypting the signature received from Alice
#============================================================
hashFromMessage = int.from_bytes(sha256(message).digest(), byteorder='big')
decryptedHash   = pow(signature, AliceKeyPair.e, AliceKeyPair.n)

if (hashFromMessage == decryptedHash):
   print("Signature is valid")
else:
   print("signature is invalid")
```

Generating Globally Unique IDs

In a blockchain application, we typically need universally unique values that identify blocks and transactions. One way to generate these global IDs is to generate a public-private key pair and then get the SHA-256 hash of the private or public key. The resultant 256-bit message digest is globally unique.[6] This means that it is computationally infeasible to generate some other public-private key pair that will generate the same message digest. Similarly, we can apply the RIPEMD-160 cryptographic hash function to a public or private key. The resultant 160-bit message hash is also a globally unique id.

Conclusion

Public key cryptography or asymmetric key encryption is a very important foundational tool of blockchain and cryptocurrency applications. In this chapter, we have delved into public key cryptography and, in particular, public-private key pairs and digital signature algorithms. We have also looked at the derivation of the RSA algorithm, which is the most popular algorithm for generating public-private key pairs. In addition, we have described a public key infrastructure which can be used to associate identities with these key pairs.

This constitutes the end of our dive into cryptography, and in the next chapter, we will proceed to the main corpus of this book, blockchain and cryptocurrency applications.

---

[6]Typically, we would convert this hash into a 512-bit hexadecimal string since the hash would include non-alphanumeric ASCII characters.

CHAPTER 6

The Constructor's Guide to Blockchains

In the last few chapters, we have studied some of the mathematical concepts of cryptography which are pertinent to blockchains and cryptocurrencies. Now that we have all of this arcane theory in our heads, we are now ready to move to the heart of the matter, the construction of blockchain and cryptocurrency applications.

In this chapter and the chapters that follow, we will examine the components which are required to build blockchain applications. Components such as blockchains, Merkle trees, peer-to-peer networks, transactions, mining, and so forth. As we proceed, I will be building a cryptocurrency called Helium from scratch in Python. The chapters that follow will typically be paired. The first chapter will expose the theory of the particular component under examination. The following chapter will develop the Python code that implements this component. The entire code pertaining to this component will also be presented in an appendix of this book. If you are primarily interested in the underlying theory, you can safely ignore the code implementation chapters.

Since this is a book about learning blockchain concepts, I use the simplest possible Python code; lucidity is favored over brevity or *Rubyesque* magic. If you are an experienced Python developer, you may find the code non-idiomatic and verbose. This is deliberately so by intention, in order to keep the barrier to this book at the lowest level possible. Secondly, I have tried to annotate the code with extensive inline comments, even at the risk of being redundant and explaining the obvious. Our friend is the KISS principle (keep it simple, stupid). It has frequently been observed that nature favors simplicity over complexity.[1] As a software developer, I have had very bad experiences

---

[1]Another articulation of KISS is Occam's razor. Occam's razor states that where several explanations of a phenomena exist, the simplest should be preferred. At the extreme end of this philosophical digression is the mathematician Gauss's hypothesis that the entire observable universe can be created from a set of axioms imposed upon the set of natural numbers {0, ,1,2,3, ...}.

© Karan Singh Garewal 2020
K. S. Garewal, *Practical Blockchains and Cryptocurrencies*, https://doi.org/10.1007/978-1-4842-5893-4_6

reading the code written by other programmers, so I want to spare you the anguish and pain of such an experience.

Alright, let us start.

Why Write a Cryptocurrency in Python?

A cryptocurrency can be developed using a variety of languages. For Helium, I considered C++, Go, and Python. The main advantage of coding Helium in C++ would be that C++ has exceptional runtime performance and can produce very high-quality production code. Equally important, we can use C++ class constructs, data encapsulation, polymorphism, and other object-oriented design principles to develop Helium in a modular way. I discarded C++ as a candidate, primarily because this is a book about learning and implementing concepts, and C++ would have restricted readership. C++ is a complex language, and developing Helium in C++ would have required a readership that is very proficient in the language.

I like Go a lot.[2] Go has been developed by programmers who were closely associated with the C language. Go is simple and easy to learn. The influence of the C programming language is manifestly evident in Go. In essence, Go is C for the Web. Go is a very minimalist language; it eschews complexity and follows the C metaprogramming principle that there should be only one way to do a particular thing. Go has many very cool features. It is a strictly typed, compiled language and is thus very fast. Like C, Go has a full-featured and high-quality standard library.[3] It has an implementation of concurrency which is hands down better than that in any other language, excepting C++. The characterization of Go as a systems language for infrastructure applications is a *canard*. Go is, in fact, a general programming language, much like C++ and Python. Go is not an object-oriented language, and in lieu thereof it offers structs and interfaces. I eliminated Go as the development language for Helium on the basis that very few developers are acquainted with this language, and thus, its usage in this book would restrict readership.

---

[2]https://golang.org/, last accessed on January 20, 2020

[3]For example, the Go standard library has all of the functions required to create a web application. In Go, we do not need to create a web framework.

When a programming language pole vaults into the rare stratosphere of the four most popular languages,[4] joining heavyweights such as C++, Java, and C, you just know that it has something going for it. Python is a powerful and expressive interpreted language that is simple to learn. Python has a huge library of software packages and is thus used in a large spectrum of cutting-edge areas, such as machine learning, neural networks, finance, virtual reality, genomics, and so forth. Python is a favorite language of scientists and academics who are not programmers. We will develop Helium in Python. Note that once you understand the architecture and algorithms typically used in blockchain applications, you can develop your application in C++, Go, or any other language for that matter. You can, of course, re-code Helium in your preferred language.

One final note is in order; my endeavor is to make the Helium code largely self-contained, and therefore, I will shun the extensive use of Python libraries.

The Computer Is the Blockchain

In 1995 or thereabouts, John Gage opined that *the network is the computer.* Gage's hypothesis was that, sometime in the future, desktop operating systems such as Windows and desktop applications would be replaced by applications running on wide area networks. It was a remarkable observation considering that it was made in 1996 when the Internet was still in a nascent stage. If blockchain technology fulfills its promise of being a foundation stone for Internet applications, we will be able to truthfully assert that *the computer is the blockchain.* So what exactly is a blockchain?

Understanding Blockchains

A blockchain is an ordered, immutable, and tamper-resistant collection of blocks of data where each block, except for the first, is related to its predecessor block using cryptographic techniques.[5] Take a look at Figure 6-1.

---

[4]www.tiobe.com/tiobe-index/, last accessed on January 10, 2020

[5]The blockchain is the invention of Satoshi Nakamoto, who is also the inventor of Bitcoin, the world's first cryptocurrency.

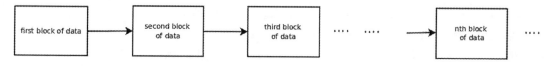

Figure 6-1. *A Blockchain*

Each block contains data which is specific to the domain of the blockchain application. Furthermore, each block is immutable once it is created. Each block is also tamper-proof; its data cannot be changed by a malicious interloper. Aside from the first block, each block is related to its previous block through a cryptographic relation. The blocks are ordered, meaning that they follow each other in a fixed, linear order. This ordered, immutable collection of blocks with cryptographic relations is called a blockchain.[6]

As more blocks are created, they are added to the head (right side) of the blockchain. In a canonical blockchain application, the blockchain keeps on increasing in size as more blocks are added on the right side. For example, the Bitcoin blockchain is over 250 GB and growing.

Canonical blockchain applications maintain a distributed blockchain. This means that there are entities on the Internet which have a copy of the blockchain. These copies need not be identical with each other, in which case it is the responsibility of each entity to synchronize its copy of the blockchain. This synchronization requires a distributed consensus mechanism that resolves the differences between these copies. Take note that this synchronization does not require any centralized entity. Distributed consensus algorithms are a very important part of blockchain applications, and we will be examining distributed consensus closely in later chapters. Since the blockchain is distributed, a blockchain is sometimes described as a distributed ledger.

Distributed consensus has important implications. There is no need for a central authority to maintain the integrity of the blockchain. This means that a blockchain is permission-less and open to the world at large. Distributed consensus solves one of the major hurdles in the creation of a distributed currency, the double-spend problem. This problem refers to a scenario where a person who owns a certain quantum of a cryptocurrency attempts to spend it twice. In centralized fiat money systems, it is trivial to prevent double-spending. However, it is a major hurdle when we are creating a

---

[6]If you are conversant with C or C++, you can visualize a blockchain as a linked list with some cryptographic constraints imposed upon it.

distributed cryptocurrency. The foregoing discussion will become crystal clear when we get into the mechanics of actually creating a cryptocurrency.

In canonical blockchain applications such as Bitcoin, time is not an important variable. Transactions are not ordered by time, and there is no central timekeeper or any need to synchronize the times of blockchain entities. Transactions can occur in any order, and the distributed consensus algorithm will sort everything out. This is a very powerful idea. By way of contrast, in a fiat money banking system, time is very important and transaction validity is typically tied to which transaction occurred first.

Blockchains are typically meant to survive over time, so they are usually persisted to a hard disk or some other media. Lastly, in the typical blockchain application, members of the public are allowed to examine the blockchain, but this need not necessarily be so.

The Genesis Block

The very first block of a blockchain is called the genesis block. It is typically initiated by the application to bootstrap the blockchain. For example, in a cryptocurrency application, the genesis block will typically include an initial distribution of the currency.

The Blockchain Database

You may be inclined to conclude that a blockchain should be implemented using a database such as PostgreSQL, Cassandra, or Redis. This is a bad practice. A blockchain application should keep its implementation at the simplest and most transparent level that is possible, especially since cryptocurrency applications involve money. A database implementation introduces too much complexity. What do we do if the data in the database is corrupted or the database crashes?

The canonical blockchain application simply persists the blocks in a blockchain as a simple text or binary files. The underlying operating system is used to write blocks to disk. A block is a write once read many times file.

This does not mean that a blockchain application does not use databases. For example, Bitcoin uses LevelDB databases to index the blocks and maintain unspent amounts. In a blockchain application, these databases always play a role ancillary to the blockchain, and the data in these databases can always be built from scratch from the blockchain.

Hash Pointers Are the Secret Ingredient

We will now examine how the blocks in a blockchain are associated through cryptographic relations. Each block in a blockchain, aside from the genesis block, looks something like Figure 6-2.

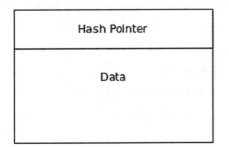

Figure 6-2. *A Block in a Blockchain*

A block consists of some application-specific data and a structure called a hash pointer. A hash pointer can be visualized as shown in Figure 6-3.

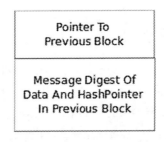

Figure 6-3. *Hash Pointer Structure*

A hash pointer is a data structure that

- Points to the location of the previous block

- Contains the message digest of the previous block's data and hash pointer

The pointer to the location of the previous block is the address of the previous block. For example, this pointer can be a path to a block file, a location in memory, or an index into a list. The pointer depends upon how the blocks are represented. Since the genesis block does not have a previous block, we simply set its hash pointer to null.

For the message digest computation, we can use SHA-256.

Thus, given a hash pointer, we can retrieve the data and message digest of the previous block. This permits us to verify that the data in the previous block has not been tampered with.

We can now represent a blockchain with hash pointers as shown in Figure 6-4.

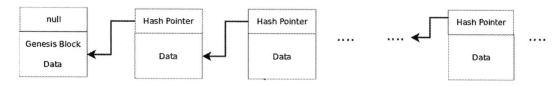

Figure 6-4. *Blockchain Structure*

Blockchain Immutability

It is quite easy to detect if a blockchain has been tampered with. Consider the blockchain represented in Figure 6-4. Suppose further that the hash pointer for each block (except for the genesis block) includes the SHA-256 message digest of the previous block's data and hash pointer.

Suppose that a malicious party changes the data or the hash pointer in the second block. An entity that is verifying that the blockchain has not been altered will compute the SHA-256 message digest of the second block. It will then compare this value with the SHA-256 message digest contained in the hash pointer of the third block. Since these two digests do not match, the entity will conclude that either the second block has been altered or the message digest in the third block has been altered.

Since the malicious party has tampered with the second block, he will also have to change the cryptographic hash in the third block so that it matches the computed hash of the second block. But then the cryptographic hash in the fourth block will not match the computed hash for the third block. This changing of hash pointers will have to be effected for all of the blocks subsequent to the block which was initially changed. Furthermore, since a blockchain is a distributed data structure, the changed blocks will have to be transmitted to all of the other nodes in the blockchain network so that they can amend their copies of the blockchain. These nodes will detect the tampering and decline to change their copies.

Making a Simple Blockchain

Let us construct a very simple blockchain in Python. Our blockchain will be a list structure (called an array in other languages):

```
blockchain = [ ]
```

We will let the data in each block be the next number in the Fibonacci sequence (0, 1, 1, 2, 3, 5, 8, 13, 21...). For each block except the genesis block, the data and the hash pointer will be represented as the following dictionary item (or map in other languages):

```
{
  'ptr':  index of the previous list element
  'hash': SHA-256 hash of the previous block as a hexadecimal string
  'data': Fibonacci number
}
```

The SHA-256 message digest of a block will be computed by converting the list element's value to a JSON string and then computing the hexadecimal value of the SHA-256 message digest of this string.

Given the foregoing specification, the genesis block is

```
blockchain[0] = {
                  'ptr': None
                  'hash': None
                  'data': 0
}
```

The second block in this blockchain is

```
blockchain[0] = {
                  'ptr': 0
                  'hash': a hexadecimal string
                  'data': 1
}
```

and so forth.

One observation to be made is that since this blockchain is a list, the pointer to the previous block can be represented simply as the index of the previous list element.

The Blockchain Universe

So far, we have taken a deep dive into the theory of blockchains; it's time to look at some of the applications of blockchains. As a general principle, we can state that any application that requires distributed consensus for decision-making is potentially a suitable candidate for the implementation of a blockchain.

The very first use of a blockchain was in the cryptocurrency Bitcoin, and cryptocurrencies still constitute a major application domain for blockchains. Another major domain is smart contract cryptocurrencies, such as Ethereum. These cryptocurrencies permit the specification of contracts which specify conditions under which value will be transferred. These contracts are specified through a programming language that a blockchain virtual machine understands.[7] Projects, such as Ripple, are concerned with automating portions of the financial services industry with the objectives of reducing the costs of transactions and the time required for their completion.

In Chapter 2, we looked at the Brave browser which proposes a radical model for the distribution of digital advertising. The Brave project enhances privacy on the Internet and also rewards all of the stakeholders in the distribution of digital advertising: the content creators, the people viewing this content, and the browser which hosts the content. All these stakeholders are rewarded with units of the BAT cryptocurrency.

Another application domain is games and digital content. TRON is an example of such a project. TRON is designed to democratize the distribution of such content by eliminating gatekeepers who host this content. The TRON project uses the BitTorrent protocol to distribute and retrieve such content.[8]

Other application domains for blockchain technology include supply chain management, tamper-proof voting systems, distributed id systems, and permission-less escrow systems. There are, of course, many more potential application domains for this technology.

---

[7]See Chapter 2.

[8]https://github.com/tronprotocol/java-tron

Conclusion

In this chapter, we have defined a blockchain and discussed its theoretical foundations and essential characteristics. We concluded by discussing some of the application domains for blockchain technology.

In the next chapter, we will start our main project, the construction of a cryptocurrency called Helium. Our first task will be to program a blockchain for Helium.

References

Antonopoulos, Andreas. Mastering Bitcoin, 2nd ed., O'Reilly Media Inc., 2017

Iyer, Kedar and Dannen, Kris. Building Games with Ethereum Smart Contracts, Apress, 2018

CHAPTER 7

The Helium Cryptocurrency Project

In this chapter, we shall begin the construction of the Helium cryptocurrency. Our implementation is going to include all of the features that you expect in a production-quality cryptocurrency. Helium is modeled after Bitcoin, which is the canonical standard. We will implement Helium in Python. Python is a simple yet powerful language whose syntax is lucid and exceptionally easy to understand. Python is an ideal language for clearly exposing the algorithms and techniques that constitute the backbone of a cryptocurrency. The downside of using Python is that it is an interpreted language and thus inherently slow. This limitation makes it unsuitable for a production environment.

The Python code implementation of Helium should provide you with a reliable blueprint to implement a cryptocurrency in some other high-performance, compiled language, such as C, C++, Go, or Rust, if you are so inclined.[1]

If you are primarily interested in the theory of blockchains and cryptocurrencies, just read the "Helium Configuration" section of this chapter.

---

[1]C++ is the most widely used language for implementing cryptocurrencies. Heuristically, C and C++ implementations should have roughly the same performance. A Go implementation should be about 15% slower than a C++ implementation, primarily because Go has garbage collection and the Go compiler does not have all of the optimizations which the GCC C++ compiler has accrued over 25 years of refinement. Python is anywhere from 10 to 100 times slower than C++. See these benchmarks at `https://benchmarksgame-team.pages.debian.net/benchmarksgame/fastest/gpp-python3.html`. Despite the hoopla, I do not think that Rust is superior to C++ and cannot displace the usage of C++ in the design and implementation of large-scale systems (see Lakos, John, *Large-Scale C++ Volume I: Process and Architecture*, Pearson Education Inc., 2020).

© Karan Singh Garewal 2020
K. S. Garewal, *Practical Blockchains and Cryptocurrencies*, https://doi.org/10.1007/978-1-4842-5893-4_7

Python Installation and the Virtual Environment

The very first order of business is the creation of a virtual environment for Helium. You are going to need a Python version greater than or equal to 3.8. Appendix 1 of this book contains the instructions for creating such a virtual environment.

You can create your virtual environment inside any directory (folder), but if you want to follow this book exactly, then I suggest creating the virtual environment in the */var/www/* directory.[2] In addition, install Python version 3.8 in your virtual environment. Your Helium virtual environment will then be inside the following directory (folder):

`/var/www/helium/`

We will call the directory */var/www/helium/* the root of the virtual environment or equivalently the root of the Helium project, and on many occasions, I will simply refer to this directory as the Helium root.

Inside the root directory, create the following 12 sub-directories: *block*, *chainstate*, *config*, *crypt*, *data*, *hnetwork*, *mining*, *simulated_network*, *testnet*, *transactions*, *unit_tests*, and *wallet*. The *block* directory will hold our blockchain implementation. The *crypt* directory will have the cryptographic functions that Helium requires, and our unit tests will reside inside the *unit_tests* directory.

The *data* directory will hold Helium blocks as well as other data. I will discuss the other directories in subsequent chapters.

In order to access the Python modules in these directories, we must add the paths to these directories to the Python search path. Make sure that you have activated your virtual environment as follows. From the root directory, do

`source virtual/bin/activate`

From the root directory, traverse to the *virtual/lib/python3.8/site-packages/* directory.[3] Create a file called *helium.pth* inside this directory, and then add the following lines to this file:

```
/var/www/helium/block/
/var/www/helium/chainstate
/var/www/helium/config/
```

---

[2]This will also save time if we implement an Ubuntu staging server at */var*/www/.
[3]If you have installed a different Python version, change the path accordingly.

```
/var/www/helium/crypt/
/var/www/helium/data/
/var/www/helium/hnetwork/
/var/www/helium/mining/
/var/www/helium/simulated_network
/var/www/helium/testnet/
/var/www/helium/transactions/
/var/www/helium/unit_tests/
/var/www/helium/wallet
```

Save this file and then deactivate and activate your environment from the root directory[4]

```
$(virtual) deactivate
$ /bin/activate
```

You should be using Git to periodically commit your work to a repository. Traverse to the root directory, initialize Git, and do an initial commit:[5]

```
$(virtual) git init
$(virtual) git add .
$(virtual) git commit -m "initial Helium commit, virtual environment
created"
```

You can view your commit history with

```
$(virtual) git log
```

git will enable you to roll back to a previous version in case you make an error. You may want to commit source code changes often.

Helium Configuration

Helium uses several vital configuration parameters that define the characteristics and behavior of this cryptocurrency. The following is a brief description of these parameters. Do not be concerned if you do not understand the meaning of some of these parameters yet. Their meaning and significance will become clearer in our subsequent exposition.

---

[4]$(virtual) indicates the system command-line prompt when the virtual environment is active.

[5]If git is not installed on your Linux system, install it with $ apt-get install git-core. This command will work on all Debian distributions, such as Ubuntu and Mint.

The Helium Version Number

`VERSION_NUMBER = 1`

This is the current version number of the Helium application.

The Maximum Number of Helium Coins

`MAX_HELIUM_COINS = 21_000_000`

This is the maximum number of Helium coins that can come into existence. We will call a helium coin a helium, and a number of helium coins will be called heliums.

A fixed number of heliums are initially created and distributed in the genesis block. The genesis block is a hard-coded block that bootstraps the block creation process. In Bitcoin, Satoshi Nakamoto created and distributed 50 bitcoins in the genesis block.

Subsequently, new heliums are created as blocks are added to the Helium blockchain. Note that the maximum number of heliums that can be created is identical to the maximum number of bitcoins that can be produced in the Bitcoin ecosystem.

The Smallest Helium Currency Unit

`HELIUM_CENT = 1/100_000_000`

HELIUM_CENT is the smallest subdivision of a helium that is possible. Observe that a hundred million Helium cents is equal to a helium. This definition corresponds to the definition of a satoshi in Bitcoin.

Helium Block Size

`MAX_BLOCK_SIZE = 1_000_000`

MAX_BLOCK_SIZE is the maximum size of a Helium block in bytes. The maximum size of a block determines the maximum number of Helium transactions that can be included in a block[6] and *a fortiori* the average number of transactions in a block.

---

[6]In Chapter 2, we discussed Bitcoin Cash and its attempt to improve performance over Bitcoin by increasing the maximum size of a block.

The Maximum Transaction Inputs

A Helium transaction collects unspent values from previous transactions and then transfers these values to one or more recipients of value. The *Max-Inputs* parameter limits the maximum number of inputs in a transaction. This limitation promotes efficient transaction processing and helps avert denial-of-service attacks:

```
MAX_INPUTS = 10
```

The Maximum Transaction Outputs

A Helium transaction transfers values to one or more recipients of value.
The *Max_Outputs* parameter limits the maximum number of recipients in a transaction:

```
MAX_OUTPUTS = 10
```

The Locktime Interval

```
MAX_LOCKTIME = 60*1440*7
```

An entity creating a transaction can specify that this transaction is not to be processed until a certain amount of time has elapsed. This will prevent miners from including this transaction in a block to be mined until this time interval has elapsed. Elapsed time is in seconds.

MAX_LOCKTIME specifies the maximum amount of time in seconds that a transaction can be locked from the time of its creation. We do not want to indefinitely lock transactions or lock transactions for very long periods of time. This can give rise to denial-of-service attacks as transaction caches maintained by miners become clogged with future transactions.

The preceding configuration parameter sets the maximum period of time that a transaction can be locked to seven days.

The Coinbase Interval

```
COINBASE_INTERVAL = 100
```

This positive integer specifies the number of new blocks that must be mined after a previous reference block, before a coinbase transaction in the reference block can be spent. When a miner mines a block, he is rewarded with the issuance of a fixed amount of new cryptocurrency. This new currency is presented to the miner in a coinbase transaction in the block. The coinbase interval parameter precludes a miner from spending a coinbase transaction until a certain number of new blocks have been added to the blockchain.

In Helium, a new block is mined every ten minutes approximately, so Helium coinbase transactions are locked for approximately 1000 minutes.

Nonce

```
NONCE = 0
```

This is a seed value. NONCE is the starting value that will be used in mining proof-of-work computations. We will discuss this use of nonces subsequently.

The Difficulty Number

```
DIFFICULTY_BITS   = 20
DIFFICULTY_NUMBER =  1/ (10 ** (256 - DIFFICULTY_BITS))
```

The DIFFICULTY_BITS parameter lets us adjust the DIFFICULTY_NUMBER. In Helium as well as Bitcoin, mining a block involves solving a difficult mathematical problem. The DIFFICULTY_NUMBER determines how difficult this problem is and hence the average amount of time it will take to solve this problem.

A block is said to be mined when this difficult problem is solved by a Helium mining node. The node that solves this problem is entitled to append the mined block to the blockchain and is entitled to a reward of freshly mined heliums as well as the transaction fees attached to all of the transactions in the mined block.

Retarget Interval

```
RETARGET_INTERVAL = 1000
```

Helium attempts to mine new blocks every ten minutes. After 1000 new blocks have been mined, Helium uses an algorithm to adjust the DIFFICULTY_NUMBER so that blocks are mined every ten minutes on average.

The Bitcoin algorithm also attempts to mine a new block every ten minutes on average. Litecoin, which is quite similar to Bitcoin, attempts to mine new blocks every two minutes on average.

The Mining Reward

MINING_REWARD = 5_000_000_000

The MINING_REWARD is the amount of new heliums in HELIUM_CENTS that are created and awarded to a mining node that successfully mines a block. The initial mining reward in Helium is five billion HELIUM_CENTS or five Helium coins (five heliums). This reward corresponds to the initial mining reward in Bitcoin.

In Helium as well as Bitcoin, the mining reward algorithm halves the mining reward periodically. The point in time when the reward is halved depends upon the number of blocks that have already been mined. Because of this periodic halving, the mining reward asymptotically approaches zero.

A cryptocurrency mining algorithm does not have to halve the reward periodically. There are cryptocurrencies where the number of coins that are created remains constant or varies according to some formula.

Bitcoin came into existence on January 3, 2009, when Satoshi Nakamoto created and mined the genesis block. The mining reward was 50 bitcoins for this block and every block that was mined thereafter. In 2012, this mining reward was halved to 25, and in 2016, the reward was again halved to 12.5 bitcoins. In 2020, the reward was halved to 6.25 bitcoins.

Since the only way to create new heliums or bitcoins is through the mining process (aside from an initial distribution in the genesis block), the mining algorithms in these two cryptocurrencies create an upper limit on the number of heliums or bitcoins that can be created. Thus, these algorithms create a scarcity of heliums and bitcoins over time, and this scarcity theoretically enhances the value of these cryptocurrencies.

Reward Interval

REWARD_INTERVAL = 210,000

The REWARD_INTERVAL determines the number of additional blocks that must be mined in order to halve the mining reward. For example, after two hundred and ten thousand new blocks have been mined, the mining reward will be halved. This number is identical to the interval used in Bitcoin.

Helium Configuration Module

We create a configuration module for Helium as follows. Create a file h*config.py* in the *config* directory and copy the following source code into this file:

```
"""

hconfig.py:  parameters that are used to configure Helium.
"""

conf = {

    # The Helium version no.
    'VERSION_NO': 1,

    # The maximum number of Helium coins that can be mined
    'MAX_HELIUM_COINS': 21_000_000,

    # The smallest Helium currency unit in terms of one Helium coin
    'HELIUM_CENT':  1/100_000_000,

    # The maximum size of a Helium block in bytes
    'MAX_BLOCK_SIZE': 1_000_000,

    # The maximum amount of time in seconds that a transaction can be locked
    'MAX_LOCKTIME': 30*1440*60,

    # The maximum number of Inputs in a Helium Transaction
    'MAX_INPUTS': 10,

    # The maximum number of Outputs in a Helium Transaction
    'MAX_OUTPUTS': 10,

    # The number of new blocks from a reference block that must be mined before
    # coinbase transaction  in the previous reference block can be spent
    'COINBASE_INTERVAL': 100,

    # The starting nonce value for the mining proof of work computations
    'NONCE': 0,
```

```
#
# Difficulty Number used in mining proof of work computations
#
'DIFFICULTY_BITS': 20,
'DIFFICULTY_NUMBER':  1/ (10 ** (256 - 20)),

#
# Retargeting interval in blocks in order to adjust the DIFFICULTY_NUMBER
#
'RETARGET_INTERVAL': 1000,

#
#Mining Reward
#
'MINING_REWARD': 5_000_000_000,

#
# Mining reward halving interval in blocks
#
'REWARD_INTERVAL': 210_000
}
```

Conclusion

In this chapter, we have commenced the construction of the Helium cryptocurrency by specifying important configuration parameters in a configuration module. These parameters bear upon the transaction processing, mining, and currency creation characteristics of Helium. They are, of course, modifiable by the software developer. Our Helium configuration is modeled after Bitcoin.

In the next chapter, we will develop the Helium cryptographic module. This module is used to sustain all of the cryptographic operations that are performed by Helium. After this, we will develop the Helium blockchain.

References

Bitcoin, retrieved from `https://github.com/bitcoin/bitcoin`, last accessed on June 29, 2020

Bitcoin Developer Reference, bitcoin.org, retrieved from `https://developer.bitcoin.org/reference/`, last accessed on June 29, 2020

Bitcoin Improvement Proposals, `https://github.com/bitcoin/bips`, last accessed on June 29, 2020

The Litecoin Project, `https://github.com/litecoin-project/litecoin/tree/master/src/leveldb`, last accessed on March 28, 2020

Dhillon V., Metcalfe D., Hooper Max, 1st ed., Blockchain Enabled Applications, Apress, 2017

CHAPTER 8

The Helium Blockchain

In this chapter, we continue forward from the last chapter and begin the construction of the Helium blockchain. Firstly, we will create the interface for the cryptographic functions that are used by Helium, and next we will develop some of Helium's blockchain functionality.

If you are primarily interested in the theory of blockchains and cryptocurrencies, please feel free to proceed to the next theory chapter.

Python Crypto Packages

Helium makes extensive use of cryptographic functions, especially SHA-256, RIPEMD-160, and digital signatures. This functionality is available in the Python *pycryptodome* package. So, let us install this package. Ensure that you are at the root of your virtual Helium environment and that the virtual environment is active. Do

```
$(virtual) pip install pycryptodome
```

We will also need some ancillary Python modules. Firstly, we will be using Python's *re* module. *re* is included in the standard Python distribution, so there is no need to install it. It is Python's regular expression parser. *re* examines strings for the presence or absence of specified sub-strings and can also perform text substitutions.

Next, we must install the *Base58* module. Base58 converts a very large string into a restricted alphanumeric string. The Base58 alphanumeric character set is

```
123456789ABCDEFGHJKLMNPQRSTUVWXYZabcdefghijkmnopqrstuvwxyz
```

A Base58-encoded string only includes characters from the preceding set.

© Karan Singh Garewal 2020
K. S. Garewal, *Practical Blockchains and Cryptocurrencies*, https://doi.org/10.1007/978-1-4842-5893-4_8

The Base58 character set differs from the ordinary alphanumeric character set, in that it excludes characters that can be easily confused. The excluded characters are I (capital I), l (lowercase L), O (capital o), and 0 (zero).[1]

We will also be using the *pdb* debugger. *pdb* enables us to set breakpoints in source code, step through our source code line by line, and examine stack frames and the values of variables.[2] *pdb* is part of the Python standard distribution, so there is no need to install it through *pip*. We will always import the *pdb* module into our Helium source code files.

rcrypt Module Walkthrough

The following module file, *rcrypt.py*, is the Helium interface into the cryptographic package *pycryptodome*. Copy the following *rcrypt* code into a file named *rcrypt.py* and save this file in *crypt* sub-directory.[3]

We are now ready for a code walkthrough of the *rcrypt* interface module:

```
"""
The rcrypt module implements various cryptographic functions that are
required by
the Helium cryptocurrency application
This module requires the pycryptodome package to be installed.
The base58 package encodes strings into base58 format.
This module uses Python's regular expression module re.
This module uses the secrets module in the Python standard library to generate
cryptographically secure hexadecimal encoded strings.
"""

# import the regular expressions module
import re
# imports from the cryptodome package
from Crypto.Hash import SHA3_256
from Crypto.PublicKey import ECC
from Crypto.PublicKey import DSA
from Crypto.Signature import DSS
```

---

[1]Base58 encoding was invented by Satoshi Nakamoto for use in Bitcoin.
[2]See https://docs.python.org/3/library/pdb.html
[3]All of the Helium source code is also available in the second last appendix of this book.

```python
from Crypto.Hash import SHA256
from Crypto.Hash import RIPEMD160

import base58
import secrets

# import Python's debugging and logging modules
import pdb
import logging
"""
   log debugging messages to the file debug.log
"""
logging.basicConfig(filename="debug.log",filemode="w", \
  format='%(asctime)s:%(levelname)s:%(message)s', level=logging.DEBUG)

def make_SHA256_hash(msg: 'string') -> 'string':
    """

    make_sha256_hash computes the SHA-256 message digest or cryptographic hash
    for a received string argument. The secure hash value that is generated
    is converted
    into a sequence of hexadecimal digits and then returned by the function.
    The hexadecimal format of the message digest is 64 bytes long.
    """

    #convert the received msg string to a sequence of ascii bytes
    message = bytes(msg, 'ascii')

    # compute the SHA-256 message digest of msg and convert to a
    hexadecimal format
    hash_object = SHA256.new()
    hash_object.update(message)
    return hash_object.hexdigest()

def validate_SHA256_hash(digest: "string") -> bool:
    """

    validate_SHA256_hash: tests whether a string has an encoding conforming
    to a
    SHA-256 message digest in hexadecimal string format (64 bytes).
```

```
    """
    # a hexadecimal SHA256 message digest must be 64 bytes long.
    if len(digest) != 64: return False

    # This regular expression tests that the received string contains only
    # hexadecimal characters
    if re.search('[^0-9a-fA-F]', digest) == None: return True
    return False

def make_RIPEMD160_hash(message: 'byte stream') -> 'string':
    """
    RIPEMD-160 is a cryptographic algorithm that emits a 20 byte message digest.
    This function computes the RIPEMD-160 message digest of a message and
    returns
    the hexadecimal string encoded representation of the message digest
    (40 bytes).
    """
    # convert message to an ascii byte stream
    bstr = bytes(message, 'ascii')
    # generate the RIPEMD hash of message
    h = RIPEMD160.new()
    h.update(bstr)
    # convert to a hexadecimal encoded string
    hash = h.hexdigest()
    return hash

def validate_RIPEMD160_hash(digest: 'string') -> 'bool':
    """
    tests that a received string has an encoding conforming to a RIPE160
    hash in
    hexadecimal format
    """
    if len(digest) != 40: return False

    # This regular expression tests that received string only contains
    # hexadecimal characters
    if re.search('[^0-9a-fA-F]+', digest) == None: return True
```

```
    return False

def make_ecc_keys():
    """

    make a private-public key pair using the elliptic curve cryptographic
    functions in the pycryptodome package.
    returns a tuple with the private key and public key in PEM format
    """

    # generate an ecc object
    ecc_key = ECC.generate(curve='P-256')
    # get the public key object
    pk_object = ecc_key.public_key()
    # export the private-public key pair in PEM format
    p = (ecc_key.export_key(format='PEM'), pk_object.export_key(format='PEM'))

    return p

def sign_message(private_key: 'String', message: 'String') -> 'string':
    """

    digitally signs a message using a private key generated using the
    elliptic curve cryptography module of the pycryptodome package.
    Receives a private key in PEM format and the message that is to be
    digitally signed.
    returns a hex encoded signature string.
    """

    # import the PEM format private key
    priv_key = ECC.import_key(private_key)

    # convert the message to a byte stream and
    # compute the SHA-256 message digest of the message
    bstr = bytes(message, 'ascii')

    hash    = SHA256.new(bstr)
    # create a digital signature object from the private key
    signer = DSS.new(priv_key, 'fips-186-3')

    # sign the SHA-256 message digest.
    signature = signer.sign(hash)
```

```
    sig = signature.hex()
    return sig

def verify_signature(public_key: 'String', msg: 'String', signature:
'string') -> 'bool':
    """
    tests whether a message is digitally signed by a private key to which a
    public key is paired.
    Receives a ECC public key in PEM format, the message that is to to be
    verified
    and the digital signature of the message.
    Returns True or False
    """

    try:
        # convert the message to a byte stream and compute the SHA-256 hash
        msg = bytes(msg, 'ascii')
        msg_hash = SHA256.new(msg)

        # signature to bytes
        signature = bytes.fromhex(signature)
        # import the PEM formatted public key and create a signature verifier
        # object from the public key
        pub_key  = ECC.import_key(public_key)
        verifier = DSS.new(pub_key, 'fips-186-3')

        # Verify the authenticity of the signed message
        verifier.verify(msg_hash, signature)
        return True

    except Exception as err:
        logging.debug('verify_signature: exception: ' + str(err))

def make_address(prefix: 'string') -> 'string':
    """
    generates a Helium address from a ECC public key in PEM format.
    prefix is a single numeric character which describes the type of
    the address. This prefix must be '1'
    """
```

```python
    key = ECC.generate(curve='P-256')
    __private_key = key.export_key(format='PEM')
    public_key = key.public_key().export_key(format='PEM')

    val = make_SHA256_hash(public_key)
    val = make_RIPEMD160_hash(val)
    tmp = prefix + val

    # make a checksum
    checksum = make_SHA256_hash(tmp)
    checksum = checksum[len(checksum) - 4:]

    # add the checksum to the tmp result
    address = tmp + checksum

    # encode addr as a base58 sequence of bytes
    address =  base58.b58encode(address.encode())

    # The decode function converts a byte sequence to a string
    address = address.decode("ascii")

    return address

def validate_address(address: 'string') -> bool:
    """

    validates a Helium address using the four character checksum appended
    to the address. Receives a base58 encoded address.
    """

    # encode the string address as a sequence of bytes
    addr = address.encode("ascii")
    # reverse the base58 encoding of the address
    addr = base58.b58decode(addr)
    # convert the address into a string
    addr = addr.decode("ascii")

    # length must be RIPEMD-160 hash length + length of checksum + 1
    if (len(addr) != 45): return False
    if (addr[0] != '1'):  return False
```

```
    # extract the checksum
    extracted_checksum = addr[len(addr) - 4:]

    # extract the checksum out of addr and compute the
    # SHA-256 hash of the remaining addr string
    tmp = addr[:len(addr)- 4]
    tmp = make_SHA256_hash(tmp)

    # get the computed checksum from tmp
    checksum = tmp[len(tmp) - 4:]

    if extracted_checksum  == checksum: return True

    return False

def make_uuid() -> 'string':
    """
    makes an universally unique 256 bit id encoded as a hexadecimal string
    that is
    used as a transaction identifier. Uses the Python standard library
    secrets module to
    generate a cryptographic strong random 32 byte string encoded as a
    hexadecimal
    string (64 bytes)
    """
    id = secrets.token_hex(32)

    return id
```

A Pytest Primer

Unit tests provide us with assurances of code correctness. Consequently, we should always strive to provide a high amount of coverage of our code with unit tests. Conceptually, a unit test tests a small discrete piece of code. This piece of code is typically a function, but it can also be something small like an expression or a collection of expressions. We will be using the Python *Pytest* module to perform unit testing on our modules.

If you are not acquainted with the *Pytest* unit test framework, you can read Appendix 3. Appendix 3 is a comprehensive tutorial on how to use *Pytest*.

All of the *Pytest* files for Helium are available in the last appendix of this book.

rcrypt Unit Tests

Install the *Pytest* module from the root of your Helium virtual environment:

```
$(virtual) pip install pytest
```

Create a file called *test_rcrypt.py* in the *unit_tests* directory of your virtual environment, and then copy the following source code into this file. Traverse to the *unit_tests* directory and run the tests with

```
$(virtual) pytest test_rcrypt.py -s
```

The -s qualifier is optional. It provides expanded output:

```
"""
pytest unit tests for the rcrypt module
"""

import pytest
import rcrypt
import pdb

@pytest.mark.parametrize("input_string, value", [
    ('hello world', True),
    ('the quick brown fox jumped over the sleeping dog', True),
    ('0', True),
    ('', True)
])
def test_make_SHA256_hash(input_string, value):
    """

    test that a SHA-256 message digest is created
    """

    ret = rcrypt.make_SHA256_hash(input_string)
    assert rcrypt.validate_SHA256_hash(ret) == value
```

```python
@pytest.mark.parametrize("input_string, value", [
    ('a silent night and a pale paper moon over the saskatchewan river', 64),
    ('Farmer Brown and the sheep-dog', 64),
    ('', 64)
])
def test_SHA256_hash_length(input_string, value):
    """

    test that the length of created SHA3-256 hash in hexadecimal format is
    is 64 bytes
    """

    assert len(rcrypt.make_SHA256_hash('hello world')) == 64

@pytest.mark.parametrize("digest, value", [
    ("123", False),
    ("644bcc7e564373040999aac89e7622f3ca71fba1d972fd94a31c3bfbf24e3938", True),
    ("644bcc7e564373040999aac89e7622f3ca71fba1d972fd94a31c3bfbf24e39380", False),
    ("644bcc7e564373040999aac89e7622f3ca71fba1d972fd94a31cZbfbf24e3938", False),
    ('', False),
    ("644bcc7e564373040999aac89e7622f3caz1fba1d972fd94a31c3bfbf24e3938", False),
])
def test_validate_SHA256_hash(digest, value):
    """

    validate whether a valid SHA-256 message digest format is generated
    """

    assert rcrypt.validate_SHA256_hash(digest) == value

@pytest.mark.parametrize("string_input, value", [
    ("0", True),
    ('andromeda galaxy', True),
    ('Farmer Brown and the sheep-dog', True),
    ('0', True)
])
def test_make_RIPEMD160_hash(string_input, value):
    """

    validate that a valid RIPEMD-160 message digest format is generated
    """
```

```
    ret = rcrypt.make_RIPEMD160_hash(string_input)
    assert rcrypt.validate_RIPEMD160_hash(ret) == value

@pytest.mark.parametrize("hash, value", [
    ('1234567890987654321690156c79FFa1200CCB1A', False),
    ("lkorkflfor4flgofmr", False),
    ('off0099ijf87', False),
    ('1234567890A87654321690156c79FFa1200CCB1A', True),
])
def test_validate_RIPEMD160_hash(hash, value):
    """

    validate whether a string is in RIPEMD-160 message digest format
    """

    assert rcrypt.validate_RIPEMD160_hash(hash) == value

def test_make_ecc_keys():
    """

    test ECC private-public key pair
    """

    ecc_keys = rcrypt.make_ecc_keys()
    assert ecc_keys[0].find("BEGIN PRIVATE KEY") >= 0
    assert ecc_keys[0].find("END PRIVATE KEY") >= 0
    assert ecc_keys[0].find("END PRIVATE KEY") > ecc_keys[0].find("BEGIN
    PRIVATE KEY")
    assert ecc_keys[1].find("BEGIN PUBLIC KEY") >= 0
    assert ecc_keys[1].find("END PUBLIC KEY") >= 0
    assert ecc_keys[1].find("END PUBLIC KEY") > ecc_keys[1].find("BEGIN
PUBLIC KEY")

@pytest.mark.parametrize("message, value", [
    ('50bfee49c706d766411777aac1c9f35456c33ecea2afb4f3c8f1033b0298bdc9', True),
    ('6e6404d8693aea119a8ef7cf82c56fe96555d8df2c36c2b9e325411fbef62014', True),
    ('ba7816bf8f01cfea414140de5dae2223b00361a396177a9cb410ff61f20015ad', True),
    ('hello world', True),
])
```

89

```python
def test_sign_message(message, value):
    """

    Digitally sign a message and then verify it
    """

    ecc_tuple = rcrypt.make_ecc_keys()
    priv_key  = ecc_tuple[0]
    pub_key   = ecc_tuple[1]

    sig = rcrypt.sign_message(priv_key, message)

    ret = rcrypt.verify_signature(pub_key, message, sig)
    assert ret == value

@pytest.mark.parametrize("prefix, value", [
    ("a", False),
    ("1", True),
    ("Q", False),
    ("qwerty", False),
    ("", False),
])
def test_make_address(prefix, value):
    """

    test the generation of Helium addresses from seeds
    """

    ret = rcrypt.make_address(prefix)
    assert rcrypt.validate_address(ret) == value

@pytest.mark.parametrize("length, ret", [
    (64, True),
    (32, False)
])
def test_make_uuid(length, ret):
    """

    test id generation
    """

    id = rcrypt.make_uuid()
    assert (len(id) == length) == ret
```

You should see 33 unit tests passing.

The Python Logger

You will notice that we make extensive use of the Python logger to assist us in debugging the source code. The following example demonstrates its usage:[4]

```
import logging

logging.basicConfig(filename="debug.log", format='%(asctime)s:%(levelname)
s:%(message)s',
    level=logging.DEBUG)

 ...
def adder(x,y):

    z = x + y

    logging.debug("This is a debug message")
    logging.info("Informational message, output = " + str(z))
    if z != x + y:
        logging.error("An error has happened!")

    return z
```

The parameters of the *logging.basicConfig* function direct that all logging output is to be written to the *debug.log* file and that all log messages with a severity level of *logging. DEBUG* or higher are to be logged. Log levels in order of increasing severity are

```
DEBUG, INFO, WARNING, ERROR, CRITICAL
```

The second parameter of the logger is optional; it specifies the format of the logger's output.

Once we have set the logger's configuration, we can specify a log message for this logger as follows:

```
logger.SEVERITY_LEVEL("Some String %s: %s", message_1, message_2)
```

SEVERITY_LEVEL is a log level: DEBUG, INFO ... CRITICAL.

---

[4]For detailed instructions, see https://docs.python.org/3/howto/logging.html

This will, for example, generate output such as this:

```
2020-02-01 16:05:03,969:SEVERITY_LEVEL:validate_block: nonce is negative
```

By default, the logger appends messages to a log file. We can instruct the logger to overwrite an existing log file by specifying an optional *filemode* parameter:

```
logging.basicConfig(filename="debug.log", filemode='w', level=DEBUG)
```

Helium Block Structure

In this section, we are going to discuss the structure of a Helium block. From Chapter 6, you will recall that a blockchain is an ordered, immutable collection of blocks that have cryptographic validation. Each Helium block is a container for transactions.

A block is the following dictionary data structure (the angle brackets describe the type of the block attribute):

```
{
    "prevblockhash":   <string>
    "version":         <string>
    "timestamp":       <integer>
    "difficulty_bits": <integer>
    "nonce":           <integer>
    "merkle_root":     <string>
    "height":          <integer>
    "tx":              <list>

}
```

In Python, an integer is a signed integer. Python 3 eliminates the difference between integers and long integers. Integers can have any size and are only limited by memory. Python can perform arithmetic operations on integers of unlimited size.

prevblockhash is the SHA-256 message digest of the previous block header in string hexadecimal format. This value is used to test whether the previous block has been tampered with. The *prevblockhash* value of the genesis block is the empty string.

The subset of block attributes *prevblockhash, version, timestamp, difficulty_bits, nonce,* and *merkle_root* is called the block header. The block header does not include the list of transactions. Because the merkle root is included in the header, we can test the validity of the entire block, inclusive of the transactions, by computing the SHA-256 message digest of the header only.

version is the version number of Helium to which this block pertains. This attribute is set in the Helium configuration module and is "1".

timestamp is the Unix timestamp (epoch time) of when the block was created. Epoch time is the number of seconds that have elapsed since midnight, January 1, 1970, Greenwich Mean Time or UTC. It marks the birth of Unix.

difficulty_bits is the DIFFICULTY_BITS as defined in the Helium configuration module. This is the value when the block was mined. Note that the DIFFICULTY_BITS parameter is periodically varied as the average time to mine a block is adjusted toward ten minutes.

nonce is a number used in the Helium mining algorithm.

merkle_root is a SHA-256 hexadecimal string. The merkle root lets us ensure that the transactions in the block have not been tampered with. It also lets us determine if a particular transaction is present in the block. We will discuss this value in a subsequent chapter.

height is the height of this block. Blocks in a blockchain are ordered in conformity with the distributed consensus algorithm and can be visualized as being stacked one on top of another. The first block, which is the genesis block, has height 0.

tx is a list of transactions. The number of transactions in the list is constrained by the maximum permissible size of a block. In the Helium configuration module, this value is set to 1 MB.

Now that we have defined a block, we can specify a Helium blockchain:

```
blockchain = []
```

The blockchain is a list and each list element is a block.[5]

Helium Blockchain Walkthrough

We are now ready to walk through our Helium blockchain code. Copy the following program code into a file named *hblockchain.py* and copy this file into the *block* directory. This is not the complete program code for the blockchain module since transactions

---

[5]We must have sufficient memory to accommodate the entire blockchain or otherwise implement code to swap portions of the blockchain in and out of memory.

and database operations have been abstracted. Since we have not developed the code for transaction and database modules as of yet, we mock operations pertaining to these modules with synthetic values.

The Helium blockchain code uses the *json* and *pickle* modules. Both of these modules are part of the Python standard library, and thus, there is no need to install them. JSON is a data interchange standard that can encode Python objects into strings and then decode these strings back into the corresponding objects. *Pickle* serializes objects by converting objects into a sequence of bytes and then writing this sequence to a file. This process is called serialization. *Pickle* can deserialize files to recover the original objects. If you have never used *Pickle* before, Appendix 5 provides a concise introduction to Pickle usage.

The *add_block* function adds a block to the Helium blockchain. This function receives a block. The function checks whether the block attributes have valid values. In particular, it verifies that the transactions included in the block are valid. In the event that the block is invalid, the function returns with a false value. If the block is valid, the function serializes the block to a raw byte file through the Pickle module. This block is then added to the blockchain list in memory.

The *serialize_block* function serializes a block to the *data* directory using Pickle. The file name is constructed as follows:

```
filename = "block_" + block_height + ".dat"
```

The *read_block* function receives an index into the blockchain and returns the block corresponding to the index. An exception will be thrown if the index is out of bounds.

The *blockheader_hash* function receives a block and returns the SHA-256 message digest of the block header as a hexadecimal string. Observe again that since the merkle root can be used to test whether the transactions in the block have been tampered with, we do not have to compute the SHA-256 cryptographic hash of the block over the entire block contents. It is sufficient to calculate this value over only the block header since it includes the merkle root.

The *validate_block* function tests whether a block has valid values. This function also validates the previous block by comparing SHA-256 message digests.

The final program code listing for *hblockchain* as well as the other Helium modules is available in Appendix 10 of this book:

```
"""

hbockchain.py: This module creates and maintains the Helium blockchain
This is a partial implementation of the module
"""

import rcrypt
import hconfig
import json
import pickle
import pdb
import logging
import os
"""

log debugging messages to the file debug.log
"""

logging.basicConfig(filename="debug.log",filemode="w",\
    format='%(asctime)s:%(levelname)s:%(message)s',level=logging.DEBUG)

"""

A block is a Python dictionary that has the following
structure. The type of an attribute is denoted in angle delimiters.

                {
                    "prevblockhash":    <string>
                    "version":          <string>
                    "timestamp":        <integer>
                    "difficulty_bits":  <integer>
                    "nonce":            <integer>
                    "merkle_root":      <string>
                    "height":           <integer>
                    "tx":               <list>
                }

The blockchain is a list where each list element is a block
This is also referred to as the primary blockchain when used
```

```
by miners.
"""

blockchain    = []

def add_block(block: "dictionary") -> "bool":
    """

    add_block: adds a block to the blockchain. Receives a block.
    The block attributes are checked for validity and each transaction in
    the block is
    tested for validity. If there are no errors, the block is written to a
    file as a
    sequence of raw bytes. Then the block is added to the blockchain.
    returns True if the block is added to the blockchain and False otherwise
    """

    try:
        # validate the received block parameters
        if validate_block(block) == False:
            raise(ValueError("block validation error"))

        # serialize the block to a file
        if (serialize_block(block) == False):
                raise(ValueError("serialize block error"))

        # add the block to the blockchain in memory
        blockchain.append(block)

    except Exception as err:
        print(str(err))
        logging.debug('add_block: exception: ' + str(err))
        return False

    return True

def serialize_block(block: "dictionary") -> "bool":
    """

    serialize_block: serializes a block to a file using pickle.
    Returns True if the block is serialized and False otherwise.
```

```
    """

    index = len(blockchain)
    filename = "block_" + str(index) + ".dat"

    # create the block file and serialize the block
    try:
        f = open(filename, 'wb')
        pickle.dump(block, f)

    except Exception as error:
        logging.debug("Exception: %s: %s", "serialize_block", error)
        f.close()
        return False

    f.close()

    return True

def read_block(blockno: 'long') -> "dictionary or False":
    """

    read_block: receives an index into the Helium blockchain.
    Returns a block or False if the block does not exist.
    """

    try:
        block = blockchain[blockno]
        return block

    except Exception as error:
        logging.debug("Exception: %s: %s", "read_block", error)
        return False

    return block

def blockheader_hash(block: 'dictionary') -> "False or String":
    """

    blockheader_hash: computes and returns SHA-256 message digest of a
    block header
    as a hexadecimal string.
    Receives a block those blockheader hash is to be computed.
```

97

Returns False if there is an error, otherwise returns a SHA-256
hexadecimal string.

The block header consists of the following block fields:
(1) version, (2)previous block hash, (3) merkle root
(4) timestamp, (5) difficulty_bits, and (6) nonce.
"""

```
try:
    hash = rcrypt.make_SHA256_hash(block['version'] +
    block['prevblockhash'] +
                        block['merkle_root'] +
                        str(block['timestamp']) +
                        str(block['difficulty_bits']) +
                        str(block['nonce']))

except Exception as error:
    logging.debug("Exception:%s: %s", "blockheader_hash", error)
    return False

return hash

def validate_block(block: "dictionary") -> "bool":
    """
```

validate_block: receives a block and verifies that all its attributes have
valid values.
Returns True if the block is valid and False otherwise.
"""

```
try:
    if type(block) != dict:
        raise(ValueError("block type error"))

    # validate scalar block attributes
    if type(block["version"]) != str:
        raise(ValueError("block version type error"))

    if block["version"] != hconfig.conf["VERSION_NO"]:
        raise(ValueError("block wrong version"))
```

```
if type(block["timestamp"]) != int:
    raise(ValueError("block timestamp type error"))

if block["timestamp"] < 0:
    raise(ValueError("block invalid timestamp"))

if type(block["difficulty_bits"]) != int:
    raise(ValueError("block difficulty_bits type error"))

if block["difficulty_bits"] <= 0:
    raise(ValueError("block difficulty_bits <= 0"))

if type(block["nonce"]) != int:
    raise(ValueError("block nonce type error"))

if block["nonce"] != hconfig.conf["NONCE"]:
    raise(ValueError("block nonce is invalid"))

if type(block["height"]) != int:
    raise(ValueError("block height type error"))

if block["height"] < 0:
    raise(ValueError("block height < 0"))

if len(blockchain) == 0 and block["height"] != 0:
        raise(ValueError("genesis block invalid height"))

if len(blockchain) > 0:

    if block["height"] != blockchain[-1]["height"] + 1:

        raise(ValueError("block height is not in order"))
# The length of the block must be less than the maximum block size that
# specified in the config module.
# json.dumps converts the block into a json format string.
if len(json.dumps(block)) > hconfig.conf["MAX_BLOCK_SIZE"]:
    raise(ValueError("block length error"))

# validate the merkle_root.

if block["merkle_root"] != merkle_root(block["tx"], True):
```

```
            raise(ValueError("merkle roots do not match"))

        # validate the previous block by comparing message digests.
        # the genesis block does not have a predecessor block

        if block["height"] > 0:
            if block["prevblockhash"] != blockheader_hash(blockchain[block[
            "height"]-1]):
                raise(ValueError("previous block header hash does not match"))
        else:
            if block["prevblockhash"] != "":
                raise(ValueError("genesis block has prevblockhash"))

        # genesis block does not have any input transactions
        if block["height"] == 0 and block["tx"][0]["vin"] !=[]:
            raise(ValueError("missing coinbase transaction"))

        # a block other than the genesis block must have at least
        # two transactions: the coinbase transaction and at least
        # one more transaction
        if block["height"] > 0 and len(block["tx"]) < 2:
            raise(ValueError("block only has one transaction"))

    except Exception as error:
        logging.error("exception: %s: %s", "validate_block",error)
        return False

    return True

def merkle_root(buffer: "List", start: "bool" = False) -> "bool or string":
    """

    merkle_tree: computes the merkle root for a list of transactions.
    Receives a list of transactions and a boolean flag to indicate whether
    the function has been called for the first time or whether it is a
    recursive call from within the function.
    Returns the root of the merkle tree or False if there is an error.
    """

    pass
```

Helium Blockchain Unit Tests

Copy the following code to a file called *test_blockchain.py* and save it in the *unit_tests* directory. You can now traverse to this directory and run all of the tests:

```
$(virtual) pytest test_blockchain.py -v -s
```

You should see 23 unit tests passing.

Since our present implementation of the Helium blockchain is not complete, the following test suite is a restricted set. The complete set of unit tests on *blockchain.py* is available in Appendix 9 of this book:

```
"""
test blockchain functionality
transaction values are synthetic.
"""

import pytest
import hblockchain
import hconfig
import rcrypt
import time
import os
import pdb
import secrets

def teardown_module():
    """
    after all of the tests have been executed, remove any blocks that were
    created
    """
    os.system("rm *.dat")
    hblockchain.blockchain.clear()

#################################################
# Make A Synthetic Random Transaction For Testing
#################################################
def make_random_transaction(block_height):
```

```
tx = {}
tx["version"] =  "1"
tx["transactionid"] = rcrypt.make_uuid()
tx["locktime"] = secrets.randbelow(hconfig.conf["MAX_LOCKTIME"])

# public-private key pair for previous transaction
prev_keys = rcrypt.make_ecc_keys()

# public-private key pair for this transaction
keys = rcrypt.make_ecc_keys()

# Build vin
tx["vin"] = []

if block_height > 0:
    ctr = secrets.randbelow(hconfig.conf["MAX_INPUTS"]) + 1
    ind = 0
    while ind < ctr:
        signed = rcrypt.sign_message(prev_keys[0], prev_keys[1])
        ScriptSig = []
        ScriptSig.append(signed[0])
        ScriptSig.append(prev_keys[1])

        tx["vin"].append({
                "txid": rcrypt.make_uuid(),
                "vout_index": ctr,
                "ScriptSig": ScriptSig
            })
        ind += 1

# Build Vout
tx["vout"] = []

ctr = secrets.randbelow(hconfig.conf["MAX_OUTPUTS"]) + 1
ind = 0
while ind < ctr:

    ScriptPubKey = []
    ScriptPubKey.append("DUP")
```

```
        ScriptPubKey.append("HASH-160")
        ScriptPubKey.append(keys[1])
        ScriptPubKey.append("EQ_VERIFY")
        ScriptPubKey.append("CHECK-SIG")

        tx["vout"] = {
                "value": secrets.randbelow(10000000) + 1000000,
                # helium cents
                "ScriptPubKey": ScriptPubKey
            }
        ind += 1

    return tx


###############################################
# Build Three Synthetic Blocks For Testing
###############################################
block_0 = {
            "prevblockhash": "",
            "version": "1",
            "timestamp": 0,
            "difficulty_bits": 20,
            "nonce": 0,
            "merkle_root": rcrypt.make_SHA256_hash('msg0'),
            "height": 0,
            "tx": [make_random_transaction(0)]
}

block_1 = {
            "prevblockhash": hblockchain.blockheader_hash(block_0),
            "version": "1",
            "timestamp": 0,
            "difficulty_bits": 20,
            "nonce": 0,
            "merkle_root": rcrypt.make_SHA256_hash('msg1'),
            "height": 1,
}
```

```
block_1["tx"] = []
block_1["tx"].append(make_random_transaction(1))
block_1["tx"].append(make_random_transaction(1))

block_2 = {
            "prevblockhash": hblockchain.blockheader_hash(block_1),
            "version": "1",
            "timestamp": 0,
            "difficulty_bits": 20,
            "nonce": 0,
            "merkle_root": rcrypt.make_SHA256_hash('msg2'),
            "height": 2,
}
block_2["tx"] = []
block_2["tx"].append(make_random_transaction(2))
block_2["tx"].append(make_random_transaction(2))

def test_block_type(monkeypatch):
    """

    tests the type of a block
    """
    monkeypatch.setattr(hblockchain, "merkle_root", lambda x, y: \ rcrypt.
    make_SHA256_hash('msg0'))
    assert hblockchain.validate_block(block_0) == True

def test_add_good_block(monkeypatch):
    """

    test add a good block
    """
    monkeypatch.setattr(hblockchain, "merkle_root", lambda x, y: \ rcrypt.
    make_SHA256_hash('msg0'))
    assert hblockchain.add_block(block_0) == True

    monkeypatch.setattr(hblockchain, "merkle_root", lambda x, y: \ rcrypt.
    make_SHA256_hash('msg1'))
    assert hblockchain.add_block(block_1) == True
    hblockchain.blockchain.clear()
```

```python
def test_missing_version(monkeypatch):
    """
    test for a missing version number
    """
    monkeypatch.setattr(hblockchain, "merkle_root", lambda x, y: \ rcrypt.
    make_SHA256_hash('msg1'))
    monkeypatch.setitem(block_1, "version", "")

    assert hblockchain.add_block(block_1) == False

def test_version_bad(monkeypatch):
    """
    test for an unknown version number
    """
    monkeypatch.setattr(hblockchain, "merkle_root", lambda x, y: \ rcrypt.
    make_SHA256_hash('msg1'))
    monkeypatch.setitem(block_1, "version", -1)

    assert hblockchain.add_block(block_1) == False

def test_bad_timestamp_type(monkeypatch):
    """
    test for a bad timestamp type
    """
    monkeypatch.setattr(hblockchain, "merkle_root", lambda x, y: \ rcrypt.
    make_SHA256_hash('msg1'))
    monkeypatch.setitem(block_1, "timestamp", "12345")

    assert hblockchain.add_block(block_1) == False

def test_negative_timestamp(monkeypatch):
    """
    test for a negative timestamp
    """
    monkeypatch.setattr(hblockchain, "merkle_root", lambda x, y: \ rcrypt.
    make_SHA256_hash('msg0'))
    monkeypatch.setitem(block_0, "timestamp", -2)

    assert hblockchain.add_block(block_0) == False
```

```
def test_missing_timestamp(monkeypatch):
    """
    test for a missing timestamp
    """
    monkeypatch.setattr(hblockchain, "merkle_root", lambda x, y: \ rcrypt.
    make_SHA256_hash('msg1'))
    monkeypatch.setitem(block_1, "timestamp", "")

    assert hblockchain.add_block(block_1) == False

def test_block_height_type(monkeypatch):
    """
    test the type of the block height parameter
    """
    monkeypatch.setattr(hblockchain, "merkle_root", lambda x, y: \ rcrypt.
    make_SHA256_hash('msg0'))
    monkeypatch.setitem(block_0, "height", "0")

    hblockchain.blockchain.clear()
    assert hblockchain.add_block(block_0) == False

def test_bad_nonce(monkeypatch):
    """
    test for a negative nonce
    """
    monkeypatch.setattr(hblockchain, "merkle_root", lambda x, y: \ rcrypt.
make_SHA256_hash('msg1'))
    monkeypatch.setitem(block_1, "nonce", -1)

    assert hblockchain.add_block(block_1) == False

def test_missing_nonce(monkeypatch):
    """
    test for a missing nonce
    """
    monkeypatch.setattr(hblockchain, "merkle_root", lambda x, y: \ rcrypt.
    make_SHA256_hash('msg0'))
    monkeypatch.setitem(block_0, "nonce", "")
```

```
    assert hblockchain.add_block(block_0) == False

def test_block_nonce_type(monkeypatch):
    """
    test nonce has the wrong type"
    """
    monkeypatch.setattr(hblockchain, "merkle_root", lambda x, y: \ rcrypt.
    make_SHA256_hash('msg0'))
    monkeypatch.setitem(block_0, "nonce", "0")

    assert hblockchain.add_block(block_0) == False

def test_negative_difficulty_bit(monkeypatch):
    """
    test for negative difficulty bits
    """
    monkeypatch.setattr(hblockchain, "merkle_root", lambda x, y: \ rcrypt.
    make_SHA256_hash('msg1'))
    monkeypatch.setitem(block_1, "difficulty_bits", -5)

    assert hblockchain.add_block(block_1) == False

def test_difficulty_type(monkeypatch):
    """
    test difficulty bits has the wrong type"
    """
    monkeypatch.setattr(hblockchain, "merkle_root", lambda x, y: \ rcrypt.
    make_SHA256_hash('msg0'))
    monkeypatch.setitem(block_0, "difficulty_bits", "20")

    assert hblockchain.add_block(block_0) == False

def test_missing_difficulty_bit(monkeypatch):
    """
    test for missing difficulty bits
    """
    monkeypatch.setattr(hblockchain, "merkle_root", lambda x, y: \ rcrypt.
    make_SHA256_hash('data'))
    monkeypatch.setitem(block_1, "difficulty_bits", '')
```

107

```
    assert hblockchain.add_block(block_1) == False

def test_read_genesis_block(monkeypatch):
    """
    test reading the genesis block from the blockchain
    """
    hblockchain.blockchain.clear()
    monkeypatch.setattr(hblockchain, "merkle_root", lambda x, y: \ rcrypt.
    make_SHA256_hash('msg0'))

    hblockchain.add_block(block_0)
    assert hblockchain.read_block(0) == block_0
    hblockchain.blockchain.clear()

def test_genesis_block_height(monkeypatch):
    """
    test genesis block height
    """
    hblockchain.blockchain.clear()
    monkeypatch.setattr(hblockchain, "merkle_root", lambda x, y: \ rcrypt.
    make_SHA256_hash('msg0'))
    block_0["height"] = 0

    assert hblockchain.add_block(block_0) == True
    blk = hblockchain.read_block(0)
    assert blk != False
    assert blk["height"] == 0
    hblockchain.blockchain.clear()

def test_read_second_block(monkeypatch):
    """
    test reading the second block from the blockchain
    """
    hblockchain.blockchain.clear()
    assert len(hblockchain.blockchain) == 0

    monkeypatch.setattr(hblockchain, "merkle_root", lambda x, y: \ rcrypt.
    make_SHA256_hash('msg0'))
```

```
    monkeypatch.setitem(block_1, "prevblockhash", hblockchain.blockheader_
    hash(block_0))

    ret = hblockchain.add_block(block_0)
    assert ret == True
    monkeypatch.setattr(hblockchain, "merkle_root", lambda x, y: \ rcrypt.
    make_SHA256_hash('msg1'))
    ret = hblockchain.add_block(block_1)
    assert ret == True
    block = hblockchain.read_block(1)
    assert block != False
    hblockchain.blockchain.clear()

def test_block_height(monkeypatch):
    """

    test height of the the second block
    """

    hblockchain.blockchain.clear()
    monkeypatch.setattr(hblockchain, "merkle_root", lambda x, y: \ rcrypt.
    make_SHA256_hash('msg0'))
    monkeypatch.setitem(block_0, "height", 0)
    monkeypatch.setitem(block_0, "prevblockhash", "")
    monkeypatch.setitem(block_1, "height", 1)
    monkeypatch.setitem(block_1, "prevblockhash", hblockchain.blockheader_
    hash(block_0))

    assert hblockchain.add_block(block_0) == True

    monkeypatch.setattr(hblockchain, "merkle_root", lambda x, y: \ rcrypt.
    make_SHA256_hash('msg1'))
    assert hblockchain.add_block(block_1) == True
    blk = hblockchain.read_block(1)
    assert blk != False
    assert blk["height"] == 1
    hblockchain.blockchain.clear()
```

```
def test_block_size(monkeypatch):
    """

    The block size must be less than hconfig["MAX_BLOCKS"]
    """

    monkeypatch.setattr(hblockchain, "merkle_root", lambda x, y: \ rcrypt.
    make_SHA256_hash('msg0'))
    arry = []
    filler = "0" * 2000000
    arry.append(filler)
    monkeypatch.setitem(block_0, "tx", arry)
    hblockchain.blockchain.clear()
    assert hblockchain.add_block(block_0) == False

def test_genesis_block_prev_hash(monkeypatch):
    """

    test that the previous block hash for the genesis block is empty
    """

    hblockchain.blockchain.clear()
    monkeypatch.setattr(hblockchain, "merkle_root", lambda x, y: \ rcrypt.
    make_SHA256_hash('msg0'))
    monkeypatch.setitem(block_0, "height", 0)
    monkeypatch.setitem(block_0, "prevblockhash", rcrypt.make_uuid() )

    assert len(hblockchain.blockchain) == 0
    assert hblockchain.add_block(block_0) == False

def test_computes_previous_block_hash(monkeypatch):
    """

    test previous block hash has correct format
    """

    val = hblockchain.blockheader_hash(block_0)
    rcrypt.validate_SHA256_hash(val) == True

def test_invalid_previous_hash(monkeypatch):
    """

    test block's prevblockhash is invalid
    """
```

```
hblockchain.blockchain.clear()

monkeypatch.setattr(hblockchain, "merkle_root", lambda x, y: \ rcrypt.
make_SHA256_hash('msg0'))
monkeypatch.setitem(block_2, "prevblockhash", \
    "188a1fd32a1f83af966b31ca781d71c40f756a3dc2a7ac44ce89734d2186f632")

hblockchain.blockchain.clear()
assert hblockchain.add_block(block_0) == True
monkeypatch.setattr(hblockchain, "merkle_root", lambda x, y: \ rcrypt.
make_SHA256_hash('msg1'))
assert hblockchain.add_block(block_1) == True

monkeypatch.setattr(hblockchain, "merkle_root", lambda x, y: \ rcrypt.
make_SHA256_hash('msg2'))
assert hblockchain.add_block(block_2) == False
hblockchain.blockchain.clear()

def test_no_consecutive_duplicate_blocks(monkeypatch):
    """
    test cannot add the same block twice consecutively to the blockchain
    """
    hblockchain.blockchain.clear()
    monkeypatch.setattr(hblockchain, "merkle_root", lambda x, y: \ rcrypt.
    make_SHA256_hash('msg0'))
    assert hblockchain.add_block(block_0) == True

    monkeypatch.setattr(hblockchain, "merkle_root", lambda x, y: \ rcrypt.
    make_SHA256_hash('msg1'))
    monkeypatch.setitem(block_1, "prevblockhash", hblockchain.blockheader_
    hash(block_0))
    assert hblockchain.add_block(block_1) == True

    monkeypatch.setitem(block_1, "height", 2)
    assert hblockchain.add_block(block_1) == False
    hblockchain.blockchain.clear()
```

Conclusion

In this chapter, we have developed the *rcrypt* module that encapsulates the cryptographic functions that are used by Helium. We also wrote unit tests for our cryptographic module. We then wrote program code for the Helium blockchain. The module *hblockchain* encapsulates Helium blockchain functionality. Finally, we wrote some unit tests to validate the blockchain module.

In the next chapter, we turn our attention to the processing of cryptocurrency transactions.

CHAPTER 9

Cryptocurrency Transaction Processing

In a cryptocurrency network such as Bitcoin or Helium, the fundamental unit of interaction is a transaction where value is transferred from one entity to another. In this type of network, the blockchain is an immutable, distributed ledger of all of the transactions that have transpired on the network. Value is transferred from one public address to another public address. We can examine and enumerate all of the transactions associated with a public address by scanning the entire blockchain for transactions that involve this address. In fact, if we scan the blockchain forward from the genesis block, then the last transaction involving this address also provides the cryptocurrency balance which is associated with this address.

The type of cryptocurrency blockchain that we have just described has no concept of a user account. The blockchain does not provide each transactor with a unique account wherein all of the account activity is recorded. Rather, the application only records transactions on the blockchain as they occur. Each transaction is comprised of one or more origin public addresses from which value is transferred to one or more destination public addresses. Thus, since an individual uses a public address to receive value and transfer away value, the transactions that involve an individual can be constructed by scanning the blockchain from the genesis block forward for transactions involving the public addresses that the person owns. This is precisely how a user's wallet is constructed. It should be mentioned that it is considered bad practice to reuse public addresses since it is essentially a zero-cost endeavor to create them offline as well as online. Furthermore, using multiple addresses obscures identity to some extent.

One thing to notice about cryptocurrency networks like Bitcoin and Helium is that the contractual relations that transfer value reside outside the network. The network does not record contractual relations. This is in contrast to Ethereum, which can encode contractual terms on the network.

© Karan Singh Garewal 2020
K. S. Garewal, *Practical Blockchains and Cryptocurrencies*, https://doi.org/10.1007/978-1-4842-5893-4_9

This chapter and the next two chapters examine cryptocurrency transactions. In this chapter, we are going to delve into cryptocurrency transactions, the validation of such transactions, and, in particular, how value is transferred securely from the hands of its rightful owner to an intended recipient. In the next chapter, we will examine merkle trees and how they can be used to validate the transactions in a block. In Chapter 11, we will write code for Helium transaction processing.

Public Address Construction

In a typical transaction, the receiver of value provides the transferor of value with a public address to which value is to be sent. Using cryptographic techniques, the receiver of value can prove that he or she generated the public address and is therefore the owner of the value that has been transferred to this address.

Henceforth and for the sake of brevity, I shall refer to the hexadecimal string-encoded output of a cryptographic hash function such as SHA-256 or RIPEMD-160 simply as a message digest or a hash.

The following algorithm enumerates the steps involved in generating a public address:

1. Generate a random private-public pair of ECC keys.[1]

2. Generate the SHA-256 message digest of the public key.

3. Generate the RIPEMD-160 message digest of the result in Step 2.

4. Add a version byte, 0x1, in front of the RIPEMD-160 hash.

5. Compute the SHA-256 message digest of the result in Step 4.

6. Extract the last four bytes of the result in Step 5. This will be our error detection checksum.

7. Concatenate the error checksum with the result of Step 4.

8. Base58 encode the result in Step 7. The result is a public address.[2]

---

[1]Use the *make_ecc_keys* function in *rcrypt.py* to create a pair of ECC keys.
[2]You can refer to the *make_address* function in rcrypt.py.

We can symbolically represent public address generation as

```
address = base58_encode("1" + RIPEMD-160(SHA256_HASH(public_key)) +
checksum)
```

Figure 9-1 shows the address generation process.

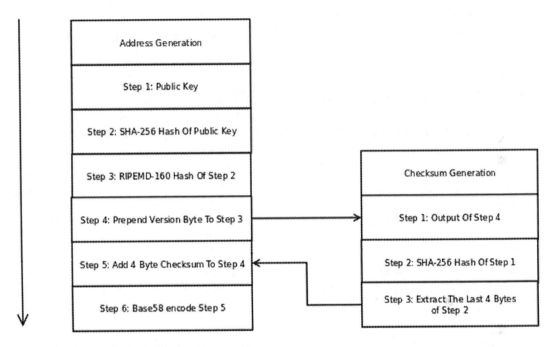

Figure 9-1. *Public Address Generation*

The version byte of Helium addresses will be fixed to the value in the *hconfig* module. The last four bytes prior to the Base58 encoding are a checksum that enables us to prove that the address is not corrupted.

This checksum is used as follows:

1. Base58 decode the public address.

2. Strip the last four bytes from the result of the previous step. These four bytes are the error checksum. We will call this the extracted checksum. The remaining portion is the prepended version byte and the RIPEMD-160 hash. We will call this portion the RIPEMD hash.

3. Take the SHA-256 hash of the RIPEMD hash and extract the last four bytes. This is our computed checksum.

4. The public address is invalid if the computed checksum is not equal to the extracted checksum.

Note that due to the random generation of the public key and the cryptographic properties of hashes, a public key will always generate a corresponding unique public address, *a fortiori*, the address is generated by some unique private-public key pair.[3]

Canonical Transaction Structure

We will now examine the canonical Python structure of a transaction. A transaction has the following dictionary structure:

```
{
    version:          <string>
    transactionid:    <string>
    locktime:         <integer>
    vin:              <list of dictionary elements>
    vout:             <list of dictionary elements>
}
```

The text that is enclosed in angle brackets specifies the type of the value corresponding to the key.

The value of the *version* key describes the version of the application software that is used to process the transaction. For Helium, this is fixed at "1".

The *transactionid* is a universally unique identifier for the transaction. We will use the *secrets* module in the Python standard library to create a random and secure cryptographic hexadecimal-encoded string that is 512 bits long.[4]

locktime is a non-negative integer. This value, if greater than zero, instructs a miner to refrain from processing the transaction until a specified amount of time has elapsed. Elapsed time is measured in seconds. A miner who caches the transaction for future processing does not include the transaction in a block until the requisite time period has

---

[3]You can refer to the *make_address* and *validate_address* functions in *rcrypt.py*.

[4]Refer to the *make_uuid* function in *rcrypt.py*.

transpired. *locktime* cannot have a value in excess of the MAX_LOCKTIME specified in the Helium configuration module.

The Transaction `vin` List

We are now in a position to discuss the vin list and unlocking previous transaction amounts. *vin* is an acronym for value in. *vin* is a list of transaction inputs that consume the outputs of previous transactions.

Each element of the *vin* list is a dictionary. This dictionary element has the following typical structure:

```
{
  txid:          <string>
  vout_index:    <integer>
  ScriptSig:     <list>
}
```

txid is the transactionid of a previous transaction, a portion of whose output is being consumed.

vout_index is an index into the previous transaction's vout array. Each vout element of a previous transaction specifies a value that can be consumed (transferred). The total value consumed is a summation of values transferred by all of the *vin* elements. Take note that the entire output in the vout element of the previous transaction must be consumed.

The *ScriptSig* script enables the transfer of value by proving ownership of the value. It is the concatenation of a digital signature and a public key. The public key is the key that was used to generate the public address to which value was transferred in the previous transaction. We will look at this script in short order.

The Transaction `vout` List

vout is an acronym for value out. Recall that when a public address receives value pursuant to a transaction, then this value can be subsequently spent in another transaction by its owner. A transaction's *vout* list specifies the values that are transferrable to one or more receivers of value. To reiterate, the vout list specifies transaction values that are available to be spent in subsequent transactions by the owners of such values.

vout is a list. Each vout list element is a dictionary that has the following representation:

```
{
  value:  <integer>,
  ScriptPubKey: <list>
}
```

value is the value of the cryptocurrency that is received by a specific public address. The string *RIPEMD-160(SHA-160(Public Key))* is *de*constructed from this public address;[5] this deconstructed string is in *ScriptPubKey*. *ScriptPubKey* is a list of symbolic unlocking operations, to be discussed subsequently. The cryptocurrency value in a *vout* element can be spent by the entity who can unlock the *ScriptPubKey* script. The only entity that can unlock the script is the entity that possesses the private key pertaining to *RIPEMD-160(SHA-160(Public Key))*. I will show this subsequently.

There are two aspects of *vout* to notice. Firstly, only integer amounts can be transferred. In the Bitcoin realm, the smallest transferable unit is one *satoshi*, or a hundred millionth of a bitcoin. In Helium, the smallest transferable unit is a *helium cent*, which is also a hundred millionth of a helium. By handling only integer arithmetic, we avoid all of the messy complications involved in decimal and floating-point arithmetic. Secondly, observe that the sum of values over the entire vout list is the total value received by public addresses that have been provided by the recipients of the transaction. Ordinarily, this amount will be slightly less than the amount transferred into this transaction. The difference is the transaction fee.

Transaction Mechanics

In Newtonian mechanics, the fundamental unit of computation is a body which has mass. Bodies have well-defined properties, and there are physical laws that govern their behavior. Analogously, the fundamental unit of computation in a cryptocurrency network is the transaction. Without transactions, there is no blockchain. Transactions have a rigid and well-defined structure, as well as fixed rules that govern their behavior.

Let us go through all of the steps that are involved in a typical transaction. Suppose that Alice wants to transfer one helium to Smith. The task before Alice is to create a

---

[5]A Base58 encoding can be reversed and the version byte and checksum stripped off to obtain this value.

transaction object (the previous dictionary structure) that enables this transfer. This transaction object must (i) unlock some of the previous *heliums* that Alice owns and (ii) lock the output helium values so that only Smith can unlock and use them. Unlocking the *heliums* that Alice owns means that she has proven her ownership of these *heliums,* and hence, they can be transferred away by her. Once these *heliums* are unlocked, they become outputs that can be delivered to Smith. Alice locks these outputs so that only Smith can unlock them. This will prove that Smith owns these *Heliums.*

Before Alice can transfer one helium to Smith, she must own at least one helium. So suppose that there is a previous transaction containing a single output of 1.08 heliums that Alice owns (one *vout* element). We suppose that the previous transaction has id

"618a125ac95ba370187c574d174eb7d618f3ee35d374899ca0007a035ba0a9e1"

Here are the steps that Alice must follow to transfer one Helium to Smith:

1. Alice requests Smith to send her a public address to which she can send one bitcoin.

2. Smith sends Alice a public address that he has created.

3. Alice creates a transaction id for her transaction. We suppose that this id is

    "d6b77f077ff700cd36df061ed75af353506f0cec6e267f0ce674eaa3b5d53217"

4. When Alice received *heliums* in the previous transaction "618...9e1", she had provided a public address to the transferor. Alice now gets the public key (say, *pPubKey*) with which this address was created and the private key (say, *PrivKey*) paired with this public key. Alice extracts the following value, which is available in the previous transaction's output (*vout* element):

MDHash = RIPEMD-160(SHA256(pPubKey))

Alice makes the digital signature of MDHash:

Sig = Signature(MDHash)

Next Alice creates a list with two elements: *Sig* and the *Public Key* string corresponding to the private key. This list is called a *ScriptSig.*

5. Using this information, Alice creates the *vin* element in the transaction's *vin* list. This list contains exactly one element. The *vout_index* element is the index into the *vout* list of the previous transaction, and it identifies the output of the previous transaction that is being consumed (let us assume it is 0). The *vin* element is

```
{
   "txid": "618a125ac95ba370187c574d174eb7d618f3ee35d374899ca0007a
   035ba0a9e1"
   "vout_index": 0
   "ScriptSig":  [Sig, PublicKey]
}
```

6. Alice next takes the public address provided by Smith and reverses the Base58 encoding and strips off the checksum. The result is

```
RESULT =  "1" + RIPEMD-160(SHA256(smith's public key))
```

She then computes the SHA256 hash of RESULT with the checksum that she has stripped off. If an error is not indicated, Alice places the following string in the *ScriptPubKey* key of first *vout* element:

```
"<DUP> <HASH-160> MDHASH <EQ_VERIFY> <CHECK_SIG>"
```

where MDHASH is `RIPEMD-160(SHA256(smith's public key))`.

7. Alice's vout element is

```
{
   "value":  1,
   "ScriptPubKey": "<DUP> <HASH-160> MDHASH <EQ_VERIFY>
   <CHECK_SIG>"
}
```

8. And Alice has now created the transaction object, which looks like this:

```
{
"version": "1"
"transactionid": "d6b77f077ff700cd36df061ed75af353506f0cec6e
267f0ce674eaa3b5d53217"
```

```
"locktime": 0
"vin": {
        "txid": "618a125ac95ba370187c574d174eb7d618f3ee35d374899ca0007a
        035ba0a9e1"
         "vout_index": 0
         "ScriptSig":  "Sig PublicKey"
         }
"vout": {
          "value":  1,
          "ScriptPubKey": [<DUP> <HASH-160> MDHASH <EQ_VERIFY>
          <CHECK_SIG>]
          }
}
```

9. Having created the transaction object, Alice serializes it into a Base58
    byte sequence and broadcasts it on the Helium peer-to-peer network.
    Miners who are listening on this network for transactions pick up the
    transaction and (may) include it in a block that they intend to mine.

Subsequently in this chapter, we will show how the *ScriptSig* script ensures that
only Alice can unlock the previous transaction output of 1.08 *heliums* and how the
ScriptPubKey script ensures that only Smith will be able to unlock the transaction output
of one helium. A transaction is only deemed to be valid if both the *ScriptSig* and the
ScriptPubKey succeed without error. Bitcoin and Helium both implement a simple stack
processor to verify that these scripts execute successfully.

You will have noticed that we unlocked 1.08 *heliums* but we transferred only 1
helium to Smith. What has happened to the remainder of 0.08 heliums? This excess
amount is called a transaction fee. It is an inducement to miners to include Alice's
transaction in a block that miners intend to mine. If a miner successfully mines a block
that contains Alice's transaction, then the miner can claim these 0.08 heliums.

The preceding logic can be applied, mutatis mutandis, to handle inputs from several
previous transactions holding outputs that Alice owns (there will be more than one
previous transaction vout list element), and the transaction can direct outputs to
several helium addresses (the transaction will have more than one vout element).

The steps that I have described earlier would typically be carried out by Alice's Helium wallet.

In a typical fiat currency transaction at a cash register, you tender some money and get some change back. Change is handled in the following manner in a cryptocurrency. Suppose that Alice has a previous transaction with 5.08 heliums in it and she intends to use these *heliums* in her transaction with Smith. Alice would create a public address and direct 4 *heliums* into this address. Thus, Smith would receive one helium to the address that he gave to Alice, Alice would get change of 4 *heliums* at the address that she has created, and the transaction fee would be 0.08 *heliums*. This aspect of a transaction would also be handled transparently by a Helium wallet.

The ScriptPubKey and ScriptSig Scripts

The *ScriptPubKey* script in a *vout* element of a transaction is used to lock the value specified in this element. Only the owner of the public address to which this value is transferred can unlock the value.

The *ScriptSig* script in a *vin* element of a transaction describes a value in a prior transaction that will be consumed in the present transaction. This value will be transferred to one or more public addresses. The consumed value can be identified completely from the transaction id of the previous transaction and the index of the *vout* element in this transaction. The *ScriptSig* script ensures that this value in the prior transaction can only be transferred by the entity that owns the value.

Notice that each *vin* element in a transaction references exactly one *vout* element in a previous transaction and such a *vin* element must consume the entirety of the value in this *vout* element.

The *ScriptPubKey* and *ScriptSig* scripts are both simple lists. They are processed by a simple stack language which I will now describe.

An element (list element) in these scripts is either an operator symbol or an operand. We will call an operator symbol an opcode. An operand is a value; for example, the integer 5 and the string *"hello world"* are both operands. Opcodes are symbolic operations that perform operations on operands. For example, the addition operator + is an opcode that operates on numbers. Each list element contains exactly one opcode or one operand. Opcodes are designated between angle brackets.

An execution stack is a list of opcodes and operands. For example, *ScriptPubKey* and *ScriptSig* are both execution stacks.

Each element of the *vin* and *vout* lists is either an opcode or an operand. Each list behaves like a stack, and hence, it permits only two operations on the stack, PUSH and POP. The POP operation pops an element from the head of a stack, and a PUSH operation pushes an element onto the head of a stack.

Finally, we also specify a result stack. An opcode on the execution stack will operate on values on the result stack, and the result of the operation may be be pushed back onto the result stack if the semantics of the opcode requires this. If the value on the execution stack is an operand, it is simply pushed onto the result stack.

Valid opcodes are DUP, HASH-160, PK_HASH, EQ-VERIFY, and CHECK-SIG. The meaning of these opcodes is described as follows. Valid operands must be strings.

This specification describes a simple stack language.

As stated previously, opcodes will be denoted by enclosing them in angle brackets. Operands, which denote values, will not be enclosed in angle brackets. The opcode that is to be executed will be indicated by an execution pointer (a fat arrow).

We are going to examine P2PKHASH (person to public key hash) scripts. These types of scripts transfer value from a single entity to another single entity. P2PKHASH scripts constitute 98% to 99% of all transactions in typical cryptocurrency networks.

ScriptSig Scripts

The ScriptSig list in each of the *vin* elements of a P2PKHASH transaction has the following structure (Figure 9-2).

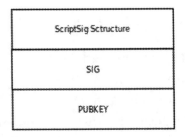

Figure 9-2. ScriptSig Structure

A *ScriptSig* script is composed of two operands. PUBKEY is the public key (hexadecimal string) that was used to create the public address that received the previous transaction output.

SIG is a signature which is created by signing the value:

```
RIPEMD-160(SHA256(public key of previous transaction input))
```

This value is also available in the *vout* element of the previous transaction.

ScriptPubKey Scripts

Consider a P2PKHASH transaction. In this type of transaction, the *ScriptPubKey* script in each of the *vout* elements of the transaction can be visualized as the stack on the left-hand side of Figure 9-3.

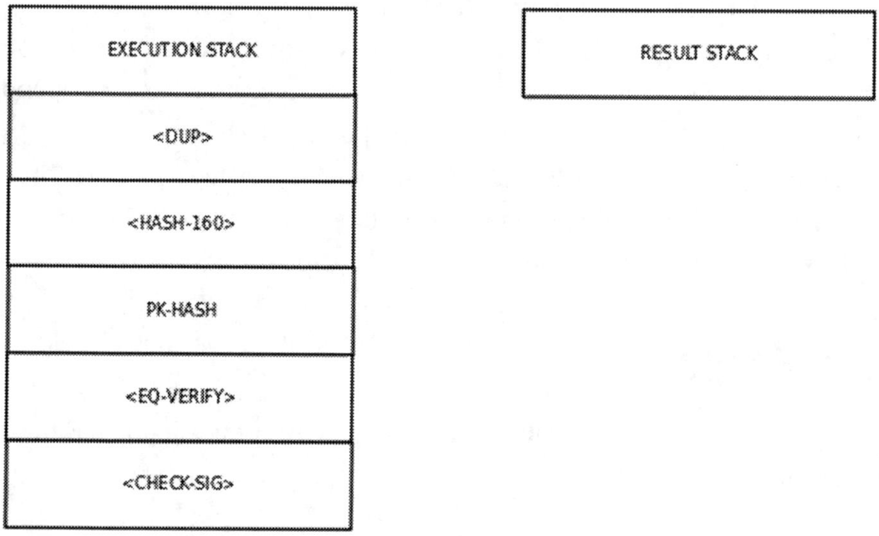

Figure 9-3. *Execution Stack for a ScriptPubKey*

This diagram also shows an empty result stack on the right side. This stack will hold operands which will be acted upon by the opcodes in the execution stack.

The meaning of the opcodes in the execution stack are as follows:

<DUP> means taking the value at the head of the result stack and pushing a copy of this value back onto the result stack.

<HASH160> means popping the value at the head of the result stack and generating the value

```
RIPEMD-160(SHA-256(popped value))
```

and then pushing the message digest onto the result stack. PK-HASH is a string.

<EQUAL_VERIFY> means popping two elements from the result stack and verifying that they are equal.

<CHECK_SIG> means popping two elements from the result stack and verifying the signature.

ScriptSig and ScriptPubKey Scripts in Action

Let us see how the *ScriptSig* and *ScriptPubKey* scripts are used to validate a P2PKHASH transaction. Such a transaction is valid if both of these scripts execute without an error. A valid transaction unlocks previous transaction outputs that are used in the transaction. We will use our previous example where Alice transfers one *helium* coin to Smith.

Firstly, we concatenate the *ScriptSig* and *ScriptPubKey* lists and get the following execution stack (the head of this list is at the top) (Figure 9-4).

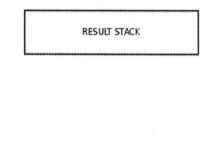

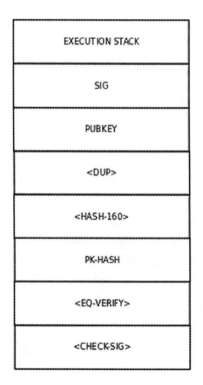

Figure 9-4. *Execution Stack for ScriptSig and ScriptPubKey*

We will now execute the opcodes on this stack. Any operands that are present in this stack will simply be pushed onto the result stack.

The execution stack will indicate the next operation to be performed with an execution pointer, which is a fat arrow (Figure 9-5).

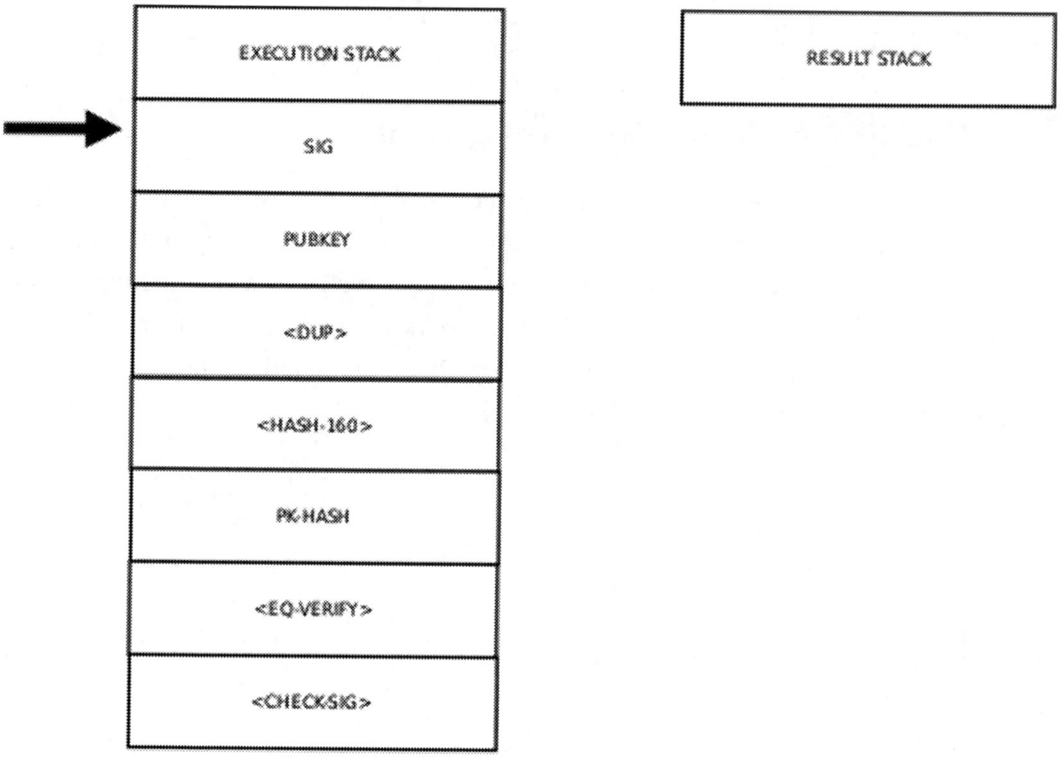

EXECUTION STACK
SIG
PUBKEY
<DUP>
<HASH-160>
PK-HASH
<EQ-VERIFY>
<CHECK-SIG>

RESULT STACK

Figure 9-5. *Step 1 of the Execution Stack*

The first operation is SIG. Alice takes the value *RIPEMD-160(SHA256(public key))* which is available in the *ScriptPubKey* element of the previous transaction's *vout* element and generates the signature of this value. This value is pushed onto the result stack. The two stacks now look like Figure 9-6.

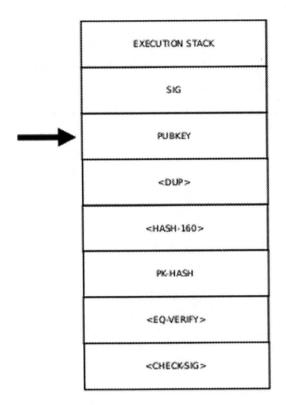

Figure 9-6. *Step 2 of the Execution Stack*

The next operation is on PUBKEY, which is the public key that Alice used to generate the address in the previous transaction whose output is being consumed by Alice. This public key hexadecimal string is pushed onto the result stack. The two stacks now look like Figure 9-7.

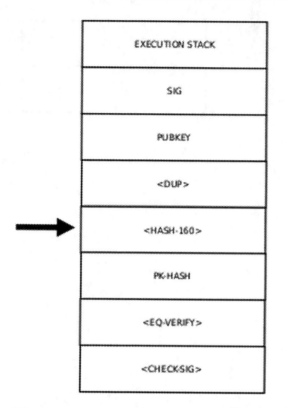
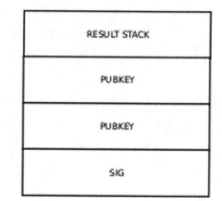

Figure 9-7. *Step 3 of the Execution Stack*

The next opcode is <DUP>. This operation requires the element at the head of the result stack to be duplicated and pushed back onto the result stack. After this operation, the two stacks look like Figure 9-8.

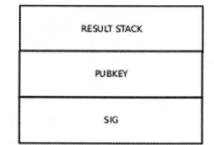

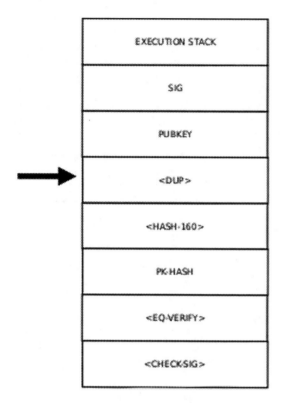

Figure 9-8. *Step 4 of the Execution Stack*

The next opcode <HASH-160> requires the value at the head of the result stack to be popped off and the value *RIPEMD-160(SHA256(popped value))* to be computed and then pushed onto the result stack. The result of this operation is in Figure 9-9.

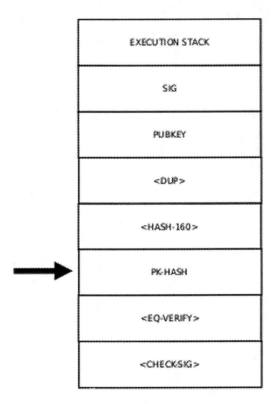
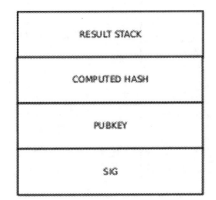

Figure 9-9. *Step 9 of the Execution Stack*

The next operation pushes the PK-HASH value onto the result stack. PK-HASH was created at the time the last transaction was created; its value is *RIPEMD-160(SHA256 (public key of previous transaction input))* in Figure 9-10.

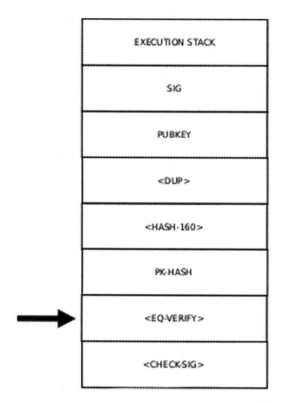
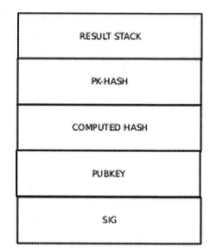

Figure 9-10. *Step 10 of the Execution Stack*

The next command on the opcode stack is <EQUAL_VERIFY>. This opcode requires us to pop the two values at the head of the result stack and compare their values. If the two RIPEMD-160 hashes are not equal, the unlocking of the input fails since the party alleging to own the value in the previous transaction has not provided the correct public key. If Alice uses the public key that she used for her previous transaction input to compute the hash, the equality verification succeeds.

If the operation succeeds, then the two stacks look like Figure 9-11.

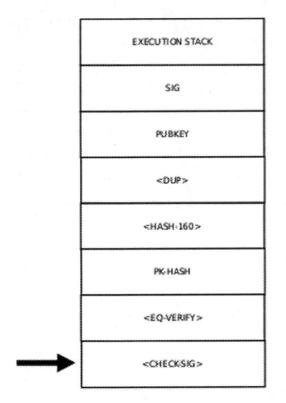

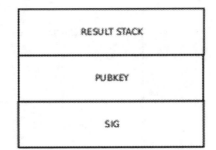

Figure 9-11. *Step 11 of the Execution Stack*

The last opcode <CHECK_SIG> verifies the previous transaction as follows:

1. Given the public key that Alice used for the prior transaction output, verify that the private key corresponding to this public key has generated the signature of the value

    ```
    RIPEMD-160(SHA256(public key))
    ```

2. If the signature is valid, pop the two elements off the result stack. The *vin* element of the transaction has validly unlocked the output of the previous transaction (Figure 9-12).

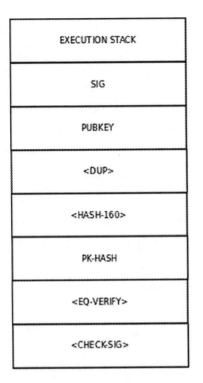

Figure 9-12. *Transaction Output Unlocked*

If all of the *vin* elements in the present transaction are unlocked, then we say that the transaction is unlocked.

Multisig Transactions

Consider a fiat currency checking account that requires both spouses to sign a check. A valid transfer of value in this case requires the signature of both spouses. The delivery of such a cheque to the drawee is a multi-signature or multisig transaction. In a cryptocurrency network, a multisig transaction refers to a transaction involving n > 1 entities, where each entity provides a public address for the transaction. Then at least m of these n entities have to provide their signatures before value will be transferred to a recipient. This type of transaction is frequently called a n:m transaction; it is implemented through a script that verifies multiple signatures. Our cheque example is a 2:2 transaction.

There are several interesting use cases for multisig transactions.

In a 2:2 escrow transaction, one of the parties is a neutral arbitrator whose function is to oversee that agreed conditions for the transfer of value have been satisfied. The arbitrator only provides his or her signature if these conditions are satisfied. We can also have m:n escrow transactions where m < n arbitrators have to sign a transaction.

In a two-factor authentication transaction, an output in the previous transaction is locked by two public addresses. The first public address is generated by an online wallet. The second address is generated from keys which are kept in cold storage.[6] The output from the previous transaction will be transferred when both signatures are verified.

The simple stack language that we have specified can be used to create scripts for multisig transactions as well as other scenarios. Note that since this stack language does not support control flow constructs (such as *if … else if …*) and loops, it is not Turing complete. This was a deliberate omission by Satoshi Nakamoto since it was a design objective to make script processing fast and simple.

Transaction Fees

A person transferring value in a transaction typically provides miners with an incentive to include the transaction in a new block to be mined. This transaction fee is the difference between the sum of the inputs and the outputs. It is not necessary to provide a transaction fee, but the failure to do so may significantly delay the processing of the transaction, as miners are not incentivized to include the transaction in candidate blocks to be mined.

Transaction Validation

Once a Helium transaction has been created, it is broadcast on the Helium peer-to-peer network. A miner who receives this new transaction can elect to include it in a block that he is mining. The miner's decision to include the transaction will be partially influenced by the transaction fee offered by the transaction.

Before including the transaction in a block, the miner will test the transaction to determine its validity. Only valid transactions will be included in the block that is to be mined.

---

[6]Cold storage refers to isolated, offline storage that is not connected to the Internet. A paper wallet is an example of cold storage.

If a miner mines a block that has an invalid transaction, other nodes in the network will refuse to incorporate this new block in their local versions of the blockchain since each node that receives a mined block tests the validity of the block as well as the transactions in the block.

Here are some of the tests that are performed on a transaction to validate it:[7]

1. The transaction's syntax is valid; this means that the required transaction fields are present and their types are valid.

2. The transaction inputs are positive integers. In particular, they are not floating-point numbers.

3. The transaction outputs are positive integers. In particular, they are not floating-point numbers.

4. Transaction inputs and outputs are not less than a Helium cent.

5. The sum of the transaction inputs is less than the value of MAX_HELIUM_COINS in the *hconfig* module.

6. The sum of the transaction outputs is less than the value of MAX_HELIUM_COINS in the *hconfig* module.

7. The sum of the transaction inputs is equal to or greater than the sum of the transaction outputs.

8. The locktime of the transaction is not less than zero.

9. The locktime is not greater than the value of LOCKTIME_INTERVAL in the *hconfig* module.

10. Each transaction is at least 100 bytes long.

11. The number of transaction inputs is less than MAX_INPUTS in the *hconfig* module.

12. The number of transaction outputs is less than MAX_OUTPUTS in the *hconfig* module.

---

[7]Constant values are in *hconfig.py*.

13.   The ScriptSig script has valid values.

14.   The ScriptPubKey script has valid values.

15.   The ScriptSig and ScriptPubKey scripts succeed in transferring value.

16.   The outputs of a *coinbase* transaction are not spent until the blockchain grows by COINBASE_INTERVAL blocks from the block in which the *coinbase* transaction is located. We will discuss coinbase transactions subsequently.

17.   A *coinbase* transaction does not have any inputs (the *vin* list is empty).

18.   The genesis block does not have any inputs.

Conclusion

The fundamental unit of computation in a cryptocurrency network is a transaction. The blocks in a blockchain contain transactions. Blocks are added to a blockchain as transactions are processed by nodes on the cryptocurrency network. These nodes are called miners, and the process of adding a block to a blockchain is called mining.

In this chapter, we have looked at the structure of a canonical cryptocurrency transaction and examined all of the steps that must be followed to unlock the inputs in previous transactions so that they can be spent. Nodes that want to add a block to the cryptocurrency blockchain must include transactions in their candidate block. These nodes must, at the outset, verify that the transactions included in a block are valid. We have examined transaction validation tests. If a mining node successfully adds a block to the blockchain, it is entitled to the transaction fees in respect to all of the transactions in the block as well as a mining reward embodied in a *coinbase* transaction.

In the next chapter, we are going to study Merkle trees. These tree structures are used to ascertain whether a list of transactions has been tampered with. Merkle trees can also be used to ascertain whether a particular transaction is in a block.

Reference

`https://github.com/bitcoin/bitcoin`, last accessed on February 8, 2020

CHAPTER 10

Merkle Trees

In the last chapter, we engaged in a comprehensive examination of cryptocurrency transactions. Transactions are the fundamental unit of computation in cryptocurrency networks. Without transactions, there is no blockchain. A block consists of several transactions as well as related data. For any block that contains transactions, we want to ascertain two properties: firstly, that these transactions have not been tampered with and, secondly, whether a particular transaction is present in the block.

You will recall from Chapter 8 that the block attribute *prevblockhash* is used to test whether the previous block has been tampered with. This hash is computed over the block header of the previous block. The transactions in the previous block are not in this block header. However, the block header contains the merkle root of these transactions. This root can be used to verify the integrity of the transactions in the block. If any of the transactions have been altered, the merkle root will change, and consequently, the hash of the previous block will not match, invalidating the transaction.

In this chapter, we will look at how merkle trees are used to verify the integrity of block transactions. After this, we will implement code for Helium merkle trees.

Tree Data Structures

In Computer Science, a tree is a collection of nodes where the nodes are related to each other through parent, child, and sibling relationships. This is best explained by means of a diagram (Figure 10-1).

© Karan Singh Garewal 2020
K. S. Garewal, *Practical Blockchains and Cryptocurrencies*, https://doi.org/10.1007/978-1-4842-5893-4_10

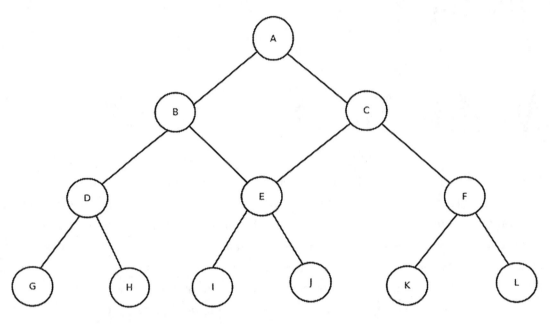

Figure 10-1. *A Tree Data Structure*

In this diagram, each node is represented by a circle. There are 12 nodes, labeled from A to L. These nodes are arranged in four layers. Each node, except for node A, is connected to a node above it with a line. The node above it is called a parent node. For example, D is a parent node of H, and C is a parent of E as well as F. Node A does not have a parent; it is called the root node. Aside from the nodes G to L, which are at the bottom of this tree structure, each node is connected to two nodes below it. These two nodes are called the children (or left and right children) of the node above (which is a parent node). For example, node E has two children, the I and J nodes. E is the parent of these nodes. The children nodes of a parent node are called siblings of each other. The nodes at the bottom of the tree do not have any children and are called leaf nodes.

This diagram is an example of a binary tree; all of the nodes except for the leaf nodes have two children. Furthermore, this is a balanced tree since all of the leaf nodes are at the same level. It is not necessary that each parent node have two children or that the tree be balanced. We can construct trees where nodes have a varying number of children and the tree is not balanced. However, balanced binary trees have very nice properties; in particular, we can do very fast insertions and deletions of nodes in the tree. Additionally, searching for a node in these trees is very fast.

Each node in a tree will typically contain pointers to its children, its parent node as well as data specific to the domain in which the tree is being used. The pointers in these nodes permit bidirectional movement through the tree.

Merkle Trees

In typical cryptocurrency implementations, the data portion of a block contains a collection of transactions. For example, a Bitcoin block may contain 2000–4000 transactions. In Helium, the transactions in a block are represented as a list. Each list element is a transaction, and each transaction has a dictionary structure. We will see shortly that we can represent this transaction list as a tree structure.

A merkle tree is a balanced binary tree where the nodes are related through cryptographic hashes. The root node of the merkle tree uniquely identifies the tree.

Suppose that we have a list of eight transactions in a block. We will construct the merkle tree of this list as follows.

For each of these transactions, compute the SHA256 cryptographic hash of the transaction as a hexadecimal string. These values will become the leaf nodes of our merkle tree (Figure 10-2).

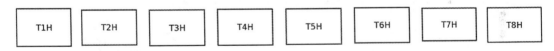

Figure 10-2. *Leaf Nodes of the Merkle Tree*

TnhH is the SHA256 hash of the nth transaction. Since a merkle tree is a balanced binary tree, it must contain an even number of leaf nodes. Therefore, if we have an odd number of transactions in the block, we will simply add the last transaction twice to the transaction list.

We can now derive the second layer of the merkle tree. Starting with the leftmost leaf node, we consider its sibling on the right side. We concatenate the two hashes, T1H and T2H, and compute the SHA256 hash of this concatenated string:

```
T12H = SHA256(T1H + T2H)
```

Then we concatenate the next pair of leaf node hashes and compute the SHA256 hash:

T34H = SHA256(T3H + T4H)

We proceed in this manner until all of the leaf nodes have been processed. This will give us a list of cryptographic hashes whose length is one half of the number of leaf nodes. The nodes in the second layer of the merkle tree are constructed from this new list (Figure 10-3).

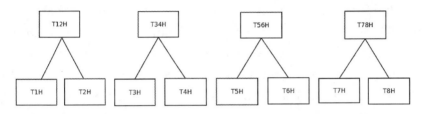

Figure 10-3. *First Two Layers of the Merkle Tree*

To derive the third layer of the merkle tree, we compute the hashes:

T1234H = SHA256(T12H + T34H)
T5678H = SHA256(T56H + T78H)

We now have the third layer of the merkle tree (Figure 10-4).

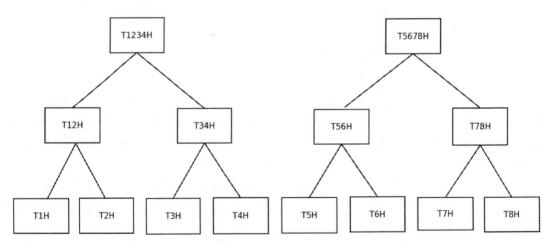

Figure 10-4. *First Three Layers of the Merkle Tree*

Finally, we concatenate the SHA256 hashes in the two nodes that are at the third level of the merkle tree:

```
T12345678H = SHA256(T1234H + T5678H)
```

This gives us the final representation of the merkle tree for the eight transactions in the block (Figure 10-5).

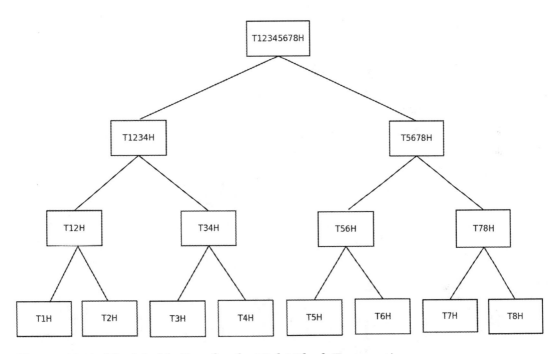

Figure 10-5. *The Merkle Tree for the Eight Block Transactions*

The hash value T12345678H is called the merkle root. It is a cryptographic hash of the transactions in the block. If any of the transactions are tampered with or if their order in the transaction list of the block is changed, the merkle root will be inconsistent with its previous value. Since the merkle root is in the block header, the block header will become inconsistent.

You may ask why we need to construct a merkle tree. The short answer is that a balanced binary tree such as a merkle tree is a remarkably efficient search structure. Consider a hypothetical list of one million block transactions. This list can be represented as a merkle tree with a depth of 20 layers. Furthermore, we can search for a particular transaction in this list in $O(\log n)$ time where n is the size of the number of transactions.

Another feature of a merkle tree is that the path to any leaf node (transaction) through the merkle tree is unique. Consider the transaction whose SHA256 hash is T6H; the path to this transaction can be represented as

T12345678 + T5678 + T56 + T6

In Figure 10-6, this path is indicated with emphasized lines.

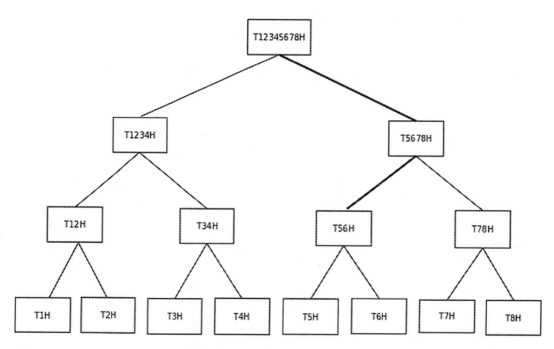

Figure 10-6. *The Path to a Block Transaction*

Deriving the Merkle Root in Helium

In Chapter 8, we wrote some of the Python code for the Helium blockchain. The function *merkle_root* in this module was stubbed out and returned a mocked value. We will now rectify this deficiency and code the function to compute and return the merkle root of a list of transactions in a block.

Remove the stubbed function *merkle_root* in your *hblockchain.py* file and add the following code to the bottom of your *hblockchain* module. The main function *merkle_root* converts dictionary values into JSON-encoded strings, so ensure that you have imported the standard Python module *json* into *hblockchain:*[1]

```
def merkle_root(buffer: "List", start: "bool" = False) -> "bool or string":
    """

    merkle_tree: computes the merkle root for a list of transactions.
    Receives a list of transactions and a boolean flag to indicate whether
    the function has been called for the first time or whether it is a
    recursive call from within the function.
    Returns the root of the merkle tree or False if there is an error.
    """

    try:
        # if start is False then we verify have a list of SHA-256 hashes
        if start == False:
            for value in buffer:
                if rcrypt.validate_SHA256_hash(value) == False:
                    raise(ValueError("tx list SHA-256 validation failure"))
                buflen = len(buffer)
                if buflen != 1 and len(buffer)%2 != 0:
                    buffer.append(buffer[-1])

        # make the merkle leaf nodes if we are entering the function
        # for the first time
        if start == True:
            tmp = buffer[:]
            tmp = make_leaf_nodes(tmp)
            if tmp == False: return False
            buffer = tmp[:]

        # if buffer has one element, we have the merkle root
        if (len(buffer) == 1):
            return buffer[0]
```

---

[1]JSON encoding and decoding is explained at https://docs.python.org/3/library/json.html, last accessed on February 7, 2020

```
        # construct the list of parent nodes from the child nodes
        index = 0
        parents = []

        while index < len(buffer):
            tmp = rcrypt.make_SHA256_hash(buffer[index] + buffer[index+1])
            parents.append(tmp)
            index += 2

        # recursively call merkle tree
        ret = merkle_root(parents, False)

    except Exception as error:
        logging.error("exception: %s: %s", "merkle_root",error)
        return False

    return ret

def make_leaf_nodes(tx_list: "list") -> "List or False":
    """
    make_leaf_nodes: makes the leaf nodes of a merkle tree.
    Receives a list of transactions. If the number of transactions is an
    odd number, appends the last transaction to the list again so that we can
    make a balanced binary tree.
    Computes the hexadecimal string encoded SHA-256 message digest of each
    transaction and appends it to a leaf node list that is initially empty.
    Returns the leaf node list or False if there is an error
    """
    try:
        # cannot have an empty transaction list
        if (len(tx_list) == 0): raise(ValueError("tx list zero length"))

        # verify we have a list type
        if type(tx_list) is not list: raise(ValueError("tx is not a list type"))

        # verify the type of each transaction is a dict
        for tx in tx_list:
            if type(tx) is not dict: raise(ValueError("tx is not a dict type"))
```

```
    # must have an even number of transactions
    if len(tx_list) % 2 == 1 or len(tx_list) == 1:
        tx_list.append(tx_list[- 1] )

    # copy the transaction list
    trx_list = list(tx_list)

    # convert each transaction into a JSON string
    tx = []

    for transaction in trx_list:
        tx.append(json.dumps(transaction))

    # make the leaf nodes
    sha256_list = []

    for transaction in tx:
        sha256_list.append(rcrypt.make_SHA256_hash(transaction))

except Exception as err:
    logging.debug('make_leaf_nodes: exception: ' + str(err))
    return False

return sha256_list
```

There are two functions: *merkle_root* and *make_leaf_nodes*. *merkle_root* receives a list of block transactions. *merkle_root* is called by the *validate_block* and *blockheader_hash* functions.

merkle_root is a recursive function; it receives a boolean flag as its second parameter. This flag is True if *merkle_root* is called from the aforementioned functions and False if this function has been called by itself. The very first thing that *merkle_root* does is to call the function *make_leaf_nodes*, whose task is to construct the leaf nodes of the merkle tree.

make_leaf_nodes performs some validation on the transaction list that it receives. If this list is empty, it returns False. An empty transaction list will have no leaf nodes. It then does some type checking to verify that it has received a list and not some other data structure. It also verifies that each list element is a dictionary type. If things are amiss, it returns a False value. Otherwise, *make_leaf_nodes* constructs the leaf nodes of the merkle tree for this transaction list and returns these values.

merkle_root then processes the leaf nodes to construct the *merkle tree* by calling itself recursively with the flag argument set to False.

As I previously indicated, Appendix 10 of this book contains the final source code for all of the Helium modules.

Pytests for the Merkle Code

We will now write some pytest unit tests to validate the merkle code. Add the following pytest code to the bottom of your *test_blockchain module.*

Once the unit test code has been added, run the tests from the unit_tests directory:

```
$(virtual) pytest test_blockchain.py -k -s
```

You should observe a total of 30 tests passing:

```
def test_empty_merkle_root(monkeypatch):
    """

    test that the merkle root of a block cannot be empty
    """

    hblockchain.blockchain.clear()
    monkeypatch.setattr(hblockchain, "merkle_root", lambda x, y: "")

    assert hblockchain.add_block(block_1) == False
    hblockchain.blockchain.clear()

def test_invalid_merkle_root(monkeypatch):
    """

    test an invalid merkle root
    """

    monkeypatch.setattr(hblockchain, "merkle_root", lambda x, y: rcrypt.
    make_SHA256_hash('msg1'))
    monkeypatch.setitem(block_1, "merkle_root", \
      "A88a1fd32a1f83af966b31ca781d71c40f756a3dc2a7ac44ce89734d2186f63z")

    assert hblockchain.add_block(block_1) == False

"""

test the merkle root
```

These merkle tests do not test the validity of transactions
"""

```
def test_merkle_root_empty_tx(monkeypatch):
    """
    test the merkle root for an empty transaction list
    """
    monkeypatch.setattr(hblockchain, "merkle_root", \
      lambda x, y: rcrypt.make_SHA256_hash('msg0'))
    monkeypatch.setitem(block_0, "tx", [])

    monkeypatch.setattr(hblockchain, "merkle_root", \
      lambda x, y: rcrypt.make_SHA256_hash('msg1'))
    monkeypatch.setitem(block_1, "tx", [])

    assert hblockchain.add_block(block_1) == False

def test_merkle_root_tx_bad_type():
    """
    test the merkle root for a bad transaction list type
    """
    assert bool(hblockchain.merkle_root ("123", True)) == False

def test_merkle_bad_flag():
    """
    test the merkle root for a bad flag parameter
    """
    assert bool(hblockchain.merkle_root ([{"a":1}], False)) == False

def test_merkle_root_transactions_dict_type():
    """
    test the merkle root for a transaction list is a dict type
    """
    assert bool(hblockchain.merkle_root ({'a': 1}, True)) == False

def test_merkle_root_random_transaction():
    """

    test merkle root for synthetic random transactions
    does not test hash of previous block
```

```
"""
hblockchain.blockchain.clear()
block_0["merkle_root"] = hblockchain.merkle_root(block_0["tx"], True)
assert hblockchain.add_block(block_0) == True

block_1["merkle_root"] = hblockchain.merkle_root(block_1["tx"], True)
block_1["prevblockhash"] = hblockchain.blockheader_hash(block_0)
assert hblockchain.add_block(block_1) == True

block_2["merkle_root"] = hblockchain.merkle_root(block_2["tx"], True)
block_2["prevblockhash"] = hblockchain.blockheader_hash(block_1)
assert hblockchain.add_block(block_2) == True
```

Conclusion

Merkle trees are important in blockchain applications for two principal reasons. Firstly, they permit us to efficiently test whether a list of transactions has been tampered with. Secondly, we can use these trees to verify whether a particular transaction is in a transaction list. In this chapter, we have examined merkle trees and written code to make a merkle tree from a list of transactions in a block.

In the next chapter, we will write transaction code for Helium and unit test this code.

CHAPTER 11

Helium Transaction Processing

This is a code-intensive chapter. In the previous two chapters, we have examined the theory of cryptocurrency transactions and seen how the *merkle root* can be used to verify that the transactions in a block have not been tampered with. In this chapter, we are going to put this theoretical knowledge into practice by implementing Python code for processing Helium transactions.

Transaction Processing Code Walkthrough

The canonical transaction processing workflow is as follows. An entity creates a transaction and then places the transaction on the Helium peer-to-peer network for processing. The transaction is then picked up by Helium mining nodes. These nodes are engaged in the activity of processing transactions and mining blocks in order to reap rewards. In the case of Bitcoin, the reward is the issuance of some new bitcoins and the transaction fees which are attached to the transactions in the block that is successfully mined by the node. A transaction may have a zero transaction fee attached to it. The quantum of the transaction fee is within the sole discretion of the entity transferring value. A miner can elect to include a transaction in a block that it is mining or decline such an inclusion. Therefore, different miners will typically be mining different blocks at the same time. If a miner succeeds in adding a block to the blockchain, we say that the miner has mined the block. The transaction processing workflow is identical in Helium.

When a miner receives a block, the very first thing that it will do is to verify the integrity of the transaction. Verification means that the transaction is examined to ascertain that it contains valid values. For example, the transaction *locktime* parameter will be invalid if it is a negative number. An important aspect of verification is to ascertain that the transferor of value is spending values that it owns. This chapter

149

K. S. Garewal, *Practical Blockchains and Cryptocurrencies*, https://doi.org/10.1007/978-1-4842-5893-4_11

addresses transaction validation. If a transaction is valid, it can become part of a block that a miner intends to mine.

After a miner has mined a block, it adds the block to its local blockchain. The miner then broadcasts the newly mined block on the Helium network. Other miners who receive this block will then add it to their local blockchain.

Let us suppose that a miner mines a block with an invalid transaction. It may maliciously add this block to its local copy of the blockchain. But other miners will decline to add the block to their local blockchains, because they will ascertain that the block contains an invalid transaction.

It is worth noting that miners on a Helium network may have local blockchains that differ from each other. But due to the distributed consensus mechanism, the network will always converge to a dominant blockchain. We will discuss this in a subsequent chapter. Because of the manner in which distributed consensus works, trust is not needed in the network. We do not care that a mining node is acting *mala fides*. This is Satoshi Nakamoto's breakthrough insight.

Alright, let us start with the code walkthrough. Copy the program code that follows into a file called *tx.py* and save it the transaction directory.

You will notice that we have typically wrapped function bodies in this module within exception blocks.

In dynamically typed languages such as Python, the debugging process consists primarily of detecting and fixing type errors at runtime. This burden rises exponentially as program size increases. This factor makes interpreted languages with dynamic typing unsuitable for large-scale program development. In contrast, Go and C++ are very strictly typed. Go and C++ programs will simply refuse to compile if there is a type error in the program. In Go, once the program has compiled, debugging runtime errors is typically very fast (probably *O(n)*).

The workhorse function in the *tx* module is *validate_transaction;* it verifies the integrity of a transaction. This function performs the following tests:

1. Verify that required transaction attributes are present.

2. The locktime is greater than or equal to zero.

3. The locktime value is less than the maximum specified in the *hconfig* module.

4. The version number is valid.

5. The transaction ID has a valid format.

6. The vin list has positive length if the transaction is not in the genesis block or if the transaction is not a coinbase transaction.

7. For genesis block transactions or a coinbase transaction, the vin list is empty.

8. The vin list is not greater than the maximum allowable length specified in the *hconfig* module.

9. The vin list has valid format.

10. The vout list has positive length.

11. The vout list is not greater than the maximum allowable length specified in the *hconfig* module.

12. The vout list elements have valid format.

13. The transaction implements a p2pkhash script.

14. The reference to a previous transaction those output is consumed is valid.

15. The total value spent is less than or equal to the total spendable value.

16. All of the spent values in a transaction are greater than zero.

17. The transaction inputs can be unlocked. That is, an entity only consumes inputs that it owns.

18. A coinbase transaction value is not consumed before its locktime has expired.

In the *tx* module, the *prevtx_value* function references an unspent value in a previous transaction. This function is mocked in the unit tests since we have not implemented a LevelDB database to get unspent transaction amounts. We will look at Helium databases in the next chapter. The *transaction_fee* function computes the transaction fee for the transaction.

The *unlock_transaction_fragment* function determines whether values in a previous transaction can be unlocked for use in the present transaction. This function implements the *p2pkhash* stack processor that was discussed two chapters previously:

```
"""
tx.py: The tx module defines the structure of Helium transactions and
implements
basic transaction validation operations.
"""
import hconfig
import hblockchain as hchain
import json
import rcrypt
import secrets
import pdb
import logging

"""
log debugging messages to the file debug.log
"""
logging.basicConfig(filename="debug.log",filemode="w", \
  format='%(asctime)s:%(levelname)s:%(message)s',level=logging.DEBUG)

"""
Each transaction is modelled as a dictionary:

            {
                "transactionid": <string>
                "version":    <integer>
                "locktime":   <integer>
                "vin":        <list<dictionary>>
                "vout":       <list<<dictionary>>
            }

transactionid is the id of the the present transaction.
vin is a list of spendable inputs that are owned by the entity spending them.
Each spendable input comes from the vout list of a previous transaction.
Each vin is a list and each element is a dictionary object with the
```

following structure:

vin element:

```
        {
          "txid":              <string>
          "vout_index":        <int>
          "ScriptSig":         <list<string>>
        }
```

txid is the transaction id of a previous transaction. vout_index is an index into this previous transaction's vout list.

vout is a list and each element in the vout list is a dictionary with the following structure:

vout element:

```
        {
            "value":  <integer>,
            "ScriptPubKey": <list<string>>

        }
"""
```

```python
def create_transaction(transaction: 'dictionary', zero_inputs:
'boolean'=False) -> 'bool':
    """
    creates a transaction. Receives a transaction object and a predicate.
    zero_inputs is True if the transaction is in the genesis block or if
    the transaction
    is a coinbase transaction, otherwise zero_inputs is False.
    Returns False if the transaction parameters are invalid. Otherwise
    returns True
    """

    if validate_transaction(transaction, zero_inputs) == False: return False
    return True
```

```
def validate_transaction(trans: "dictionary", zero_inputs: "boolean"=False)
-> "bool":
    """
```

    verifies that a transaction has valid values.
    receives a transaction and a predicate.
    zero_inputs is True if the transaction is in the genesis block or if
    the transaction
    is a coinbase transaction, otherwise zero_inputs is False.

    The following transaction validation tests are performed:
        (1) The required attributes are present.
        (2) The locktime is greater than or equal to zero.
        (3) The locktime is less than a prescribed value.
        (4) The version number is valid.
        (5) The transaction ID has a valid format.
        (6) The vin list has positive length for transactions that are not in
             the genesis block and are not coinbase transactions.
        (7) The vin list is empty for coinbase transactions.
        (8) The genesis block does not have any inputs
        (9) The vin list is not greater than the maximum allowable length.
        (10) The vin list has valid format.
        (11) The vout list has positive length.
        (12) The vout list is not greater than the maximum allowable length.
        (13) The vout list elements have valid format.
        (14) The The vout list implements a p2pkhash script.
        (15) The reference to a previous transaction ID is valid.
        (16) The total value spent is less than or equal to the total
             spendable value.
        (17) The spent values are greater than zero.
        (18) The index values in the vin array reference valid elements in the
             vout array of the previous transaction.
        (19) The transaction inputs can be spent

    """

```
try:
    if type(trans) != dict:
        raise(ValueError("not dict type"))

    # Verify that required attributes are present
    if trans.get("transactionid") == None: return False
    if 'version' not in trans: return False
    if trans['locktime'] == None: return False
    if trans['vin'] == None: return False
    if trans['vout'] == None: return False

    # validate the format of the transaction id
    if rcrypt.validate_SHA256_hash(trans['transactionid']) == False:
        raise(ValueError("not SHA-256 hash error"))

    # validate the transaction version and locktime values
    if trans['version'] != hconfig.conf["VERSION_NO"]:
        raise(ValueError("improper version no"))

    if trans['locktime'] < 0:
        raise(ValueError("invalid locktime"))

    # genesis block or a coinbase transaction does not have any inputs
    if zero_inputs == True and len(trans["vin"]) > 0:
        raise(ValueError("genesis block cannot have inputs"))

    # validate the vin elements
    # there are no vin inputs for a genesis block transaction
    spendable_fragments = []

    for vin_element in trans['vin']:
        if validate_vin(vin_element) == False: return False
        tx_key = vin_element['txid'] + '_' + str(vin_element['vout_index'])

        spendable_fragment = prevtx_value(tx_key)

        if spendable_fragment == False:
            raise(ValueError("invalid spendable input for transaction"))
```

```
        else:
            spendable_fragments.append(spendable_fragment)

    # validate the transaction's vout list
    if len(trans['vout']) > hconfig.conf['MAX_OUTPUTS'] or
    len(trans['vout']) <= 0:
        raise(ValueError("vout list length error"))

    for vout_element in trans['vout']:
        if validate_vout(vout_element) == False: return False

    # validate the transaction fee
    if zero_inputs == False:
        if (transaction_fee(trans, spendable_fragments)) == False:
        return False

    # test that the transaction inputs are unlocked
    ctr = 0
    for vin in trans['vin']:
        if unlock_transaction_fragment(vin, spendable_fragments[ctr])
        == False:
            raise(ValueError("failed to unlock transaction"))
        ctr += 1

except Exception as err:
    logging.debug('validate_transaction: exception: ' + str(err))
    return False

return True

def validate_vin(vin_element: 'dictionary') -> bool:
    """

    tests whether a vin element has valid values
    returns True if the vin is valid, False otherwise
    """

    try:
        if vin_element['vout_index'] < 0: return False
        if len(vin_element['ScriptSig']) != 2: return False
        if len(vin_element['ScriptSig'][0]) == 0: return False
```

```python
        if len(vin_element['ScriptSig'][1]) == 0: return False

        if rcrypt.validate_SHA256_hash(vin_element['txid']) == False:
            raise(ValueError("txid is invalid"))

    except Exception as err:

        print("validate_vin exception" + str(err))
        logging.debug('validate_vin: exception: ' + str(err))
        return False

    return True

def validate_vout(vout_element: 'dictionary') -> bool:
    """

    tests whether a vout element has valid values
    returns True if the vout is valid, False otherwise
    """

    try:
        if vout_element['value'] <= 0:
            raise(ValueError("value is <= 0"))

        # validate the p2pkhash script
        if len(vout_element["ScriptPubKey"]) != 5:
            raise(ValueError("ScriptPubKey length error"))

        if vout_element["ScriptPubKey"][0] != '<DUP>':
            raise(ValueError("ScriptPubKey <DUP> error"))

        if vout_element["ScriptPubKey"][1] != '<HASH-160>':
            raise(ValueError("ScriptPubKey <HASH-160> error"))

        if vout_element["ScriptPubKey"][3] != '<EQ-VERIFY>':
            raise(ValueError("ScriptPubKey <EQ-VERIFY> error"))

        if vout_element["ScriptPubKey"][4] != '<CHECK-SIG>':
            raise(ValueError("ScriptPubKey <CHECK-SIG> error"))

        if len(vout_element["ScriptPubKey"][2]) == 0:
            raise(ValueError("ScriptPubKey RIPEMD-160 hash error"))
```

```
        except Exception as err:
            print("validate_vout exception" + str(err))
            logging.debug('validate_vout: exception: ' + str(err))
            return False

    return True

def prevtx_value(txkey: "string") -> 'bool':
    """

    examines the chainstate database and returns the transaction fragment:
        {
            "pkkhash":   <string>,
            "value":     <int>,
            "spent":     <bool>,
            "tx_chain": <string>
        }

    receives a transaction fragment key:
            "previous txid" + "_" + str(prevtx_vout_index)

    Returns False if the transaction if does not exist, or if the
    value has  been spent or if the value is not a positive integer
    otherwise returns the previous transaction fragment data
    """
    return "mocked value"

def transaction_fee(trans: 'dictionary', value_list: 'list<dictionary>' )
-> 'integer or bool':
    """

    calculates the transaction fee for a transaction.
    Receives a transaction and a list of chainstate transaction fragments
    Returns the transaction fee (in helium_cents) or False if there is an
    error.
    There is no transaction fee for the genesis block or coinbase
transactions.
    """

    try:
        spendable_value = 0
```

```
        spent_value      = 0

        for val in value_list:
            spendable_value += val["value"]

        for vout in trans['vout']:
            spent_value += vout['value']

        if spendable_value <= 0:
            raise(ValueError("spendable value <= 0 "))

        if spent_value <= 0:
            raise(ValueError("spent value <= 0 "))

        if spendable_value < spent_value:
            raise(ValueError("spendable value < spent value"))

    except Exception as err:
        logging.debug('transaction_fee: exception: ' + str(err))
        return False

    return spendable_value - spent_value


def unlock_transaction_fragment(vinel: "dictionary", fragment:
"dictionary") -> "boolean":
    """

    unlocks a previous transaction fragment using the p2pkhash script.
    Executes the script and returns False if the transaction is not unlocked
    Receives: the consuming vin and the previous transaction fragment consumed
    by the vin element.
    """

    try:
        execution_stack = []
        result_stack = []

        # make the execution stack for a p2pkhash script
        # since we only have one type of script in Helium
        # we can use hard-coded values
        execution_stack.append('SIG')
```

```
        execution_stack.append('PUBKEY')
        execution_stack.append('<DUP>')
        execution_stack.append('<HASH_160>')
        execution_stack.append('HASH-160')
        execution_stack.append('<EQ-VERIFY>')
        execution_stack.append('<CHECK_SIG>')

        # Run the p2pkhash execution stack
        result_stack.insert(0, vinel['ScriptSig'][0])
        result_stack.insert(0, vinel['ScriptSig'][1])
        result_stack.insert(0, vinel['ScriptSig'][1])

        hash_160 = rcrypt.make_SHA256_hash(vinel['ScriptSig'][1])
        hash_160 = rcrypt.make_RIPEMD160_hash(hash_160)

        result_stack.insert(0, hash_160)
        result_stack.insert(0, fragment["pkhash"])

        # do the EQ_VERIFY operation
        tmp1 = result_stack.pop(0)
        tmp2 = result_stack.pop(0)

        # test for RIPEMD-160 hash match
        if tmp1 != tmp2:
            raise(ValueError("public key match failure"))

        # test for a signature match
        ret = rcrypt.verify_signature(vinel['ScriptSig'][1], \
            vinel['ScriptSig'][1], vinel['ScriptSig'][0])
        if ret == False:
            raise(ValueError("signature match failure"))

    except Exception as err:
        logging.debug('unlock_transaction_fragment: exception: ' + str(err))
        return False

    return True
```

Transaction Processing Unit Tests

Copy the following code into a file named *test_tx.py* and copy this file into the *unit_tests* directory. Traverse to the *unit_tests* directory and run the tests:[1]

```
$(virtual) pytest test_tx.py -s
```

You will note that at the outset we create a symbolic transaction as well as a symbolic previous transaction that is used by the unit tests to create a pair of transactions with randomized values. The *randomize_list* function provides randomized access to *vin* and *vout* list elements for our unit tests. This module makes extensive use of pytest mocks, so if you are not conversant with this technology, you will want to review Appendix 3. The last two unit tests are noteworthy for your consideration; they test the unlocking of previous transaction outputs.

After executing the command line, you should see 35 unit tests passing:

```
"""
test_tx.py: implements unit tests for the transactions module
"""
import rcrypt
import hconfig
import hblockchain as bchain
import tx
import pytest
import pdb
import secrets
import random

previous_tx = None
prev_tx_keys = []
num_prev_tx_outputs = 0

###################################
# Synthetic Previous Transaction
###################################

def make_synthetic_previous_transaction(num_outputs):
```

---

[1]Note these are not strictly unit tests; they are akin to integration tests.

```
    """
    makes synthetic previous transaction with randomized values
    we abstract away the inputs to the previous transaction.
    """
    transaction = {}
    transaction['version'] = 1
    transaction['transactionid'] = rcrypt.make_uuid()
    transaction['locktime'] = 0
    transaction['vin'] = []
    transaction['vout'] = []

    def make_synthetic_vout():
        """
        make a synthetic vout object.
        returns a vout dictionary item
        """
        key_pair = rcrypt.make_ecc_keys()
        global prev_tx_keys
        prev_tx_keys.append([key_pair[0],key_pair[1]])
        vout = {}
        vout['value'] = secrets.randbelow(1000000) + 1000   # helium cents

        tmp = []
        tmp.append('<DUP>')
        tmp.append('<HASH-160>')
        tmp.append(key_pair[1])
        tmp.append('<EQ-VERIFY>')
        tmp.append('<CHECK-SIG>')
        vout['ScriptPubKey'] = tmp
        return vout

    ctr = 0
    while ctr < num_outputs:
        ret = make_synthetic_vout()
        transaction['vout'].append(ret)

        ctr += 1
```

```
        return transaction


##################################
# Synthetic Transaction
##################################
def make_synthetic_transaction(num_outputs):
    """

    makes a synthetic transaction with randomized values
    """

    transaction = {}
    transaction['version'] = 1
    transaction['transactionid'] = rcrypt.make_uuid()
    transaction['locktime'] = 0
    transaction['vin'] = []
    transaction['vout'] = []

    ctr = 0
    while ctr < num_outputs:
        vout = make_synthetic_vout()
        transaction['vout'].append(vout)
        ctr += 1

    # randomize how many of the previous transaction outputs
    # are consumed and the order in which they are consumed
    num_inputs = secrets.randbelow(num_prev_tx_outputs) + 1
    indices = list(range(num_inputs))
    random.shuffle(indices)

    for ctr in indices:
        vin = make_synthetic_vin(previous_tx["transactionid"], ctr)
        transaction['vin'].append(vin)
        ctr += 1

    return transaction
```

```python
#############################
# make a synthetic vin list
#############################

def make_synthetic_vin(prev_txid, prev_tx_vout_index):
    """
    makes a vin object.
    receives a previous transaction id and an index into the vout list.
    returns the vin element
    """
    vin = {}
    vin['txid'] = prev_txid
    vin['vout_index'] = prev_tx_vout_index
    vin['ScriptSig'] = []

    global prev_tx_keys

    vin['ScriptSig'].append(rcrypt.sign_message(prev_tx_keys[prev_tx_vout_
    index][0],

                                        prev_tx_keys[prev_tx_vout_
                                        index][1]))
    vin['ScriptSig'].append(prev_tx_keys[prev_tx_vout_index][1])
    return vin

#############################
# make a synthetic vout list
#############################

def make_synthetic_vout():
    """
    make a randomized vout element
    receives a public key
    returns the vout dict element
    """
    vout = {}
    vout['value'] = 1  # helium cents

    tmp = []
```

```python
    tmp.append('<DUP>')
    tmp.append('<HASH-160>')
    tmp.append(secrets.token_hex(64))
    tmp.append('<EQ-VERIFY>')
    tmp.append('<CHECK-SIG>')

    vout['ScriptPubKey'] = tmp
    return vout

###############################
# randomize access to a list
###############################

def randomize_list(lst: "list"):
    """

    randomly shuffles the indexes into a list
    returns the randomized index list
    """

    ctr = len(lst)
    p = 0
    index = []
    while p < ctr: index.append(p);p += 1
    random.shuffle(index)
    return index

###########################################
# Make a synthetic previous transaction
###########################################

num_prev_tx_outputs = secrets.randbelow(3) + 1
previous_tx = make_synthetic_previous_transaction(num_prev_tx_outputs)

"""

test the transactions
"""

def test_type_transaction():
    """

    test transaction type
```

```
    """

    assert tx.validate_transaction([]) == False

def test_missing_transactionid():
    """

    test missing transaction id
    """

    trns = make_synthetic_transaction(1)
    del trns["transactionid"]
    assert tx.validate_transaction(trns) == False

def test_bad_transactionid():
    """

    test transaction id with an invalid length
    """

    trns = make_synthetic_transaction(1)
    # replace the last char with an invalid char
    trns["transactionid"] = trns["transactionid"][:-1] + "z"
    assert tx.validate_transaction(trns) == False

def test_zero_version_number():
    """

    test zero version no
    """

    trns = make_synthetic_transaction(1)
    trns["version"] = 0
    assert tx.validate_transaction(trns) == False

def test_negative_locktime():
    """

    test for a negative locktime
    """

    trns = make_synthetic_transaction(1)
    trns["locktime"] = -1
    assert tx.validate_transaction(trns) == False
```

```python
def test_invalid_vout_length():
    """

    test that the vout list length is not greater than
    the maximum allowed by the Helium config
    """

    trn = make_synthetic_transaction(11)
    assert tx.validate_transaction(trn) == False

def test_no_prev_tx_reference():
    """

    test that the transaction's vin element has a
    reference to a previous transaction.
    """

    txn = make_synthetic_transaction(1)
    indices = randomize_list(txn["vin"])

    for ctr in list(range(len(indices))):
        txn['vin'][indices[ctr]]['txid'] = ""
        assert tx.validate_transaction(txn) == False

def test_empty_scriptSig():
    """

    test that ScriptPubKey element is not empty
    """

    txn = make_synthetic_transaction(8)
    indices = randomize_list(txn['vin'])

    for ctr in list(range(len(indices))):
        txn['vin'][indices[ctr]]['ScriptSig'] = []
        vin = txn['vin'][indices[ctr]]
        assert tx.validate_vin(vin) == False

def test_scriptsig_length_error():
    """

    test if the ScriptSig list has invalid length
    """

    txn = make_synthetic_transaction(2)
    indices = randomize_list(txn['vin'])
```

```python
    keys = rcrypt.make_ecc_keys()

    for ctr in list(range(len(indices))):
        txn["vin"][indices[ctr]]['ScriptSig'].append(keys[1])
        assert tx.validate_vin(txn['vin'][indices[ctr]]) == False
def test_empty_scriptSig_sig():
    """

    test that ScriptSig signature field is not empty
    """

    txn = make_synthetic_transaction(2)
    indices = randomize_list(txn['vin'])

    for ctr in list(range(len(indices))):
        txn['vin'][indices[ctr]]['ScriptSig'][0] = ''
        vin = txn['vin'][indices[ctr]]
        assert tx.validate_vin(vin) == False
def test_empty_scriptSig_pubkey():
    """

    test that ScriptSig public key field is not empty
    """

    txn = make_synthetic_transaction(2)
    indices = randomize_list(txn['vin'])

    for ctr in list(range(len(indices))):
        txn['vin'][indices[ctr]]['ScriptSig'][1] = ''
        assert tx.validate_transaction(txn) == False
def test_scriptpubkey_length_error():
    """

    test that ScriptPubKey list has a valid length
    """

    txn = make_synthetic_transaction(4)
    indices = randomize_list(txn['vout'])

    for ctr in list(range(len(indices))):
        element = txn['vout'][indices[ctr]]['ScriptPubKey'][1]
        txn['vout'][indices[ctr]]['ScriptPubKey'].append(element)
```

```
        assert tx.validate_transaction(txn) == False

@pytest.mark.parametrize("index, value, ret", [
    (0, 'DUP', False),
    (0, '<DUP>', True),
    (1, '<HASH-160',False),
    (1, '<HASH-160<',False),
    (1, '<HASH-160>',True),
    (1, '<HASH160>', False),
    (3, '<VERIFY>', False),
    (3, '<EQ-VERIFY>', True),
    (4, '<CHECKSIG>', False),
    (4, '<CHECK-SIG>', True),
])
def test_bad_scriptpubkey_script(monkeypatch, index, value, ret):
    """

    test if ScriptPubKey has an invalid element
    """

    monkeypatch.setattr(tx, "transaction_fee", 5)
    monkeypatch.setattr(tx, "unlock_transaction_fragment", True)

    txn = make_synthetic_transaction(7)
    indices = randomize_list(txn['vout'])

    txn['vout'][indices[0]]['ScriptPubKey'][index] = value
    assert tx.validate_vout(txn['vout'][indices[0]]) == ret

def test_pubkeyhash():
    """

    test a public key hash in scriptpubkey for a
    valid RIPEMD-160 format
    """

    txn = make_synthetic_transaction(5)

    indices = randomize_list(txn['vout'])

    for ctr in list(range(len(indices))):
        val = txn['vout'][indices[ctr]]['ScriptPubKey'][2]
```

```
        val = rcrypt.make_RIPEMD160_hash(rcrypt.make_SHA256_hash(val))
        assert rcrypt.validate_RIPEMD160_hash(val) == True

def test_invalid_txid():
    """

    test the format of a previous transaction
    """

    txn = make_synthetic_transaction(2)
    id = rcrypt.make_uuid()
    id = "j" + id[1:]

    indices = randomize_list(txn['vin'])


    ctr = secrets.randbelow(len(indices))
    txn['vin'][indices[ctr]]['txid'] = id
    assert tx.validate_transaction(txn) == False

def test_invalid_txid_length():
    """

    test a previous transaction id for length
    """

    txn = make_synthetic_transaction(2)
    id = rcrypt.make_uuid()
    id = "p" + id[0:]
    indices = randomize_list(txn['vin'])

    ctr = secrets.randbelow(len(indices))
    txn['vin'][indices[ctr]]['txid'] = id
    assert tx.validate_transaction(txn) == False

def test_bad_transaction_inputs(monkeypatch):
    """

    tests that the inputs received are valid.
    fails if the previous transaction does not exist,
    or previous value has been spent, or is negative
    """

    monkeypatch.setattr(tx, 'prevtx_value', lambda x: False)
    assert tx.prevtx_value("stubbed function") == False
```

```
def test_transaction_inputs(monkeypatch):
    """

    tests that the inputs received are valid
    fails if the previous transaction does not exist,
    or previous value has been spent, or is negative
    """

    txn = make_synthetic_transaction(2)
    monkeypatch.setattr(tx, 'prevtx_value', lambda x:
            [{
            "txid_vout": txn['vin'][0]['txid'] + '_' + str(txn['vin'][0]
            ['vout_index']),
            "value": 210,
            "pkhash": previous_tx['vout'][0]['ScriptPubKey'][2],
            "block": 100,
            "spent": False
        },

        {

            "txid_vout": txn['vin'][0]['txid'] + '_' + str(txn['vin'][0]
            ['vout_index']),
            "value": 38,
            "pkhash": previous_tx['vout'][0]['ScriptPubKey'][2],
            "block": 29,
            "spent": False
        }]
    )

    assert bool(tx.prevtx_value(txn)) == True

def test_zero_output_value(monkeypatch):
    """

    test a zero transaction output value
    """

    txn = make_synthetic_transaction(4)

    indices = randomize_list(txn['vout'])
    ctr = secrets.randbelow(len(indices))
```

171

```python
    monkeypatch.setitem(txn['vout'][indices[ctr]], 'value', 0 )
    assert tx.validate_transaction(txn) == False

def test_negative_output_value(monkeypatch):
    """

    test a negative transaction output value
    """

    txn = make_synthetic_transaction(4)

    indices = randomize_list(txn['vout'])
    ctr = secrets.randbelow(len(indices))

    monkeypatch.setitem(txn['vout'][indices[ctr]], 'value', -456712)
    assert tx.validate_transaction(txn) == False

def test_transaction_fee(monkeypatch):
    """

    test various transaction fees
    """

    txn = make_synthetic_transaction(2)
    txn['vout'][0]["value"] = 10
    txn['vout'][1]["value"] = 203

    value_list = [{
        "txid_vout": txn['vin'][0]['txid'] + '_' + str(txn['vin'][0]['vout_
        index']),
        "value": 210,
        "pkhash": previous_tx['vout'][0]['ScriptPubKey'][2],
        "block": 100,
        "spent": False
    },

    {
        "txid_vout": txn['vin'][0]['txid'] + '_' + str(txn['vin'][0]['vout_
        index']),
        "value": 38,
        "pkhash": previous_tx['vout'][0]['ScriptPubKey'][2],
        "block": 29,
```

```
        "spent": False
        }
    ]

    assert tx.transaction_fee(txn, value_list) != False

def test_negative_transaction_fee(monkeypatch):
    """

    test a negative transaction fee
    """

    txn = make_synthetic_transaction(3)
    monkeypatch.setitem(txn['vout'][0], 'value', 10000)

    value_list = [{
        "txid_vout": txn['vin'][0]['txid'] + '_' + str(txn['vin'][0]['vout_
        index']),
        "value": 210,
        "pkhash": previous_tx['vout'][0]['ScriptPubKey'][2],
        "block": 100,
        "spent": False
    },

    {
        "txid_vout": txn['vin'][0]['txid'] + '_' + str(txn['vin'][0]['vout_
        index']),
        "value": 38,
        "pkhash": previous_tx['vout'][0]['ScriptPubKey'][2],
        "block": 29,
        "spent": False
    }
    ]

    assert tx.transaction_fee(txn, value_list) == False

def test_unlock_bad_hash(monkeypatch):
    """

    test unlocking previous transaction output with
    bad RIPEMD-160 hash p2pkhash value
```

```
    """

    global prev_tx_keys

    prev_tx_keys.clear()
    txn1 = make_synthetic_previous_transaction(4)
    txn2 = make_synthetic_transaction(2)

    # make a transaction fragment where the first vin element
    # of txn2 consumes the value of the first vout element of txn1

    # synthetic consuming vin element in tx2
    vin = {}
    vin['txid'] = txn1["transactionid"]
    vin['vout_index'] = 0
    vin['ScriptSig'] = {}

    signature = rcrypt.sign_message(prev_tx_keys[1][0], prev_tx_keys[1][1])
    pubkey = prev_tx_keys[1][1]
    sig = []
    sig.append(signature)
    sig.append(pubkey + "corrupted")
    vin['ScriptSig'] = sig

    # use the wrong public key hash in txn2
    key_pair = rcrypt.make_ecc_keys()
    ripemd_hash = rcrypt.make_RIPEMD160_hash(rcrypt.make_SHA256_hash(key_pair[1]))

    fragment = {
        "value": 210,
        "pkhash": ripemd_hash,
        "spent": False,
        "tx_chain": txn2["transactionid"] + "_" + "0",
        "checksum":    rcrypt.make_SHA256_hash(txn1["transactionid"])
    }

    assert tx.unlock_transaction_fragment(vin, fragment) == False

def test_unlock_bad_signature(monkeypatch):
    """
```

```
    test unlocking a transaction with a bad signature
    """

    global prev_tx_keys

    prev_tx_keys.clear()
    txn1 = make_synthetic_previous_transaction(4)
    txn2 = make_synthetic_transaction(2)

    # make a transaction fragment where the first vin element
    # of txn2 consumes the value of the first vout element of txn1

    # synthetic consuming vin element in tx2
    vin = {}
    vin['txid'] = txn1["transactionid"]
    vin['vout_index'] = 0
    vin['ScriptSig'] = {}

    # use wrong private key to sign
    key_pair = rcrypt.make_ecc_keys()

    signature = rcrypt.sign_message(key_pair[0], prev_tx_keys[1][1])
    pubkey = prev_tx_keys[1][1]
    sig = []
    sig.append(signature)
    sig.append(pubkey + "corrupted")
    vin['ScriptSig'] = sig

    # public key hash in txn2
    ripemd_hash = rcrypt.make_RIPEMD160_hash(rcrypt.make_SHA256_hash(prev_
    tx_keys[1][1]))

    fragment = {
        "value": 210,
        "pkhash": ripemd_hash,
        "spent": False,
        "tx_chain": txn2["transactionid"] + "_" + "0",
        "checksum":   rcrypt.make_SHA256_hash(txn1["transactionid"])
    }

    assert tx.unlock_transaction_fragment(vin, fragment) == False
```

```python
def test_unlock_bad_pubkey():
    """
    test unlocking a transaction with a bad public key
    """
    global prev_tx_keys

    prev_tx_keys.clear()
    txn1 = make_synthetic_previous_transaction(4)
    txn2 = make_synthetic_transaction(2)

    # make a transaction fragment where the first vin element
    # of txn2 consumes the value of the first vout element of txn1

    # synthetic consuming vin element in tx2
    vin = {}
    vin['txid'] = txn1["transactionid"]
    vin['vout_index'] = 0
    vin['ScriptSig'] = {}

    signature = rcrypt.sign_message(prev_tx_keys[1][0], prev_tx_keys[1][1])
    pubkey = prev_tx_keys[1][1]
    sig = []
    sig.append(signature)
    sig.append(pubkey + "corrupted")
    vin['ScriptSig'] = sig

    # public key hash in txn2
    ripemd_hash = rcrypt.make_RIPEMD160_hash(rcrypt.make_SHA256_hash(prev_
    tx_keys[1][1]))

    fragment = {
        "value": 210,
        "pkhash": ripemd_hash,
        "spent": False,
        "tx_chain": txn2["transactionid"] + "_" + "0",
        "checksum":   rcrypt.make_SHA256_hash(txn1["transactionid"])
    }

    assert tx.unlock_transaction_fragment(vin, fragment) == False
```

```python
def test_unlock_good():
    """
    test unlocking a transaction with a good private-public key pair
    """

    global prev_tx_keys

    prev_tx_keys.clear()
    txn1 = make_synthetic_previous_transaction(4)
    txn2 = make_synthetic_transaction(2)

    # make a transaction fragment where the first vin element
    # of txn2 consumes the value of the first vout element of txn1

    # synthetic consuming vin element in tx2
    vin = {}
    vin['txid'] = txn1["transactionid"]
    vin['vout_index'] = 0
    vin['ScriptSig'] = {}

    signature = rcrypt.sign_message(prev_tx_keys[1][0], prev_tx_keys[1][1])
    pubkey = prev_tx_keys[1][1]
    sig = []
    sig.append(signature)
    sig.append(pubkey)
    vin['ScriptSig'] = sig

    # public key hash in txn2
    ripemd_hash = rcrypt.make_RIPEMD160_hash(rcrypt.make_SHA256_hash(prev_
tx_keys[1][1]))

    fragment = {
        "value": 210,
        "pkhash": ripemd_hash,
        "spent": False,
        "tx_chain": txn2["transactionid"] + "_" + "0",
        "checksum":    rcrypt.make_SHA256_hash(txn1["transactionid"])
    }

    assert tx.unlock_transaction_fragment(vin, fragment) == True
```

Update the Helium Blockchain Module

Now that we have a functional transaction module; we update the *hblockchain* module to validate transactions in a block. Ensure that you import the *tx* module into *hblockchain*. Remove the *add_block* function from the *hblockchain* module and add the following variant in lieu thereof:

```
def add_block(block: "dictionary") -> "bool":
    """

    add_block: adds a block to the blockchain. Receives a block.
    The block attributes are checked for validity and each transaction
    in the block is tested for validity. If there are no errors, the block
    is written to a file as a sequence of raw bytes. Then the block is added
    to the blockchain.
    returns True if the block is added to the blockchain and False
    otherwise.
    """

    try:
        # validate the received block parameters
        if validate_block(block) == False:
            raise(ValueError("block validation error"))

        # validate the transactions in the block
        for trx in block['tx']:
            # first transaction in the block is a coinbase transaction
            if block["height"] == 0 or block['tx'][0] == trx: zero_inputs =
            True
            else: zero_inputs = False

            if tx.validate_transaction(trx, zero_inputs) == False:
                raise(ValueError("transaction validation error"))

        # serialize the block to a file
        if (serialize_block(block) == False):
                raise(ValueError("serialize block error"))

        # add the block to the blockchain in memory
        blockchain.append(block)
```

```
except Exception as err:
    print(str(err))
    logging.debug('add_block: exception: ' + str(err))
    return False

return True
```

This validates all of the transactions in a block before the block is added to the blockchain.

Conclusion

In this chapter, we have written program code to validate Helium transactions. We have also written unit tests for our transaction program code. Lastly, we have refined the Helium blockchain code to verify transactions before a block is added to the blockchain.

You will have noticed that we have not implemented any code to retrieve unspent transaction values from previous transactions. This feature was mocked in our unit tests. The next chapter addresses this matter.

We will implement two databases for Helium. In the same manner as Bitcoin, we are going to implement a LevelDB database to verify and get unspent transaction amounts. We will also implement a second LevelDB database that lets us quickly determine the block in which a particular transaction is located.

CHAPTER 12

The Chainstate

In the previous chapter, we implemented program code that validated the integrity
of transactions. There was a significant omission in this code, we did not address the
issue of how unspent values from a previous transaction are obtained, and we also did
not address the matter of validating the unspent values in previous transactions. The
reason for this omission is that unspent values are implemented in a key-value store.
In this chapter, we will rectify this deficiency by implementing a key-value store for
transactions. We will also implement a key-value store that lets us determine the block
which contains a particular transaction.

In brief, a key-value store is a data structure which maps keys to values.[1] Given a
key, we can obtain the value associated with it. The keys in the store are unique. If you
are inclined to think of an analogy, then a telephone directory is a good example of an
analogue key-value store. The primary and significant benefit of key-value stores is that
they provide random access to the store. Thus, getting, mutating, and deleting key values
is extremely fast. A very large persistent key-value store can search and fetch a value in
one disk access.

In Bitcoin, the key-value store of unspent transaction values is implemented as
a LevelDB database. Helium also uses LevelDB in its implementation. Appendix 2 of
this book contains a good introduction to installing and using LevelDB. You should go
through this appendix if you are not familiar with LevelDB. LevelDB is a particularly
simple key-value store. It is so, deliberately by design. The LevelDB design objective is to
implement a very simple and very fast persistent store which has extreme reliability. You
will observe, for example, that LevelDB only supports string keys and string values and
has a tiny API footprint.

---

[1] A key-value store is called a dictionary in Python. In other languages, such as Ruby, it's called a
map. In C++, it's called an associative container.

© Karan Singh Garewal 2020
K. S. Garewal, *Practical Blockchains and Cryptocurrencies*, https://doi.org/10.1007/978-1-4842-5893-4_12

Finding Unspent Transaction Values

In Bitcoin and Helium, blocks are stored on disk as ordinary text files. Blocks are not stored in a database. This is a deliberate design feature. The design objective in Bitcoin is to keep the cryptocurrency implementation at the simplest level possible. This maximizes reliability. By simply storing blocks to disk as ordinary binary files, it becomes the responsibility of the operating system to ensure that blocks are successfully written to disk. Furthermore, the operating system must ensure that these files are not corrupted. The cryptocurrency application needs to only examine the response of the operating system to a request to write a block to disk. There is an additional reason for such a file-based block storage implementation. In Bitcoin and Helium, all of the databases and other needed data structures can be built from scratch from these block files. The only significant point of failure is thus any missing or corrupted block files. Since a blockchain is an immutable structure, block files must also be immutable, write once, and read many times structures. It is primarily the responsibility of the operating system to ensure the integrity of block files. This implementation of block storage is significantly less complex than storing blocks in a SQL or NoSQL database.

There is, however, an intrinsic deficiency in this file-based block storage model. Consider a transaction where we want to spend a value in some previous transaction. Suppose further that we only have the transaction id corresponding to this value. We will have to retrieve the transaction from the block that contains this transaction and then determine if the value is unspent. Since the blocks are not indexed, this will entail searching all of the block files for this particular transaction and then searching for a subsequent transaction that has spent this value. If, for example, the blockchain is composed of ten million block files, then it is patently obvious that such a search will be unacceptably slow. In a real-world application, there may be thousands of transactions per second.

A transaction store can solve this scalability problem by maintaining transaction metadata in a memory key-value store. Every time a transaction occurs, the application saves metadata pertaining to the transaction in the key-value store and also persists this data to disk.[2] Now, if the application needs to interrogate the blockchain about a transaction, it searches the key-value store, and since such a store provides random access, the response will be more or less instantaneous. We are going to build a LevelDB

---

[2]To be precise, the store persists data to disk but also maintains a dictionary in memory of the most recently used keys. This memory structure is called a cache.

database implementation that provides such a capability for transactions and a second LevelDB database that lets us query it for the block that contains a particular transaction.

Chainstate Database Design

We will call the LevelDB database that provides the capability to query the unspent status of transaction outputs, a Chainstate database or simply Chainstate. Chainstate will let us determine whether a particular transaction exists and whether a particular transaction value is unspent. In addition, Chainstate will provide other metainformation that is useful for transaction processing.

A Chainstate database is also invaluable in constructing wallets. Bitcoin-like cryptocurrencies do not maintain an account for each entity that conducts transactions. Instead, the cryptocurrency network maintains a distributed ledger that records transactions as they occur. Clients that use such a cryptocurrency must maintain their own wallets to conduct transactions. Such a wallet will contain the user's public-private key pairs and the unspent values available at public addresses that the wallet holder has created. A wallet will provide a history of transactions that the wallet holder has consummated. Finally, a wallet will also let the user create public-private keys for use in transactions. You will note that in the absence of such a wallet, the client would have to maintain a local copy of the entire blockchain and query the blockchain every time she wanted to engage in a transaction.

The following is the record structure for the Chainstate Database:

```
key: "transaction_index" + "_" + "vout_index"
value:  {
                    "pkhash":                    <string>
                    "value":                     <int>
                    "spent":                     <bool>
                    "tx_chain"                   <string>
        }
```

The key, called a transaction key, is the concatenation of a transaction id and an index into the *vout list* at which a value of interest is located. These two pieces of information are sufficient to identify a value in a previous transaction. Due to the properties of transaction IDs, a transaction key is guaranteed to be universally unique.

The value associated with a key is a dictionary. We call this key value a transaction fragment. Its fields are interpreted as follows.

value is a positive number. It is the quantum of helium cents spendable in this transaction, which is pointed to by the *transactionid* and *vout index* in the transaction key. *value* is an integer.

pk_hash is the string of the form

$$\text{"pk\_hash": RIPEMD\_160(SHA-256(public\_key))}$$

pk_hash is constructed from the public address that the recipient of the value has provided to the transferor of the value.[3]

spent is a boolean type. It is True if the value has been spent and False otherwise.

tx_chain points to the transaction input that has spent this output. *tx_chain* will be empty if the output has not been spent.

Since a LevelDB database only accepts string keys and values, we must convert the transaction fragment dictionary to a string before insertion into the database.[4] In Python, this can be easily accomplished with the *dumps* function in the *json* module.

Our Chainstate Database will have five interface functions:

```
open_chainstate(directory_path: "string")
close_chainstate()
put_transaction(key: "string", value: "dictionary") => "bool"
get_transaction(key: "string") => "bool or string"
transaction_update(key: "string") => "bool"
```

The *open_chainstate* function opens the Helium LevelDB Chainstate database and creates it if it does not exist. This function receives a full or partial file path parameter, inclusive of the database name. *close_chainstate* closes the database.

The *get_transaction* function receives a transaction key which has the form "transaction id" + "_"+ str(vout_index). This function returns the transaction fragment pertaining to this key or False if the key does not exist in *Chainstate*.

The *put_transaction* function adds a key-value pair to *Chainstate*. This function receives a transaction key and a transaction fragment as arguments. It returns True if

---

[3]Please refer to Chapter 9.

[4]To be precise, LevelDB databases only handle byte strings; Python strings must be converted into byte strings before they are handed over to the database interface function. Similarly, LevelDB databases only return byte strings.

the key-value pair is added to Chainstate and False otherwise. *put_transaction* performs synchronous writes into the Chainstate.

The LevelDB API expects byte string arguments and returns byte strings. A byte string is a length-prefixed string (as opposed to a string that has a null terminator '\0'. This is required to ensure transmission portability across networks. These conversions are handled internally by our interface functions. The LevelDB API also contains functions that permit key-value pairs to be batched before they are written into the store; this is a performance feature.

The *transaction_update* function updates the Chainstate database when a transaction value is spent. This function ensures that the previous transaction fragment, whose value is being spent, does in fact exist. It prevents "double-spending" of a spent value. This function marks a transaction fragment as spent and sets the fragment attribute *tx_chain* to the transaction fragment that has received the spendable value. This function receives a transaction as its argument.

We can now implement program code for the chainstate module.

Chainstate Database Code

Make sure that you have compiled and installed the LevelDB database. Additionally, ensure that you have installed the LevelDB Python interface, the *plyvel* module, in your virtual Helium environment. Instructions for this are in Appendix 2.

Next, we will create an empty Helium LevelDB database. This database will be located in the *data* sub-directory of the root of Helium. Traverse to the root of your virtual environment, enter the Python shell, and do

```
 $(virtual) python
>>> import plyvel

# create the Helium Chainstate key-value store
>>> db = plyvel.DB('data/heliumdb/')
```

If you traverse to the *data* directory, you will see a *heliumdb* sub-directory. This sub-directory contains the Chainstate files.

We are now ready for a walkthrough to the Helium Chainstate program code. Copy the following code into a file called *hchaindb.py* and then copy this file into the *chainstate* sub-directory of the root.

Helium has a particularly simple implementation for tracking and summarizing transactions. The *open_hchainstate* function receives a full or partial file path including the name of the LevelDB database. It opens the Helium Chainstate database that is named in the path and creates this database if it does not exist. This function does not create any sub-directories listed in the file path if they do not exist. If the function succeeds, it returns a handle to the Chainstate database. In the event of a failure, the function returns False.

The *close_hchainstate* function receives a handle to the Chainstate and closes the database in an orderly fashion.

The *put_transaction* function receives a transaction key and a transaction fragment as its arguments. *put_transaction* returns True if it succeeds in inserting the *transactionid, transaction fragment* key-value pair into the Chainstate database. Otherwise, *put_transaction* returns False.

The *get_transaction* function has a transaction key argument and returns the transaction fragment associated with this key (along with the checksum). If the transaction key is fictitious, *get_transaction* returns False.

The *update_transaction* function updates the Chainstate when previous unspent values are spent. In particular, it prevents double-spending an unspent value two or more times. This function has a transaction as its argument:

```
"""

Implementation of the Helium chainstate key-value store. This store lets us
access information about transaction fragments through a transaction key.
"""

import hconfig
import rcrypt
import plyvel
import logging
import json
import pdb

"""

log debugging messages to the file debug.log
```

```
"""
logging.basicConfig(filename="debug.log",filemode="w", \
 format='%(asctime)s:%(levelname)s:%(message)s', level=logging.DEBUG)

# handle to the Helium Chainstate Database
hDB = None

def open_hchainstate(filepath: "string") -> "db handle or False":
    """
    opens the Helium Chainstate key-value store and returns a handle to
    it. The database will be created if it does not exist.  All of the
    directories in filepath must exist.
    Returns a handle to the database or False
    """

    try:
        global hDB
        hDB = plyvel.DB(filepath, create_if_missing=True)

    except Exception as err:
        logging.debug('open_hchainstate: exception: ' + str(err))
        return False

    return hDB

def close_hchainstate() -> "bool":
    """
    close the Helium Chainstate store
    Returns True if the database is closed, False otherwise
    """
    global hDB
    try:
        hDB.close()
        if hDB.closed != True: return False

    except Exception as err:
        logging.debug('close_hchainstate: exception: ' + str(err))
        return False

    return True
```

```python
def put_transaction(txkey: "string", tx_fragment: "dictionary") -> "bool":
    """

    creates a key-value pair in the Chainstate Database
    Receives a transaction key and a transaction_fragment.
    The transaction key is: transactionid + "_" + str(vout_index)

    The tx_fragment parameter received is:
    {
                "pkhash":                   <string>
                "value":                    <int>
                "spent":                    <bool>
                "tx_chain"                  <string>
    }

    Returns True if the key-value pair is created and False otherwise
    """
    try:
        # if transaction key already exists delete because
        # the transaction fragment is going to be updated
        encoded_key = str.encode(txkey)
        hDB.delete(encoded_key)

        keyvalue = json.dumps(tx_fragment)
        # save the txkey-fragment pair to the store
        hDB.put(encoded_key, str.encode(keyvalue))

    except Exception as err:
        print(str(err))
        logging.debug('put_transaction: exception: ' + str(err))
        return False

    return True

def get_transaction(key: "string") -> "False or dictionary":
    """

    Receives a transaction key (transactionid + "_" + str(vout_index))
    for a transaction fragment
    returns False or the key value. The transaction fragment returned has
```

```
    form:
    {
                "pkhash":                   <string>
                "value":                    <string>
                "spent":                    <string>
                "tx_chain"                  <string>

    }
    """

    try:
        # get the transaction fragment corresponding to the transaction
        # key, return False if the key does not exist
        fragment = hDB.get(str.encode(key))
        if fragment == None:
            raise(ValueError("transaction fragment not found"))

        fragment = json.loads(fragment.decode())

    except Exception as err:
        logging.debug('get_transaction: exception: ' + str(err))
        return False

    return fragment

def transaction_update(trx: "transaction")-> "bool":
    """

        receives a transaction. Updates the chainstate database to
        reflect the transaction. Sets previous transaction fragments
        to indicate that they have been spent. Updates these fragments
        to indicate the transaction id of the consuming transaction.
        returns True or False if there is an error
    """

    try:
        # collect all of the outputs of previous transactions and set them
          to spent
        # specify the transaction key consuming the previous transaction inputs
        for vin in trx["vin"]:
```

```
# fetch a previous transaction fragment. It must exist
prev_tx_key = vin["txid"] + "_" + str(vin["vout_index"])

tx_fragment = get_transaction(prev_tx_key)
if tx_fragment == False:
    print("vin fragment not found: " + prev_tx_key)
    raise(ValueError("transaction fragment not found"))

# double spend error
# should be detected prior to writing to the Chainstate
if tx_fragment["spent"] == True:
    print("fragment is double spend error: " + prev_tx_key)
    raise(ValueError("transaction fragment double spend error:
    " + prev_tx_key))

# set the spent values to True in the previous transaction
# fragment
tx_fragment["spent"] = True

# set the reference to the consuming transaction
tx_fragment["tx_chain"] = trx["transactionid"] + "_" +
str(vin["vout_index"])

# save to HeliumDB
ret = put_transaction(prev_tx_key, tx_fragment)
if ret == False:
    raise(ValueError("failed to update spent tx fragment"))

# put the fragments of the consuming transaction into the HeliumDB
ctr = 0
for vout in trx["vout"]:
    tx_fragment = {}
    txkey = trx["transactionid"] + "_" + str(ctr)
    tx_fragment["pkhash"] = vout["ScriptPubKey"][2]
    tx_fragment["value"] = vout["value"]
    tx_fragment["spent"] = False
    tx_fragment["tx_chain"] = ""

    if put_transaction(txkey, tx_fragment) == False:
```

```
            raise(ValueError("failed to insert consuming transaction
            fragment"))

        ctr += 1

except Exception as err:
    print(str(err))
    logging.debug('transaction_update: exception: ' + str(err))
    return False

return True
```

Pytests for the Chainstate Database

Copy the following unit test code into the file *test_hchaindb.py* and save this file in the *unit_tests* directory. Traverse to the *unit_tests* directory and run the tests in the virtual Helium environment:

`$(virtual): pytest test_hchaindb.py -s`

The *setup_module* function in *test_hchaindb.py* opens the Chainstate database before any tests are run. The *teardown_module* closes the database after the tests have been executed. There are two helper functions that generate a pair of adjacent, randomized, synthetic transactions. There are tests for *put_transaction*, *get_transaction*, and *transaction_update* functionality. The *put_transaction* function tests various random values for *pkhash*, *value*, and *spent*. With *get_transaction*, we test in particular that trying to get the value of a non-existent transaction key fails. The *update_transaction* function tests the creation of unspent fragments and tests that double-spending cannot occur.

When you execute these tests, you should see six tests passing:

```
"""
pytest unit tests for the hchaindb module
"""

import hchaindb as chain
import rcrypt
import pytest
import json
```

```python
import random
import secrets
import pdb
import os

def setup_module():
    assert bool(chain.open_hchainstate("heliumdb")) == True

def teardown_module():
    assert chain.close_hchainstate() == True
    if os.path.isfile("heliumdb"):
        os.remove("heliumdb")

###############################################
# Globals for a synthetic previous transaction
###############################################
prev_tx = None
prev_tx_keys = []

def make_keys():
    """
    makes a private-public key pair for the synthetic
    previous transaction
    """
    prev_tx_keys.clear()
    key_pair = rcrypt.make_ecc_keys()
    prev_tx_keys.append([key_pair[0],key_pair[1]])
    return

# instantiate a key pair
make_keys()

def make_synthetic_previous_transaction(num_outputs):
    """
    makes synthetic previous transaction with randomized values
    we abstract away the inputs to the previous transaction.
    """
    transaction = {}
```

```
    transaction['version'] = 1
    transaction['transactionid'] = rcrypt.make_uuid()
    transaction['locktime'] = 0
    transaction['vin']  = []
    transaction['vout'] = []

    def make_synthetic_vout():
        """

        make a synthetic vout object.
        returns a vout dictionary item
        """

        vout = {}
        vout['value'] = secrets.randbelow(1000000) + 1000  # helium cents

        tmp = []
        tmp.append('<DUP>')
        tmp.append('<HASH-160>')
        tmp.append(prev_tx_keys[0][1])
        tmp.append('<EQ-VERIFY>')
        tmp.append('<CHECK-SIG>')
        vout['ScriptPubKey'] = tmp
        return vout

    ctr = 0
    while ctr < num_outputs:
        ret = make_synthetic_vout()
        transaction['vout'].append(ret)

        ctr += 1

    return transaction

####################################
# Synthetic Transaction
####################################
def make_synthetic_transaction(prev_tx: "dictionary"):
    """

    makes a synthetic transaction with randomized values and that
```

```
    draws inputs from the previous transaction
    """

    transaction = {}
    transaction['version'] = 1
    transaction['transactionid'] = rcrypt.make_uuid()
    transaction['locktime'] = 0
    transaction['vin'] = []
    transaction['vout'] = []

    num_outputs = max(1, secrets.randbelow(9))

    ctr = 0
    while ctr < num_outputs:
        vout = make_synthetic_vout()
        transaction['vout'].append(vout)
        ctr += 1

    # randomize how many of the previous transaction outputs
    # are consumed and the order in which they are consumed
    num_inputs = max(secrets.randbelow(len(prev_tx["vout"])), 1)
    indices = list(range(num_inputs))
    random.shuffle(indices)

    for ctr in indices:
        vin = make_synthetic_vin(prev_tx["transactionid"], ctr)
        transaction['vin'].append(vin)
        ctr += 1

    return transaction

##############################
# make a synthetic vin list
##############################

def make_synthetic_vin(prev_txid, prev_tx_vout_index):
    """

    make a vin object, receives a previous transaction id
    and an index into the vout list
```

```
    returns the vin element
    """

    vin = {}
    vin['txid'] = prev_txid
    vin['vout_index'] = prev_tx_vout_index
    vin['ScriptSig'] = []
    vin['ScriptSig'].append(rcrypt.sign_message(prev_tx_keys[0][0], prev_
tx_keys[0][1]))
    vin['ScriptSig'].append(prev_tx_keys[0][1])
    return vin

#############################
# make a synthetic vout list
#############################

def make_synthetic_vout():
    """

    make a randomized vout element
    receives a public key
    returns the vout dict element
    """

    vout = {}
    vout['value'] = 1  # helium cents

    tmp = []
    tmp.append('<DUP>')
    tmp.append('<HASH-160>')
    tmp.append(secrets.token_hex(64))
    tmp.append('<EQ-VERIFY>')
    tmp.append('<CHECK-SIG>')

    vout['ScriptPubKey'] = tmp
    return vout

def make_transactionid():
    """

    makes a random transaction id
    """
```

```
    return rcrypt.make_uuid()

def make_vout_index():
    """
    makes a random vout index
    """
    return random.randrange(10)

def make_pkhash():
    """
    creates a random pkhash value
    """
    id = rcrypt.make_uuid()
    return rcrypt.make_RIPEMD160_hash(rcrypt.make_SHA256_hash(id))

def make_value():
    """
    creates a random value
    """
    return random.randrange(1000000)

def make_spent():
    """
    creates a random spent boolean
    """
    sbool = random.randrange(10) % 2
    if sbool: return False
    return True

def test_put_keyvalue():
    """
    put a key-value pair into the chainstate database
    values have already been validated by validate_transaction
    """
    ctr = 0
    while ctr < 10:
        txid = make_transactionid()
        vout_index = make_vout_index()
```

```python
        keyvalue = {
            "pkhash": make_pkhash(),
            "value":  make_value(),
            "spent":  make_spent(),
            "tx_chain": ""
        }

        assert chain.put_transaction(txid + "_" + str(vout_index),
        keyvalue) == True
        ctr += 1

def test_get_keyvalue():
    """

    get a key value for an existing key
    """

    txid = make_transactionid()
    vout_index = make_vout_index()

    keyvalue = {
        "pkhash": make_pkhash(),
        "value":  make_value(),
        "spent":  make_spent(),
        "tx_chain": ""
    }

    assert chain.put_transaction(txid + "_" + str(vout_index), keyvalue) == True

    key = txid + "_" + str(vout_index)
    ret = chain.get_transaction(key)
    assert ret != False
    assert type(ret) == dict

def test_get_for_fake_key():
    """

    attempt to get a key value for a fictitious key
    """

    txid = make_transactionid()
    vout_index = make_vout_index()
```

```
    keyvalue = {
        "pkhash": make_pkhash(),
        "value":  make_value(),
        "spent":  make_spent(),
        "tx_chain": ""
    }

    assert chain.put_transaction(txid + "_" + str(vout_index), keyvalue) == True

    key = "junk_" + str(vout_index)
    ret = chain.get_transaction(key)
    assert ret == False

def test_transaction_update():
    """

    updates the HeliumDB to reflect a transaction
    """
    # make a synthetic previous transaction
    num_prev_tx_outputs = secrets.randbelow(5) + 1
    previous_tx = make_synthetic_previous_transaction(num_prev_tx_outputs)

    #reflect this previous transaction in HeliumDB
    ctr = 0
    for vout in previous_tx["vout"]:
        #pdb.set_trace()
        fragment = {}
        fragment["pkhash"] = vout["ScriptPubKey"][2]
        fragment["spent"] = False
        fragment["value"] = max(secrets.randbelow(1000000), 10)
        fragment["tx_chain"] = ""

        txid = previous_tx["transactionid"] + "_" + str(ctr)
        chain.put_transaction( txid, fragment)
        ctr += 1

    # make a transaction consuming some previous transaction outputs
    trx = make_synthetic_transaction(previous_tx)

    #update the Helium Chainstate
```

```
    assert chain.transaction_update(trx) == True

def test_double_spend():
    """

     tests transaction update when a previous transaction fragment
     has been spent
    """

    # make a synthetic previous transaction
    num_prev_tx_outputs = secrets.randbelow(5) + 1
    previous_tx = make_synthetic_previous_transaction(num_prev_tx_outputs)

    #reflect this previous transaction in HeliumDB
    ctr = 0
    for vout in previous_tx["vout"]:
        #pdb.set_trace()
        fragment = {}
        fragment["pkhash"] = vout["ScriptPubKey"][2]
        fragment["spent"] = True
        fragment["value"] = max(secrets.randbelow(1000000), 10)
        fragment["tx_chain"] = ""

        txid = previous_tx["transactionid"] + "_" + str(ctr)
        chain.put_transaction( txid, fragment)
        ctr += 1

    # make a transaction consuming some previous transaction outputs
    trx = make_synthetic_transaction(previous_tx)

    #update the Helium Chainstate
    assert chain.transaction_update(trx) == 0

def test_previous_tx_non_existent():
    """

     tests transaction update when a previous transaction does
     not exist
    """

    # make a synthetic previous transaction
    num_prev_tx_outputs = secrets.randbelow(5) + 1
```

```
    previous_tx = make_synthetic_previous_transaction(num_prev_tx_outputs)

    #reflect this previous transaction in HeliumDB
    ctr = 0
    for vout in previous_tx["vout"]:
        #pdb.set_trace()
        fragment = {}
        fragment["pkhash"] = vout["ScriptPubKey"][2]
        fragment["spent"] = False
        fragment["value"] = max(secrets.randbelow(1000000), 10)
        fragment["tx_chain"] =   ""

        txid = previous_tx["transactionid"] + "_" + str(ctr)
        chain.put_transaction( txid, fragment)
        ctr += 1

    # make a transaction consuming some previous transaction outputs
    trx = make_synthetic_transaction(previous_tx)
    trx["vin"][0]["txid"] = "bad previous tx id"
    #update the Helium Chainstate
    assert chain.transaction_update(trx) == False
```

Updating the tx Module

Now that we have a functional Chainstate module, we can update the *tx* module to get previous transaction fragments. Make sure to import the *hchaindb* and *json* modules into *tx*. In the *tx* module, remove the *prevtx_value* function and insert the following function in lieu thereof:

```
def prevtx_value(txkey: "string") -> 'bool':
    """

    examines the chainstate database and returns the transaction fragment
    corresponding to txkey:
        {
            "pkkhash":  <string>,
            "value":    <int>,
            "spent":    <bool>,
```

```
        "tx_chain": <string>
    }
```

receives a transaction fragment key:
```
        "previous txid" + "_" + str(prevtx_vout_index)
```

Returns False if the transaction if does not exist, or if the value has been spent or if value is not a positive integer otherwise returns the previous transaction fragment data
```
    """
    try:
        fragment = hchaindb.get_transaction(txkey)
        if fragment == False:
            raise(ValueError("cannot get fragment from chainstate"))

        # return False if the value has been spent or if the value is
        # not positive

        if fragment["spent"] == True:
            raise(ValueError("cannot respend fragment in chainstate: " +
            txkey))

        if fragment["value"] <= 0:
            raise(ValueError("fragment value <= 0"))

    except Exception as err:
        logging.debug('prevtx_value: exception: ' + str(err))
        return False

    return fragment
```

prevtx_value returns False if it is unable to get a transaction fragment from the Chainstate. Chainstate will return False if the transaction key is fictitious. *prevtx_value* also returns False if the value item in the returned dictionary is not a positive integer or if the value has been spent.

The blk_index Database

The *blk_index* database permits us to determine the block that contains a particular transaction. This is a LevelDB database.

The *blk_index* database has five interface functions:

```
open_blk_index(directory_path: "string")
close_blk_index()
get_blockno(key: "string") => "bool or integer"
put_index(key: "string", value: "integer") => "bool"
delete_index(key: "string") => "bool"
```

The *open_blk_index* function opens the Helium LevelDB blk_index database and creates it if it does not exist. This function receives a full or partial file path parameter, inclusive of the database name. *close_blk_index* closes the database.

The *get_blockno* function has a transaction key argument. This function returns the block number (or block height) that contains this transaction or False if the transaction key does not exist in *blk_index*. Note that this is a transaction id, not a pointer to a transaction fragment.

The *put_index* function adds a key-value pair to *blk_index*. This function receives a transaction id key and a block number (or block height) as arguments. It returns True if the key-value pair is added to *blk_index* and False otherwise. Note that the genesis block has height zero.

delete_index receives a transaction key and deletes the transaction key, block number pair from *blk-index*, if the pair exists. This function returns False if the key does not exist or if there is some other error. Otherwise, the function returns True.

The blk_index Code Walkthrough

We will create an empty Helium *blk_index* database. This database will be located in the *data* sub-directory of the root of the Helium application. Traverse to the root of your virtual environment, enter the Python shell, and do

```
# create the Helium blk_index key-value store
>>> db = plyvel.DB('data/blk_index')
```

If you traverse to the *data* directory, you will see a *blk_index* sub-directory has been created. This sub-directory contains the Helium *blk_index* database.

Copy the following program code into the file *blk_index.py* and copy this file into the chainstate directory:

```
"""

Implementation of the Helium block index key-value store
lets us search for the block that contains a transaction
"""

import plyvel
import pdb
import logging
import json
import rcrypt

"""

log debugging messages to the file debug.log
"""

logging.basicConfig(filename="debug.log",filemode="w", format='%(asctime)
s:%(levelname)s:%(message)s',
    level=logging.DEBUG)

# handle to the Helium blk_index key-value store
bDB = None

def open_blk_index(filepath: "string") -> "db handle or False":
    """

    opens the Helium blk_index store and returns a handle to
    the database. Any directories in filepath must exist. The
    database will be created if it does not exist.
    Returns a handle to the database or False
    """

    try:
        global bDB
        bDB = plyvel.DB(filepath, create_if_missing=True)
        print("blk_index opened")
    except Exception as err:
```

```
        print("open_blk_index: exception: " + str(err))
        logging.debug("open_blk_index: exception: " + str(err))
        return False

    return bDB

def close_blk_index() -> "bool":
    """

    close the Helium block index store
    Returns True if the database is closed, False otherwise
    """

    try:
        bDB.close()
        if bDB.closed != True: return False

    except Exception as err:
        logging.debug("close_blk_index: exception: " + str(err))
        return False

    return True

def get_blockno(txid: "string") -> "False or integer":
    """

    Receives a transaction id (not a transaction fragment id)
    returns the block no. of the block that contains the transaction:
    """

    try:
        # get the block no, return False if the
        # transaction does not exist in the store
        block_no = bDB.get(str.encode(txid))
        if block_no == None:
            raise(ValueError("txid does not have a block no."))

        block_no = block_no.decode()
        block_no = int(block_no)

    except Exception as err:
        logging.debug('get_blockno: exception: ' + str(err))
```

```
        return False

    return block_no


def put_index(txid: "string", blockno: "integer") -> "bool":
    """
    Returns True if the trainsactionid_block_no key-value pair is created
    and False otherwise
    """
    try:
        if len(txid.strip()) != 64:
            raise(ValueError("txid invalid length"))

        if len(str(blockno).strip()) == 0:
            raise(ValueError("blockno field is empty"))

        if blockno < 0:
            raise(ValueError("negative blockno"))

        # save the transactionid-block no pair in the store
        bDB.put(str.encode(txid), str.encode(str(blockno)))

    except Exception as err:
        logging.debug('put_blockno: exception: ' + str(err))
        return False

    return True

def delete_index(txid: "string"):
    """
    deletes a (txid, blockno) pair from the blk_index store
    """
    try:
        bDB.delete(str.encode(txid))

    except Exception as err:
        logging.debug('delete_tx_blockno: exception: ' + str(err))
        return False

    return True
```

Pytests for the blk_index Database

Copy the following unit test code into the file *test_blk_index.py* and save this file in the *unit_tests* directory. Traverse to the *unit_tests* directory and run the tests in the virtual Helium environment:

```
$(virtual): pytest test_blk_index.py -s
```

You should observe nine tests passing:

```python
"""
pytest unit tests for the blk_index module
"""
import blk_index as blkindex
import rcrypt
import pytest
import json
import random
import secrets
import pdb
import os

def setup_module():
    assert bool(blkindex.open_blk_index("hblk_index")) == True
    if os.path.isfile("hblk_index"):
        os.remove("hblk_index")

def teardown_module():
    assert blkindex.close_blk_index() == True

@pytest.mark.parametrize("txid, value, ret", [
    ("",   9, False),
    ("abc", "", False),
    ('290cfd3f3e5027420ed483871309d2a0780b6c3092bef3f26347166b586ff89f',
    10899, True),
    (rcrypt.make_uuid(), 9, True),
    (rcrypt.make_uuid(), -1, False),
    (rcrypt.make_uuid(), -56019, False),
```

```
        (rcrypt.make_uuid(), 90890231, True),
])
def test_put_index(txid, value, ret):
    """

        tests putting valid and invalid transaction_index and blockno pairs
        into the blk_index store
    """

    assert blkindex.put_index(txid, value) == ret

def test_get_existing_tx():
    """

    test getting a block for an existing transaction
    """

    txid = rcrypt.make_uuid()
    blkindex.put_index(txid, 555)
    assert blkindex.get_blockno(txid) == 555

def get_faketx():
    """

    test getting a block for a fake transaction
    """

    assert blkindex.get_blockno("dummy tx") == False

def test_delete_tx():
    txid = rcrypt.make_uuid()
    blkindex.put_index(txid, 555)
    assert blkindex.delete_index(txid) == True
    assert blkindex.get_blockno(txid) == False
```

Updating the Blockchain Module

Now that we have functional code for the Chainstate and the *blk_index* databases, we can use these databases to index the blockchain. The *blk_index* algorithm is particularly simple. Every time a block is added to the blockchain, do

```
for transaction in block:
    add blk_index[transaction id] = block["height"]
```

Delete the *add_block* function in the *hblockchain* module, and add the following function code in its stead:

```python
def add_block(block: "dictionary") -> "bool":
    """

    add_block: adds a block to the blockchain. Receives a block.
    The block attributes are checked for validity and each transaction in
    the block is
    tested for validity. If there are no errors, the block is written to a
    file as a
    sequence of raw bytes. Then the block is added to the blockchain.
    The chainstate database and the blk_index databases are updated.
    returns True if the block is added to the blockchain and False otherwise
    """

    try:
        # validate the received block parameters
        if validate_block(block) == False:
            raise(ValueError("block validation error"))

        # validate the transactions in the block
        # update the chainstate database

        for trx in block['tx']:
            # first transaction in the block is a coinbase transaction
            if block["height"] == 0 or block['tx'][0] == trx:
            zero_inputs = True
            else: zero_inputs = False

            if tx.validate_transaction(trx, zero_inputs) == False:
                raise(ValueError("transaction validation error"))

            if hchaindb.transaction_update(trx) == False:
                raise(ValueError("chainstate update transaction error"))

        # serialize the block to a file
        if (serialize_block(block) == False):
                raise(ValueError("serialize block error"))
```

```
    # add the block to the blockchain in memory
    blockchain.append(block)

    #  update the blk_index
    for transaction in block['tx']:
        blockindex.put_index(transaction["transactionid"], block["height"])

except Exception as err:
    print(str(err))
    logging.debug('add_block: exception: ' + str(err))
    return False

return True
```

Make sure to import the *blk_index* module:

```
import blk_index as blockindex
```

Conclusion

In this chapter, we have looked at the *raison d'etre* for the Helium Chainstate database, and we have written code to interface with it. We can query this database and obtain answers to pertinent questions such as (i) has a transaction value been spent? and (ii) what is the RIPEMD-160 hash of the public key that can unlock this transaction? As we have seen, the Chainstate database is also important for the construction of client wallets. We have also constructed a *blk_index* key-value store that associates block heights with transaction IDs. This permits us to discover the block in which a particular transaction is contained.

We have written unit tests for the *chainstate* and *blk_index* databases. Furthermore, we have added code to the *hblockchain* module to keep the *blk_index* and chainstate databases updated as new blocks are added to the blockchain. Finally, we have updated code in the *tx* module to fetch and validate previous transaction values.

In the next chapter, we will come to a central pillar of cryptocurrency applications. This is the mining of cryptocurrency blocks and the creation of new currency units in a distributed manner which is outside the control of any particular entity, *mala fides* or otherwise.

CHAPTER 13

Mining Cryptocurrency

We now come to mining a cryptocurrency, which is one of the central pillars of any cryptocurrency implementation. Mining performs three essential tasks:

1. It validates transactions occurring on the cryptocurrency network

2. It adds blocks to the blockchain

3. It creates new currency units

All of these activities occur in a distributed manner outside the control of any particular node on the cryptocurrency network. Blocks are added to the blockchain through distributed consensus.

In this chapter, we will examine how mining is carried out in a Bitcoin-like currency and how the distributed consensus algorithm adds blocks to the blockchain.

A caveat is in order. In this chapter, you will sometimes see the phrase "the blockchain" used. There is in actuality no single authoritative blockchain held by some supernode. There are blockchains held by various nodes, and some of these nodes may hold blockchains that differ from those held by other nodes. The blockchain is a distributed structure. We refer to the blockchains held by various network nodes as local blockchains. The blockchain is an aggregated abstraction of all local blockchains. The distributed consensus algorithm ensures that all divergent blockchains will converge to a single authoritative blockchain.

The Mining Process

Why would an entity engage in mining? After all, mining is an expensive process that consumes a lot of CPU cycles and hence electricity. This incentive comes from the transaction fees and the mining reward that a miner receives for successfully mining

© Karan Singh Garewal 2020
K. S. Garewal, *Practical Blockchains and Cryptocurrencies*, https://doi.org/10.1007/978-1-4842-5893-4_13

a block. This remuneration is substantial. Any entity that has a local blockchain can engage in mining a cryptocurrency. Let us see how mining works.

Consider an individual who initiates a transaction that will transfer some units of a cryptocurrency. After the transaction has been consummated, the transferor of the cryptocurrency broadcasts the transaction on the cryptocurrency peer-to-peer network.[1] Miners (mining nodes), who have a local blockchain, are listening for transactions that are propagating across this network.

The task before a miner is to construct a prospective new block that can be added to the blockchain. The miner adds transactions to a candidate block and then mines this block.

Consider a miner who receives a transaction. The miner verifies that the transaction is valid. If it is invalid, the miner discards the transaction. Otherwise, the miner broadcasts this incoming transaction to other mining nodes that this miner has discovered.

The miner then examines the locktime of the received transaction. If the transaction is to be processed at some future time, the miner places it into a local cache of transactions that are to be processed in the future. This cache is called a memcache. If the miner decides to include this particular transaction in the candidate block that he intends to mine, he adds it to the block. Otherwise, the miner adds the transaction to the memcache.

The miner accesses the memcache as well as incoming transactions to add transactions to his candidate block. Subject to the constraint on the maximum size of a block, it is completely within the discretion of a miner as to which transactions and how many transactions it is going to include in a candidate block. Each transaction may have a transaction fee attached to it. It is within the sole discretion of the transferor of value to specify the transaction fee, if any. The miner obviously wants to maximize the transaction fees that he will receive if he successfully mines the candidate block.

Once the miner has decided that there are enough transactions in the candidate block, it adds a special transaction to the block. This transaction is called a coinbase transaction. It is the first transaction in the candidate block's list of transactions. The coinbase transaction contains the quantum of new cryptocurrency that will be created if the miner succeeds in mining the block. This value is called the mining reward. The miner is entitled to the mining reward. Thus, the mining reward and the total transaction

---

[1]We will discuss the topology of cryptocurrency networks in a subsequent chapter.

fees for the transactions included in the block are what the miner will receive if it successfully mines the block.

In Bitcoin and Helium, the amount of the mining reward is determined by an algorithm that depends on the number of blocks that have already been mined. Periodically the mining reward is halved as the size of the blockchain increases. The mining reward approaches zero asymptotically. Note that since a mining reward is new currency, it has no corresponding vin element.

The Bitcoin mining algorithm implies that a maximum of 21 million bitcoins can be produced. This suggests that Bitcoin is asymptotically deflationary; its value (purchasing power) must rise over time. Other cryptocurrencies can implement different currency creation algorithms. For example, the mining reward can be constant or vary in accordance with the volume of transactions per fixed unit of time. The TRON cryptocurrency has the dubious distinction of permitting the creation of an unlimited number of currency units by ostensibly distributed committee consensus. Helium follows the Bitcoin algorithm.

After adding the coinbase transaction to the candidate block, the miner builds the block header of this block. Recall that a Helium block has the following dictionary structure. The sub-dictionary with the exclusion of the *tx* list is called a block header:

```
{
        "prevblockhash":    <string>
        "version":          <string>
        "timestamp":        <integer>
        "difficulty_bits":  <integer>
        "nonce":            <integer>
        "merkle_root":      <string>
        "height":           <integer>
        "tx":               <list>
}
```

The miner calculates the SHA-256 hash of the header of the most recent block in its blockchain and pairs this value with the *prevblockhash* key of the candidate block. It next computes the merkle root of the transactions in the block and also inserts this value into the block header. Similarly, the miner puts the current Unix time, difficulty bits, initial nonce value, and version number into the block header. Recall that the genesis block has height 0, the succeeding block has height 1, and so forth.

After the miner has specified the block header, it is ready to mine the candidate block.

Mining a Block

Now that the miner has a candidate block ready for mining, it can start the actual process. The header block of a candidate block has a number called a nonce; this is a non-negative integer initialized to zero. The nonce starts the mining process and is incremented as the process proceeds.

The miner computes the SHA-256 hexadecimal digest of the block header, which includes the nonce. This hexadecimal string is converted into a (very large) number and compared with the current difficulty number specified for the network. If the computed value is less than the difficulty number, the block is said to be mined.[2] If the SHA-256 hash is greater than or equal to the difficulty number, then the nonce is incremented and the SHA-256 hash is recomputed and again compared to the difficulty number. This process continues until a hashed value less than the difficulty number is obtained.

In Bitcoin, the nonce is a 32-bit integer, and it frequently happens that the computed value will fail to fall below the difficulty number as the computation runs through the entire range of $2**32 - 1$ nonces. If this occurs, the nonce is again initialized at 0 and is placed in the transaction id field of the first vin list element of the coinbase transaction. This is not a concern for our Python implementation since Python can perform arithmetic on arbitrarily large numbers.

Figure 13-1 shows the flowchart for mining a block.

---

[2]For Helium, this difficulty number is obtained from the Helium configuration module.

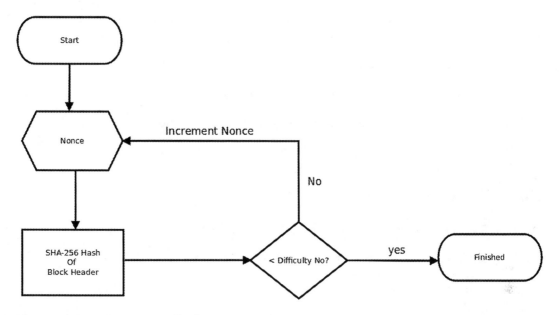

Figure 13-1. *Mining a Block*

While the miner is mining its candidate block, other miners are also mining blocks. The blocks that the other miners are mining need not contain the same transactions as the candidate block of our miner. Indeed, some miners may have local blockchains that differ from the blockchains of other miners.

If a miner succeeds in mining a candidate block, it will add the new block to its local blockchain and then broadcast the mined block on the cryptocurrency network. This is an invitation for other nodes to include this block in their local blockchains.

Nodes that receive the newly mined block will run a number of tests to validate the block. These tests are

1. The correct difficulty number has been used.

2. The block has a computed hash that is less than the difficulty number for the nonce in the block header.

3. The block height of the new block is valid.

4. The merkle root of the block transactions matches the merkle root in the block header.

5. No transaction in the block is locked.

6. The transactions in the block are valid.

7. If a transaction transfers a coinbase value, then a required minimum number of blocks have been added to the blockchain since the block which contained this coinbase transaction.

8. There is a *prevblockhash* match as discussed in the following.

If the mined node passes this suite of validation tests, the node can add this block to its blockchain.

Block Height Validation

The node receiving the new block checks the value of the height key in the block:

1. If the height is negative or zero, the block is rejected.

2. If the height value is less than the height of the node's blockchain, the block is rejected.

3. If the block height is equal to the node's blockchain height plus 2, the block is placed in an orphan list.

4. If the block height is greater than the node's blockchain height plus 2, the block is placed in an orphan list. The node's blockchain may be outdated. The node requisitions other nodes for the latest block(s), so that it can bring its blockchain up to date, if so required.

Previous Block Validation

A node that has received and validated a new block can now add the new block. The following algorithm enumerates the steps in adding the block to a blockchain.

Definitions

Let *previousblockhash* be the value of the *prevblockhash* key in the mined block.

Let block_name[latest] be the latest block on a blockchain that is named "block_name".

Let block_name[latest-1] be the second latest block on a blockchain that is named "block_name".

Let hash(block_name[x]) be the SHA-256 hash of the block header of the block named block_name, where x is *latest* or *latest-1*.

If the node has one blockchain, then name it *primary_blockchain*.

If the node has two blockchains, name one the *primary blockchain* and the other one the *secondary_blockchain*.

Algorithm

1. If the node has one blockchain and

    `previousblockhash == hash(primary_blockchain[latest])`

    then append the mined block to the primary blockchain.

2. Else if the node has one blockchain and

    `previousblockhash == hash(primary_blockchain[latest -1]`

    then

    (a) Make a new blockchain called secondary_blockchain by removing the latest element of primary_blockchain

    (b) Append the mined block to secondary_blockchain

3. If the node has two blockchains, then

    ```
    if previousblockhash == primary_blockchain[latest]
        then add the mined block to primary blockchain
    else if previousblockhash == secondary_blockchain[latest]
        then add the mined block to the secondary blockchain
    ```

4. If none of the aforementioned is possible, then the node places the block and is added to an orphan blocks list.

Note that in the second case the node has two blockchains which are competing to become the dominant blockchain.

If a node that receives a newly mined block is a miner, it will check to see if any transactions in the mined block are also in the block that it has been mining. If this is the case, the miner will discard the block that it has been mining and return the transactions in this block to the mempool. If this is not the case, it can keep on mining its candidate block. The miner next updates its memcache by removing any transactions in the mempool that are also in the mined block that has been received.

Finally, the node broadcasts the new block that it has received on the cryptocurrency network so that other nodes can verify the block and add it to their local blockchains.

Proof of Work

Mining a block is a computationally intensive task. When a block is mined, the inclusion of the nonce and the difficulty number in the block enables other miners to verify that the miner has in fact mined the block. This verification is called proof of work. A block which fails this proof of work will not be used by other miners to extend their local blockchains.

The Difficulty Number

The difficulty number is not some fixed number. It dynamically changes over time. For example, in Bitcoin the constraint is that a block should be mined approximately every ten minutes. The purpose of the difficulty number is to ensure that on average a block is mined in this time period. In the Bitcoin ecosystem, the difficulty number is adjusted every two weeks to ensure that blocks are mined approximately every ten minutes. Helium follows this model.

In Helium, after a fixed number of blocks have been mined, the mining nodes check to determine the frequency with which blocks are being mined. If the rate is too high, the difficulty number is adjusted downward, and if the blocks are being produced too slowly, the difficulty number is increased. Each node adjusts its difficulty number. When a mining node receives a mined block, it checks to determine that the correct difficulty number has been used.

In Helium, a new block should be mined, on average, every ten minutes. The Helium difficulty number is calibrated by the following algorithm[3] every 1000 blocks:

```
time_initial    = timestamp of the block that is 1000 blocks earlier
time_now        = timestamp of latest block
elapsed_seconds = time_now - time_old

blocks_expected_to_be_mined = elapsed_seconds / 600
actual blocks mined = 1000

discrepancy = 1000 - blocks_expected_to_be_mined
```

---

[3]The Helium config module fixes the number of blocks that must be mined before the difficulty number is recalibrated.

```
new difficulty no = old_difficulty_number - old_difficulty_number * \
        (20/100)*(discrepancy/(1000 + blocks_expected_to_be_mined))
```

The fraction 20/1000 constrains the new difficulty number to vary by no more than 20% from its previous value.

Hash Power Computations

Mining a block involves computing the SHA-256 hash of the current value of the block header. Given the hardware which a miner has available to him, this miner can perform a fixed number of hashes per second. The total hash power of the cryptocurrency network is the total number of hashes which all of the miners in the network can perform in a second given their hardware configurations. Consequently, the probability of a miner mining a block is

```
probBlock = (miner's hash power) / (total hash power of the network)
```

The average amount of time that it will take for a miner to mine a block (*minerAvgTime*) is calculated as follows:

```
let blockTime = average amount of time to mine a block in the network
```

```
then:
minerAvgTime = blockTime / probBlock
```

For the Bitcoin network, the average time to mine a block is 600 seconds, so:

```
minerAvgTime = 600/probBlock
```

The Distributed Consensus Algorithm

We are now ready to discuss how nodes on a cryptocurrency network arrive at a consensus as to the dominant blockchain on the network.

Each full node in a cryptocurrency network maintains its own blockchain.[4] Furthermore, such a node does not know what the blockchains of other full nodes look like. Conceivably, these local blockchains can differ from each other. The distributed

---

[4]A full node maintains a blockchain; it need not be a mining node.

consensus algorithm decides how blocks will be added to these local blockchains when different nodes in the cryptocurrency network have blockchains which differ from each other. This algorithm implements a distributed consensus that converges the nodes to the same blockchain without requiring any node to trust any other node. This distributed consensus algorithm constitutes the single most important innovation in the implementation of Bitcoin by Satoshi Nakamoto.

To be precise, the distributed consensus algorithm that we are discussing is called the proof-of-work distributed consensus algorithm to distinguish it from the proof-of-stake distributed consensus algorithm.

Before we begin our examination of this distributed consensus algorithm, note that there is no clock or timekeeper in the system and there is also no concept of the ordering of transactions on the basis of time or otherwise. A node processes blocks as they are received, and these blocks need not arrive in the order that they were produced. A node may not receive a block for any number of reasons including a temporary partition in the network.

Mining is a costly endeavor and requires the expenditure of CPU cycles (electricity) to solve a difficult mathematical problem. A miner is only willing to undertake the cost of mining if it can be compensated by an adequate mining reward and transaction fees. It is this incentive for profit which impels miners to converge to the same view of the blockchain. As we shall see, this incentive compels nodes to be honest and follow the blockchain consensus algorithm.

Consider a cryptocurrency network where all of the nodes initially have the same view of the blockchain.

In Figure 13-2, each circle represents a node in the cryptocurrency network. The rectangle in each node represents the head of the local blockchain of the node. Since all of these shapes are the same, we interpret this to mean that each of the nodes has the same blockchain.

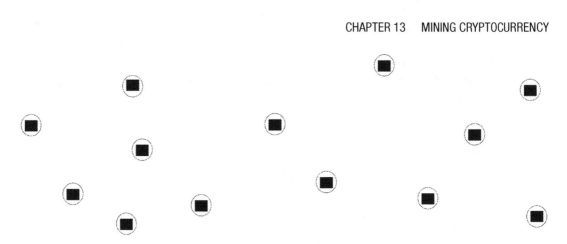

Figure 13-2. *Nodes in a Cryptocurrency Network*

Now, node X successfully mines a block and adds it to the head of its local blockchain. X then broadcasts the block, and its immediate neighbors append the new block to the head of their respective local blockchains. The nodes that have appended the new block to their blockchains are indicated by a circle with a star inside. Some of the nodes in the network have not received the new block or for some reason have not appended it to their local blockchains. The shape of these nodes remains unchanged (Figure 13-3).

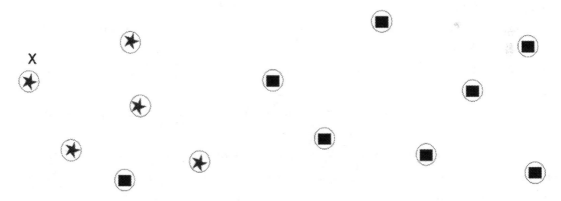

Figure 13-3. *Node X Mines a Block*

At this point in time, there are two views of the blockchain since some nodes have not yet appended the new block to their blockchains. These nodes are effectively one block behind.

Now a very short time after X mined its block, node Y mines a block, and after adding it to its blockchain, it broadcasts the new block on the network. A number of nodes receive this block and append the block to their blockchains (Figure 13-4). The nodes that have appended Y's mined block to their blockchains are depicted as the nodes with an angled rectangle inside a circle.

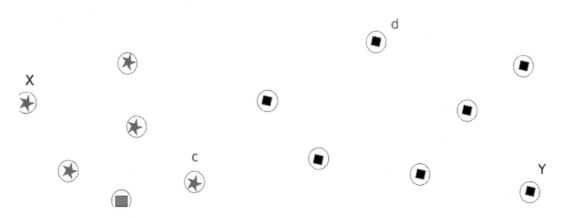

Figure 13-4. Node Y Mines a Block

Now the block mined by Y reaches node C. Node C notices that it cannot add this block to the head of its version of the blockchain since the previous block hash value does not match. Node C also observes that this block could be added if the block before the block at the head of the blockchain was in fact at the head of the blockchain. So node C creates a secondary blockchain by removing the node at the head of the blockchain and adding the new block to this secondary blockchain. At this stage, node C has a primary blockchain and a secondary blockchain, and the heads of these blockchains are different.

All of the nodes with a star follow the same logic and create primary and secondary blockchains as node Y's block reaches them.

Similarly, as the block mined by X reaches the nodes with the angled rectangles, these nodes accept the incoming block but have to create primary and secondary blockchains.

Now both of the blocks mined by X and Y reach the node with a rectangle, and it too creates a primary and secondary blockchain.

Next, node d successfully mines a block and broadcasts it on the network. This time, no other mining node on the network is able to mine a node quickly enough, so the block mined by node d reaches all of the nodes on the network (Figure 13-5). Some of these nodes can add the block to their primary blockchains (these are the nodes that received the block mined by Y first). These nodes add the block to their primary blockchain. The shorter blockchain is cleared, provided it is two blocks or more blocks shorter than the longer blockchain.

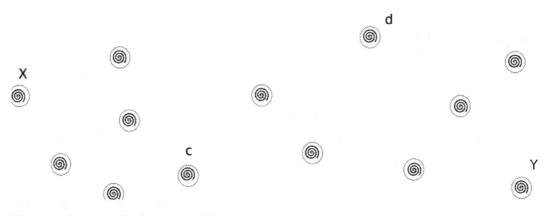

Figure 13-5. *Node d Mines a block*

Similarly, the nodes that received the block from node X first can add the new block to their secondary blockchains. These nodes add the block to their secondary blockchains and delete their primary blockchains and designate the secondary blockchain as the primary blockchain. Notice once again that the shorter blockchain is deleted.

At this stage, all of the nodes on the network have converged to the same view of the blockchain. The preceding process describes the distributed consensus algorithm which was implemented first by Satoshi Nakamoto for Bitcoin. The reason why all miners will follow the longest blockchain is because if they do not, the majority of miners will add blocks to the longest blockchain and the dissenting miners will discover that though they can mine blocks, they will not be able to persuade other miners to add these blocks to the shorter blockchain and thus they will be unable to collect mining rewards and transaction fees.

Because the longest blockchain has the most hashing power expended on it, nodes consider this blockchain to be the correct one and will work on extending it.

As we have just seen, when the two forked blockchains, the primary blockchain and the secondary blockchain, re-converge, one of these blockchains is deleted. So what happens to the transactions in the deleted blockchain? Let's assume that the primary blockchain is deleted because the secondary blockchain is one block ahead of it. Since the secondary blockchain was created from the primary blockchain with the exclusion of the latest block on the primary blockchain, we only have to consider the transactions in this particular block. We simply put those transactions in this block which are also not in the the latest block of the secondary blockchain, back into the mempool.

Malicious Nodes

We can note three aspects of malicious nodes. A malicious node cannot create a transaction that steals someone's cryptocurrency because it needs the private key of this individual in order to digitally sign the malicious transaction.

Secondly, a malicious mining node may decide not to process a transaction. But this is a useless action since other mining nodes that receive the transaction will include it in their candidate blocks.

Lastly, a number of malicious nodes acting in concert cannot impose their common blockchain as the dominant blockchain on the network unless they control at least 51% of the total hashing power. The reason for this is that if these nodes have at least 51% of the total hashing power, then the probability that the next block will be produced by them and added to their version of the blockchain is at least 51%. Thus, since they control the majority of the hashing power, they will be able to extend their version of the blockchain and impose it as the primary blockchain on the network.

Transaction Confirmations

When a block is mined and added to the blockchain, we say that the transactions in the block have one confirmation. When another block is added, the transactions in the previous block are said to have two confirmations. As the number of blocks added to the blockchain keeps on increasing, so do the confirmations. In Bitcoin, transactions that receive six confirmations are considered to be irreversible because of the prohibitively expensive hashing power that would be required for the network to undo a transaction in a block that is six blocks deep. A malicious node would have to control the majority of the hashing power of the network to undo these blocks and build an alternate longest blockchain.

The Double-Spend Problem

Consider the following scenario. Alice has one helium coin and she transmits it to Smith. Alice propagates the transaction on the network and a miner starts mining a block that contains this transaction. Now Alice goes somewhere else and spends the same helium again. Since no miner has yet mined a block containing Alice's first transaction, the second transaction also propagates on the network, and some miners add it to their candidate blocks and start mining these blocks. This is the double-spend problem. Alice has apparently spent her helium twice.

The first miner successfully mines its block and broadcasts the block on the network. This block contains Alice's first transaction. A very short time after, a second miner also successfully mines a block and propagates it on the network. This block contains Alice's second transaction.

Consider a node that receives one of these blocks. This node will extend its blockchain with the received block and update its Chainstate database. If a short time later it receives the second block, it will reject this block because a query on the Chainstate database will show that Alice does not have the required value for the transaction. Due to the examination of the Chainstate, a node will only have one of the two blocks containing a transaction by Alice. This is true even if a node has bifurcated to a primary and secondary blockchain.

This example shows why transaction confirmations are important. For small value transactions, two confirmations are sufficient (20 minutes on the bitcoin network on average). For large value transactions, at least six confirmations should be obtained (about one hour on the bitcoin network).

Conclusion

In this chapter, we have examined how the cryptocurrency mining process works. Mining performs a very important function in distributed cryptocurrencies that are modeled similarly to Bitcoin. Mining nodes verify transactions and add blocks to local blockchains. These nodes also reach a distributed consensus on the primary or dominant blockchain without any reliance on trust, a centralized clock, or a supernode coordinator. We have studied the manner in which blockchains in the network converge to one view of the blockchain through the application of the distributed consensus algorithm. Lastly, we have examined how distributed cryptocurrencies solve the "double-spend" problem.

In the next chapter, we will write program code for a Helium mining node.

References

https://github.com/bitcoin/bitcoin

Antonopoulos, Andreas. Mastering Bitcoin, 1st ed., 2015, O'Reilly Media, Inc.

CHAPTER 14

Helium Mining

In the previous chapter, we have examined the cryptocurrency mining process in detail. Mining is a critical aspect of distributed cryptocurrencies that are modeled after Bitcoin. As you will recall, mining produces three results:

1. Attaches new blocks to the blockchain

2. Achieves distributed consensus on the content of the blockchain and hence distributed consensus on the transactions in the network

3. Creates fresh units of cryptocurrency that are distributed to miners

In this chapter, we will implement the theoretical concepts pertaining to distributed consensus in the form of mining nodes that implement consensus by solving a difficult mathematical problem. Solving this problem is called proof of work, and it lets a mining node attach a block to the blockchain and hence collect a substantial mining reward as well as transaction fees. Mining is a computationally intensive task and hence consumes a substantial quantum of electricity. Nodes compete with each other to obtain the financial benefits of mining. The only way to maximize profit is to mine as many blocks as possible and attach them to the longest blockchain. Longer blockchains have more computational effort extended upon them. Miners will not attempt to attach newly mined blocks to a shorter secondary blockchain as this blockchain will eventually be deleted by other miners.

In this chapter, we will write the Python program code for a Helium mining node. As usual, we will buttress this code with *pytest* unit tests. So without further ado, let us commence this task.

© Karan Singh Garewal 2020
K. S. Garewal, *Practical Blockchains and Cryptocurrencies*, https://doi.org/10.1007/978-1-4842-5893-4_14

Distributed Consensus Algorithm in Detail

In Chapter 13, we described how blocks are processed in the Helium network and how the network arrives at a distributed consensus as to the blockchain. We are now going to provide the precise algorithm that a mining node uses to process transactions and blocks and achieve distributed consensus:

Handling Incoming Transactions

A transaction arrives at a miners interface. There are two cases:

Case A: If the transaction is valid, add it to the mempool. In particular, since the transaction is valid, it does not spend transaction fragments in the Chainstate database which have already been spent.

Adding Transactions to a Candidate Block

As transactions are added to a candidate block, we maintain a temporary list of prior transaction fragments that are going to be spent by these transactions. If a transaction selected for the candidate block tries to spend a fragment that is in this list, it is rejected for inclusion in the block and also deleted from the mempool.

Case B: The transaction is invalid. For example, the miner checks the Chainstate database and sees that this transaction references one or more previous transaction fragments that have already been spent. The transaction is rejected.

Handling Incoming Blocks

A block arrives at a mining node interface:

Get the block height of the incoming block. There are then five possible cases:

Case A: The block height is less than the height of the blockchain.   Reject the block; it is stale. A block at this height has already been mined.

Case B: The block height is greater than the height of the blockchain + 1.   Put the block in the *orphan_blocks* list. We will process this block later once our blockchain height increases.

Case C: The block height is equal to the height of the blockchain + 1.   We can add the block to the primary blockchain or the secondary blockchain (if it exists) depending upon the value of the *prevblockhash* attribute (see the following note).

(continued)

Handling Incoming Transactions

Case D:	The block height is equal to the current block height.	If the *prevblock* hash of the new block matches the block header hash of the parent of the block at the head of the primary blockchain, then fork the blockchain. Otherwise, reject the block (see the following note).
Case E:	A block arrives which is greater than the blockchain height + 1.	Trigger a call to update our blockchain if a number of such blocks have been received by the miner. The blockchain is possibly behind the blockchain of other miners.
Note:		Suppose that the head of our blockchain has a transaction that consumes a transaction fragment and the incoming block also has a transaction that consumes the same transaction fragment, then unless the miner that mined the incoming block is acting mala fides, the new block cannot have a *prevblockhash* value that points to the head of our primary blockchain.
		The new block must either sit on top of a secondary blockchain (if it exists) or have a *prevblockhash* that matches the block that is the parent of the head block at the head of our blockchain. In the latter case, we will have a fork of the primary blockchain. But in either case, two double-spending transactions cannot exist on one blockchain. One will exist on the primary blockchain, and the second will exist on the secondary blockchain. This solves the double-spend problem.
		Suppose further that we have a primary and secondary blockchain and a block arrives that has a *prevblockhash* value that matches the parent of the head on one of these blockchains. This block will be rejected, as it is in effect matching the block hash of the grandparent of the block at the head of the blockchain before it was forked (exercise: think this through with some diagrams).

Helium Mining Code Walkthrough

Create a file called *hmining.py* in the mining sub-directory and copy the following Python code into this file. Our walkthrough of the data structures and functions in the *hmining* module follows the program code.

```
"""
    hmining.py: The code in this module implements a Helium mining node.
    The node constructs candidate blocks with transactions in them and then
    mines these
    blocks
"""

import blk_index
import hconfig
import hblockchain as bchain
import hchaindb
import networknode
import rcrypt
import tx
import asyncio
import json
import math
import sys
import time
import threading
import pdb
import logging

"""
    log debugging messages to the file debug.log
"""
logging.basicConfig(filename="debug.log",filemode="w",  \
    format='%(asctime)s:%(levelname)s:%(message)s',
    level=logging.DEBUG)

"""
address list of nodes on the Helium network
"""

address_list = []

"""
    specify a list container to hold transactions which are received by the miner.
```

```
"""

mempool         = []
"""

   blocks mined by other miners which are received by this mining node
   and are to intended to be appended to this miner's blockchain.
"""

received_blocks = []
"""

   blocks which are received and cannot be added to the head of the
   blockchain
   or the parent of the block at the head of the blockchain.
"""

orphan_blocks = []
"""

list of transactions in a block that have been mined and are to be removed
from the
memcache
"""

remove_list = []

semaphore = threading.Semaphore()

def mining_reward(block_height:"integer") -> "non-negative integer":
    """

    The mining_reward function determines the mining reward.
    When a miner successfully mines a block he is entitled to a reward which
    is a number of Helium coins.
    The reward depends on the number of blocks that have been mined so far.
    The initial reward  is hconfig.conf["MINING_REWARD"] coins.
    This reward halves every hconfig.conf["REWARD_INTERVAL"] blocks.
    """

    try:
        # there is no reward for the genesis block
        sz = block_height
```

```
        sz = sz // hconfig.conf["REWARD_INTERVAL"]
        if sz == 0:   return hconfig.conf["MINING_REWARD"]

        # determine the mining reward
        reward = hconfig.conf["MINING_REWARD"]
        for __ctr in range(0,sz):
            reward = reward/2

        # truncate to an integer
        reward = int(round(reward))

        # the mining reward cannot be less than the lowest denominated
        # currency unit
        if reward < hconfig.conf["HELIUM_CENT"]: return 0

    except Exception as err:
        print(str(err))
        logging.debug('mining reward: exception: ' + str(err))
        return -1

    return reward

def receive_transaction(transaction: "dictionary") -> "bool":
    """

    receives a transaction propagating over the P2P cryptocurrency network
    this function executes in a thread
    """
    # do not add the transaction if:
    #     it already exists in the mempool
    #     it exists in the Chainstate
    #     it is invalid

    try:
        # if the transaction is in the mempool, return
        for trans in mempool:
            if trans == transaction: return False

        # do not add the transaction if it has been accounted for in
        # the chainstate database.
```

```
        tx_fragment_id = transaction["transactionid"] + "_" + "0"

        if hchaindb.get_transaction(tx_fragment_id) != False:
            return True

        # verify that the incoming transaction is valid
        if len(transaction["vin"]) >  0: zero_inputs = False
        else: zero_inputs = True
        if tx.validate_transaction(transaction, zero_inputs) == False:
            raise(ValueError("invalid transaction received"))

        # add the transaction to the mempool
        mempool.append(transaction)

        # place the transaction on the P2P network for further
        # propagation
        propagate_transaction(transaction)

    except Exception as err:
        logging.debug('receive_transaction: exception: ' + str(err))
        return False

    return True

def make_candidate_block() -> "dictionary || bool":
    """

    makes a candidate block for inclusion in the Helium blockchain.
    A candidate block is created by:
            (i)  fetching transactions from the  mempool and adding them to
                 the candidate blocks transaction list.
            (ii) specifying the block header.

    returns the candidate block or returns False if there is an error or if
    the mempool is empty.
    Executes in a Python thread
    """

    try:
        # if the mempool is empty then no transactions can be put into
        # the candidate block
```

233

```
if len(mempool) == 0: return False

# make a public-private key pair that the miner will use to receive
# the mining reward as well as the transaction fees.
key_pair = make_miner_keys()

block = {}

# create a incomplete candidate block header
block['version']    = hconfig.conf["VERSION_NO"]
block['timestamp'] = int(time.time())
block['difficulty_bits']    = hconfig.conf["DIFFICULTY_BITS"]
block['nonce']      = hconfig.conf["NONCE"]

if len(bchain.blockchain) > 0:
    block['height'] = bchain.blockchain[-1]["height"] + 1
else:
    block['height'] = 0

block['merkle_root'] = ""

# get the value of the hash of the previous block's header
# this induces tamperproofness for the blockchain
if len(bchain.blockchain) > 0:
    block['prevblockhash'] = bchain.blockheader_hash(bchain.
    blockchain[-1])
else:
    block['prevblockhash'] = ""

# calculate the  size (in bytes) of the candidate block header
# The number 64 is  the byte size of the SHA-256 hexadecimal
# merkle root. The merkle root is computed after all the
# transactions are included in the candidate block
# reserve 1000 bytes for the coinbase transaction
block_size =  sys.getsizeof(block['version'])
block_size += sys.getsizeof(block['timestamp'])
block_size += sys.getsizeof(block['difficulty_bits'])
block_size += sys.getsizeof(block['nonce'])
block_size += sys.getsizeof(block['height'])
```

```
block_size += sys.getsizeof(block['prevblockhash'])
block_size += 64
block_size += sys.getsizeof(block['timestamp'])
block_size += 1000

# list of transactions in the block
block['tx'] = []

# get the Unix Time now
now = int(time.time())

# add transactions from the mempool to the candidate block until
# the transactions in the mempool are exhausted or the block
# attains its maximum permissible size
for memtx in mempool:
        # do not process future transactions
        if memtx['locktime'] > now: continue

        memtx = add_transaction_fee(memtx, key_pair[1])

        # add the transaction to the candidate block
        block_size += sys.getsizeof(memtx)
        if block_size <= hconfig.conf['MAX_BLOCK_SIZE']:
            block['tx'].append(memtx)
            remove_list.append(memtx)
        else:
            break

# return if there are no transactions in the block
if len(block["tx"]) == 0: return False

# add a coinbase transaction
coinbase_tx = make_coinbase_transaction(block['height'], key_
pair[1])
block['tx'].insert(0, coinbase_tx)

# update the length of the block
block_size += sys.getsizeof(block['tx'])
```

```
        # calculate the merkle root of this block
        ret = bchain.merkle_root(block['tx'], True)

        if ret == False:
            logging.debug('mining::make_candidate_block - merkle root error')
            return False

        block['merkle_root'] = ret

        ####################################
        # validate the candidate block
        ####################################
        if bchain.validate_block(block) == False:
            logging.debug('mining::make_candidate_block - invalid block
            header')
            return False

        ##################################################
        # remove transactions from the mempool
        ##################################################
        remove_mempool_transactions(remove_list)

    except Exception as err:
        logging.debug('make_candidate_block: exception: ' + str(err))

    # At this stage the candidate block has been created and it can be mined
    return block

def make_miner_keys():
    """

    makes a public-private key pair that the miner will use to receive
    the mining reward and the transaction fee for each transaction.
    This function writes the  keys to a file and returns hash:
    RIPEMD160(SHA256(public key))
    """

    try:
        keys    = rcrypt.make_ecc_keys()
        privkey = keys[0]
```

```
        pubkey  = keys[1]

        pkhash  = rcrypt.make_SHA256_hash(pubkey)
        mdhash  = rcrypt.make_RIPEMD160_hash(pkhash)

        # write the keys to file with the private key as a hexadecimal string
        f = open('coinbase_keys.txt', 'a')
        f.write(privkey)
        f.write('\n')        # newline
        f.write(pubkey)
        f.write('\n')
        f.close()

    except Exception as err:
        logging.debug('make_miner_keys: exception: ' + str(err))

    return mdhash

def add_transaction_fee(trx: 'dictionary', pubkey: 'string') ->
'dictionary':
    """

    directs the transaction fee of a transaction to the miner.
    Receives a transaction and a miner's public key.
    Amends and returns the transaction so that it consumes the transaction
    fee.
    """

    try:
        # get the previous transaction fragments
        prev_fragments = []

        for vin in trx["vin"]:
            fragment_id = vin["txid"] + "_" + str(vin["vout_index"])
            prev_fragments.append(hchaindb.get_transaction(fragment_id))

        #  Calculate the transaction fee
        fee = tx.transaction_fee(trx, prev_fragments)

        if fee > 0:
            vout = {}
```

```
            vout["value"] = fee
            ScriptPubKey = []
            ScriptPubKey.append('SIG')
            ScriptPubKey.append(rcrypt.make_RIPEMD160_hash(rcrypt.make_
            SHA256_hash(pubkey)))
            ScriptPubKey.append('<DUP>')
            ScriptPubKey.append('<HASH_160>')
            ScriptPubKey.append('HASH-160')
            ScriptPubKey.append('<EQ-VERIFY>')
            ScriptPubKey.append('<CHECK_SIG>')
            vout["ScriptPubKey"] = ScriptPubKey

            trx["vout"].append(vout)


    except Exception as err:
        logging.debug('add_transaction_fee: exception: ' + str(err))
        return False

    return trx

def make_coinbase_transaction(block_height: "integer", pubkey: "string") ->
'dict':
    """

    makes a coinbase transaction, this is the miner's reward for mining
    a block. Receives a public key to denote ownership of the reward.
    Since this is a fresh issuance of heliums there are no vin elements.
    locks the transaction for hconfig["COINBASE_INTERVAL"] blocks.
    Returns the coinbase transaction.
    """

    try:
        # calculate the mining reward
        reward = mining_reward(block_height)

        # create a coinbase transaction
        trx = {}
        trx['transactionid'] = rcrypt.make_uuid()
        trx['version']  = hconfig.conf["VERSION_NO"]
```

```
    # the mining reward cannot be claimed until approximately 100
    blocks are mined
    # convert into a time interval
    trx['locktime'] = hconfig.conf["COINBASE_INTERVAL"]*600
    trx['vin']  = []
    trx['vout'] = []

    ScriptPubKey = []
    ScriptPubKey.append('SIG')
    ScriptPubKey.append(rcrypt.make_RIPEMD160_hash(rcrypt.make_SHA256_
    hash(pubkey)))
    ScriptPubKey.append('<DUP>')
    ScriptPubKey.append('<HASH_160>')
    ScriptPubKey.append('HASH-160')
    ScriptPubKey.append('<EQ-VERIFY>')
    ScriptPubKey.append('<CHECK_SIG>')

    # create the vout element with the reward
    trx['vout'].append({
                        'value':  reward,
                        'ScriptPubKey': ScriptPubKey
                 })

except Exception as err:
    logging.debug('make_coinbase_transaction: exception: ' + str(err))

return trx

def remove_mempool_transactions(block: 'dictionary') -> "bool":
    """

    removes the transactions in the candidate block from the mempool
    """
    try:
        for transaction in block["tx"]:
            if transaction in mempool:
                mempool.remove(transaction)

    except Exception as err:
```

```
        logging.debug('remove_mempool_transactions: exception: ' + str(err))
        return False

    return True

def mine_block(candidate_block: 'dictionary') -> "bool":
    """

    Mines a candidate block.
    Returns the solution nonce as a hexadecimal string if the block is
    mined and False otherwise

    Executes in a Python thread
    """

    try:
        final_nonce = None
        save_block = dict(candidate_block)

        # Loop until block is mined
        while True:
            # compute the SHA-256 hash for the block header of the
            # candidate block
            hash = bchain.blockheader_hash(candidate_block)
            # convert the SHA-256 hash string to a Python integer
            mined_value = int(hash, 16)
            mined_value = 1/mined_value

            # test to determine whether the block has been mined
            if mined_value < hconfig.conf["DIFFICULTY_NUMBER"]:
                final_nonce = candidate_block["nonce"]
                break

            # if a received block contains a transaction that is also in the
            # candidate block then terminate mining this block
            with semaphore:
                if len(received_blocks) > 0:
                    if compare_transaction_lists(candidate_block) == False:
                        return False
```

```
            # failed to mine the block so increment the
            # nonce and try again
            candidate_block['nonce'] += 1

        logging.debug('mining.py: block has been mined')

        # add block to the received_blocks list and process list
        received_blocks.append(save_block)
        ret = process_received_blocks()
        if ret == False:
            raise(ValueError("failed to add mined block to blockchain"))

    except Exception as err:
        logging.debug('mine_block: exception: ' + str(err))
        return False

    return hex(final_nonce)

def proof_of_work(block):
    """

    Proves whether a received block has in fact been mined.
    Returns True or False
    """

    try:
        if block['difficulty_bits'] != hconfig.conf["DIFFICULTY_BITS"]:
            raise(ValueError("wrong difficulty bits used"))

        # compute the SHA-256 hash for the block header of the candidate block
        hash = bchain.blockheader_hash(block)
        # convert the SHA-256 hash string to a Python integer to base 10
        mined_value = int(hash, 16)
        mined_value = 1/mined_value

        # test to determine whether the block has been mined
        if mined_value < hconfig.conf["DIFFICULTY_NUMBER"]: return True
```

```
    except Exception as err:
        logging.debug('proof_of_work: exception: ' + str(err))
        return False

    return False

def receive_block(block):
    """

    Maintains the received_blocks list.
    Receives a block and returns False if:

    (1)  the block is invalid
    (2)  the block height is less than (blockchain height - 2)
    (3)  block height > (blockchain height + 1)
    (4)  the proof of work fails
    (5)  the block does not contain at least two transactions
    (6)  the first block transaction is not a coinbase transaction
    (7)  transactions in the block are invalid
    (8)  block is already in the blockchain
    (9)  the block is already in the received_blocks list

    Otherwise (i)  adds the block to the received_blocks list
              (ii) propagates the block

    Executes in a python thread
    """

    try:
        # test if block is already in the received_blocks list
        with semaphore:
            for blk in received_blocks:
                if blk == block: return False

        # verify the proof of work
        if proof_of_work(block) == False:
            raise(ValueError("block proof of work failed"))

        # restore the Nonce to its initial value
        block["nonce"] = hconfig.conf["NONCE"]
```

```
    # validate the block and block transactions
    if bchain.validate_block(block) == False: return False
    for trx in block["tx"]:
        if block["height"] == 0 or block["tx"][0] == trx: flag = True
        else: flag = False
        if tx.validate_transaction(trx, flag) == False: return False

    if len(bchain.blockchain) > 0:
        # do not add stale blocks to the blockchain
        if block["height"] < bchain.blockchain[-1]["height"] - 2:
            raise(ValueError("block height too old"))

        # do not add blocks that are too distant into the future
        if block["height"] > bchain.blockchain[-1]["height"] + 1:
            raise(ValueError("block height beyond future"))

    # test if block is in the primary or secondary blockchains
    if len(bchain.blockchain) > 0:
        if block == bchain.blockchain[-1]: return False

    if len(bchain.blockchain) > 1:
      if block == bchain.blockchain[-2]: return False

    if len(bchain.secondary_blockchain) > 0:
        if block == bchain.secondary_blockchain[-1]: return False

    if len(bchain.secondary_blockchain) > 1:
        if block == bchain.secondary_blockchain[-2]: return False

    # add the block to the blocks_received list
    with semaphore:
        received_blocks.append(block)

    process_received_blocks()

except Exception as err:
    logging.debug('receive_block: exception: ' + str(err))
    return False

return True
```

```
def process_received_blocks() -> 'bool':
    """
```

processes mined blocks that are in the in the received_blocks
list and attempts to add these blocks to a blockchain.

Algorithm:
  (1) get a block from the received blocks list.

  (2) if the blockchain is empty and the block has an empty
  prevblockhash
        field then add the block to the blockchain.

  (3) Compute the block header hash of the last block on the
  blockchain.
        if blkhash == block["prevblockhash"] then add the block to the
        blockchain.

  (4) if the blockchain has at least two blocks, then if:
          let blk_hash be the hash second-latest block of the blockchain,
          then if:

          block["prevblockhash"] == blk_hash

          create a secondary block consisting of all of the blocks of
          the blockchain
          except for the latest. Append the block to the secondary
          blockchain.

  (5) Otherwise move the block to the orphans list.

  (6) If the received block was attached to a blockchain, for each block in
        the orphans list, try to attach the orphan block to the primary
        blockchain or
        the secondary blockchain if it exists.

  (7) If the received block was attached to a blockchain and the
        secondary blockchain
        has elements then swap the blockchain and the secondary blockchain
        if the

length of the secondary blockchain is greater.

(8)   if the receive block was attached and the secondary blockchain has
      elements
      then clear the secondary blockchain if its length is more than two
      blocks
      behind the primary blockchain.

Note: Runs In A Python thread
"""

```
while True:
    # process all of the blocks in the received blocks list
    add_flag = False

    # get a received block
    with semaphore:
        if len(received_blocks) > 0:
            block = received_blocks.pop()
        else:
            return True

        # try to add block to the primary blockchain
        if bchain.add_block(block) == True:
            logging.debug('receive_mined_block: block added to primary
            blockchain')
            add_flag = True

        # test whether the primary blockchain must be forked
        # if the previous block hash is equal to the hash of the parent
        block of
        # the block at the head of the blockchain add the block as a
        child of the
        # parent and create a secondary blockchain. This constitutes a
        fork of the
        # primary blockchain
        elif len(bchain.blockchain) >= 2 and  block['prevblockhash'] == \
            bchain.blockheader_hash(bchain.blockchain[-2]):
```

```
                logging.debug('receive_mined_block: forking the blockchain')
                ret = fork_blockchain(block)
                if ret == True: add_flag = True

        # try to add add block to the secondary blockchain
        elif len(bchain.secondary_blockchain) > 0 and
        block['prevblockhash'] == \
                bchain.blockheader_hash(bchain.secondary_blockchain[-1]):
                if append_secondary_blockchain(block) == True: add_flag = True

        # cannot attach the block to a blockchain add to the orphan list,
        else:
                if add_flag == False: orphan_blocks.append(block)

        if add_flag == True:
                if block["height"] % hconfig.conf["RETARGET_INTERVAL"] == 0:
                        retarget_difficulty_number(block)
                handle_orphans()
                swap_blockchains()
                propagate_mined_block(block)

        # remove any transactions in this block that are also
        # in the the mempool
        remove_mempool_transactions(block)

    return True

def fork_blockchain(block: 'list') -> 'bool':
    """

    forks the primary blockchain and creates a secondary blockchain from
    the primary blockchain and then adds the received block to the
    secondary block
    """

    try:
        bchain.secondary_blockchain = list(bchain.blockchain[0:-1])
        if append_secondary_blockchain(block) == False: return False

        # switch the primary and secondary blockchain if required
```

```
        swap_blockchains()

    except Exception as err:
        logging.debug('fork_blockchain: exception: ' + str(err))
        return False

    return True

def swap_blockchains() -> 'bool':
    """

    compares the length of the primary and secondary blockchains.
    The longest blockchain is designated as the primary blockchain and
    the other blockchain is designated as the secondary blockchain.
    if the primary blockchain is ahead of the secondary blockchain by at
    least two blocks then clear the secondary blockchain.
    """

    try:
        # if the secondary blockchain is longer than the primary
        # blockchain designate the secondary blockchain as the primary
        # blockchain and the primary blockchain as the secondary blockchain
        if len(bchain.secondary_blockchain) > len(bchain.blockchain):
            tmp = list(bchain.blockchain)
            bchain.blockchain = list(bchain.secondary_blockchain)
            bchain.secondary_blockchain = list(tmp)

        # if the primary blockchain is ahead of the secondary blockchain by
        # at least two blocks then clear the secondary blockchain
        if len(bchain.blockchain) - len(bchain.secondary_blockchain) > 2:
            bchain.secondary_blockchain.clear()

    except Exception as err:
        logging.debug('swap_blockchains: exception: ' + str(err))
        return False

    return True

def append_secondary_blockchain(block):
    """
```

```
        append a block to the the secondary blockchain
        """

        with semaphore:
            tmp = list(bchain.blockchain)
            bchain.blockchain = list(bchain.secondary_blockchain)
            bchain.secondary_blockchain = list(tmp)
            ret = bchain.add_block(block)
            if ret == True: swap_blockchains()

        return ret


def handle_orphans() -> "bool":
    """

    tries to attach an orphan block to the head of the primary or secondary
    blockchain.
    Sometimes blocks are received out of order and cannot be attached to
    the primary
    or secondary blockchains. These blocks are placed in an orphan_blocks
    list and as
    new blocks are added to the primary or secondary blockchains, an
    attempt is made to
    add orphaned  blocks to the blockchain(s).
    """
    try:
        # iterate through the orphan blocks attempting to append an orphan
        # block to a blockchain

        for block in orphan_blocks:
            if bchain.add_block(block) == True:
                orphan_blocks.remove(block)
                continue

            # try to append to the primary blockchain
            if len(bchain.blockchain) > 1 and len(bchain.secondary_
            blockchain) == 0:
                if block['prevblockhash'] == \
                    bchain.blockheader_hash(bchain.blockchain[-1]):
```

```
                if block["height"] == bchain.blockchain[-1]["height"] + 1:
                    if fork_blockchain(block) == True:
                        orphan_blocks.remove(block)
                        continue

            # try to append to the secondary blockchain
            if len(bchain.secondary_blockchain) > 0:
                if block['prevblockhash']  == \
                    bchain.blockheader_hash(bchain.secondary_
                    blockchain[-1]):
                    if block["height"] == bchain.secondary_blockchain[-1]
                    ["height"] + 1:
                        if append_secondary_blockchain(block) == True:
                            orphan_blocks.remove(block)
                            continue

        orphan_blocks.remove(block)

    except Exception as err:
        logging.debug('handle_orphans: exception: ' + str(err))
        return False

    return True


def remove_received_block(block: 'dictionary') -> "bool":
    """
    remove a block from the received blocks list
    """
    try:
        with semaphore:
            if block in received_blocks:
                received_blocks.remove(block)

    except Exception as err:
        logging.debug('remove_received_block: exception: ' + str(err))
        return False

    return True
```

```python
def retarget_difficulty_number(block):
    """

    recalibrates the difficulty number every hconfig.conf["RETARGET_INTERVAL"]
    blocks
    """

    if block["height"] == 0: return

    old_diff_no   = hconfig.conf["DIFFICULTY_NUMBER"]
    initial_block = bchain.blockchain[(block["height"] - \
        hconfig.conf["RETARGET_INTERVAL"])]
    time_initial  = initial_block["timestamp"]
    time_now      = block["timestamp"]

    elapsed_seconds = time_now - time_initial
    # the average time to mine a block is 600 seconds
    blocks_expected_to_be_mined = int(elapsed_seconds / 600)
    discrepancy = 1000 - blocks_expected_to_be_mined

    hconfig.conf["DIFFICULTY_NUMBER"] =  old_diff_no - \
        old_diff_no * (20/100)*(discrepancy /(1000 + blocks_expected_to_be_
        mined))

    return

def propagate_transaction(txn: "dictionary"):
    """

    propagates a transaction that is received
    """

    if len(address_list) % 20 == 0: get_address_list()
    cmd = {}
    cmd["jsonrpc"] = "2.0"
    cmd["method"]  = "receive_transaction"
    cmd["params"]  = {"trx":txn}
    cmd["id"] = 0

    for addr in address_list:
        rpc = json.dumps(cmd)
        networknode.hclient(addr,rpc)
```

```
    return

def propagate_mined_block(block):
    """

    sends a block to other mining nodes so that they may add this block
    to their blockchain.
    We refresh the list of known node addresses periodically
    """

    if len(address_list) % 20 == 0: get_address_list()

    cmd = {}
    cmd["jsonrpc"] = "2.0"
    cmd["method"]  = "receive_block"
    cmd["params"]  = {"block":block}
    cmd["id"] = 0

    for addr in address_list:
        rpc = json.dumps(cmd)
        networknode.hclient(addr,rpc)

    return

def get_address_list():
    '''

    update the list of node addresses that are known
    AMEND IP ADDRESS AND PORT AS REQUIRED.
    '''

    ret = networknode.hclient("http://127.0.0.69:8081",
            '{"jsonrpc":"2.0","method":"get_address_
list","params":{},"id":1}')
    if ret.find("error") != -1: return
    retd = json.loads(ret)

    for addr in retd["result"]:
        if address_list.count(addr) == 0:
            address_list.append(addr)

    return
```

```python
def compare_transaction_lists(block):
    """

    tests whether a transaction in a received block is also in a candidate
    block that is being mined
    """

    for tx1 in block["tx"]:
        for tx2 in remove_list:
            if tx1 == tx2: return False

    return True


def start_mining():
    """

    assemble a candidate block and then mine this block
    """

    while True:
        candidate_block = make_candidate_block()
        if candidate_block() == False:
            time.sleep(1)
            continue
        # remove transactions in the mined block from the mempool
        if mine_block(candidate_block) != False:
            remove_mempool_transactions(remove_list)
        else: time.sleep(1)
```

Helium Mining Data Structures

mempool

mempool is a list containing transactions that have been received but are not in any
mined block.

received_blocks

This is a list of blocks mined by other mining nodes and meant to be included in the
receiving node's blockchain.

orphan_blocks

This is a list of valid blocks which have been received from other nodes but which could not be appended to the receiving miner's blockchain.

Blockchain

This is the local blockchain that is being maintained by this mining node. It is located in the *hblockchain* module. This blockchain is also referred to as the primary blockchain.

Secondary Blockchain

This is an alternate blockchain that is maintained by the miner when the primary blockchain is forked.

Helium Mining Functions

mining_reward

A miner who successfully mines a block is entitled to a reward which consists of the issuance of new helium coins. The mining reward determines the quantum of fresh currency awarded to the miner. This reward halves periodically. Both the initial reward and the halving period are set out in the *hconfig* module.

The initial reward is *hconfig.conf["MINING_REWARD"]* coins. This reward halves every *hconfig.conf["REWARD_INTERVAL"]* blocks.

receive_transaction

The function *receive_transaction* receives a transaction propagating on the Helium P2P network. This function checks to determine whether the transaction is in the mempool. The function discards the transaction if it is already in the *mempool*.

In the next step, *receive_transaction* verifies the validity of the transaction. If the transaction is valid, it is added to *mempool*; otherwise, the transaction is discarded. If the transaction is added to the *mempool*, it is sent for further propagation on the Helium network.

receive_transaction is meant to run in a Python thread.[1]

---

[1]See Appendix 4 for an exposition of Python threads and concurrent programming.

make_candidate_block

The purpose of *make_candidate_block* is to create a block that can be mined. If the *mempool* is empty, the function just returns.

make_candidate_block creates a partial header for a block and then draws transactions from the *mempool* and appends them to *tx* field of this block. Any number of algorithms can be used to draw transactions from the *mempool*. *make_candidate_block* uses a simple FIFO (First-In, First-Out) algorithm and keeps on drawing transactions until the maximum block size of 1 MB is almost reached or the *mempool* is exhausted. For each transaction, this function inserts a *vout* transaction fragment giving itself the transaction fee.

After *make_candidate_block* has finished its draw from *mempool*, it creates a *coinbase* transaction. The *coinbase* transaction is the first transaction in the *tx* list. For each block, this function creates a fresh public-private key pair that is used to create the *coinbase* transaction and the transaction fee fragment.

Finally, *make_candidate_block* computes the merkle root of the transactions and inserts it into the merkle field of the block header. It then tests the validity of the constructed block. If the block is valid, it removes the transactions in the block from the *mempool*. The candidate block is now ready to be mined.

make_miner_keys

This function creates a public-private key pair and saves these keys to a text file. *make_candidate_block* uses the public key to create the RIPEMD160(SHA256(public key)) hash that is inserted into the ScriptPubKey portion of the coinbase transaction and each transaction fee vout fragment.

add_transaction_fee

add_transaction_fee is called from *make_candidate_block*. It receives a transaction and the miner's public key. This function calculates the transaction fee, updates the Chainstate, and creates a transaction fragment that directs the transaction fee to the holder of the private key corresponding to the public key.

make_coinbase_transaction

make_coinbase_transaction is called from *make_candidate_block*. It receives the height of the candidate block and the miner's public key. This function computes the block reward and then creates and returns a coinbase transaction.

remove_mempool_transactions

This function removes transactions from the mempool and hence prevents transactions from being included more than once in different candidate blocks.

mine_block

mine_block receives a candidate block and initiates mining this block. The SHA256 hash of the nonce in the block header is computed. The block is said to be mined if the computed SHA-256 hash is less than the difficulty number in the Helium h*config* module. If the value is greater than or equal to the difficulty number, then the nonce is incremented and the computational result is compared once again to the difficulty number. This process continues until the block is mined or the computational loop is exited.

Once the block is mined, it is attached to the miner's blockchain and then propagated on the Helium P2P network so that other miners can append it to their blockchains.

proof_of_work

Before a block received from another miner can be included in a local blockchain, the node must verify the integrity of the block and its transactions and also verify that the nonce supplied in the block header is less than the difficulty number in this node's *hconfig* file. This function implements the proof of work for the received block.

receive_block

receive_block receives a block mined by some other miner. If the block is valid, the mining node adds the block to its *received_blocks* list. The block is invalid if any of the following conditions occur:

1.   The block is invalid.

2.   The block height is less than (blockchain height – 2).

3. The proof of work fails.

4. The block does not contain at least two transactions.

5. The first block transaction is not a coinbase transaction.

6. Transactions in the block are invalid.

7. Block is already in the blockchain.

8. The block is already in the *received_blocks* list.

If the received block is valid, it is added to the *received_blocks* list and the block is propagated on the Helium P2P network so that other nodes can attach it to their blockchains.

receive_block is meant to be executed as a Python thread.

process_received_blocks

process_received_blocks draws blocks from the *received_blocks* list and attempts to attach them to the blockchain. This function implements distributed consensus. Note that since miners are impelled to make a profit, they will always extend their longest blockchain. The algorithm for processing the received blocks is as follows:

1. Get a block from the *received blocks* list.

2. If the blockchain is empty and the block has an empty *prevblockhash* field, then add the block to the blockchain (this is a genesis block).

3. Compute the block header hash of the last block on the blockchain (*blkhash*)

   ```
   if blkhash == block["prevblockhash"]
   ```

   and then add the block to the blockchain.

4. If the blockchain has at least two blocks, let *blk_hash* be the hash of the block header of the second latest block in the blockchain, and then if

   ```
   block["prevblockhash"] == blk_hash
   ```

create a secondary block consisting of all of the blocks of the blockchain except for the latest. Append the block to this secondary blockchain.

5.   Otherwise, move the block to the *orphan_blocks* list.

6.   If the received block was attached to a blockchain, then for each block in the *orphan_blocks* list, try to attach the orphan block to the primary blockchain or the secondary blockchain, if it exists.

7.   If the received block was attached to a blockchain and the secondary blockchain has elements, then swap the primary blockchain and the secondary blockchain if the length of the secondary blockchain is greater.

8.   If the received block was attached and the secondary blockchain has elements, then clear the secondary blockchain if its length is more than two blocks behind the primary blockchain.

process_receive_block is meant to run in a concurrent thread.

fork_blockchain

This function creates the secondary blockchain by forking the primary blockchain. *fork_blockchain* receives a block parameter which it attaches to the secondary blockchain.

swap_blockchains

swap_blockchains swaps the primary and secondary blockchains so that the primary blockchain is the longer blockchain.

handle_orphans

handle_orphans draws orphaned blocks from the orphans list and attempts to attach them to the primary blockchain. Orphaned blocks that are more than two blocks distant from the head of the blockchain are deleted.

remove_received_block

This function removes a block from the *received_blocks* list.

retarget_difficulty_number

This function is invoked every *hconfig.conf["RETARGET_INTERVAL"]* number of blocks. It recalibrates the difficulty number. The purpose of this function is to ensure that blocks are mined every ten minutes on the average. This function implements the algorithm set out in Chapter 13.

Miscellany

The remaining functions in the *hmining* module handle concurrent mining and will be discussed in the next chapter.

Changes to the Helium Blockchain Module

In order to handle secondary blockchains, add the following top-level attribute to the *hblockchain* module:

```
"""
secondary block used by mining nodes
"""
secondary_blockchain = []
```

Helium Mining Unit Tests

We are now ready to run unit tests on the mining module. Copy the following code into a file called *test_hmining.py* and save it in the *unit_tests* directory. Execute the tests in your virtual Python environment with

```
$ pytest test_hmining.py -s
```

You should see 40 unit tests passing:

```
"""
    pytest unit tests for hmining module
"""
import hmining
import hblockchain
```

```python
import tx
import hchaindb
import blk_index
import hconfig
import rcrypt
import plyvel
import random
import secrets
import time
import pytest
import pdb
import os

def teardown_module():
    #hchaindb.close_hchainstate()
    if os.path.isfile("coinbase_keys.txt"):
        os.remove("coinbase_keys.txt")

####################################
# Synthetic Transaction
####################################
def make_synthetic_transaction():
    """

    makes a synthetic transaction with randomized values
    """

    transaction = {}
    transaction['version'] = hconfig.conf["VERSION_NO"]
    transaction['transactionid'] = rcrypt.make_uuid()
    transaction['locktime'] = 0
    transaction['vin'] = []
    transaction['vout'] = []

    # make vin list
    vin = {}
    vin["txid"] = rcrypt.make_uuid()
    vin["vout_index"] = 0
```

```python
    vin["ScriptSig"] = []
    vin["ScriptSig"].append(rcrypt.make_uuid())
    vin["ScriptSig"].append(rcrypt.make_uuid())
    transaction['vin'].append(vin)

    # make vout list
    vout = {}
    vout["value"] = secrets.randbelow(10000000) +1000
    vin["ScripPubKey"] = []
    transaction['vout'].append(vout)

    return transaction

def make_synthetic_block():
    """

    make synthetic block for unit testing
    """

    block = {}
    block["transactionid"] = rcrypt.make_uuid()
    block["version"] = hconfig.conf["VERSION_NO"]
    block["difficulty_bits"] = hconfig.conf["DIFFICULTY_BITS"]
    block["nonce"] = hconfig.conf["NONCE"]
    block["height"] = 1024
    block["timestamp"] = int(time.time())
    block["tx"] = []

    # add transactions to the block
    num_tx = secrets.randbelow(6) + 2
    for __ctr in range(num_tx):
        trx = make_synthetic_transaction()
        block["tx"].append(trx)

    block["merkle_root"] = hblockchain.merkle_root(block["tx"], True)
    block["prevblockhash"] =rcrypt.make_uuid()

    return block

@pytest.mark.parametrize("block_height, reward", [
    (0, 50),
```

```
        (1, 50),
        (11, 25),
        (29, 12),
        (31, 12),
        (34, 6),
        (115,0 )
])
def test_mining_reward(block_height, reward):
    """

    test halving of mining reward
    """

    # rescale to test
    hconfig.conf["REWARD_INTERVAL"] = 11
    hconfig.conf["MINING_REWARD"] = 50
    assert hmining.mining_reward(block_height) == reward
    hconfig.conf["MINING_REWARD"] = 5_000_000

def test_tx_in_mempool(monkeypatch):
    """

    test do not add transaction to mempool if it is
    already in the mempool
    """

    hmining.mempool.clear()
    monkeypatch.setattr(tx, "validate_transaction", lambda x: True)
    monkeypatch.setattr(hchaindb, "get_transaction", lambda x: True)

    syn_tx = make_synthetic_transaction()
    hmining.mempool.append(syn_tx)
    assert hmining.receive_transaction(syn_tx) == False
    assert len(hmining.mempool) == 1
    hmining.mempool.clear()

def test_tx_in_chainstate(monkeypatch):
    """

    test do not add transaction if it is accounted for in the
    Chainstate
    """
```

```
    hmining.mempool.clear()
    monkeypatch.setattr(hchaindb, "get_transaction", lambda x: {"mock":
    "fragment"})
    syn_tx = make_synthetic_transaction()
    assert hmining.receive_transaction(syn_tx) == True
    hmining.mempool.clear()

def test_invalid_transaction(monkeypatch):
    """

    tests that an invalid transaction is not added to the mempool
    """

    monkeypatch.setattr(hchaindb, "get_transaction", lambda x: False)
    monkeypatch.setattr(tx, "validate_transaction", lambda x: False)
    hmining.mempool.clear()
    syn_tx = make_synthetic_transaction()
    assert hmining.receive_transaction(syn_tx) == False
    assert len(hmining.mempool) == 0

def test_valid_transaction(monkeypatch):
    """

    tests that a valid transaction is added to the mempool
    """

    monkeypatch.setattr(hchaindb, "get_transaction", lambda x: False)
    monkeypatch.setattr(tx, "validate_transaction", lambda x, y: True,
    False)
    hmining.mempool.clear()
    syn_tx = make_synthetic_transaction()
    assert hmining.receive_transaction(syn_tx) == True
    assert len(hmining.mempool) == 1
    hmining.mempool.clear()

def test_make_from_empty_mempool():
    """

    test cannot make a candidate block when the mempool is empty
    """

    hmining.mempool.clear()
    assert hmining.make_candidate_block() == False
```

```
def test_future_lock_time(monkeypatch):
    """

    test that transactions locked into the future will not be processed"
    """

    monkeypatch.setattr(tx, "validate_transaction", lambda x: True)
    monkeypatch.setattr(hchaindb, "get_transaction", lambda x: True)

    hmining.mempool.clear()
    tx1 = make_synthetic_transaction()
    tx1["locktime"] = int(time.time()) + 86400
    hmining.mempool.append(tx1)

    assert(bool(hmining.make_candidate_block())) == False


def test_no_transactions():
    """

    test that candidate blocks with no transactions are not be processed"
    """

    hmining.mempool.clear()
    tx1 = make_synthetic_transaction()
    tx1[tx] = []
    assert hmining.make_candidate_block() == False

def test_add_transaction_fee(monkeypatch):
    """

    tests that a transaction includes a miner's transaction fee
    """

    monkeypatch.setattr(tx, "validate_transaction", lambda x: True)
    monkeypatch.setattr(hchaindb, "get_transaction", lambda x: True)
    monkeypatch.setattr(tx, "transaction_fee", lambda x,y: 12_940)
    trx = make_synthetic_transaction()

    trx = hmining.add_transaction_fee(trx, "pubkey")
    vout_list = trx["vout"]
    vout = vout_list[-1]
    assert vout["value"] == 12_940

def test_make_coinbase_transaction():
```

```
    """
    tests making a coinbase transaction
    """
    ctx = hmining.make_coinbase_transaction(10, "synthetic pubkey")
    assert len(ctx["vin"]) == 0
    assert len(ctx["vout"]) == 1
    hash = rcrypt.make_RIPEMD160_hash(rcrypt.make_SHA256_hash("synthetic
    pubkey"))
    assert ctx["vout"][0]["ScriptPubKey"][1] == hash

def test_mine_block(monkeypatch):
    """
    test that a good block can be mined
    """
    block = make_synthetic_block()

    monkeypatch.setattr(hchaindb, "get_transaction", lambda x: False)
    monkeypatch.setattr(hchaindb, "transaction_update", lambda x: True)
    monkeypatch.setattr(hblockchain, "validate_block", lambda x: True)
    monkeypatch.setattr(tx, "validate_transaction", lambda x,y: True)
    monkeypatch.setattr(blk_index, "put_index", lambda x,y: True)

    # make the mining easier
    hconfig.conf["DIFFICULTY_NUMBER"] = 0.0001
    assert hmining.mine_block(block) != False

def test_receive_bad_block(monkeypatch):
    """
    test that received block is not added to the received_blocks
    list if the block is invalid
    """
    monkeypatch.setattr(hchaindb, "get_transaction", lambda x: False)
    monkeypatch.setattr(tx, "validate_transaction", lambda x,y: True)
    monkeypatch.setattr(hblockchain, "validate_block", lambda x: False)
    hmining.received_blocks.clear()
    block = make_synthetic_block()
    assert hmining.receive_block(block) == False
```

```
    assert len(hmining.received_blocks) == 0

def test_receive_stale_block(monkeypatch):
    """
    test that received block is not added to the received_blocks
    list if the block height is old
    """
    monkeypatch.setattr(hblockchain, "validate_block", lambda x,y: True)
    monkeypatch.setattr(hchaindb, "get_transaction", lambda x: True)
    monkeypatch.setattr(tx, "validate_transaction", lambda x,y: True)

    hmining.received_blocks.clear()
    for ctr in range(50):
        block = make_synthetic_block()
        block["height"] = ctr
        hblockchain.blockchain.append(block)

    syn_block = make_synthetic_block()
    syn_block["height"] = 47

    assert hmining.receive_block(syn_block) == False
    hblockchain.blockchain.clear()

def test_receive_future_block(monkeypatch):
    """
    test that received block is not added to the received_blocks
    list if the block height is too large
    """
    monkeypatch.setattr(hblockchain, "validate_block", lambda x,y: True)
    monkeypatch.setattr(tx, "validate_transaction", lambda x,y: True)
    monkeypatch.setattr(hchaindb, "get_transaction", lambda x: True)

    hmining.received_blocks.clear()
    for ctr in range(50):
        block = make_synthetic_block()
        block["height"] = ctr
        hblockchain.blockchain.append(block)

    syn_block = make_synthetic_block()
```

```
    syn_block["height"] = 51

    assert hmining.receive_block(syn_block) == False
    hblockchain.blockchain.clear()

def test_bad_difficulty_number(monkeypatch):
    """
    test that the proof of work fails if the difficulty no
    does not match
    """
    monkeypatch.setattr(hblockchain, "validate_block", lambda x,y: True)
    monkeypatch.setattr(hmining, "proof_of_work", lambda x: False)

    block= make_synthetic_block()
    block["difficulty_no"] = -1
    block["nonce"] = 60
    assert hmining.proof_of_work(block) == False

def test_invalid_block(monkeypatch):
    """
    test that received block is not added to the received_blocks
    list if the block is invalid
    """
    monkeypatch.setattr(hblockchain, "validate_block", lambda x,y: False)
    monkeypatch.setattr(tx, "validate_transaction", lambda x,y: True)
    monkeypatch.setattr(hchaindb, "get_transaction", lambda x: True)

    hmining.received_blocks.clear()
    block = make_synthetic_block()
    assert hmining.receive_block(block) == False
    assert len(hmining.received_blocks) == 0

def test_block_receive_once(monkeypatch):

    """
    test that a received block is not added to the received_blocks
    list if the block is already in the list
    """
```

```
    monkeypatch.setattr(hblockchain, "validate_block", lambda x: True)
    monkeypatch.setattr(tx, "validate_transaction", lambda x,y: True)
    monkeypatch.setattr(hchaindb, "get_transaction", lambda x: True)

    hmining.received_blocks.clear()
    block1 = make_synthetic_block()
    hmining.received_blocks.append(block1)

    assert hmining.receive_block(block1) == False
    assert len(hmining.received_blocks) == 1
    hmining.received_blocks.clear()

def test_num_transactions(monkeypatch):
    """

    a received block must contain at least two transactions
    """

    monkeypatch.setattr(hblockchain, "validate_block", lambda x: True)
    monkeypatch.setattr(tx, "validate_transaction", lambda x,y: True)
    monkeypatch.setattr(hchaindb, "get_transaction", lambda x: True)

    hmining.received_blocks.clear()
    block1 = make_synthetic_block()
    block1["tx"] = []
    block1["tx"].append(make_synthetic_transaction())

    hmining.received_blocks.append(block1)

    assert hmining.receive_block(block1) == False
    assert len(hmining.received_blocks) == 1
    hmining.received_blocks.clear()

def test_coinbase_transaction_present(monkeypatch):
    """

    a received block must contain a coinbase transaction
    """

    monkeypatch.setattr(hblockchain, "validate_block", lambda x: True)
    monkeypatch.setattr(tx, "validate_transaction", lambda x,y: True)
    monkeypatch.setattr(hchaindb, "get_transaction", lambda x: True)
```

```
        hmining.received_blocks.clear()
        block1 = make_synthetic_block()
        block1["tx"] = []

        hmining.received_blocks.append(block1)

        assert hmining.receive_block(block1) == False
        assert len(hmining.received_blocks) == 1
        hmining.received_blocks.clear()

def test_block_in_blockchain(monkeypatch):
        """

        test if a received block is in the blockchain
        """

        monkeypatch.setattr(hblockchain, "validate_block", lambda x: True)
        monkeypatch.setattr(tx, "validate_transaction", lambda x,y: True)
        monkeypatch.setattr(hchaindb, "get_transaction", lambda x: True)

        block1 = make_synthetic_block()
        block2 = make_synthetic_block()
        hblockchain.blockchain.append(block1)
        hblockchain.blockchain.append(block2)

        assert len(hblockchain.blockchain) == 2
        assert hmining.receive_block(block2) == False
        hblockchain.blockchain.clear()

def test_block_in_secondary_blockchain(monkeypatch):
        """

        test if a received block is in the secondary blockchain
        """

        monkeypatch.setattr(hblockchain, "validate_block", lambda x: True)
        monkeypatch.setattr(tx, "validate_transaction", lambda x,y: True)
        monkeypatch.setattr(hchaindb, "get_transaction", lambda x: True)

        block1 = make_synthetic_block()
        block2 = make_synthetic_block()
        hblockchain.secondary_blockchain.append(block1)
```

```
        hblockchain.secondary_blockchain.append(block2)

        assert len(hblockchain.secondary_blockchain) == 2
        assert hmining.receive_block(block2) == False
        hblockchain.secondary_blockchain.clear()

def test_add_block_received_list(monkeypatch):
        """

        add a block to the received blocks list. test for a block
        coinbase tx
        """

        monkeypatch.setattr(hblockchain, "validate_block", lambda x: True)
        #monkeypatch.setattr(tx, "validate_transaction", lambda x,y: True)
        monkeypatch.setattr(hchaindb, "get_transaction", lambda x: True)
        monkeypatch.setattr(hchaindb, "transaction_update", lambda x: True)
        monkeypatch.setattr(blk_index, "put_index", lambda x,y: True)

        block = make_synthetic_block()
        trx = make_synthetic_transaction()
        block["tx"].insert(0, trx)
        assert hmining.receive_block(block) == False
        assert len(hblockchain.blockchain) == 0

        hmining.received_blocks.clear()
        hblockchain.blockchain.clear()

def test_fetch_received_block(monkeypatch):
        """

        a block in the received_blocks list can be fetched
        for processing
        """

        monkeypatch.setattr(hblockchain, "validate_block", lambda x: True)
        monkeypatch.setattr(tx, "validate_transaction", lambda x,y: True)
        monkeypatch.setattr(hchaindb, "get_transaction", lambda x: True)
        monkeypatch.setattr(hchaindb, "transaction_update", lambda x: True)
        block = make_synthetic_block()
        hmining.received_blocks.append(block)
```

```
    assert hmining.process_received_blocks() == True
    assert len(hmining.received_blocks) == 0
    hmining.received_blocks.clear()
    hblockchain.blockchain.clear()

def test_remove_received_block():
    """

    test removal of a received block from the received_blocks list
    """

    block = make_synthetic_block()
    hmining.received_blocks.append(block)

    assert len(hmining.received_blocks) == 1
    assert hmining.remove_received_block(block) == True
    assert len(hmining.received_blocks) == 0

def test_remove_mempool_transaction():
    """

    test removal of a transaction in the mempool
    """

    block = make_synthetic_block()
    hmining.mempool.append(block["tx"][0])

    assert len(hmining.mempool) == 1
    assert hmining.remove_mempool_transactions(block) == True
    assert len(hmining.mempool) == 0

def test_fork_primary_blockchain(monkeypatch):
    """

    test forking the primary blockchain
    """

    monkeypatch.setattr(hblockchain, "validate_block", lambda x: True)
    monkeypatch.setattr(tx, "validate_transaction", lambda x,y: True)
    monkeypatch.setattr(hchaindb, "get_transaction", lambda x: True)
    monkeypatch.setattr(hchaindb, "transaction_update", lambda x: True)

    hblockchain.blockchain.clear()
    hblockchain.secondary_blockchain.clear()
```

```
    hmining.received_blocks.clear()

    block1 = make_synthetic_block()
    block2 = make_synthetic_block()
    block3 = make_synthetic_block()
    block4 = make_synthetic_block()
    block4["prevblockhash"] = hblockchain.blockheader_hash(block2)

    hblockchain.blockchain.append(block1)
    hblockchain.blockchain.append(block2)
    hblockchain.blockchain.append(block3)
    assert len(hblockchain.blockchain) == 3

    hmining.received_blocks.append(block4)
    assert len(hmining.received_blocks) == 1

    hmining.process_received_blocks()
    assert len(hblockchain.blockchain) == 4
    assert len(hblockchain.secondary_blockchain) == 0

    hblockchain.blockchain.clear()
    hblockchain.secondary_blockchain.clear()
    hmining.received_blocks.clear()

def test_append_to_primary_blockchain(monkeypatch):
    """

    test add a received block to the primary blockchain
    """

    monkeypatch.setattr(hblockchain, "validate_block", lambda x: True)
    monkeypatch.setattr(tx, "validate_transaction", lambda x,y: True)
    monkeypatch.setattr(hchaindb, "get_transaction", lambda x: True)
    monkeypatch.setattr(hchaindb, "transaction_update", lambda x: True)

    hblockchain.blockchain.clear()
    hblockchain.secondary_blockchain.clear()
    hmining.received_blocks.clear()

    block1 = make_synthetic_block()
    block2 = make_synthetic_block()
```

```
    block3 = make_synthetic_block()
    block4 = make_synthetic_block()
    block4["prevblockhash"] = hblockchain.blockheader_hash(block3)

    hblockchain.blockchain.append(block1)
    hblockchain.blockchain.append(block2)
    hblockchain.blockchain.append(block3)
    assert len(hblockchain.blockchain) == 3

    hmining.received_blocks.append(block4)
    assert len(hmining.received_blocks) == 1

    hmining.process_received_blocks()
    assert len(hblockchain.blockchain) == 4
    assert len(hblockchain.secondary_blockchain) == 0

    hblockchain.blockchain.clear()
    hblockchain.secondary_blockchain.clear()
    hmining.received_blocks.clear()

def test_add_orphan_block(monkeypatch):
    """

    test add_orphan_block
    """

    hblockchain.blockchain.clear()
    hblockchain.secondary_blockchain.clear()
    hmining.received_blocks.clear()
    hmining.orphan_blocks.clear()

    monkeypatch.setattr(hblockchain, "blockheader_hash", lambda x: "mock_hash")
    monkeypatch.setattr(tx, "validate_transaction", lambda x,y : True)
    monkeypatch.setattr(hchaindb, "transaction_update", lambda x : True)
    monkeypatch.setattr(blk_index, "put_index", lambda x,y : True)

    block0 = make_synthetic_block()
    block1 = make_synthetic_block()
    block1["height"] = block0["height"] + 1
    block1["prevblockhash"] = "mock_hash"
```

```python
    hblockchain.blockchain.append(block0)
    hmining.received_blocks.append(block1)
    assert len(hmining.received_blocks) == 1

    hmining.process_received_blocks()
    assert len(hmining.orphan_blocks) == 0
    assert len(hblockchain.blockchain) == 2
    assert len(hblockchain.secondary_blockchain) == 0

    hblockchain.blockchain.clear()
    hblockchain.secondary_blockchain.clear()
    hmining.received_blocks.clear()

def test_swap_blockchain():
    """

    test swap the primary and secondary blockchains
    """

    hblockchain.blockchain.clear()
    hblockchain.secondary_blockchain.clear()
    hmining.received_blocks.clear()

    block1 = make_synthetic_block()
    block2 = make_synthetic_block()
    block3 = make_synthetic_block()
    block4 = make_synthetic_block()
    block4["prevblockhash"] = hblockchain.blockheader_hash(block3)

    hblockchain.blockchain.append(block1)
    hblockchain.secondary_blockchain.append(block2)
    hblockchain.secondary_blockchain.append(block3)
    hblockchain.secondary_blockchain.append(block4)
    assert len(hblockchain.blockchain) == 1
    assert len(hblockchain.secondary_blockchain) == 3

    hmining.swap_blockchains()
    assert len(hblockchain.blockchain) == 3
    assert len(hblockchain.secondary_blockchain) == 1

    hblockchain.blockchain.clear()
```

273

```
    hblockchain.secondary_blockchain.clear()

def test_clear_blockchain():
    """
    test clear the secondary blockchains
    """
    hblockchain.blockchain.clear()
    hblockchain.secondary_blockchain.clear()
    hmining.received_blocks.clear()

    block1 = make_synthetic_block()
    block2 = make_synthetic_block()
    block3 = make_synthetic_block()
    block4 = make_synthetic_block()
    block5 = make_synthetic_block()

    hblockchain.blockchain.append(block1)
    hblockchain.blockchain.append(block2)
    hblockchain.secondary_blockchain.append(block3)
    hblockchain.blockchain.append(block4)
    hblockchain.blockchain.append(block5)
    assert len(hblockchain.secondary_blockchain) == 1
    assert len(hblockchain.blockchain) == 4

    hmining.swap_blockchains()
    assert len(hblockchain.blockchain) == 4
    assert len(hblockchain.secondary_blockchain) == 0

    hblockchain.blockchain.clear()
    hblockchain.secondary_blockchain.clear()

def test_remove_stale_orphans(monkeypatch):
    """
    test to remove old orphan blocks
    """
    hblockchain.blockchain.clear()
    hblockchain.secondary_blockchain.clear()
    hmining.received_blocks.clear()
```

```
    hmining.orphan_blocks.clear()

    block1 = make_synthetic_block()
    block1["height"] = 1290
    block2 = make_synthetic_block()
    block2["height"] = 1285

    monkeypatch.setattr(hblockchain, "blockheader_hash", lambda x: "mock_hash")
    monkeypatch.setattr(tx, "validate_transaction", lambda x,y : True)
    monkeypatch.setattr(hchaindb, "transaction_update", lambda x : True)
    monkeypatch.setattr(blk_index, "put_index", lambda x,y : True)

    hblockchain.blockchain.append(block1)
    assert len(hblockchain.blockchain) == 1
    hmining.orphan_blocks.append(block2)
    assert len(hmining.orphan_blocks) == 1

    hmining.handle_orphans()
    assert len(hmining.orphan_blocks) == 0
    assert len(hblockchain.blockchain) == 1
    assert len(hblockchain.secondary_blockchain) == 0

    hblockchain.blockchain.clear()
    hblockchain.secondary_blockchain.clear()
    hmining.orphan_blocks.clear()

def test_add_orphan_to_blockchain(monkeypatch):
    """

    test to add orphan block to blockchain
    """

    hmining.orphan_blocks.clear()
    hblockchain.blockchain.clear()
    hblockchain.secondary_blockchain.clear()
    hmining.received_blocks.clear()

    monkeypatch.setattr(hblockchain, "validate_block", lambda x: True)
    monkeypatch.setattr(hblockchain, "blockheader_hash", lambda x:
"mockvalue")
    monkeypatch.setattr(tx, "validate_transaction", lambda x, y: True)
```

```
    monkeypatch.setattr(hchaindb, "transaction_update", lambda x: True)
    monkeypatch.setattr(blk_index, "put_index", lambda x, y: True)

    block0 = make_synthetic_block()
    block1 = make_synthetic_block()
    block1["height"] = 1290
    block2 = make_synthetic_block()
    block2["height"] = 1291

    hblockchain.blockchain.append(block0)
    hblockchain.blockchain.append(block1)
    assert len(hblockchain.blockchain) == 2
    hmining.orphan_blocks.append(block2)
    assert len(hmining.orphan_blocks) == 1

    block2["prevblockhash"] = "mockvalue"

    hmining.handle_orphans()
    assert len(hmining.orphan_blocks) == 0
    assert len(hblockchain.blockchain) == 3
    assert len(hblockchain.secondary_blockchain) == 0

    hblockchain.blockchain.clear()
    hmining.orphan_blocks.clear()

def test_add_orphan_to_secondary_blockchain(monkeypatch):
    """
    test to add orphan block to the secondary blockchain
    """
    hmining.orphan_blocks.clear()
    hblockchain.blockchain.clear()
    hblockchain.secondary_blockchain.clear()
    hmining.received_blocks.clear()

    #monkeypatch.setattr(hblockchain, "validate_block", lambda x: True)
    monkeypatch.setattr(tx, "validate_transaction", lambda x, y: True)
    monkeypatch.setattr(hchaindb, "transaction_update", lambda x: True)
    monkeypatch.setattr(blk_index, "put_index", lambda x, y: True)
```

```python
block0 = make_synthetic_block()
hblockchain.blockchain.append(block0)

block1 = make_synthetic_block()
block1["height"] = 1290
block2 = make_synthetic_block()
block2["height"] = 1291
block3 = make_synthetic_block()
block3["height"] = 1292

block3["prevblockhash"] = hblockchain.blockheader_hash(block2)


hblockchain.secondary_blockchain.append(block1)
hblockchain.secondary_blockchain.append(block2)
assert len(hblockchain.secondary_blockchain) == 2
hmining.orphan_blocks.append(block3)
assert len(hmining.orphan_blocks) == 1
hmining.handle_orphans()
assert len(hmining.orphan_blocks) == 0
assert len(hblockchain.secondary_blockchain) == 1
assert len(hblockchain.blockchain) == 3

hblockchain.blockchain.clear()
hblockchain.secondary_blockchain.clear()
hmining.orphan_blocks.clear()

def test_append_to_secondary_blockchain(monkeypatch):
    """

    test add a received block to the primary blockchain
    """

    #monkeypatch.setattr(hblockchain, "validate_block", lambda x: True)
    monkeypatch.setattr(tx, "validate_transaction", lambda x,y: True)
    monkeypatch.setattr(hchaindb, "get_transaction", lambda x: True)
    monkeypatch.setattr(hchaindb, "transaction_update", lambda x: True)

    hblockchain.blockchain.clear()
    hblockchain.secondary_blockchain.clear()
    hmining.received_blocks.clear()
```

```
block1 = make_synthetic_block()
hblockchain.blockchain.append(block1)

block2 = make_synthetic_block()
block3 = make_synthetic_block()
block4 = make_synthetic_block()
block4["prevblockhash"] = hblockchain.blockheader_hash(block3)

hblockchain.secondary_blockchain.append(block2)
hblockchain.secondary_blockchain.append(block3)
assert len(hblockchain.blockchain) == 1
assert len(hblockchain.secondary_blockchain) == 2
block4["height"] = block3["height"] + 1
block4["prevblockhash"] = hblockchain.blockheader_hash(block3)
hmining.received_blocks.append(block4)
assert len(hmining.received_blocks) == 1

hmining.process_received_blocks()
assert len(hblockchain.blockchain) == 3
assert len(hblockchain.secondary_blockchain) == 1

hblockchain.blockchain.clear()
hblockchain.secondary_blockchain.clear()
hmining.received_blocks.clear()
```

Conclusion

At this stage, we have implemented a substantial portion of a Helium mining node. But our implementation of a mining node is not over. We have yet to implement portions of the *hmining* module as concurrent processes and interface the mining node with the external Helium peer-to-peer network. This is the matter that will be handled next.

CHAPTER 15

The Helium Network

In this chapter, we are going to examine the topology of peer-to-peer networks and contrast this with the client-server model, which is the dominant model of computing on the Internet. After this, we will set up a Helium peer-to-peer network on the localhost loopback address 127.0.x.x. This network is useful for testing Helium.

In the previous chapter, we built most of the functionality of a Helium mining node. However, we did not expose mining nodes to the Helium network or indicate how this can be done. There are a number of outstanding questions concerning mining nodes. How does a mining node receive transactions? How does a node handle blocks that are mined by other nodes? How does a mining node inform other nodes that it has just mined a block? How does a new mining node that does not have a blockchain get a copy of the distributed blockchain? In this chapter, we are going to answer these questions by building a canonical API interface that enables nodes on the Helium cryptocurrency peer-to-peer network to interoperate with each other.

In order to follow this chapter, you will need to be familiar with concurrent Python programming as well as JSON remote procedure calls. You can consult Appendixes 4 and 6, if required. These appendixes provide you with all of the required knowledge in these areas.

The Client-Server Model

The client-server model is the dominant network topology on the Internet. In this topological model, nodes on the Internet are either servers or clients. A client that wants a task performed contacts a server and makes a request. The server can elect to respond to the request or ignore it. Some of the servers may also be clients that are served by other servers.

This topology can be illustrated as shown in Figure 15-1.

© Karan Singh Garewal 2020
K. S. Garewal, *Practical Blockchains and Cryptocurrencies*, https://doi.org/10.1007/978-1-4842-5893-4_15

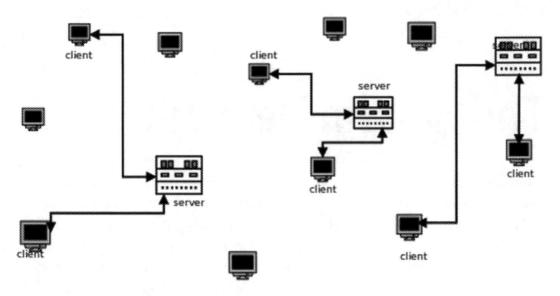

Figure 15-1. *Client-Server Topology*

This diagram shows clients interacting with servers. The lines represent bidirectional lines of communication between a client and a server (request-response). Clients make requests and servers respond to these requests. For example, a web browser (client) requests a web page from a server, and the server responds by sending an HTML page to the client.

For our purposes, we need to only observe that there is a degree of centralization in this topology. There are two types of nodes, servers and clients. The servers respond to requests and can choose to ignore some of the requests that are made. The servers control the flow of information in the network.

Peer-to-Peer Networks

A blockchain network or a cryptocurrency network for that matter is a peer-to-peer network. In a peer-to-peer network (P2P), all of the nodes on the network are equal in capability and there are no supernodes.

In a P2P network, nodes are peers of each other. In the context of Helium, this means that typically all of the nodes maintain a full blockchain and have the capability to mine blocks. Of course, some nodes may elect not to engage in mining, and other nodes may, for their own purposes, choose to maintain only a portion of the blockchain. As we have seen previously, Helium nodes do not trust each other, but the network can nevertheless converge to a consensus as to the state of the network, that is, the blockchain.

This lack of centralization in the network is why blockchain networks are resilient and cannot be shut down. This is in contrast to client-server networks, where the entire network can be degraded by simply shutting down the servers.

Figure 15-2 shows the gross topology of a blockchain network.

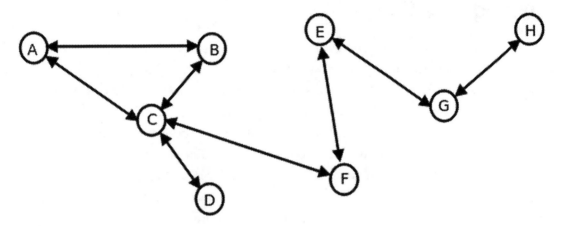

Figure 15-2. *A Peer-to-Peer Network*

This diagram shows a number of nodes that are identical to each other in terms of functionality, interacting on a network. The lines represent bidirectional channels of communication between peer nodes. This type of topology is called a peer-to-peer network and sometimes a mesh network. Nodes can come into the system and exit from it without degrading the efficacy of the network. Furthermore, nodes form communication links with other nodes on a transient basis.

Previous attempts to set up alternate currency networks were based on the client-server model. These currency systems were easy to identify and shut down. Furthermore, they attracted motivated criminal prosecution, often founded on dubious political jurisprudence. Bitcoin's cardinal strength is that it cannot be shut down. Satoshi Nakamoto, being aware of the potentiality of criminal litigation, vanished from the scene after putting the Bitcoin network into a functional running state in 2011.

Nodes in a P2P network do not have globally unique IDs that distinguish one node from another. All of the nodes are conceptually peers of each other. Nodes can only be differentiated from one another on the basis of their IP addresses. One of the consequences of this node anonymity is that the network is vulnerable to Sybil attacks. In a Sybil attack, a node masquerades as another node or a number of other nodes.

Booting Up a Node

When a node on a peer-to-peer network boots up, it connects to one or more seed nodes and queries these nodes for the addresses of other nodes on the network. A seed node acts like a directory server that maintains addresses of nodes. A query to a directory server permits a node to join the P2P network and communicate with a subset of nodes. Different nodes may contact different seed nodes during the bootstrap phase, and consequently, each of these nodes will probably have a different view of the network. Each node on a P2P network maintains a list of node addresses that it knows and can thus also act as a directory server, if it so wishes. These nodes can respond to a query to provide node addresses by providing their list of node addresses.

Distributed hash tables (DHT) are the most general manner in which node addresses can be provided in a P2P network. In such a P2P network, a subset of the nodes on the network, if not all of them, maintain a distributed hash table of addresses.[1] A DHT is a key-value store that maps a keyspace into an address space. Any node on the network can elect to maintain a portion of the DHT. A node that is booting up floods the P2P network searching for nodes that maintain a distributed hash table of addresses. These nodes are seed nodes in a DHT type network.

For our purposes, we will simply designate one or more P2P nodes to act as directory servers that respond to queries for node addresses.[2] An implementation of DHT for the Helium network, though not difficult, will take us to far afield.

---

[1]See, for example, `http://bnrg.cs.berkeley.edu/~adj/publications/paper-files/tapestry_jsac.pdf`, `https://github.com/haojin2/Chord-p2p-DHT`, `http://nms.lcs.mit.edu/papers/chord.pdf` and Pastry: Scalable, Decentralized Object Location and Routing for Large-Scale Peer-to-Peer Systems: `www.cs.rice.edu/~druschel/publications/Pastry.pdf`

[2]This is the Napster model. Napster was a P2P MP3 file sharing service and a pioneer in the development of P2P networks. Since it relied upon a centralized directory server, it was vulnerable to being shut down. See `https://github.com/gkiran315/Napster-style-peer-to-peer-P2P-file-sharing-system/blob/master/Design.pdf`

In Figure 15-3, node A requests a directory server (seed) to provide it with a list of addresses of other nodes on the network. The directory server replies with a list of node addresses and also adds the address of the querying node to its list of nodes. The nodes provided by the directory server become the neighbors of the requesting node.

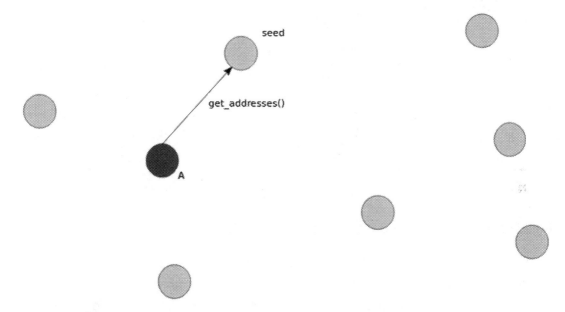

Figure 15-3. *Booting Up a Node with a Directory Server on a Peer-to-Peer Network*

Data Propagation on a P2P Network

In the Bitcoin and Helium networks, transactions and newly mined blocks propagate throughout the network by a process called flooding. Each node on the network listens on a specific port for transactions occurring on the network and for new blocks that have been mined. When a node receives a new transaction or a new block, it processes the new block or transaction and may also transmit it to other nodes in its address list. Figure 15-4 shows a transaction being propagated on a network.

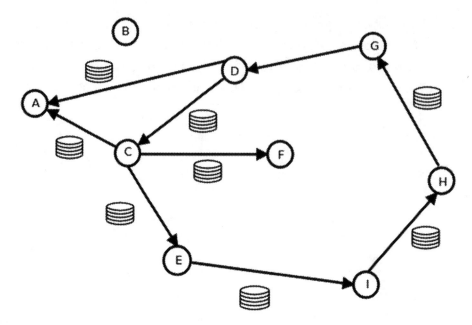

Figure 15-4. *Transaction Propagation on a P2P Network*

This diagram shows a transaction, represented by four stacked disks, being propagated from node D. Node D consults its address list and delivers the transaction to nodes A and C. Node C consults its address list and delivers the transaction to nodes E and F. The propagation continues as indicated by the arrows in the diagram.

This flooding process permits transactions and new blocks to rapidly propagate through the network. Of course, and as we discussed in the last chapter, nodes validate blocks and transactions before forwarding a transaction or a newly mined block to a neighbor.

You may be concerned that transactions and blocks will propagate endlessly on the network. There are two ways to ensure that this does not occur. The conventional way is to include a time-to-live (TTL) parameter with each transaction or block. Consider, for example, a fresh transaction. The metadata for this transaction will have a time-to-live (TTL) counter, with a value of 256, for example. When a node receives this transaction, it decrements the TTL and then re-broadcasts the transaction. If a node receives a transaction with a TTL of 0, it simply discards the transaction.

The second approach is the manner in which Bitcoin and Helium handle transaction routing. A Bitcoin node discards the incoming transaction if (i) the node has this transaction in its cache of transactions waiting to be processed (the *mempool*), (ii) if the transaction is already in the blockchain, or if (iii) the transaction is invalid. Otherwise, the node re-broadcasts the transaction to the nodes in its address list.

Note that the transaction propagation mechanism also provides each node receiving a transaction with the address of the node propagating the transaction. The receiving node can add this address to its address list. This feature enables receiving nodes to expand their view of the network by adding previously unknown addresses to their address lists.

Due to the flooding algorithm, each node will typically have a different set of transactions that it is processing, and in particular, a node may not receive some transactions being propagated across the network. A node may completely cease receiving transactions if there is a temporary network partition or if the node goes down.

Note that nodes may receive transactions in an order different than the time at which they were created.

Concurrent Mining

As indicated in the last chapter, some of the functions in the mining module are meant to operate concurrently with RPC servers. In order to facilitate this, add the *async* keyword to the following two functions in the *hmining* module, *make_candidate_block* and *mine_block*, for example:

```
async def mine_block(candidate_block: 'dictionary')
async def make_candidate_block()
```

With this simple change, these two functions become capable of concurrent operation.

The *start_mining* function is a concurrent thread that starts the mining of blocks. Add the following block of code to the end of the *hmining* module:

```
#####################################
# start mining in a thread:
# $(virtual) python hmining.py
#####################################

if __name__ == "__main__":
    #Create the Threads
    t1 = threading.Thread(target=start_mining, args=(), daemon=True)
    t1.start()
    t1.join()
```

Starting this module from the command line will start the mining of blocks on a thread.

Simulating the Helium Network on Localhost

In this chapter, we will be simulating and testing Helium mining nodes on a peer-to-peer network hosted on a localhost network (127.0.x.x).[3] You should have already created a *simulated_network* sub-directory under the Helium root (see Chapter 7). The *simulated_network* directory must be in the path of your Python interpreter.[4] Create a directory called *node_1* under the *simulated_network* directory. Next, copy all of the sub-directories under the Helium root with the exception of the *unit_tests* directory and the *simulated_network* directory into the *simulated_network/node_1* sub-directory. Delete all of the files in the *simulated_network/node_1/data* sub-directory. The *node_1* directory tree contains all of the necessary Python code for a node running on the simulated Helium network.

Next, create a sub-directory tree *seed_1/hnetwork* under the *simulated_network* directory. Copy the following program code into a file called *directory_server.py*, and save this file in the *seed_1/hnetwork* sub-directory. This code specifies a directory server on the Helium network.

At this stage, we have specified a seed node and a Helium mining node for our simulated network. You can now copy and paste the *node_1* directory tree into the *simulated_network* directory as many times as you want to and rename the root of these sub-trees as may be desired. This will give you a sub-directory for each Helium node on the simulated network. You can also specify more than one seed node, mutatis mutandis.

We can also use Docker images and containers to set up the Helium network on localhost. Docker is a quasi-virtualization solution that builds applications in containers. Containers can be deployed to multiple hosts without requiring any complicated deployment pipelines or any source code changes to the containers. You can refer to the following Docker resource for more information: *Ian Miell and Aidan Sayers, Docker in Practice, Manning Publications, 2016.*

---

[3]In creating and programming in the simulated network, you may find it useful to use a multi-window shell such as tmux: `https://github.com/tmux/tmux/wiki`

[4]See Appendix 1, if necessary.

Let's look at the *directory_server* module code. This program code is in the *seed_1/
hnetwork* sub-directory:

```
'''
start a directory server on 127.0.0.69:8081
'''

import hmining
from tornado import ioloop, web
from jsonrpcserver import method, async_dispatch as dispatch
import ipaddress
import json
import threading
import pdb
import logging

# A Fake list of addresses for testing only
address_list = ["127.0.0.10:8081", "127.0.0.11:8081", "127.0.0.12:8081",
                "127.0.0.13:8081", \
           "127.0.0.14:8081", "127.0.0.15:8081", "127.0.0.16:8081",
           "127.0.0.17:8081", \
           "127.0.0.18:8081", "127.0.0.19:8081", "127.0.0.20:8081" ]

logging.basicConfig(filename="debug.log",filemode="w", \
format='server: %(asctime)s:%(levelname)s:%(message)s', level=logging.DEBUG)

@method
async def get_address_list():
    with hmining.semaphore:
        ret = address_list
    return ret

@method
async def register_address(address: "string"):
    global address_list
    try:
        # validate IP address and port format: addr:port
        if address.find(":") == -1: return "error-invalid address"
```

```
        addr_list = address.split(":")
        addr_list[1]=addr_list[1].strip()
        if len(addr_list[0]) == 0 or len(addr_list[1]) == \
            0: return "error-invalid address"
        if int(addr_list[1]) <= 0 or int(addr_list[1]) >= \
            65536: return "error-invalid address"

        _ = ipaddress.ip_address(addr_list[0])
        addr = addr_list[0] + ":" + addr_list[1]
        if addr not in address_list:
            with hmining.semaphore:
                address_list.append(addr)
        return address

    except Exception as err:
        logging.debug('directory server::register address - ' + str(err))
        return "error-register address"

class MainHandler(web.RequestHandler):
    async def post(self):
        request = self.request.body.decode()
        logging.debug('decoded server request =  ' + str(request))
        response = await dispatch(request)
        print(response)
        self.write(str(response))

app = web.Application([(r"/", MainHandler)])

# start the network interface for a node on the local loop: 127.0.0.69:8081
if __name__ == "__main__":
    app.listen(address="127.0.0.69", port="8081")
    logging.debug('server running')
    print("directory server started at 127.0.0.69:8081")
    ioloop.IOLoop.current().start()
```

This Python script will start an asynchronous JSON-RPC directory server on the localhost network at IP address 127.0.0.69 and port 8081. You will want to refer to Appendix 6 if you are not acquainted with JSON remote procedure call servers and clients. This directory server maintains a list called *address_list* of the IP addresses and ports on which other Helium nodes are listening.[5] This directory server performs two tasks: (i) provides the addresses of RPC servers (Helium mining nodes) on the network, when so requested, and (ii) registers the addresses of RPC server nodes.

Note that the shared resource *address_list* is protected from data races through the use of semaphores. You can refer to Appendix 4 if you need to review the theory of Python concurrency and resource locking.

In order to start this directory server, traverse to the *seed_1/hnetwork* directory and execute the *directory-server.py* script in your Helium virtual environment:

```
$(virtual) python directory_server.py
```

Each Helium node that is not a directory server maintains a JSON-RPC client and a JSON-RPC server. RPC clients make requests to other RPC servers on the Helium P2P network and process the responses that are received. Similarly, RPC servers respond to requests that are made by other RPC clients on the network.

For each node directory (*node_1, node_2...*) that you have created (other than the *seed* directories), copy the following program code into the file *networknode.py* and save this file into the respective *node_x/hnetwork* sub-directories.

Let's take a look at this program code:

```
'''
netnode: implementation of a synchronous RPC-Client node that makes remote
procedure calls to RPC servers using the JSON RPC protocol version 2, and
a JSON-RPC server that responds to requests from RPC client nodes.
'''
import blk_index as blkindex
import hblockchain
import hchaindb
import hmining
import networknode
from    tornado import ioloop, web
from    jsonrpcserver import method, async_dispatch as dispatch
from    jsonrpcclient.clients.http_client import HTTPClient
import ipaddress
```

---

[5]For testing purposes only, we have hard-coded some fictitious node addresses.

```python
import threading
import json
import pdb
import logging
import os
import sys

logging.basicConfig(filename="debug.log",filemode="w",  \
format='server: %(asctime)s:%(levelname)s:%(message)s', level=logging.DEBUG)

####################################
# JSON-RPC Client
####################################

def hclient(remote_server, json_rpc):
    '''

    sends a synchronous request to a remote RPC server
    '''

    try:
        client = HTTPClient(remote_server)

        response = client.send(json_rpc)
        valstr = response.text
        val = json.loads(valstr)
        print("result: " + str(val["result"]))
        print("id:   " + str(val["id"]))
        return valstr

    except Exception as err:
        logging.debug("node_client: " + str(err))
        return '{"jsonrpc": "2.0", "result":"error", "id":"error"}'

########################################
# JSON-RPC Server
########################################

address_list = []

@method
```

```
async def receive_transaction(trx):
    """

    receives a transaction that is propagating on the Helium network
    """

    try:
        hmining.semaphore.acquire()
        ret = hmining.receive_transaction(trx)
        hmining.semaphore.release()
        if ret == False: return "error: invalid transaction"
        return "ok"
    except Exception as err:
        return "error: " + err


@method
async def receive_block(block):
    """

    receives a block that is propagating on the Helium network
    """

    try:
        ret = hmining.receive_block(block)
        if ret == False: return "error: invalid block"
        return "ok"
    except Exception as err:
        return "error: " + err


@method
async def get_block(height):
    """

    returns the block with the given height or an error if the block
    does not exist
    """

    with hmining.semaphore:
        if len(hblockchain.blockchain) == 0:
            return ("error: empty blockchain")

        if height < 0 or height > hblockchain.blockchain[-1]["height"]:
            return "error-invalid block height"
```

```
        block = json.dumps(hblockchain.blockchain[height])
        return block

@method
async def get_blockchain_height():
    """

    returns the height of the blockchain. Note that the first block has
    height 0
    """

    with hmining.semaphore:
        if hblockchain.blockchain == []: return -1
        height = hblockchain.blockchain[-1]["height"]

    return height


@method
async def clear_blockchain():
    """

    clears the primary and secondary blockchains.
    """

    pdb.set_trace()
    with hmining.semaphore:
        hblockchain.blockchain.clear()
        hblockchain.secondary_blockchain.clear()
    return "ok"

class MainHandler(web.RequestHandler):
    async def post(self):
        request = self.request.body.decode()
        logging.debug('decoded server request =  ' + str(request))
        response = await dispatch(request)
        print(response)
        self.write(str(response))

def startup():
    '''

    start node related systems
```

```
    '''

    try:
        # remove any locks
        os.system("rm -rf ../data/heliumdb/*")
        os.system("rm -rf ../data/hblk_index/*")
        # start the Chainstate Database
        ret = hchaindb.open_hchainstate("../data/heliumdb")
        if ret == False: return "error: failed to start Chainstate
database"
        else: print("Chainstate Database running")
        # start the LevelDB Database blk_index
        ret = blkindex.open_blk_index("../data/hblk_index")
        if ret == False: return "error: failed to start blk_index"
        else: print("blkindex Database running")

    except Exception:
        return "error: failed to start Chainstate database"

    return True


app = web.Application([(r"/", MainHandler)])


############################################################
# start the network interface for the server node on
# the localhost loop: 127.0.0.19:8081
############################################################
if __name__ == "__main__":
    app.listen(address="127.0.0.51", port="8081")
    logging.debug('server node is running')
    print("network node starting at 127.0.0.19:8081")

    ###############################
    # start this node
    ###############################

    if startup() != True:
        logging.debug('server node resource failure')
```

```
        print("stopping")
        sys.exit()

    logging.debug('server node is running')
    print('server node is running')

    ###############################
    # start the event loop
    ###############################
    ioloop.IOLoop.current().start()
```

This code base leverages our JSON-RPC implementation in Appendix 6. Notice that this particular node is listening on 27.0.019:8081. Each network node on your simulated network must listen on a unique IP address (on localhost).

A request made by an RPC client has the following syntactical format:

```
rpc   = json.dumps({"jsonrpc":"2.0","method":"receive_
block","params":{"block": blocks[0]}, "id":21})
ret = networknode.hclient("http://127.0.0.51:8081", rpc)
```

The argument to the *dumps* function is the remote procedure call in JSON-RPC v. 2 format. The value of the second argument is the method that is to be invoked on the remote server (*receive_block*). The value of the third argument are the arguments to be passed to the remote function. The arguments are a Python dictionary. The third argument will be the empty dictionary, {}, if we invoke a remote method which does not take any function parameters. The fourth argument is a numeric id that identifies our request. The remote server will return this id with its response. This JSON-RPC command is packaged as a string by j*son.dumps* before it is placed on the network.

We are now ready to send this command to the remote server. *networknode* is the Python module containing the RPC client and server. The function *networknode.hclient* will send the command to the remote server. The first argument of the *networknode. hclient* function is the IP address and port of the remote JSON-RPC server that is being called. Notice that the address includes the protocol (*http*) that is used to communicate with this server. The second argument is our packaged RPC command.

The remote JSON server will typically reply with a response with this type of syntactical format:

```
'{"jsonrpc": "2.0", "result": ["127.0.0.10:8081",
"127.0.0.11:8081"],"id":5}'
```

This is a JSON object encoded as a string. We can convert this into a Python dictionary with the function *json.loads()*.

The first key item specifies the *json rpc* version that is used to format the response. The second key item is "*result*". The value of this key is what we are interested in. The third key, *id*, identifies the id of the request to which this response pertains.

In the event of an error, the server will respond in the following format:

```
'{"jsonrpc": "2.0", "error": "message", "id": 5 }'
or:
'{"jsonrpc": "2.0", "result": "error: message", "id": 5 }'
```

The second portion of the *networknode* module is the JSON-RPC server. Examine the *app.listen* call in this module:

```
app.listen(address="127.0.0.19", port="8081")
```

This specifies that the server will listen on port 8081 at IP address 127.0.0.19. Each network node must listen on a unique IP address and port combination.

Finally, note that shared resources are protected from data races through the use of semaphores.

In order to start this server on the simulated network, traverse to the *hnetwork* directory of the node and execute the *networknode.py* script in the Helium virtual environment:

```
$(virtual) python networknode.py
```

Network Interface for Helium Nodes

Nodes on the Helium cryptocurrency P2P network perform the following network tasks:

1. Query for node addresses and obtain address lists from one or more directory servers.

2. Provide their address lists to other requesting nodes.

3. Query other nodes for blocks and process the blocks received.

4. Get the height of a node's blockchain.

5. Receive transactions and blocks propagating on the network and propagate them to other nodes.

The specification for the Helium network interface is as follows. All of the functions in the interface are implemented as JSON remote procedure calls.[6] A procedure on a JSON-RPC server is invoked using HTTP.[7] The RPC server processes remote procedure calls asynchronously. Each Helium mining node implements all of the functions described as follows in its *networknode* module, and hence, it is both a JSON-RPC server and a client.

Helium Bootup Scripts

```
directory_server.py
networknode.py
```

There are two types of bootup scripts: a directory server bootup script called *directory_server.py* and a node bootup script called *networknode.py*.

directory_server.py boots up a directory server that provides requesting nodes with a list of Helium node addresses.

networknode.py is a Python script that boots up a Helium node and puts the RPC server node into an operational state on the P2P network. As indicated previously, each such node on the Helium network that is not a directory server implements an RPC server and a client.

Address Resolution

```
get_address_list() -> "string"
register_address(address: "string") -> "string"
```

get_address_list: This invokes a seed node (directory server) with a request to send a list of node addresses. The remote server returns a stringified list of P2P node addresses.

---

[6]See Appendixes 4 and 6.

[7]In our implementation, we will refrain from the use of HTTPS in order to keep the focus on the architecture of our implementation.

register_address: A node registers its address (such as 127.0.0.34:8081) with a seed node or a directory server.

Blockchain Initialization

```
clear_blockchain() -> "string"
```

This clears the primary and secondary blockchains of a node. It returns the string "*ok*" if the blockchains are cleared.

Blockchain Query

There are two remote procedure calls to make blockchain queries:

```
get_blockchain_height() -> "integer"
get_block(block_no: "int") ->  "stringified block or an error string"
```

get_blockchain_height: This requests a remote node to provide the height of its blockchain. The requestor receives an integer reply. This function is used by a node to determine if its blockchain is in sync with the blockchain of some other node or to populate an empty blockchain. An out-of-sync condition will arise if the height of a node's blockchain is substantially less than the height of the blockchains of other nodes due to conditions such as downtime or a network failure.

get_block: This requests a remote node to send the block which has a certain block height. This function returns a block or an error string if a request is made for a non-existent block. An error string will contain the word *error*.

Block Propagation

```
receive_block(block: "string") -> "ok or an error string"
```

receive_block: A node (acting as a JSON-RPC client) sends a block to a remote node (acting as a JSON-RPC server). The function argument is a stringified block. The block can be a newly mined block or a block that is propagating on the P2P Helium network. The function returns an error string in the event of an error. An error string will contain the word *error*.

Transaction Propagation

```
receive_transaction(transaction: "string")  ->   "ok or an error string"
```

A node receives a transaction through a remote procedure call initiated by a remote node acting as a JSON-RPC client. This function returns an error string in the event of an error. An error string will contain the word *error*.

Node Process Space

Our simulated P2P network is for all practical purposes identical to a Helium network running on the Internet. One aspect to bear in mind is that the JSON-RPC server and client for each node executes in its own process space, and in particular, there is no shared memory or program code even though everything is running on one machine. Clients can only communicate with servers through the HTTP and JSON-RPC version 2.0 protocols. To elaborate further, each *networknode* module and all of the modules that it imports execute in its own process space.

Pytests for the Helium Network Interface

To initiate testing, make sure that you have created the simulated network as described earlier and started a few server nodes and one or more directory server nodes. Make sure that you are in the virtual Helium environment when you instantiate the servers and that each server is listening on a unique address. Our Pytest code uses a directory server listening at 127.0.0.69:8081 and a JSON-RPC server for a remote mining node that is listening at 127.0.0.51:8081. Finally, copy networknode.py into the unit_tests directory and start a server at 127.0.0.19:8081.

Copy the following Pytest program code into a file called *test_hnetwork.py* and save this file in the *unit_tests* sub-directory of the Helium root directory.

The tests in this file are integration tests, that is, they execute the remote procedure calls on an actual simulated network and return the actual results obtained. They do not mock any functions involved in a test. In order to effect this, the tests build an actual synthetic blockchain with the help of the functions *make_blocks* and *make_random_ transaction*. Appendix 7 discusses the creation of simulated blockchains of arbitrary height.

Traverse to the *unit_tests* directory of the Helium root and run the tests with

```
$(virtual) pytest test_hnetwork.py -s
```

Note: Do not instantiate the *hmining* module from the command line and execute *mine_blocks* when testing the module with these unit tests.

Note   You can get expanded output for a test by using the -s option, for example:

```
$(virtual) pytest test_hnetwork.py -s -k test_get_address_list
```

The -k option only tests *test_get_address_list* and ignores the other tests. The -s option gives expanded output, which is otherwise suppressed. For this particular test, the -s option will print the address list received on the terminal screen. The command

```
$(virtual) pytest test_hnetwork.py -s
```

will execute all of the tests and provide expanded output.

You should see six tests passing. Note that executing these tests will emit the transaction fragments of the simulated network as it is built.

```
########################################################################
# test a helium network
########################################################################
import blk_index as blkindex
import hchaindb
import hmining
import hconfig
import hblockchain
import networknode
import rcrypt
import tx
import json
import logging
import pdb
import pytest
```

```python
import os
import secrets
import sys
import time

"""
    log debugging messages to the file debug.log
"""

logging.basicConfig(filename="debug.log",filemode="w",  \
format='client: %(asctime)s:%(levelname)s:%(message)s', level=logging.
DEBUG)

def setup_module():
        os.system("rm -rf ../data/heliumdb/*")
        os.system("rm -rf ../data/hblk_index/*")
        os.system("rm *.log")

        # start the Chainstate Database
        ret = hchaindb.open_hchainstate("../data/heliumdb")
        if ret == False: return "error: failed to start Chainstate
database"
        else: print("Chainstate Database running")
        # start the LevelDB Database blk_index
        ret = blkindex.open_blk_index("../data/hblk_index")
        if ret == False: return "error: failed to start blk_index"
        else: print("blkindex Database running")

def teardown_module():
    """
    remove the debug logs, close databases
    """

    hchaindb.close_hchainstate()
    blkindex.close_blk_index()

# unspent transaction fragment values [{fragmentid:value}]
unspent_fragments = []
```

```
"""
    log debugging messages to the file debug.log
"""
logging.basicConfig(filename="debug.log",filemode="w", \
format='client: %(asctime)s:%(levelname)s:%(message)s', level=logging.
DEBUG)

def startup():
    """
    start the databases
    """
    # start the Chainstate Database
    ret = hchaindb.open_hchainstate("heliumdb")
    if ret == False: return "error: failed to start Chainstate database"
    else: print("Chainstate Database running")
    # start the LevelDB Database blk_index
    ret = blkindex.open_blk_index("hblk_index")
    if ret == False: return "error: failed to start blk_index"
    else: print("blkindex Database running")

def stop():
    """
    stop the databases
    """
    hchaindb.close_hchainstate()
    blkindex.close_blk_index()

# unspent transaction fragment values [{fragmentid:value}]
unspent_fragments = []

#########################################################
# Make A Synthetic Random Transaction For Testing
# receives a block no and a predicate indicating
# whether the transaction is a coinbase transaction
#########################################################
def make_random_transaction(blockno, is_coinbase):
```

```
txn = {}
txn["version"] =  "1"
txn["transactionid"] = rcrypt.make_uuid()
if is_coinbase == True: txn["locktime"] = hconfig.conf["COINBASE_LOCKTIME"]
else: txn["locktime"] = 0

# the public-private key pair for this transaction
transaction_keys = rcrypt.make_ecc_keys()

# previous transaction fragments spent by this transaction
total_spendable = 0

########################
# Build the vin array
########################
txn["vin"] = []

# genesis block transactions have no prior inputs.
# coinbase transactions do not have any inputs
if (blockno > 0) and (is_coinbase != True):
    max_inputs = secrets.randbelow(hconfig.conf["MAX_INPUTS"])
    if max_inputs == 0: max_inputs = hconfig.conf["MAX_INPUTS"] - 1

    # get some random previous unspent transaction
    # fragments to spend
    ind = 0
    ctr = 0

    while ind < max_inputs:
        # get a random unspent fragment from a previous block
        index = secrets.randbelow(len(unspent_fragments))
        frag_dict = unspent_fragments[index]
        key = [*frag_dict.keys()][0]
        val = [*frag_dict.values()][0]
```

```python
        if val["blockno"] == blockno:
            ctr += 1
            if ctr == 10000:
                print("failed to get random unspent fragment")
                return False
            continue

    unspent_fragments.pop(index)

    total_spendable += val["value"]
    tmp = hchaindb.get_transaction(key)
    if tmp == False:
        print("cannot get fragment from chainstate: " + key)

    assert tmp != False
    assert tmp["spent"] == False
    assert tmp["value"] > 0

    # create a random vin element
    key_array = key.split("_")

    signed = rcrypt.sign_message(val["privkey"], val["pubkey"])
    ScriptSig = []
    ScriptSig.append(signed)
    ScriptSig.append(val["pubkey"])

    txn["vin"].append({
            "txid": key_array[0],
            "vout_index": int(key_array[1]),
            "ScriptSig": ScriptSig
        })

    ctr = 0
    ind += 1

#####################
# Build Vout list
#####################
txn["vout"] = []
```

```
# genesis block
if blockno == 0:
    total_spendable = secrets.randbelow(10_000_000) + 50_000

# we need at least one transaction output for non-coinbase
# transactions
if is_coinbase == True: max_outputs = hconfig.conf["MAX_OUTPUTS"]
else:
    max_outputs = secrets.randbelow(hconfig.conf["MAX_OUTPUTS"])
    if max_outputs <= 1: max_outputs = 2

ind = 0

while ind < max_outputs:
    tmp = rcrypt.make_SHA256_hash(transaction_keys[1])
    tmp = rcrypt.make_RIPEMD160_hash(tmp)

    ScriptPubKey = []
    ScriptPubKey.append("<DUP>")
    ScriptPubKey.append("<HASH-160>")
    ScriptPubKey.append(tmp)
    ScriptPubKey.append("<EQ-VERIFY>")
    ScriptPubKey.append("<CHECK-SIG>")

    if is_coinbase == True:
        value = hmining.mining_reward(blockno)
    else:
        amt = int(total_spendable/max_outputs)
        value = secrets.randbelow(amt)    # helium cents
        if value == 0:
            value = int(amt / 10)
        total_spendable -= value
        assert value > 0
        assert total_spendable >= 0

    txn["vout"].append({
            "value": value,
            "ScriptPubKey": ScriptPubKey
        })
```

```
            # save the transaction fragment
            fragid = txn["transactionid"] + "_" + str(ind)
            fragment = {}
            fragment[fragid] = { "value":value,
                                 "privkey":transaction_keys[0],
                                 "pubkey":transaction_keys[1],
                                 "blockno": blockno
                               }
            unspent_fragments.append(fragment)
            #print("added to unspent fragments: " + fragid)

            if total_spendable <= 0: break
            ind += 1

    return txn

############################################################
# Build some random Synthetic Blocks For Testing.
# Makes num_blocks, sequentially linking each
# block to the previous block through the prevblockhash
# attribute.
# Returns an array of synthetic blocks
############################################################

def make_blocks(num_blocks):

    ctr = 0
    blocks = []

    global unspent_fragments
    unspent_fragments.clear()
    hblockchain.blockchain.clear()

    while ctr < num_blocks:
        block = {
                "prevblockhash": "",
                "version": "1",
                "timestamp": int(time.time()),
                "difficulty_bits": 20,
```

```
            "nonce": 0,
            "merkle_root": "",
            "height": ctr,
            "tx": []
        }

    # make a random number of transactions for this block
    # genesis block is ctr == 0
    if ctr == 0: num_transactions = 200
    else:
        num_transactions = secrets.randbelow(50)
        if num_transactions == 0: num_transactions = 40

    txctr = 0
    while txctr < num_transactions:
        if ctr > 0 and txctr == 0: is_coinbase = True
        else: is_coinbase = False

        trx = make_random_transaction(ctr, is_coinbase)
        assert trx != False
        block["tx"].append(trx)
        txctr += 1

    if ctr > 0:
        block["prevblockhash"] = \
            hblockchain.blockheader_hash(hblockchain.blockchain[ctr - 1])

    ret = hblockchain.merkle_root(block["tx"], True)
    assert ret != False
    block["merkle_root"] = ret

    ret = hblockchain.add_block(block)
    assert ret == True
    blocks.append(block)
    ctr+= 1
return blocks
```

```python
def test_register_address():
    '''

    test address registration with the directory server at 127.0.0.69:8081'
    '''

    #test 1
    ret = networknode.hclient("http://127.0.0.69:8081",
    '{"jsonrpc":"2.0","method":"register_address","params":{"address":
    "127.0.0.19:8081"},"id":1}')

    result = (json.loads(ret))["result"]
    print(result)
    assert result.find("error") == -1

    #test 2
    ret = networknode.hclient("http://127.0.0.69:8081",
    '{"jsonrpc":"2.0","method":"register_address","params":{"address":
    "127.0.0.19"},"id":2}')

    result = (json.loads(ret))["result"]
    print(result)
    assert result.find("error") >= 0

    #test 3
    ret = networknode.hclient("http://127.0.0.69:8081",
    '{"jsonrpc":"2.0","method":"register_address","params":{"address":
    "127.0.0:8081"},"id":3}')

    result = (json.loads(ret))["result"]
    print(result)
    assert result.find("error")  >= 0

def test_get_address_list():
    '''

    get an address list from a directory server. These are synthetic
    addresses,
    servers are not running at these addresses.
    '''
```

```python
    ret = networknode.hclient("http://127.0.0.69:8081",
            '{"jsonrpc":"2.0","method":"get_address_
            list","params":{},"id":4}')
    assert (ret.find("error")) == -1
    retd = json.loads(ret)
    assert "127.0.0.10:8081" in retd["result"]
    print(ret)

def test_get_blockchain_height():
    """ test get the height of some node's blockchain"""

    blocks = make_blocks(2)
    assert len(blocks) == 2

    # clear the primary and secondary blockchains for this test
    ret = networknode.hclient("http://127.0.0.51:8081",
            '{"jsonrpc": "2.0", "method": "clear_blockchain",
            "params": {}, "id": 10}')
    assert ret.find("ok") != -1

    rpc   = json.dumps({"jsonrpc":"2.0","method":"receive_block",
        "params":{"block": blocks[0]}, "id":11})
    ret = networknode.hclient("http://127.0.0.51:8081",rpc)
    assert ret.find("ok") != -1

    ret = networknode.hclient("http://127.0.0.51:8081",
            '{"jsonrpc": "2.0", "method": "get_blockchain_height",
            "params": {}, "id": 12}')
    assert ret.find("error") == -1
    height = (json.loads(ret))["result"]
    assert height == 0

    rpc   = json.dumps({"jsonrpc":"2.0","method":"receive_block",
        "params":{"block": blocks[1]}, "id":13})
    ret = networknode.hclient("http://127.0.0.51:8081",rpc)
    assert ret.find("ok") != -1
```

```
    ret = networknode.hclient("http://127.0.0.51:8081",
            '{"jsonrpc": "2.0", "method": "get_blockchain_height",
            "params": {}, "id": 14}')
    assert ret.find("error") == -1
    height = (json.loads(ret))["result"]
    assert height == 1

def test_receive_block():
    """

    send a block to a remote node. The remote node returns ok
    if the block is appended to its received_blocks list,
    otherwise returns an error string
    """

    blocks = make_blocks(2)
    assert len(blocks) == 2

    # clear the primary and secondary blockchains for this test
    ret = networknode.hclient("http://127.0.0.51:8081",
            '{"jsonrpc": "2.0", "method": "clear_blockchain",
            "params": {}, "id": 10}')
    assert ret.find("ok") != -1

    rpc   = json.dumps({"jsonrpc":"2.0","method":"receive_block",
        "params":{"block": blocks[0]}, "id":8})
    ret = networknode.hclient("http://127.0.0.51:8081",rpc)
    assert ret.find("ok") != -1

    rpc   = json.dumps({"jsonrpc":"2.0","method":"receive_block",
        "params":{"block": blocks[1]}, "id":9})
    ret = networknode.hclient("http://127.0.0.51:8081",rpc)
    assert ret.find("ok") != -1

def test_receive_transaction():
    """

    send a transaction to a remote node. The remote node returns ok
    if the transaction is appended to its mempool.
    Otherwise returns an error string
    """
```

```
    blocks = make_blocks(2)
    assert len(blocks) == 2

    # clear the primary and secondary blockchains for this test
    ret = networknode.hclient("http://127.0.0.51:8081",
            '{"jsonrpc":"2.0", "method": "clear_blockchain", "params": {},
            "id": 15}')
    assert ret.find("ok") >= 0

    rpc   = json.dumps({"jsonrpc":"2.0","method":"receive_transaction",
        "params":{"trx":blocks[0]["tx"][0]},"id":16})
    ret = networknode.hclient("http://127.0.0.51:8081",rpc)
    assert ret.find("ok") >= 0

    rpc   = json.dumps({"jsonrpc":"2.0","method":"receive_transaction",
        "params":{"trx": blocks[0]["tx"][1]}, "id":17})
    ret = networknode.hclient("http://127.0.0.51:8081",rpc)
    assert ret.find("ok") >= 0

def test_clear_blockchain(monkeypatch):
    """
    builds and clears the primary and secondary blockchains of a node
    """
    # clear the primary and secondary blockchains for this test
    ret = networknode.hclient("http://127.0.0.51:8081",
            '{"jsonrpc":"2.0", "method": "clear_blockchain", "params": {},
            "id": 19}')
    assert ret.find("ok") >= 0

    monkeypatch.setattr(tx, "validate_transaction", lambda x,y: True)

    num_blocks = 20
    blocks = make_blocks(num_blocks)
    assert len(blocks) == num_blocks

    tmp = hblockchain.blockheader_hash(blocks[0])
    assert tmp == blocks[1]["prevblockhash"]
    assert blocks[1]["height"] == 1
```

```
rpc    = json.dumps({"jsonrpc":"2.0","method":"receive_block",
    "params":{"block": blocks[0]}, "id":21})
ret = networknode.hclient("http://127.0.0.51:8081",rpc)
assert ret.find("ok") != -1

ret = networknode.hclient("http://127.0.0.51:8081",
        '{"jsonrpc": "2.0", "method": "get_blockchain_height",
        "params": {}, "id": 22}')
assert ret.find("error") == -1
height = (json.loads(ret))["result"]
# value of height attribute of the latest block in the blockchain
# meaning there is one block in the blockchain
assert height == 0

rpc    = json.dumps({"jsonrpc":"2.0","method":"receive_block",
    "params":{"block": blocks[1]}, "id":23})
ret = networknode.hclient("http://127.0.0.51:8081",rpc)
assert ret.find("ok") != -1

ret = networknode.hclient("http://127.0.0.51:8081",
        '{"jsonrpc": "2.0", "method": "get_blockchain_height",
        "params": {}, "id": 24}')
assert ret.find("error") == -1
height = (json.loads(ret))["result"]
# value of height attribute of the latest block in the blockchain
# meaning there are two blocks in the blockchain
assert height == 1

# clear the primary and secondary blockchains for this test
ret = networknode.hclient("http://127.0.0.51:8081",
        '{"jsonrpc":"2.0", "method": "clear_blockchain", "params": {},
        "id": 25}')
assert ret.find("ok") >= 0
```

Conclusion

In this chapter, we have discussed the two principal network topologies on the Internet, the client server topology and the peer-to-peer topology (P2P). We have also developed the program code necessary to interface Helium nodes to the Helium P2P network. In effecting this, we constructed a JSON-RPC server and JSON-RPC client interface for each mining node. We also created a directory server or seed node. Our interface code allows a mining node to do the following:

1. Obtain the addresses of other nodes from a directory server.

2. Receive transactions from the network and propagate them further.

3. Receive blocks propagating on the network and propagate them further.

4. Get the height of a node's blockchain.

5. Request a node to send it a certain block.

6. Clear the primary and secondary blockchains.

In the next chapter, we will address the issue of serializing the blockchain to disk. We will also show how a node can rebuild its entire blockchain environment including databases from a serialized blockchain.

CHAPTER 16

Blockchain Maintenance

In this chapter, we will examine Helium blockchain maintenance. The following topics will be discussed:

1. How a new Helium node with an empty blockchain acquires blocks from the Helium network and synchronizes itself with the distributed blockchain. This procedure for acquiring blocks also applies if a node goes down or if there is a temporary network partition.

2. Rebuilding the Chainstate database.

3. Rebuilding the blk_index database.

Blockchain Maintenance

A new node that joins the Helium peer-to-peer network will need to obtain a blockchain. Furthermore, the blockchain held by a node may need synchronization if it goes down or if there is a temporary network partition.

The Helium network interface provides two remote procedure calls to handle these use cases:

```
get_blockchain_height() -> "integer"
get_block(block_no: "int") ->  "stringified block or an error string"
```

get_blockchain_height obtains the height of the blockchain held by a remote node. The call *get_block* obtains a specific block from a remote node. Both of these remote procedure calls were discussed in the previous chapter.

I will leave it to you to develop tests to obtain blocks. In a production setting and in order to improve performance, you will want to enhance the code to provide for the concurrent downloading of blocks from several remote nodes.

© Karan Singh Garewal 2020
K. S. Garewal, *Practical Blockchains and Cryptocurrencies*, https://doi.org/10.1007/978-1-4842-5893-4_16

Reliability Engineering in Helium

An application that manages financial transactions must have extreme reliability. The cardinal principle is that the application should implement the simplest architectural patterns possible to achieve its objectives.

In the previous chapter, we saw that the distributed peer-to-peer architecture of Helium creates a network architecture that cannot be easily degraded. All of the nodes in the ecosystem are equal in capability, and anyone can instantiate a node and join the Helium network. Furthermore, Bitcoin and Helium have very modest requirements and thus can run on inexpensive commodity hardware. It is entirely feasible to run a Helium or Bitcoin node on a laptop.

Furthermore, we saw in the previous section that a Helium node can always synchronize its blockchain with the distributed blockchain in the event that the node goes down or if there is an unexpected network partition.

Aside from these reliability features, Helium and Bitcoin implement a single point of failure architecture. This point of failure is the block file, which is a simple, encoded text file. A blockchain is the collection of these files.

A Helium node can rebuild all of the data structures and databases that it needs for its operation from the blockchain (the collection of block files). Helium uses two key-value stores, the *Chainstate Database* and the *blk_index database*, and ensures by design that these databases are not critical points of failure. In other words, Helium can always rebuild these databases as long as it has all of the block files.

Helium blocks are encoded text files that are read-only. Since a blockchain is an immutable structure, block file updates and deletes are not required or supported. The create and read operations are handled by the underlying operating system. The following code snippet from the *hblockchain* module shows how block persistence is implemented in Helium:

```
def add_block(block: "dictionary") -> "bool":
    """

    add_block: adds a block to the blockchain. Receives a block. The block
    attributes are checked for validity and each transaction in the block is
    tested for validity. If there are no errors, the block is written to a file
    as asequence of raw bytes. Then the block is added to the blockchain.
    The chainstate database and the blk_index databases are updated.
    returns True if the block is added to the blockchain and False otherwise
```

```
        """
        try:
            # validate the received block parameters
            if validate_block(block) == False:
                raise(ValueError("block validation error"))

            # validate the transactions in the block
            # update the chainstate database

            for trx in block['tx']:
                # first transaction in the block is a coinbase transaction
                if block["height"] == 0 or block['tx'][0] == trx: zero_inputs = True
                else: zero_inputs = False

                if tx.validate_transaction(trx, zero_inputs) == False:
                    raise(ValueError("transaction validation error"))

                if hchaindb.transaction_update(trx) == False:
                    raise(ValueError("chainstate update transaction error"))

            # serialize the block to a file
            if (serialize_block(block) == False):
                    raise(ValueError("serialize block error"))

            # add the block to the blockchain in memory
            blockchain.append(block)

            #  update the blk_index
            for transaction in block['tx']:
                blockindex.put_index(transaction["transactionid"], block["height"])

        except Exception as err:
            print(str(err))
            logging.debug('add_block: exception: ' + str(err))
            return False

        return True

def serialize_block(block: "dictionary") -> "bool":
    """
```

```
serialize_block: serializes a block to a file using pickle.
Returns True if the block is serialized and False otherwise.
"""
index = len(blockchain)
filename = "block_" + str(index) + ".dat"

# create the block file and serialize the block
try:
    f = open(filename, 'wb')
    pickle.dump(block, f)

except Exception as error:
    logging.debug("Exception: %s: %s", "serialize_block", error)
    f.close()
    return False

f.close()

return True
```

Once a block has been validated, it is persisted to a specific directory.[1] You will want the blocks written into the *data* directory. The function *serialize_block* writes a block into a directory. As you will notice, it is exceptionally simple. Each block is written to a file named

```
"block" + "height of block " + ".dat"
```

This simple naming scheme indexes the block files by height. The genesis block has height zero.

The collection of all of the blocks in the directory is the blockchain.

---

[1]The block filename can be specified as a full or partial path. Otherwise, we can start the *networknode* script from a specific directory, such as the data directory. As you may have noticed, our unit tests were executed from the unit_tests directory and the Helium blocks were thus written into this directory.

Constructing a Simulated Blockchain

The following program code builds a simulated blockchain with a height of 500 blocks. Such a synthetic blockchain can be very useful for a number of use cases:

1. Testing blockchains during the development phase

2. Examining the behavior of the blockchain when its parameters are changed

3. Examining the resiliency and reliability of the blockchain

Copy this code into a Python file called *simulated_blockchain.py* and save it in the *unit_tests* directory. After this, execute it in the Helium virtual environment, with

```
$(virtual) simulated_blockchain.py
```

You should see a blockchain of 500 blocks in the *unit_tests* directory. You can build blockchains of arbitrary height by providing the requisite height parameter to the *make_blocks* function.

A caveat is in order. As transactions occur on the simulated blockchain, the proportion of fragmented transactions with very small outputs will increase. Due to this fragmentation, builds of the blockchain for very high heights will fail. Consolidation of fragmented transaction outputs is typically handled by wallets. You are invited to build a fragmented transaction consolidator for our simulated blockchain. This will provide you with very valuable insight into how blockchains are built and evolve over time.

```
#########################################################
# simulated blockchain constructor
#########################################################
import blk_index as blkindex
import hchaindb
import hmining
import hconfig
import hblockchain
import rcrypt
import tx
import json
import logging
import pdb
```

```python
import os
import secrets
import sys
import time

"""
    log debugging messages to the file debug.log
"""
logging.basicConfig(filename="debug.log",filemode="w",   \
format='client: %(asctime)s:%(levelname)s:%(message)s', level=logging.DEBUG)

def startup():
    """
    start the databases
    """
    # start the Chainstate Database
    ret = hchaindb.open_hchainstate("heliumdb")
    if ret == False: return "error: failed to start Chainstate database"
    else: print("Chainstate Database running")
    # start the LevelDB Database blk_index
    ret = blkindex.open_blk_index("hblk_index")
    if ret == False: return "error: failed to start blk_index"
    else: print("blkindex Database running")

def stop():
    """
    stop the databases
    """
    hchaindb.close_hchainstate()
    blkindex.close_blk_index()

# unspent transaction fragment values [{fragmentid:value}]
unspent_fragments = []

##########################################################
# Make A Synthetic Random Transaction For Testing
# receives a block no and a predicate indicating
# whether the transaction is a coinbase transaction
```

```python
##########################################################
def make_random_transaction(blockno, is_coinbase):

    txn = {}
    txn["version"] =   "1"
    txn["transactionid"] = rcrypt.make_uuid()
    if is_coinbase == True: txn["locktime"] = hconfig.conf["COINBASE_
    LOCKTIME"]
    else: txn["locktime"] = 0

    # the public-private key pair for this transaction
    transaction_keys = rcrypt.make_ecc_keys()

    # previous transaction fragments spent by this transaction
    total_spendable = 0

    ########################
    # Build the vin array
    ########################
    txn["vin"] = []

    # genesis block transactions have no prior inputs.
    # coinbase transactions do not have any inputs
    if (blockno > 0) and (is_coinbase != True):
        max_inputs = secrets.randbelow(hconfig.conf["MAX_INPUTS"])
        if max_inputs == 0: max_inputs = hconfig.conf["MAX_INPUTS"] - 1

        # get some random previous unspent transaction
        # fragments to spend
        ind = 0
        ctr = 0

        while ind < max_inputs:
            # get a random unspent fragment from a previous block
            index = secrets.randbelow(len(unspent_fragments))
            frag_dict = unspent_fragments[index]
            key = [*frag_dict.keys()][0]
            val = [*frag_dict.values()][0]
            if val["blockno"] == blockno:
```

```
            ctr += 1
            if ctr == 10000:
                print("failed to get random unspent fragment")
                return False
            continue

        unspent_fragments.pop(index)

        total_spendable += val["value"]
        tmp = hchaindb.get_transaction(key)
        if tmp == False:
            print("cannot get fragment from chainstate: " + key)

        assert tmp != False
        assert tmp["spent"] == False
        assert tmp["value"] > 0

        # create a random vin element
        key_array = key.split("_")

        signed = rcrypt.sign_message(val["privkey"], val["pubkey"])
        ScriptSig = []
        ScriptSig.append(signed)
        ScriptSig.append(val["pubkey"])

        txn["vin"].append({
                "txid": key_array[0],
                "vout_index": int(key_array[1]),
                "ScriptSig": ScriptSig
            })

        ctr = 0
        ind += 1

####################
# Build Vout list
####################
txn["vout"] = []

# genesis block
```

```
if blockno == 0:
    total_spendable = secrets.randbelow(10_000_000) + 50_000

# we need at least one transaction output for non-coinbase
# transactions
if is_coinbase == True: max_outputs = 1
else:
    max_outputs = secrets.randbelow(hconfig.conf["MAX_OUTPUTS"])
    if max_outputs == 0: max_outputs = 6

ind = 0

while ind < max_outputs:
    tmp = rcrypt.make_SHA256_hash(transaction_keys[1])
    tmp = rcrypt.make_RIPEMD160_hash(tmp)

    ScriptPubKey = []
    ScriptPubKey.append("<DUP>")
    ScriptPubKey.append("<HASH-160>")
    ScriptPubKey.append(tmp)
    ScriptPubKey.append("<EQ-VERIFY>")
    ScriptPubKey.append("<CHECK-SIG>")

    if is_coinbase == True:
        value = hmining.mining_reward(blockno)
    else:
        amt = int(total_spendable/max_outputs)
        value = secrets.randbelow(amt)    # helium cents
        if value == 0:
            pdb.set_trace()
            value = int(amt / 10)
        total_spendable -= value
        assert value > 0
        assert total_spendable >= 0

    txn["vout"].append({
            "value": value,
            "ScriptPubKey": ScriptPubKey
        })
```

```
        # save the transaction fragment
        fragid = txn["transactionid"] + "_" + str(ind)
        fragment = {}
        fragment[fragid] = { "value":value,
                             "privkey":transaction_keys[0],
                             "pubkey":transaction_keys[1],
                             "blockno": blockno
                            }
        unspent_fragments.append(fragment)
        print("added to unspent fragments: " + fragid)

        if total_spendable <= 0: break
        ind += 1

    return txn

############################################################
# Build some random Synthetic Blocks For Testing.
# Makes num_blocks, sequentially linking each
# block to the previous block through the prevblockhash
# attribute.
# Returns an array of synthetic blocks
############################################################

def make_blocks(num_blocks):

    ctr = 0
    blocks = []

    global unspent_fragments
    unspent_fragments.clear()
    hblockchain.blockchain.clear()

    while ctr < num_blocks:
        block = {
                "prevblockhash": "",
                "version": "1",
                "timestamp": int(time.time()),
                "difficulty_bits": 20,
```

```
            "nonce": 0,
            "merkle_root": "",
            "height": ctr,
            "tx": []
        }

    # make a random number of transactions for this block
    # genesis block is ctr == 0
    if ctr == 0: num_transactions = 200
    else:
        num_transactions = secrets.randbelow(50)
        if num_transactions == 0: num_transactions = 40
        num_transactions = 2

    txctr = 0
    while txctr < num_transactions:
        if ctr > 0 and txctr == 0: is_coinbase = True
        else: is_coinbase = False

        trx = make_random_transaction(ctr, is_coinbase)
        assert trx != False
        block["tx"].append(trx)
        txctr += 1

    if ctr > 0:
        block["prevblockhash"] = \
            hblockchain.blockheader_hash(hblockchain.blockchain[ctr - 1])

    ret = hblockchain.merkle_root(block["tx"], True)
    assert ret != False
    block["merkle_root"] = ret

    ret = hblockchain.add_block(block)
    assert ret == True
    blocks.append(block)
    ctr+= 1

return blocks
```

```
###################################################
# make the simulated blockchain
###################################################
startup()
make_blocks(500)
print("finished synthetic blockchain construction")
stop()
```

Directory File Constraints

A running Helium node will accumulate a large number of block files in its *data* directory. This raises the issue of the maximum number of files that can be written into a directory. This constraint depends upon the underlying operating system. In Linux with the *ext4* filesystem, there is no theoretical limit on the number of files that can be written to a directory. We can nevertheless elect to write blocks into a number of sub-directories using a sharding algorithm, such as the following:

```
create n sub-directories of the data directory: 0, 1,2,3,...n-1
for each block:
    compute the SHA-256 hash of the block.
    convert this hash into an integer: hash_num.
    compute the n-modulus of hash_num: hash_mod = hash_num%n
    write the block into directory hash_mod
```

Chainstate Maintenance

In a typical cryptocurrency transaction, an entity spends previous transaction values that have been received and not spent. The *Chainstate database* keeps track of all of the spent and unspent values in the cryptocurrency ecosystem. Each such value is represented as a transaction fragment. At each point in time, the *Chainstate* provides a snapshot of the spent and unspent fragments in the system. You can refer to Chapter 12 to review the theory of the *Chainstate*.

If a Helium node has the blockchain, it can always rebuild the *Chainstate database*. The following algorithm in pseudo-code accomplishes this:

```
for each block:
        for each transaction in the block:
            let transaction id be trnid.
            let ctr = 0.
            for each vout element in the transaction:
                    fragment_id = trnid + "_" + string(ctr)
                    value = vout["value"]
                    hash = RIPEMD160(SHA256(public_key))
                    chainstate[fragment_id] = {"value": value,
                                                "spent": False,
                                                "tx_chain": "",
                                                "pkhash": hash
                                                }
            ctr += 1

        for each vin element in the transaction:
                fragment_id = vin["txid] + "_" + vin["vout_index"]
                chainstate[fragment_id] = {"value": value,
                                            "spent": True,
                                            "tx_chain": some_fragment,
                                            "pkhash": hash
                                            }
```

The following program code rebuilds the *Chainstate database* from scratch from the collection of block files. You will notice that this code leverages the *hchaindb* module and, in particular, uses the *update_transaction* function in this module to build the *Chainstate database*.

In order to exercise this code, copy this code into the file *build_chainstate.py* and save it in the *unit_tests* directory. Then make a simulated blockchain with a height of 500 blocks in the *unit_tests* directory. Finally, delete the *Chainstate* database, *helium_db* in the *unit_tests/helium* sub-directory (*rm -rf heliumdb*), if it exists. The following command will rebuild the Chainstate:

```
$(virtual) python build_chainstate.py
```

```python
################################################################################
# build_chainstate: Builds the chainstate database from the blockchain files.
################################################################################
import hblockchain
import hchaindb
import pickle
import os.path
import pdb

def startup():
    """
    start the chainstate database
    """
    # start the Chainstate Database
    ret = hchaindb.open_hchainstate("heliumdb")
    if ret == False:
        print("error: failed to start Chainstate database")
        return
    else: print("Chainstate Database running")

def stop():
    """
    stop the chainstate database
    """
    hchaindb.close_hchainstate()

def build_chainstate():
    '''
    build the Chainstate database from the blockchain files
    '''
    blockno  = 0
    tx_count = 0

    try:
        while True:
            # test whether the block file exists
            block_file = "block" + "_" + str(blockno) + ".dat"
```

```
        if os.path.isfile(block_file)== False: break

        # load the block file into a dictionary object
        f = open(block_file, 'rb')
        block = pickle.load(f)

        # process the vout and vin arrays for each block transaction
        for trx in block["tx"]:
            ret = hchaindb.transaction_update(trx)
            tx_count += 1
            if ret == False:
                raise(ValueError("failed to rebuild chainstate. block
                no: " + \
                    str(blockno)))

        blockno += 1

    except Exception as err:
        print(str(err))
        return False

    print("transactions processed: " + str(tx_count))
    print("blocks processed: " +  str(blockno))

    return True


# start the chainstate build
print("start build chainstate")
startup()
build_chainstate()
print("chainstate rebuilt")
stop()
```

The *build_chainstate* is available in Appendix 9.

blk_index Maintenance

In Chapter 12, we discussed the *blk_index database*. This is a key-value store that determines the block in which a particular transaction is located. The keys are the transaction IDs and the values are the block heights.

Like the *Chainstate database*, the *blk_index database* can be rebuilt from the blockchain files.

The following pseudo-code rebuilds *blk_index* from the blockchain:

```
for block in blockchain:
    for transaction in block:
        blk_index[transaction[transactionid]] = block["height"]
```

The following module, *build_blk_index*, rebuilds the *blk_index* store. Copy the following code into the *build_blk_index.py* file and save it in the *unit_tests* directory. Delete the *hblk_index* sub-directory, if it exists.

We can now rebuild the *blk_index* database:

```
$(virtual) python build_index.py
```

```
################################################################
# build_blk_index: rebuilds the blk_index database from the blockchain
################################################################
import blk_index
import pickle
import os.path
import pdb

def startup():
    """

    start/create the blk_index database
    """

    # start the blk_index Database
    ret = blk_index.open_blk_index("hblk_index")
    if ret == False:
        print("error: failed to start blk_index database")
        return
```

```python
    else: print("blk_index Database running")
    return True

def stop():
    """
    stop the blk_index database
    """
    blk_index.close_blk_index()

def build_blk_index():
    '''
    build the blk_index database from the blockchain
    '''
    blockno = 0
    tx_count = 0

    try:
        while True:
            # test whether the block file exists
            block_file = "block" + "_" + str(blockno) + ".dat"
            if os.path.isfile(block_file)== False: break

            # load the block file into a dictionary object
            f = open(block_file, 'rb')
            block = pickle.load(f)

            # process the transactions in the block
            for trx in block["tx"]:
                ret = blk_index.put_index(trx["transactionid"], blockno)
                tx_count += 1
                if ret == False:
                    raise(ValueError("failed to rebuild blk_index. block
                    no: " \
                        + str(blockno)))

            blockno += 1

    except Exception as err:
        print(str(err))
```

```
        return False

    print("transactions processed: " + str(tx_count))
    print("blocks processed: " +  str(blockno))

    return True

# start the build_index build
print("start build blk_index")
ret = startup()
if ret == False:
    print("failed to open blk_index")
    os._exit(-1)
build_blk_index()
print("blk_index rebuilt")
stop()
```

Conclusion

In this chapter, we have considered some of important maintenance aspects of Helium. These have included obtaining a blockchain for a new node and synchronizing the blockchain held by a node if a node goes down or if there is a temporary network partition. We have also exposed code to rebuild the *Chainstate* database and the *blk_index* database from the blockchain files.

In the next chapter, we will develop a user wallet for Helium.

## CHAPTER 17

Helium Wallet Construction

Introduction

In this chapter, we will examine the construction of Helium wallets. In particular, we discuss the following topics:

1. What is a wallet

2. The Helium wallet interface

3. Helium wallet program code

4. Helium wallet Pytest code

The Bitcoin reference wallet implementation relies upon access to the complete Bitcoin blockchain. Similarly, any Helium node that has the complete Helium blockchain or has access to this blockchain can create and maintain a wallet.

This chapter creates a basic command-line Helium wallet that implements core functionality. Once we have an implementation of core functionality, we can embellish our wallet with additional capabilities. For example, we can wrap a GUI around our command-line wallet.

What Is a Wallet

A Helium wallet is an object that performs the following functions:

1. Creates and maintains private-public key pairs

2. Records the heliums received by the wallet holder

3. Records the heliums transferred to other entities

© Karan Singh Garewal 2020

K. S. Garewal, *Practical Blockchains and Cryptocurrencies*, https://doi.org/10.1007/978-1-4842-5893-4_17

4. Records the final helium balance of the wallet holder (as of the time of the query)

5. Creates transactions and propagates them on the Helium network

6. Saves wallet data to files

The Helium Wallet Interface

A Helium wallet maintains the following dictionary data structure:

```
wallet_state = {
            "keys": [],              # list of private-public key tuples
            "received": [],          # values received by the wallet holder
            "spent": [],             # values transferred by the wallet holder
            "received_last_block_scanned": 0,
            "spent_last_block_scanned": 0
              }
```

wallet_state describes the state of the the wallet at a given point in time.

wallet["keys"] is a list of the private-public key-pair tuples owned by the wallet holder. The wallet application can create private-public keys.

wallet["received"] is a list of all the values received by the wallet holder. Each element in this list has the structure:

```
{
   "value": value
   "blockno": block_height
   "fragmentid: transaction["transactionid"] + "_" + str(index)
   "public_key" = key_pair[1]
}
```

wallet["spent"] is a list of all the values transferred by the wallet holder. Each element in this list has the same structure as *wallet["received"]*.

wallet["received_last_block_scanned"] is the last block of the blockchain that was scanned when the blockchain was scanned for values received.

wallet["spent_last_block_scanned"] is the last block of the blockchain that was scanned when the blockchain was scanned for values transferred by the wallet holder.

Our Helium wallet contains the following interface functions:

Key Management

```
create_keys() -> "public, private key tuple"
```

This function creates a public-private key pair that can be used in a transaction.

Transaction Record

```
value_received(block_height -> "integer" = 0) ->    "boolean"
```

value_received creates a list of helium values that have been received by the wallet holder. *block_height* is an optional parameter that directs the function to get the values received since and including the block with the given height. This function returns False if the function fails and True otherwise.

value_received creates or updates the *wallet_state["received"]* key value.

The algorithm for this function relies upon the observation that a *vout* element of a transaction that transfers value to the wallet holder contains a public key generated by the wallet holder in the encoded form `RIPEMD-160(SHA-256(public_key))`.

The pseudo-code for this function is

```
let values_received = []

for each block where block["height"] >= block_height:
    for each transaction trx in the block:
        for each vout array element in trx:
            for each public_key, pk, owned by the wallet holder:
                if RIPEMD-160(SHA-256(pk)) == vout_element["ScriptPubKey][3]:
                    values_received.append {
                                        value: vout_element[value]
                                        block: block["height"]
                                        transaction: trx[transactionid]
                                        public_key: pk
                                        }
```

The function *value_spent* creates a list of helium values that have been transferred by the wallet holder to other entities. *block_height* is an optional parameter that directs the function to get the values transferred after the block with the given height (inclusive of this block).

```
value_spent(block_height -> "integer" = 0) ->    "list"
```

This function relies on the observation that each value transferred by the wallet holder to some entity will be identified by a *vin* element in the transaction that contains the wallet holder's public key. The following pseudo-code implements this functionality:

```
let values_spent = []

for each block where block["height"] >= block_height:
    for each transaction trx in the block:
        for each vin list element, vin_element, in trx:
            for each public_key, pk, owned by the wallet holder:
                if pk == vin_element["ScriptPubKey][1]:
                    pointer = vin_element[transactionid] + "_" + \
                              vin_element[vout_index]
                    values_spent.append {
                                            value: vin_element[value],
                                            block: block["height"],
                                            transaction: pointer,
                                            public_key: pk
                    }
```

Persistence

```
save_wallet() → "boolean"
```

The *save_wallet* function saves *wallet_state*. In particular, *wallet_state* is persisted to the disk file *wallet.dat*:

```
load_wallet()   -> "dictionary"
```

This function loads all of the wallet data from w*allet.dat* into the *wallet_state* structure.

Note that because the state of the wallet is persisted, we do not have to interrogate the entire blockchain to update the wallet. We simply need to examine the blocks from parameters r*eceived_last_block_scanned* and *spent_last_block_scanne*d onward.

The Helium Wallet Program Code

Copy the following program code into a file called *wallet.py* and save it in the *wallet* directory:

```
############################################################################
# wallet.rb: a command-line wallet for Helium
############################################################################
import hblockchain
import rcrypt
import pdb
import pickle

# the state of the wallet
wallet_state = {
                "keys": [],          # list of private-public key tuples
                "received": [],      # values received by wallet holder
                "spent": [],         # values transferred by the wallet
                holder
                "received_last_block_scanned": 0,
                "spent_last_block_scanned": 0
               }

def create_keys():
    key_pair = rcrypt.make_ecc_keys()
    wallet_state["keys"].append(key_pair)

def initialize_wallet():
    wallet_state["received"] = []
    wallet_state["spent"] = []
    wallet_state["received_last_block_scanned"] = 0
    wallet_state["spent_last_block_scanned"] = 0

def value_received(blockno:"integer"=0) -> "list" :
    """

    obtains all of the helium values received by the wallet holder by examining
    transactions in the blockchain. Updates the wallet state.
    {
```

```
        value:  <integer>,
        ScriptPubKey: <list>
    }
    """

    hreceived = []
    rvalue = {}

    # get values received from the blockchain
    for block in hblockchain.blockchain:
        for transaction in block["tx"]:
            ctr = -1
            for vout in transaction["vout"]:
                ctr += 1
                for key_pair in wallet_state["keys"]:
                    if rcrypt.make_RIPEMD160_hash(rcrypt.make_SHA256_
                    hash(key_pair[1])) \ == vout["ScriptPubKey"][2]:
                        rvalue["value"] = vout["value"]
                        rvalue["blockno"] = block["height"]
                        rvalue["fragmentid"] = transaction["transactionid"]
                        + "_" + str(ctr)
                        rvalue["public_key"] = key_pair[1]
                        hreceived.append(rvalue)
                        break

    # update the wallet state
    if block["height"] > wallet_state["received_last_block_scanned"]:
        wallet_state["received_last_block_scanned"] = block["height"]

    for received in hreceived:
        wallet_state["received"].append(received)

    return

def value_spent(blockno:"integer"=0):
    """

    obtains all of the helium values transferred by the wallet holder by
    examining
    transactions in the blockchain. Update the wallet state.
```

```
    """
    hspent = []
    tvalue = {}

    # get values spent from  blockchain transactions
    for block in hblockchain.blockchain:
        for transaction in block["tx"]:
            ctr = -1
            for vin in transaction["vin"]:
                ctr += 1
                for key_pair in wallet_state["keys"]:
                    if rcrypt.make_RIPEMD160_hash(rcrypt.make_SHA256_
                    hash(key_pair[1])) \ == vin["ScriptSig"][1]:
                        tvalue["value"] = vin["value"]
                        tvalue["blockno"] = block["height"]
                        tvalue["fragmentid"] = transaction["transactionid"]
                        + "_" +  str(ctr)
                        tvalue["public_key"] = key_pair[1]
                        hspent.append(tvalue)
                        break

    # update the wallet state
    if block["height"] > wallet_state["spent_last_block_scanned"]:
        wallet_state["spent_last_block_scanned"] = block["height"]

    for spent in hspent:
        wallet_state["spent"].append(spent)

    return

def save_wallet() -> "bool":
    """

    saves the wallet state to a file
    """
    try:
        f = open('wallet.dat', 'wb')
        pickle.dump(wallet_state, f)
        f.close()
```

337

```
        return True

    except Exception as error:
        print(str(error))
        return False

def load_wallet() -> "bool":
    """
    loads the wallet state from a file
    """
    try:
        f = open('wallet.dat', 'rb')
        global wallet_state
        wallet_state = pickle.load(f)
        f.close()
        return True

    except Exception as error:
        print(str(error))
        return False
```

wallet.py contains functions that scan the blockchain and constructs a list of all of
the transaction values received as well as the transaction values sent. Since the wallet
state maintains the markers for the last block that has been scanned when these lists
are constructed (*received_last_block_scanned* and *spent_last_block_scanned*), we do not
need to re-scan the portion of the blockchain that is scanned to create these lists as long
as the wallet only uses private-public keys that are created using the wallet's *create_keys*
function.

The *initialize_wallet* function can be called in the event that we decide to scan the
blockchain again from the genesis block.

I will leave it as an exercise for the reader to write the code for a wallet function
that receives a Helium address and creates a transaction that is propagated on the
Helium network (refer to Chapter 9 for the algorithm that creates and transforms
Helium addresses). Another piece of functionality that can be added to this wallet is to
automatically consolidate small input values that are owned by the wallet holder into a
larger value.

Helium Wallet Pytest Code

The following program code implements Pytests for our Helium wallet. These tests are integration tests that use a simulated blockchain. Copy this code into a file called *test_wallet.py* and save the file in the *unit_tests* directory. As usual, we can run these tests with

```
(virtual) $ pytest test_wallet.rb
```

Execution of these tests should indicate 13 passing tests:

```
######################################################
# test_wallet.rb
######################################################
import hchaindb
import hmining
import hconfig
import hblockchain
import rcrypt
import tx
import wallet
import json
import logging
import os
import pdb
import pytest
import secrets
import sys
import time

"""
    log debugging messages to the file debug.log
"""
logging.basicConfig(filename="debug.log",filemode="w",  \
format='client: %(asctime)s:%(levelname)s:%(message)s', level=logging.DEBUG)

def setup_module():
    """
```

```
    start the databases
    """

    # start the Chainstate Database
    ret = hchaindb.open_hchainstate("heliumdb")
    if ret == False:
        print("error: failed to start Chainstate database")
        return
    else: print("Chainstate Database running")

    # make a simulated blockchain with height 5
    make_blocks(5)

def teardown_module():
    """

    stop the databases
    """

    hchaindb.close_hchainstate()

# unspent transaction fragment values [{fragmentid:value}]
unspent_fragments = []

keys = []

#########################################################
# Make A Synthetic Random Transaction For Testing
# receives a block no and a predicate indicating
# whether the transaction is a coinbase transaction
#########################################################
def make_random_transaction(blockno, is_coinbase):

    txn = {}
    txn["version"] =   "1"
    txn["transactionid"] = rcrypt.make_uuid()

    if is_coinbase == True: txn["locktime"] = hconfig.conf["COINBASE_
    LOCKTIME"]
    else: txn["locktime"] = 0

    # the public-private key pair for this transaction
```

```
transaction_keys = rcrypt.make_ecc_keys()
global keys
keys.append(transaction_keys)

# previous transaction fragments spent by this transaction
total_spendable = 0

#######################
# Build the vin array
#######################
txn["vin"] = []

# genesis block transactions have no prior inputs.
# coinbase transactions do not have any inputs
if (blockno > 0) and (is_coinbase != True):
    max_inputs = secrets.randbelow(hconfig.conf["MAX_INPUTS"])
    if max_inputs == 0: max_inputs = hconfig.conf["MAX_INPUTS"] - 1

    # get some random previous unspent transaction
    # fragments to spend
    ind = 0
    ctr = 0

    while ind < max_inputs:
        # get a random unspent fragment from a previous block
        index = secrets.randbelow(len(unspent_fragments))
        frag_dict = unspent_fragments[index]

        if frag_dict["blockno"] == blockno or frag_dict["value"] < 10:
            ctr += 1
            if ctr == 10000:
                print("failed to get random unspent fragment")
                return False
            continue

        key = frag_dict["key"]
        unspent_fragments.pop(index)
        assert unspent_fragments.count(frag_dict) == 0
```

```
            total_spendable += frag_dict["value"]
            tmp = hchaindb.get_transaction(key)
            if tmp == False:
                print("cannot get fragment from chainstate: " + key)

            assert tmp["spent"] == False
            assert tmp["value"] > 0

            # create a random vin element
            key_array = key.split("_")

            signed = rcrypt.sign_message(frag_dict["privkey"], frag_
            dict["pubkey"])
            ScriptSig = []
            ScriptSig.append(signed)
            ScriptSig.append(frag_dict["pubkey"])

            txn["vin"].append({
                    "txid": key_array[0],
                    "vout_index": int(key_array[1]),
                    "ScriptSig": ScriptSig
                })

            ctr = 0
            ind += 1

####################
# Build Vout list
####################
txn["vout"] = []

# genesis block
if blockno == 0:
    total_spendable = secrets.randbelow(10000000) + 50000

# we need at least one transaction output for non-coinbase
# transactions
if is_coinbase == True: max_outputs = 1
else:
```

```
        max_outputs = secrets.randbelow(hconfig.conf["MAX_OUTPUTS"])
        if max_outputs == 0: max_outputs = hconfig.conf["MAX_OUTPUTS"]

ind = 0

while ind < max_outputs:
    tmp = rcrypt.make_SHA256_hash(transaction_keys[1])
    tmp = rcrypt.make_RIPEMD160_hash(tmp)

    ScriptPubKey = []
    ScriptPubKey.append("<DUP>")
    ScriptPubKey.append("<HASH-160>")
    ScriptPubKey.append(tmp)
    ScriptPubKey.append("<EQ-VERIFY>")
    ScriptPubKey.append("<CHECK-SIG>")

    if is_coinbase == True:
        value = hmining.mining_reward(blockno)
    else:
        amt = int(total_spendable/max_outputs)
        if amt == 0: break
        value = secrets.randbelow(amt)    # helium cents
        if value == 0: value = int(amt)
        total_spendable -= value
        assert value > 0
        assert total_spendable >= 0

    txn["vout"].append({
            "value": value,
            "ScriptPubKey": ScriptPubKey
        })

    # save the transaction fragment
    fragid = txn["transactionid"] + "_" + str(ind)
    fragment = {
                "key": fragid,
                "value":value,
                "privkey":transaction_keys[0],
```

```
                        "pubkey":transaction_keys[1],
                        "blockno": blockno
                }
        unspent_fragments.append(fragment)
        print("added to unspent fragments: " + fragment["key"])

        if total_spendable <= 50: break
        ind += 1

    return txn

############################################################
# Build some random Synthetic Blocks For Testing.
# Makes num_blocks, sequentially linking each
# block to the previous block through the prevblockhash
# attribute.
# Returns an array of synthetic blocks
############################################################

def make_blocks(num_blocks):

    ctr = 0
    total_tx = 0
    blocks = []

    global unspent_fragments
    unspent_fragments.clear()
    hblockchain.blockchain.clear()

    while ctr < num_blocks:
        block = {}
        block["prevblockhash"] = ""
        block["version"] = hconfig.conf["VERSION_NO"]
        block["timestamp"] = int(time.time())
        block["difficulty_bits"] = hconfig.conf["DIFFICULTY_BITS"]
        block["nonce"] = hconfig.conf["NONCE"]
        block["merkle_root"] = ""
        block["height"] = ctr
        block["tx"] = []
```

```
        # make a random number of transactions for this block
        # genesis block is ctr == 0
        if ctr == 0: num_transactions = 200
        else:
            num_transactions = secrets.randbelow(50)
            if num_transactions <= 1: num_transactions = 25

        txctr = 0
        while txctr < num_transactions:
            if ctr > 0 and txctr == 0: coinbase_trans = True
            else: coinbase_trans = False

            trx = make_random_transaction(ctr, coinbase_trans)
            assert trx != False
            block["tx"].append(trx)
            total_tx += 1
            txctr += 1

        if ctr > 0:
            block["prevblockhash"] = \
                hblockchain.blockheader_hash(hblockchain.blockchain[ctr - 1])

        ret = hblockchain.merkle_root(block["tx"], True)
        assert ret != False
        block["merkle_root"] = ret

        ret = hblockchain.add_block(block)
        assert ret == True
        blocks.append(block)

        ctr+= 1

    print("blockchain height: " + str(blocks[-1]["height"]))
    print("total transactions count: " + str(total_tx))

    return blocks

def test_no_values_received():
    """

    get all of the transaction values received by the wallet-holder
```

345

```
    when the holder has no keys.
    """

    wallet.wallet_state["keys"] = []
    wallet.value_received(0)
    assert wallet.wallet_state["received"] == []

@pytest.mark.parametrize("index", [
    (0),
    (1),
    (11),
    (55),
])
def test_values_received(index):
    """

    test that each value received by the wallet owner pertains to a
    public key owned by the wallet owner.
    Note: At least 55 private-public keys must have been generated.
    """

    wallet.initialize_wallet()
    wallet.wallet_state["keys"] = []
    my_key_pairs = keys[:]

    for _ in range(index):
        key_index = secrets.randbelow(len(my_key_pairs))
        wallet.wallet_state["keys"].append(keys[key_index])

    # remove any duplicates
    wallet.wallet_state["keys"] = list(set(wallet.wallet_state["keys"]))

    my_public_keys = []
    for key_pair in wallet.wallet_state["keys"]:
        my_public_keys.append(key_pair[1])

    wallet.value_received(0)
    for received in wallet.wallet_state["received"]:
        assert received["public_key"] in my_public_keys

def test_one_received():
```

```
    """
    test that for a given public key owned by the wallet-holder, at least one
    transaction fragment exists in the wallet.
    """

    wallet.initialize_wallet()
    wallet.wallet_state["keys"] = []

    key_index = secrets.randbelow(len(keys))
    wallet.wallet_state["keys"].append(keys[key_index])

    ctr = 0

    wallet.value_received(0)

    for received in wallet.wallet_state["received"]:
        if received["public_key"] == wallet.wallet_state["keys"][0][1]:
        ctr  += 1
    assert ctr >= 1

@pytest.mark.parametrize("index", [
    (0),
    (1),
    (13),
    (49),
    (55)
])
def test_values_spent(index):
    """
    test that values spent pertain to public keys owned by the wallet owner.
    Note: At least 55 private-public keys must have been generated.
    """

    wallet.initialize_wallet()
    wallet.wallet_state["keys"] = []
    my_key_pairs = keys[:]

    for _ in range(index):
        key_index = secrets.randbelow(len(my_key_pairs))
        wallet.wallet_state["keys"].append(keys[key_index])
```

```python
    # remove any duplicates
    wallet.wallet_state["keys"] = list(set(wallet.wallet_state["keys"]))

    my_public_keys = []
    for key_pair in wallet.wallet_state["keys"]:
        my_public_keys.append(key_pair[1])

    wallet.value_spent(0)
    for spent in wallet.wallet_state["spent"]:
        assert spent["public_key"] in my_public_keys

def test_received_and_spent():
    """

    test that if a transaction fragment is spent then it has also been
    received by the wallet owner.
    """

    wallet.initialize_wallet()
    wallet.wallet_state["keys"] = []

    key_index = secrets.randbelow(len(keys))
    wallet.wallet_state["keys"].append(keys[key_index])

    wallet.value_received(0)
    wallet.value_spent(0)
    assert len(wallet.wallet_state["received"]) >= 1

    for spent in wallet.wallet_state["spent"]:
        ctr = 0
        assert spent["public_key"] == wallet.wallet_state[keys][0][1]
        ptr = spent["fragmentid"]
        for received in wallet.wallet_state["received"]:
            if received["fragmentid"] == ptr: ctr += 1
        assert ctr == 1
        ctr = 0

def test_wallet_persistence():
    """

    test the persistence of a wallet to a file.
    """
```

```
wallet.initialize_wallet()
wallet.wallet_state["keys"] = []
my_key_pairs = keys[:]

for _ in range(25):
    key_index = secrets.randbelow(len(my_key_pairs))
    wallet.wallet_state["keys"].append(keys[key_index])

# remove any duplicates
wallet.wallet_state["keys"] = list(set(wallet.wallet_state["keys"]))
wallet.value_spent(0)
wallet.value_received(0)

wallet_str = json.dumps(wallet.wallet_state)
wallet_copy = json.loads(wallet_str)

assert wallet.save_wallet() == True
assert wallet.load_wallet() == True

assert wallet.wallet_state["received"] == wallet_copy["received"]
assert wallet.wallet_state["spent"] == wallet_copy["spent"]
assert wallet.wallet_state["received_last_block_scanned"] == \
      wallet_copy["received_last_block_scanned"]
assert wallet.wallet_state["spent_last_block_scanned"] == \
      wallet_copy["spent_last_block_scanned"]

max = len(wallet_copy["keys"])
ctr = 0

for ctr in range(max):
    assert wallet.wallet_state["keys"][ctr][0] == wallet_copy["keys"]
    [ctr][0]
    assert wallet.wallet_state["keys"][ctr][1] == wallet_copy["keys"]
    [ctr][1]
```

Conclusion

In this chapter, we have constructed a basic command-line wallet from a blockchain. This wallet implements all of the core functionality that is required in a wallet. The wallet can be embellished by encrypting the disk file that persists the state of the wallet, wrapping the wallet in a GUI interface as well as providing other convenience features.

In the next and final chapter, we will return to the matter of creating a test network for the Helium network.

## CHAPTER 18

The Helium Testnet

In this short concluding chapter, we will briefly discuss two matters that pertain to testing a Helium P2P network:

1. The implementation of a Helium test network on the Internet

2. Helium faucets

Implementing a Helium Testnet

In Chapter 15, we implemented a Helium peer-to-peer network on the localhost network. In this implementation, network nodes listen on loopback addresses (127.0.0.x). The relevant portion of the code in the file *networknode.py* that enables this is[1]

```
##########################################################
# start the network interface for the server node on
# the localhost loop: 127.0.0.19:8081
##########################################################
if __name__ == "__main__":
    app.listen(address="127.0.0.19", port="8081")
    logging.debug('server node is running')
    print("network node starting at 127.0.0.19:8081")
```

We can easily change this implementation so that nodes listen on routable Internet addresses. Each network node edits its *networknode.py* file by replacing the address parameter of the *app.listen* function with a unique routable IP address that it owns.

This simple change enables us to set up a Helium testnet on the Internet that listens on some designated common port.

---

[1]Directory servers also have a similar code fragment.

© Karan Singh Garewal 2020

K. S. Garewal, *Practical Blockchains and Cryptocurrencies*, https://doi.org/10.1007/978-1-4842-5893-4_18

Implementing a Helium Faucet

Once we have a Helium testnet on the Internet, we need to provide network nodes with Helium cryptocurrency so that they can create and propagate test transactions on the network. This can be accomplished by creating a Helium faucet. A faucet is a network node that

1. Creates a private-public key pair

2. Creates and propagates a transaction that transfers a fixed amount of Helium coins to the owner of the key pair that has been created

A faucet works as follows. A requestor asks the faucet to give it some free Helium coins through a JSON remote procedure call to the faucet JSON-RPC server. The faucet generates a private-public key tuple and sends it back to the requestor. The faucet then creates a coinbase type transaction whereby a fixed number of Helium coins are transferred to the requestor, using the key pair that has been provided to the requestor. Finally, the faucet propagates this transaction on the Helium network. Eventually, this transaction will be added to a block and the block will be mined. Upon being mined, the requestor has spendable helium coins that were created by the faucet.

We can also implement a faucet as a web service. A visitor who comes to the faucet website is provided with a private-public key tuple. The website then invokes the JSON-RPC faucet server, which creates and propagates a Helium transaction that uses the key pair that has been provided to the website visitor.

Conclusion

If you are reading this, then congratulations. You have reached the terminal point of this book. We have completed a long journey from the cryptographic foundations of blockchains and cryptocurrencies to the construction of transactions, blockchains, mining nodes, and cryptocurrency networks. Along the way, we have learned the key algorithms that operate in this space. You should now have the facility to confidently architect and program blockchain and cryptocurrency applications in the language of your choice.

In the *metaphysiks* of the Sikh race, the material world is characterized as the terrifying world ocean. And each time the ferryman ferries someone safely over to the distant shore, a quantum of goodness is added to the equation. With your hard-acquired knowledge, you too are a master of the ferry and the power of goodness is with you.[2] Thank you for your kind consideration. Good hunting.

Karan Singh

Attorney-at-law

---

[2]See Dr. Vandana Shiva (nuclear physicist) on Bill Gates and Biopiracy (speech at UNRISD, Geneva) (www.youtube.com/watch?v=Ek2M-obq9LE&t=364s), Dr. Vandana Shiva on Democracy Now (www.youtube.com/watch?v=GwxOxQ1AOEg), and Bill Gates and the War on Cash: https:// sputniknews.com/analysis/202005071079213583-bill-gates-and-his-war-against-cash- are-a-threat-to-our-liberty-economist-warns/

APPENDIX 1

Environment

A Python virtual environment is an isolated environment for the development of a Python project. This virtual environment contains the Python interpreter that is used for the project, the packages and dependencies of the project, as well as all of the project's source code. In this appendix, I will show you how to set up a virtual environment for the Helium cryptocurrency project. The instructions that follow are for a Linux host environment. If you are using a Mac or Windows machine, the instructions are analogous and available on the Internet.

My Development Environment

This is my development environment for the Helium project. The host environment is Linux Mint release 19.3 Tricia, a 64-bit distribution running on a Lenovo ThinkPad. Mint is a distribution forked from Ubuntu. The windows manager is a Gnome version 2 fork, called Mate by the Linux Mint development team. Mint has a reputation for protecting privacy rights and espousing progressive politics.[1] I have created 24 virtual desktops on the laptop with Mate.[2] Typically, my IDE will be running in one virtual desktop. In another desktop, a terminal will be open with the Python interpreter ready to run the application. A third virtual desktop will have Git available at a terminal prompt. Another desktop will have a database client GUI open. A virtual desktop will have the Firefox

---

[1]I would encourage you to use Linux in preference to Microsoft Windows and in this regard would refer you to Dr. Vandana Shiva's critique of Bill Gates and his agenda. Dr. Shiva is a nuclear physicist and an eco-feminist. I would also refer you to Dr. Richard Stallman, inventor of the open source software movement and the inventor/maintainer of GNU C++. The C++ compiler is probably the most complex piece of software ever devised and programmed. Both authors are accessible on the Internet. I have not used Microsoft Windows in any form since 2002. This book was written using LibreOffice v. 6.07.

[2]The Mate GUI makes it very easy to create this virtual desktop environment. Each desktop can have multiple windows open, and each desktop can be running multiple applications.

© Karan Singh Garewal 2020
K. S. Garewal, *Practical Blockchains and Cryptocurrencies*, https://doi.org/10.1007/978-1-4842-5893-4

browser pointing to the *localhost* address of the Helium application. LibreOffice will be open on another desktop for editing this book. A desktop may have VLC paused on a movie I am watching. A ribbon at the bottom of the screen displays icons for all of these virtual desktops. I can switch between these desktops by simply clicking one of these icons. This is the big picture. It is a very efficient development environment.

I periodically deploy Helium to a Linux Ubuntu server staging environment. Deployment is easy since the development and staging environments are closely related Linux distributions. My IDE is Visual Code and the version control system is Git. I use *rsync* to move files to the staging server. The staging server runs on a VPS (virtual private server). My laptop typically has a terminal with an active SSH (secure shell) connection to the VPS root shell.

This development environment is not very fancy, but it is dead simple and it works well.

Preliminary Steps

Check whether the *pip3* tool is installed. *pip3* (the Python Index Package Tool) is used to install, update, and remove Python packages and libraries.[3]

In your Linux operating system, you can drop into a command shell by opening a terminal window. This permits us to type in shell commands. In the exposition that follows, I shall denote a system command shell prompt with a $.

Open a terminal and do

```
$ which pip3            # returns the path where pip3 is installed
or:
$ pip3  --version
```

If pip3 is not installed, install it on Debian-derived Linux distributions, such as Mint and Ubuntu, as follows:

```
$ sudo apt-get update
$ sudo apt-get -y install python3-pip
```

---

[3]As this book is being written, we are in a transition period where Python 2.x versions are being deprecated, hence the usage of pip3. In due course of time, the identifier pip3 will be supplanted by pip.

This will install the latest version of Python. Test whether Python3 is installed:

```
$ which python3
or:
$ python3 -V
```

The first command returns the path where a Python version 3 is installed. The second command will display the version of Python that is installed.

We need a Python version that is 3.8 or greater. If Python is not present or we do not have a conforming version, we must install a valid Python version. We can install a specific version from the *deadsnakes* repository. To install version 3.8 of Python on your Ubuntu-derived Linux distribution, do

```
$ sudo apt install software-properties-common
$ sudo add-apt-repository ppa:deadsnakes/ppa
$ sudo apt-get update
$ sudo apt install python3.8
```

When executed from the terminal command line, this sequence of commands will install Python version 3.8 on your Ubuntu-derived distribution.

Create a Virtual Environment for the Project

virtualenv is a tool that creates isolated Python environments. *virtualenv* creates a directory tree and a virtual environment for our project. Install *virtualenv* in your host environment:

```
$ pip3 install virtualenv
```

Next, test that *virtualenv* has been successfully installed:

```
$ virtualenv --version
```

Now that we have installed *virtualenv*, we create a project directory called *helium* and create a virtual Python environment inside this directory:

```
$ mkdir helium
$ cd helium
$ virtualenv -p /usr/bin/python3.8  virtual
```

This sequence of commands will create a directory *helium* under your present directory. It will then create a *virtual* sub-directory inside the *helium* directory and install Python version 3.8 inside this virtual directory.

Note   You must have already installed Python version 3.8 into the host environment, as previously indicated.

The *virtual* folder will contain the Python interpreter, the *pip* library, as well as other modules and dependencies. *pip3* will be used to install additional modules and packages inside the virtual environment. The name of the virtual environment (in this case *helium*) can be anything.

The *preceding virtualenv* command installs Python version 3.8 in the directory *virtual/bin*.

Now that we have created a virtual environment for the Helium project, we need to activate the environment in order to work in it. Drop down into the Helium directory and then enter

```
$ source virtual/bin/activate
```

The command-line prompt will prepend the string (*virtual*) to itself to indicate that we are in an active virtual environment. We can now install packages inside the environment with pip3, as usual, for example:

```
# do not install
(virtual) $ pip install requests
```

This command will install the *requests* module into the Helium virtual environment. After we have finished working in the virtual environment, we deactivate it:

```
$(virtual) deactivate
```

We can freeze the virtual environment by entering the following command inside the root directory of the virtual environment (*helium*) as follows:

```
$(virtual) pip freeze > requirements.txt
```

This command will create a *requirements.txt* text file, which contains a simple list of all the installed modules in the current environment and their respective versions.

We can view the list of modules installed inside the virtual environment with

```
$(virtual) pip3 list
```

We can install the package versions listed in *requirements.txt* as follows:

```
$ (virtual) pip3 install -r requirements.txt
```

APPENDIX 2

Installing LevelDB for Helium

LevelDB is a key-value store implemented as a library. It was primarily developed by Sanjay Ghemawat during his tenure at Google.[1] LevelDB is a lightweight, high-performance keystore. Its outstanding performance is primarily due to the simplicity of its construction and its limited design objectives.[2] LevelDB is single threaded and only supports string keys and string values. Keys and values can be arbitrarily long.

LevelDB has three basic operations:

```
Put(key,value)
Get(key)
Delete(key)
```

LevelDB does not have any indexes; in lieu thereof, the keys in the store are maintained in a sorted lexicographic order.

In this appendix, we will install LevelDB and Plyvel. Plyvel is a Python interface module for the LevelDB library.

---

[1]https://github.com/google/leveldb, last accessed on January 20, 2020

[2]The following article discusses the performance of LevelDB: http://highscalability.com/blog/2011/8/10/leveldb-fast-and-lightweight-keyvalue-database-from-the-auth.html, last accessed on January 20, 2020

361

LevelDB Installation

Install the *libsnappy* compression development library:[3]

```
$ sudo apt-get install libsnappy-dev
```

Install git:

```
$ sudo apt-get install git-core
```

If git has been successfully installed, then the following command will display help on the terminal screen:

```
$ git
```

Change to the */tmp* directory (or any other suitable directory) and clone LevelDB from its Github directory:[4]

```
$ git clone https://github.com/google/leveldb
```

We are now ready to compile the LevelDB source code. LevelDB uses cmake to compile the source and produce binaries. Install cmake:

```
$ sudo apt-get install cmake
```

Change to the *tmp/leveldb* directory and compile the source code:

```
$ cd leveldb
$ cmake -DCMAKE_BUILD_TYPE=Release .
$ cmake --build .
```

Install the LevelDB binary and include files:

```
$ cp --preserve=links libleveldb.* /usr/local/lib
$ cp -r include/leveldb /usr/local/include/
$ ldconfig
```

---

[3]These instructions are for a Debian-derived distribution, such as Ubuntu and Mint. If you are installing for Windows or Mac, refer to documentation on the Internet. The $ symbol represents the operating system terminal prompt.

[4]The URL for the git LevelDB git repository is https://github.com/google/leveldb

Build and Install Plyvel

The package Plyvel is a Python interface for the LevelDB library. Traverse to the root of your Helium virtual environment and activate it. Now we can install Plyvel:

```
$(virtual) pip install plyvel
```

We next test that plyvel has been successfully installed. Start the Python interpreter in the virtual environment:

```
$(virtual) python
```

At the interpreter command-line prompt, enter

```
>>> import plyvel
```

If the import generates an error, LevelDB has not been properly installed. It's most likely that plyvel cannot find the levelDB library. This is a path issue.

You can also test the plyvel installation with

```
$(virtual) python -c 'import plyvel'
```

This command will not generate any output if the LevelDB and Plyvel installation were both successful.

A Plyvel Primer

Plyvel is remarkably easy to use. The following commands in the Python interpreter shell demonstrate its usage:

```
$(virtual) python
>>> import plyvel

# create a key-value store
>>> db = plyvel.DB('/tmp/testdb/', create_if_missing=True)

# put a few keys and values as byte strings
>>> db.put(b"farm", b"green acres")
>>> db.put(b"dog", b"wolf")

# get a key value
```

```
>>> db.get(b"farm")
>>> "green acres"
```

```
# try to retrieve a non-existent key
>> db.get(b"hens")
>> None
```

```
# delete a key
>>> db.delete(b"dog")
```

```
# close the database
>>> db.close()
```

```
# delete the database
>>> delete db
```

Iterating over the LevelDB Keyspace

Since LevelDB is a sorted keyspace, we can iterate over its keys:

```
>>> for key, value in db:
...       print(key)
...       print(value)
```

```
>>> b"farm"
>>> b"wolf"
...
```

We can also iterate over restricted key ranges:

```
>>> for key, value in db.iterator(start=b'key 6', stop=b'key 45'):
...       print(key)
```

By default, Plyvel will start the iterator at the key *b'key 6'* and stop at the key which is before *b'key 45'*. This matches default Python behavior.

We can omit either the first argument or the last argument of db.iterator in order to iterate from the first key or iterate to the last key.

To iterate in reverse order, simply reverse the start and stop keys; do

```
>>> for key, value in db.iterator(start=b'key 45', stop=b'key '6'):
...     print(key)
```

We can also iterate over keys which have a certain prefix:

```
>>> for key, value in db.iterator(prefix=b'fa'):
...     print(key)
```

In this example, we iterate over keys which have the prefix bytes 'fa'.
We can create iterators and use them as follows:

```
>>> iter = db.iterator()
...
>>> iter.close()
```

APPENDIX 3

Unit Tests with Pytest

Unit tests validate functions and methods. In particular, they verify that functions and methods return correct values for given inputs. We should always strive to provide maximal unit test coverage for our code. This will provide us with assurances of code correctness as well as quality.

For the Helium cryptocurrency application, we will use the *pytest* module for writing unit tests. *pytest* is the de facto Python standard for implementing unit tests.

Install pytest in your Helium virtual environment as follows:

```
$(virtual) pip install pytest
```

Running Unit Tests with Pytest

To run unit tests, traverse to a directory containing the tests, and execute pytest from the command line:

```
$(virtual) pytest test_rcrypt.py
```

This command will cause pytest to run all of the unit tests in the *test_rcrypt.py* file. The command-line option *-v* causes pytest to generate verbose output:

```
$(virtual) pytest test_rcrypt.py -v
```

If we are in a directory containing pytest files, we can run all of the unit tests in all of the pytest files in this directory with

```
$(virtual) pytest
or
$(virtual) pytest -v
```

© Karan Singh Garewal 2020

K. S. Garewal, *Practical Blockchains and Cryptocurrencies*, https://doi.org/10.1007/978-1-4842-5893-4

In general, we can run all of the tests in a directory with

```
$(virtual) pytest path/to/directory/ -v
```

A pytest file is a Python file that contains pytest functions. pytest file names must be in either of these two forms: *test_*.py* or **_test.py* (* is a wildcard, meaning any sequence of alphanumeric characters or underscores). For example, *test_trig.py* and *trig_test.py* are valid names for a pytest file.

A test function in a pytest file must begin with the prefix *test_* or end with the suffix *_test*. For example, *test_arithmetic* and *arithmetic_test* are valid names for pytest functions.[1]

If we are debugging a single function or method, it is frequently very useful to only run a single test in a pytest file:

```
$(virtual) pytest path/to/test_file.py -k test_adder
```

This command executes the unit test called *test_adder* in the pytest file *test_file.py*. The parameter to *k* can be a sub-string instead of the whole name of a test function, for example:

```
$(virtual) pytest path/to/test_file.py -k arithmetic -v
```

This command will execute all of the pytest functions in the file *test_file.py;* those names contain the sub-string *arithmetic*.

Writing Pytest Tests

pytest uses the *assert* function to test whether a unit test passes or fails. *assert()* tests an expression and returns True or False. The following code shows the structure of a simple *pytest* unit test module with a single test in it:

```
# file test_functions.py
import pytest

def test_capital_case():
        assert "python".upper == "PYTHON"
```

---

[1]A pytest file can contain functions which are not pytest functions, but these functions cannot be directly executed by pytest. However, a pytest function can invoke such functions.

Since the expression *"python".upper() == "PYTHON"* is True, the assert function returns True and the test passes. Similarly, the following test fails if x does not equal 0:

```python
import pytest
import my_module

def test_arithmetic():
    x = my_module.arithmetic_func(1)
    assert x == 0
```

Note that a test function does not have any arguments (with the exception of fixtures and pytest parametrized tests, which are discussed subsequently).

Floating-Point Numbers and Tests for Approximation

In cases where we are handling floating-point numbers, it is typically necessary to test that a floating-point number is within a certain tolerance interval of another number. In *pytest*, we test for such an approximation as follows:

```python
# my_module.py
def div(x, y):
    return x/y

# test_sample.py module
import pytest
import my_module

def test_approx():
    x = my_module.div(22,7)
    assert x == pytest.approx(3.3, 1.5)
```

This tests whether the number x returned by the *div* function in *my_module* is within 1.5 of the reference number 3.3. The tolerance interval is 1.5.

Testing Exceptions

The following *pytest* code demonstrates how to test that an exception has been raised by a function:

```
# my_module.py
def div(x, y ):
    return x/y

# test_my_module.py
import pytest
import my_module

def test_division():
    with pytest.raises(Exception):
            z = my_module.div(5, 0)
```

In this example, we are using the *test_division* function in the pytest file *test_my_module.py* to test the function *div* in *my_module*. The function *div(x, y)* throws an exception if the divisor is zero. This exception is trapped in the *with* block of *test_division*. Since the test correctly traps the exception, the test passes.

Setup and Teardown

If a *pytest* module contains any of the following functions: *setup_module()* or *teardown_module(),* then the *setup_module* function will be executed before any of the tests in the pytest module are run. Similarly, after all of the tests in the pytest module have been executed, the *teardown_module* function, if present, will be executed. The *setup_module* function allows us to perform initialization tasks before any of the tests are executed. Similarly, the *teardown_module* function performs cleanup tasks after the tests have run.

Here is an example:

```
# my_module.py
def init():
    # some initialization tasks
    database.start()
```

```
def finish():
    # perform cleanup
    database.stop()

# test_sample.py
import pytest
import my_module

# setup_module runs once in the test module
# before all tests

def setup_module():
    my_module.init()

# teardown_module runs once in the test module
# after all tests have been executed

def teardown_module():
    my_module.finish()

def test_func():
    assert 1 == True
```

Pytest Fixtures

A fixture is a function which returns a predetermined value. Pytest fixtures are created by prefixing the fixture function with the decorator *@pytest.fixture*. A test function can use a fixture by specifying the fixture name as a function argument (in the test function).

Here is an example of using fixtures:

```
# test_sample.py
import pytest

# creates a fixture called db_connection
# simulates a valid connection to a database
@pytest.fixture
def db_connection():
    return True
```

```
def test_is_connected(db_connection):
    response = db_connection
    assert response == True
```

Fixtures allow us to replace functions in our code with fixtures that return predetermined values.

Parametrized Test Functions

Parametrized test functions are one of the best features of pytest. This feature lets us test various scenarios easily. In other words, we can test the correctness of a large number of function inputs with ease.

The following example will demonstrate how this feature works:

```
# my_module.py

class Account:

    def __init__(self, balance):
        self.balance = balance

    def deposit(self, amount):
        self.balance += amount

    def spend(self, amount):
        self.balance -= amount
```

```
# test_sample.py
import pytest
import my_module

@pytest.mark.parametrize("deposit, spent, balance", [
    (30, 10, 20),
    (20, 2, 18),
    (95, 25, 70),
    (0, 0, 0)
])
```

```
def test_transactions(deposit, spent, balance):

    my_account = my_module.Account(0)
    #use a parametrized deposit
    my_account.deposit(deposit)

    # use a parametrized spend value
    my_account.spend(spent)

    # test the actual account balance against the
    # parametrized balance
    assert my_account.balance == balance
```

The decorator function is @pytest.mark.parametrize("deposit, spent, balance", [...]).

This parametrization has three variables: *deposit*, *spent*, and *balance*. Each tuple *(deposit, spent, balance)* is a particular scenario. In our case, there are four scenarios.

The test function *test_transactions(deposit, spent, balance)* uses the parameter values for each of the scenarios specified in the decorator function. This function uses the deposit and spent values and then compares the actual balance in the account object with the parametrized balance value.

Note that Python syntax requires that the parametrized test function *test_transactions(deposit, spent, balance)* follow immediately after the decorator.

Mocks

A mock replaces an attribute with a synthetic attribute that we have created or pretends that the attribute does not exist. The mocked attribute can be a function, method, dictionary value, an environmental variable, or any other top-level attribute in a module. Mocking permits us to substitute a mocked attribute for the real attribute. In pytest, mocking is accomplished with the *monkeypatch()* function.

Stubbing or mocking the return value of a function or method is a major use case of mocking. Suppose that we want to mock the function *employee_record(id)* in the *employee* module. Suppose further that this function has an id parameter and returns an employee name, then we can mock this function as follows:

```
monkeypatch.setattr(employee, "employee_record", lambda x: "alice smith")
```

The first *monkeypatch* function parameter is the module that contains the function that is to be mocked; the second parameter is the name of the function that is being mocked (as a string.)

Here we have mocked the *employee_record* function in the employee module to return "alice smith".

The lambda function takes a number of symbolic parameters that is equal to the number of parameters in the mocked function. Since *employee_record* has one parameter, the lambda has one symbolic parameter x.

We can also write this function mock more concisely as

```
monkeypatch.setattr("employee.employee_record", lambda x: "alice smith")
```

Take a look at the following more complex mocked function implementation:

```
 monkeypatch.setattr(block, "make_hash", lambda x, y: fake.hash(5,6))
```

This mocks the function *make_hash* in the *block* module. *make_hash* has two parameters; therefore, lambda has two symbolic parameters. The mock function returns the value produced by the function call *fake.hash(5,6)*, where *hash* is a function in the *fake* module.

Suppose that we want to mock delete a top-level attribute in a module. The syntax for effecting this is

```
monkeypatch.delattr(module_name, "attribute")
```

For example,

```
monkeypatch.delattr(employee, "employee_record")
```

will mock delete the function *employee_record* in the *employee* module. Thus, in the context of the test environment, this attribute does not exist. We can also specify such an attribute deletion more concisely with

```
monkeypatch.delattr("employee.employee_record")
```

Monkeypatching dictionary values is also a prominent use case. Suppose that we have a dictionary called *travel* and a key in this dictionary which is called "*airline*". We can mock the value for this key as follows:

```
monkeypatch.setitem(travel, "airline", mocked_value)
```

or

```
monkeypatch.setitem("travel.airline", mocked_value)
```

This will set the value of the *airline* key to *mocked_value*.

The following is the syntax to mock the deletion of a dictionary key:

```
monkeypatch.delitem(some_dictionary, "key")
```

or:

```
monkeypatch.delitem("some_dictionary.key")
```

We can also mock environmental variables. In the following example, we mock the value of an environment variable called COLOR:

```
monkeypatch.setenv(COLOR, value)
```

We can mock the deletion of an environment variable called "shell" as follows:

```
monkeypatch.delenv("shell")
```

The functions *monkeypatch.setattr, monkeypatch.delattr, monkeypatch.delitem*, and *monkeypatch.delenv* raise an exception if the target does not exist. The attribute that is being mocked must exist. This is default behavior. If you specify *False* as the last parameter to any of these functions, then an exception will not be raised.

Using Monkeypatching in Unit Tests

A test function that uses monkeypatching must pass *monkeypatch* as a parameter, for example:

```
def test_missing_difficulty_bit(monkeypatch):
    """
    test for missing difficulty bits
    """
    monkeypatch.setattr(tx, "validate_transaction", lambda x, y: True)
    monkeypatch.setitem(block_1, "difficulty_bits", '')

    assert hblockchain.add_block(block_1) == False
```

Note that in this example the dictionary key value for *difficulty_bits* is being mocked as an empty string.

APPENDIX 4

Making Concurrent Python Programs

A set of processes, tasks, or events is said to be concurrent if we do not know which one will finish first. A thread can be thought of as a block of code in a program that runs independently of other code in the program. We say that threads execute concurrently.

When a Python program begins execution, it runs in a main thread of execution. This thread may spawn additional threads in order to perform certain tasks. Hence, a program may consist of the main thread and several concurrently executing threads. For example, we could have a program where one thread is computing and printing Fibonacci numbers, and the second thread is searching for prime numbers and printing them. Because a CPU is extremely fast, it appears to a user that these two threads are executing simultaneously.

Aside from possibly increasing the speed at which a program is executed, one of the main benefits of implementing concurrency in a program is that it can improve program organization by partitioning code into separate tasks that can each run in a separate thread.

Thread Implementation in Python

To get up to speed with concurrency, we are going to write a concurrent Python program with two threads. The first thread will compute and print Fibonacci numbers, and the second thread will search for prime numbers and print them.

A Fibonacci sequence is a set of numbers where the first two numbers are 0 and 1. Each subsequent Fibonacci number is the sum of the previous two numbers. So our Fibonacci sequence looks like this:

```
0,1,1,2,3,5,8,13,21...
```

© Karan Singh Garewal 2020
K. S. Garewal, *Practical Blockchains and Cryptocurrencies*, https://doi.org/10.1007/978-1-4842-5893-4

A prime number is a natural number that is only divisible by itself and 1.

In order to implement threads, our program has to import the threading module:

```
import threading
```

In order to implement Python concurrency, we need Python 3.6 or later.

The fibonacci function is

```
import threading
import time

def fibonacci():
    ctr  = 2
    fib1 = 1
    fib2 = 2
    print("fibonacci number 0 = " + "0")
    print("fibonacci number 1 = " + "1")

    while True:
        tmp  = fib1 + fib2
        fib1 = fib2
        fib2 = tmp
        print("fibonacci no: " + str(ctr) + "  = " + str(fib2))
        ctr += 1
        time.sleep(1)
```

You will notice that this function is an infinite loop. After printing a fibonacci number, the function sleeps for one second and then continues its task when it wakes up.

The prime number function is

```
def prime():
    number = 3
    half   = 3

    while True:
        for ctr in range(half):
            divided = False
```

```
        if ctr < 2: continue
        if number%ctr == 0:
            divided = True
            break

    if divided == False:
        print("next prime number: " + str(number))

    number += 1
    half = int(number/2) + 1
    time.sleep(1)
```

Like the fibonacci function, this is an infinite loop; it sleeps for one second after printing a prime number.

Our program starts and runs in a main thread. The Python code for the main thread is

```
if __name__ == "__main__":
    print("starting program in main thread")

    #Create the Threads
    t1 = threading.Thread(target=fibonacci, args=(), daemon=True)
    t2 = threading.Thread(target=prime, args=(), daemon=True)

    # start the threads
    t1.start()
    t2.start()

    #t1.join()
    #t2.join()

    time.sleep(20)
    print("ending program")
```

The *threading.Thread* function creates a thread that can be executed. The first parameter is the name of the function that will be executed concurrently. The second parameter is a tuple of arguments that is passed to the function. Since our concurrent functions do not have any parameters, we specify empty tuples. The third argument *daemon=True* is optional. If this argument is included, the main program thread will terminate the concurrent threads *t1* and *t2* before it exits.

The two *start* functions initiate the execution of the *t1* and *t2* threads.

379

Put all of the preceding code into a Python script file named *fibprime.py*. Make sure that the program's main thread code is at the bottom of this file and that you have included the *threading* and *time* modules. Now execute this script in your virtual environment:

```
$(virtual) python fibprime.py
```

You should see the fibonacci and prime numbers being printed on your terminal. The main thread creates the fibonacci and prime threads and then sleeps for 20 seconds. After awakening, it terminates the two threads and exits.

The join statement *t1.join* instructs the main thread not to terminate until the *t1* thread has finished with its processing. To be precise, the thread to which the *t1* thread is joined will not terminate until t1 has finished its work; similarly for the t2 thread.

Resource Access with Mutual Exclusion

A mutex synchronizes access to a shared resource. The following code demonstrates how to prevent improper concurrent access to a resource with a mutex:

```
from threading import Lock
balance = 0
hmutex = Lock()

def balance():
        global balance
        hmutex.acquire()
        bal = balance
        hmutex.release()
        return bal
```

We must import the *Lock* module.

We create a lock object called *hmutex*. The *hmutex.acquire* and *hmutex.release* functions wrap around the resource that is to be protected with mutual exclusion. While *hmutex* is in an acquired state, no other concurrent thread will be able to access the balance until the lock is released. The portion of the code that is enclosed by the mutex is called a critical region.

It is important to release a lock after we have finished using the common resource. Failure to do so will result in resource starvation as threads that need the resource keep on waiting for the lock to be released.

The balance function can be written with a context manager; this ensures the release of the mutex:

```
def balance():
    global balance
    with hmutex:
        return balance
```

The lock is automatically released once the code block under the context manager (*with hmutex*) has finished execution.

Deadlocks caused by improper resource locks are another dangerous pitfall in concurrent systems. Consider two concurrently executing threads T1 and T2, which each needs two resources R1 and R2. T1 acquires a lock on R2, and T2 acquires a lock on R1. T1 keeps on waiting for T2 to release its lock, and T2 keeps on waiting for T1 to release its lock. At this point, both threads are deadlocked.

Race Conditions

A data race occurs when two or more threads attempt to access a common resource at the same time. Data races typically occur infrequently and are difficult to debug. The classic exposition of a data race is the bank account bug. This is a canonical type of bug in concurrent systems. It's worthwhile to examine this bug carefully. Take a look at the following pseudo-code:

```
balance = 0

function Deposit(amount) { balance = Balance() + amount }
function Balance() { return balance }

// Alice Bank Account:
function AliceAccount(amount) {
    balance = Balance() + amount
}

// Alice:
AliceAccount(200)
// Smith
Deposit(1000)
```

Consider this scenario; Alice decides to deposit 200 dollars, so she calls the function *AliceAccount* which executes on a concurrent thread (*Alice thread*). The *balance()* function is called and the balance of 0 dollars is read. At this point in time, Smith decides to deposit 1000 dollars in Alice's account; the *Deposit* function is called on another thread. The *Deposit* function calls the *Balance* function to read Alice's bank balance, which is 0 dollars. The thread now completes the deposit action, and at this point, Alice has a balance of 1000 dollars. Now the processor switches back to the *Alice thread* and resumes execution of the code and sets the final balance to 200 dollars. In other words, Smith's deposit of 1000 dollars has been lost. This is a data race condition caused by improper concurrent access to the balance resource.

There are three ways to avoid a data race condition: (1) do not have shared variables, (2) design in such a way that only one function has access to a shared variable, and (3) allow many concurrent threads to access a shared variable, but only one at a time. The third approach is known as mutual exclusion, and the object that implements mutual exclusion is called a *mutex*.

Resource Access with Semaphores

A semaphore is a non-negative integer that synchronizes access to a shared resource. Semaphores are atomic, meaning that the operating system guarantees that an operation changing the value of a semaphore will not be interrupted.

A semaphore is initialized with a value which designates the maximum number of threads that can have concurrent access to the resource which is guarded by the semaphore. A semaphore is decremented each time a lock is acquired, and it is incremented each time a lock is released. If the semaphore has a value of 0, a lock cannot be acquired by any thread until some other thread releases its semaphore lock. It should be clear that a semaphore cannot exceed its initialization value.

The mutex object that we encountered in the last section is in actuality a semaphore initialized with 1.

The following code fragment demonstrates semaphore usage:

```
import threading
balance = 0
semaphore = threading.Semaphore()

def balance():
      global balance
```

```
    semaphore.acquire()
    bal = balance
    semaphore.release()
    return bal
```

We obtain a semaphore object with *threading.Semaphore*. Since we have not specified a value when the semaphore is created, the default value of one is used. The *acquire* and *release* functions wrap around the resource that is to be protected.

It is important to release a semaphore after we are finished with it. The use of a semaphore context manager releases the semaphore automatically once the context block is exited:

```
def balance():
    global balance
    with semaphore:
        return balance
```

Concurrent Asynchronous Functions

Consider the following design pattern that frequently arises in the context of concurrent applications. We have two concurrently executing functions: F() and G(). F() suspends execution waiting for G() to return a result to it. When F() gets the result, it resumes execution. F() is called an asynchronously executing function. We will see this pattern several times in Helium.

We will use the Python *asyncio* package to implement asynchronous, concurrent functions. To examine how *asyncio* works, let us implement our *fibprime* program so that a function called *print_number* prints the fibonacci or prime number after sleeping for a few seconds:

```
import asyncio
import threading
import time
import secrets

async def fibonacci():
    ctr  = 2
    fib1 = 1
    fib2 = 2
```

```python
        print("fibonacci number 0"  + "  = "  + "0")
        print("fibonacci number 1"  + "  = " + "1")

        while True:
            tmp  = fib1 + fib2
            fib1 = fib2
            fib2 = tmp
            message = await print_number(fib2, "F")
            ctr += 1
            time.sleep(1)

async def prime():
    number = 3
    half   = 3

    while True:
        for ctr in range(half):
            divided = False

            if ctr < 2: continue
            if number%ctr == 0:
                divided = True
                break

        if divided == False:
            message = await print_number(number, "P")

        number += 1
        half = int(number/2) + 1
        time.sleep(1)

async def print_number(number: "int", number_type: "F or P" ):
    #F: fibonacci number, P: Prime Number
    nap = secrets.randbelow(3)
    await asyncio.sleep(nap)

    if number_type == "F":
        print("fibonacci no:     " + " = " + str(number))
```

```
    else:
        print("prime number no: " + " = " + str(number))
    return "task executed"
async def main():
    await asyncio.gather(fibonacci(), prime())

if __name__ == "__main__":
    print("starting program in main thread")
    asyncio.run(main())
    print("ending program")
```

The important changes in the source code are emphasized. Copy the previous program into a file called *fibprime2.py* and execute it in your virtual environment:

```
$(virtual) fibprime2.py
```

The module *asyncio* must be imported. There is one cardinal rule with *asyncio*. If a function is to be executed concurrently with this module, then the function declaration has to be preceded with the keyword *async*.

The statement

```
asyncio.run(main())
```

instructs *asyncio* to create an event loop and call *main()*. All concurrent functions will execute under this loop.

The statement in *main()*

```
await asyncio.gather(fibonacci(), prime())
```

directs *asyncio* to execute the *fibonacci* and *prime* functions as concurrent threads under the control of the event loop. The *await* keyword directs the event loop to wait for these two functions to complete.

Now consider the statement

```
result = await print_number(number, "P")
```

in *prime()*. This statement suspends the execution of the *prime* function and passes control back to the event loop. Furthermore, it instructs the event loop to only return to it once the *print_number* function has finished. When *print_number* finishes execution, it passes the result back to the event loop and the event loop sends the result to *prime()*. *prime()* now has the value returned by *print_number,* and it resumes execution.

APPENDIX 5

Object Persistence with Pickle

This appendix introduces you to the Pickle module. Helium uses Pickle to serialize blocks to files. This enables blocks to be read into memory from files. Pickle persists a Python object by converting the object into a sequence of bytes and then storing this raw byte sequence to a file.

Aside from native Python types such as strings, numbers, lists, tuples, sets, and dictionaries, Pickle can convert almost any type of Python object into a sequence of bytes. This conversion is called serialization of the object.

Using Pickle

Here is an example of pickle usage:

```
# pickle_example.py

import pickle
dct = {
        "prevblockhash":    "31651d"
        "version": "1.0"
        "timestamp":  1580399346
        "difficulty_bits": 20
        "nonce": 0
        "merkle_root": "2EECC5"
        "height": 0
        "tx": []

}
```

© Karan Singh Garewal 2020
K. S. Garewal, *Practical Blockchains and Cryptocurrencies*, https://doi.org/10.1007/978-1-4842-5893-4

```
f = open('block_0.dat', 'wb')
pickle.dump(dct, f)
f.close()
```

As this example shows, we open or create a file called *block_0.dat*. The mode '*wb*' means that the file is opened for writing in binary mode and the file will be truncated if it exists and created if it does not exist. Once the file has been opened, we use the *pickle.dump* function to serialize the dictionary *dct* to the file *block_0.dat*. Pickle will throw an exception if serialization fails.

We can use Pickle to retrieve the serialized object from the file *data.pkl* as follows:

```
f = open('block_0.dat', 'rb')
block_0  = pickle.load(f)
```

The file *block_0.dat* is opened in read binary mode. Then the function *pickle.load* is called with the file handle *f* as its argument. pickle deserializes the bytes in the file and recreates the block that was originally serialized.

APPENDIX 6

Helium Remote Procedure Calls

In this appendix, we are concerned with calling functions in remote modules. You should have familiarity with the content in Appendix 4 on concurrent Python programs.

A remote procedure call permits a node on a network to invoke a function on some other remote node and receive the result of this function execution. The request to execute the remote function is encoded as a JSON object and transmitted over the network to a JSON server that is running on the remote node. The server decodes the request and executes the function. Once the function has finished execution, the server packs the return value into a JSON object and sends the reply back to the RPC client that has made the request. Figure A6-1 shows this functionality at work.

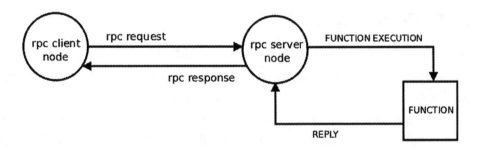

Figure A6-1. *JSON Remote Procedure Calls*

A JSON request and response are both packaged in accordance with the JSON-RPC protocol. This is a very simple text-based protocol. We will use version 2 of this protocol. A request is packaged as the following JSON object:

```
{"jsonrpc": "2.0", "method": "add", "params": {"x": 5, "y": 23}, "id": 3}
```

389

© Karan Singh Garewal 2020

K. S. Garewal, *Practical Blockchains and Cryptocurrencies*, https://doi.org/10.1007/978-1-4842-5893-4

As you will notice, this object is also a Python dictionary object. For all practical purposes, JSON objects and Python dictionaries are indistinguishable.

The particular request earlier is asking the remote server to invoke the function *add* to add two numbers 5 and 23. The *method* attribute in the JSON object specifies the function that is to be executed as a string type. The *params* attribute specifies the function parameters as a JSON object. Note that these are positional parameters. If the function does not have any parameters, we will not send a params attribute. The *id* parameter specifies an identification number that the server will use when it encodes its reply. When the RPC client receives a reply, it uses this *id* to identify the request to which the reply pertains. The *jsonrpc* attribute sets out the version of the JSON-RPC protocol that is being used in the encoding of the request.

An RPC server responds to the request to execute the *add* function by encoding its reply as the following JSON object:

```
{"jsonrpc": "2.0", "result": 28, "id": 3}
```

The *result* attribute is the return value emitted by the *add* function. The *id* attribute identifies the request to which the response pertains. The *jsonrpc* attribute specifies the protocol version number that has been used to encode the result.

Both Bitcoin and Helium use the JSON-RPC protocol to execute remote functions.

Making an RPC Server

In this section, we are going to create an asynchronous JSON-RPC server and demonstrate canonical client-server remote procedure call usage. This model will be used to implement peer-to-peer network functionality in Helium. A function call is synchronous if the caller waits for the function to return a value before proceeding to the execution of the next instruction. A function call is asynchronous if the caller does not wait for the called function to return a value but immediately continues with its processing after making the function call. The caller will process the function value returned (if any) when it arrives some time in the future.

Tornado is a highly scalable, asynchronous networking library.[1] *jsonrpcserver* is a JSON-RPC server built on top of Tornado.[2] Traverse to the root of your Helium environment and install both of these applications:

```
$(virtual) pip install tornado, jsonrpcserver
```

Next, install a JSON-RPC client that will be used to communicate with the server:

```
$(virtual) pip install "jsonrpcclient[tornado]"
```

Go to the root of your Helium virtual environment and make a directory named *tmp* in the Helium root. Copy the following program code to the file *rpc_server.py* and then save this code in the *tmp* directory. This is the code for our JSON-RPC server:

```python
from tornado import ioloop, web
from jsonrpcserver import method, async_dispatch as dispatch

@method
async def fibonacci(m, n):
    n = n+m
    x1 = 0
    x2 = 1
    while True:
        if x2 >= n: return {"method":"fibonacci", "result": x2, "error":
        "none"}
        tmp = x2
        x2 = x2 + x1
        x1 = tmp

class MainHandler(web.RequestHandler):
    async def post(self):
        request = self.request.body.decode()
        response = await dispatch(request)
        print(response)
        if response.wanted:
            self.write(str(response))
```

---

[1]See www.tornadoweb.org/en/stable/
[2]See https://bcb.github.io/jsonrpc/tornado

```
app = web.Application([(r"/", MainHandler)])

if __name__ == "__main__":
    app.listen(address="127.0.0.24", port="8081")
    ioloop.IOLoop.current().start()
```

We have imported modules from *Tornado* and *jsonrpcserver*.

ioloop implements event loop functionality for Tornado, while the *web* module implements an HTTP framework. The *method* module handles functions which are callable through a remote procedure call, while *async_dispatch* handles asynchronous calls to these functions.

A function that is remotely callable must be prefaced with the decorator *@method*, and since the function returns its result asynchronously, the function definition must be prefaced with the *async* keyword.

The *MainHandler* class implements the asynchronous *post* method. This method handles a request by an RPC client for a function invocation. *post* invokes the function and packages function return value as a response which is sent back to the RPC client.

This RPC server has a callable method *fibonacci*.

The *fibonacci* function receives two numbers m and n. It sums these two numbers and computes the first fibonacci number that is greater than this sum. The *fibonacci* function returns a JSON object of the form:

```
{"method":"fibonacci", "result": fib_number, "error": "none"}
```

The *app.listen* function sets the IP address and port on which the server will listen. The *ioloop* statement creates an event-handling loop and starts the server.

Start the RPC server in your virtual environment with

```
$(virtual) python rpc_server.py
```

An RPC client is said to be synchronous if it makes a remote procedure call and then waits for a reply before proceeding. An asynchronous client does not wait for a reply and proceeds with other processing right after making the call. The client processes the reply when it arrives at some point later in time.

The program code for a synchronous JSON RPC client is

```
from jsonrpcclient.clients.http_client import HTTPClient
import json

try:
    client = HTTPClient("http://127.0.0.24:8081")
    print("RPC client is ready")

    response = client.send('{"jsonrpc": "2.0", "method": "fibonacci", \
            "params":{ "m":100, "n":200}, "id":31 }')
    print("have json fibonacci response from server: " + response.text)

    val = response.text
    val = json.loads(val)
    print("result: " + str(val["result"]))
    print("id:   " + str(val["id"]))
    print("fibonacci number is: " + str(val["result"]["result"]))

except Exception as error:
    print(error)
```

This code instantiates an RPC client, connects to the RPC server at 127.0.0.24:8081, and then sends two synchronous requests encoded in the JSON-RPC protocol to the server.

Place this code in a file named *rpc_client.py* and save it in the *tmp* directory. With the RPC server listening, open a new terminal session, traverse to the *tmp* directory, and execute this client in your virtual environment with

```
$(virtual) python rpc_client.py
```

You should see the following terminal output:

```
RPC client is ready
have json fibonacci response from server: {"jsonrpc": "2.0", "result":
{"method": "fibonacci", "result": 377, "error": "none"}, "id": 31}
result: {'method': 'fibonacci', 'result': 377, 'error': 'none'}
id:  31
fibonacci number is: 377
```

The RPC client can also be executed in asynchronous mode. The client RPC program code for this is

```python
import json
from tornado import ioloop
from jsonrpcclient.clients.tornado_client import TornadoClient

try:
    client = TornadoClient("http://127.0.0.24:8081/")

    async def main():
        response = await client.send('{"jsonrpc": "2.0", "method":
        "fibonacci", \
                    "params":{ "m":100, "n":200}, "id":41 }')

        print("have json fibonacci response from server: " + response.text)

    ioloop.IOLoop.current().run_sync(main)

except Exception as error:
    print(error)
```

APPENDIX 7

Simulated Blockchain Automation

The following program code implements a simulated Helium cryptocurrency blockchain that can be automatically created by a user. The user needs to only specify the desired height of the blockchain. This simulated blockchain makes full use of all of the Helium cryptocurrency modules. Furthermore, this synthetic blockchain is created using randomized values.

A simulated blockchain is useful for a number of purposes, including

1. Creating integration tests

2. Examining how blocks in a blockchain relate to each other

3. Experimenting with blockchains that have different characteristics

---

In Chapter 15, a simulated blockchain is used by the Pytest code to test the functionality of the Helium network.

Simulated Blockchain Code Walkthrough

The simulated blockchain constructor requires access to all of the Helium modules including *blk_index*, *hchaindb*, *hmining*, *hconfig*, *hblockchain*, *rcrypt*, and *tx*. The *Chainstate* and *blk_index* databases must be in a running state. The *startup* function starts the *Chainstate* and *blk_index* databases.

© Karan Singh Garewal 2020
K. S. Garewal, *Practical Blockchains and Cryptocurrencies*, https://doi.org/10.1007/978-1-4842-5893-4

Note   The final versions of the Helium modules *blk_index*, *hchaindb*, *hmining*, *hconfig*, *hblockchain*, *rcrypt*, and *tx* are required. See Appendix 10.

The following program code creates a simulated blockchain with 500 blocks.

The function *make_blocks* creates a blockchain. *make_blocks* receives a parameter that specifies the height of the blockchain. This synthetic blockchain simulates the actions of an arbitrary number of users who are conducting transactions on the network. The *make_blocks* function calls the *make_random_transaction* function to create Helium transactions with randomized values. Transactions and blocks are passed through the Helium modules for validation. Valid blocks are attached to the simulated blockchain. The *Chainstate* and *blk_index* databases are updated as required.

It must be noted that as transactions occur over time, the proportion of transaction fragments with very small helium amounts will increase. In an ordinary wallet, the wallet holder can consolidate these small values into one transaction fragment. The simulated blockchain does not do this. The effect of this fragmentation is to cause the blockchain to fail when the desired block height is large. This failure is strictly a consequence of the lack of a function to consolidate transaction fragments with very small helium outputs. I would invite you to write such a consolidation function; this exercise will provide you with a good exposure to blockchain mechanics.

I have used simulated blockchains with a height of 500 in testing.

Copy the following program code into a file called *simulated_blockchain.py* and save it in the *unit_tests* directory. Traverse to the *unit_tests* directory and execute the following command in order to build a simulated blockchain with a height of 500:

```
$(virtual) python simulated_blockchain.py
```

```
#########################################################
# simulated blockchain constructor
#########################################################
import blk_index as blkindex
import hchaindb
import hmining
```

```python
import hconfig
import hblockchain
import rcrypt
import tx
import json
import logging
import pdb
import os
import secrets
import sys
import time

"""

    log debugging messages to the file debug.log
"""

logging.basicConfig(filename="debug.log",filemode="w",  \
format='client: %(asctime)s:%(levelname)s:%(message)s', level=logging.DEBUG)

def startup():
    """

    start the databases
    """

    # start the Chainstate Database
    ret = hchaindb.open_hchainstate("heliumdb")
    if ret == False: return "error: failed to start Chainstate database"
    else: print("Chainstate Database running")
    # start the LevelDB Database blk_index
    ret = blkindex.open_blk_index("hblk_index")
    if ret == False: return "error: failed to start blk_index"
    else: print("blkindex Database running")

def stop():
    """

    stop the databases
    """

    hchaindb.close_hchainstate()
    blkindex.close_blk_index()
```

```python
# unspent transaction fragment values [{fragmentid:value}]
unspent_fragments = []

#######################################################
# Make A Synthetic Random Transaction For Testing
# receives a block no and a predicate indicating
# whether the transaction is a coinbase transaction
#######################################################
def make_random_transaction(blockno, is_coinbase):

    txn = {}
    txn["version"] =   "1"
    txn["transactionid"] = rcrypt.make_uuid()
  if is_coinbase == True: txn["locktime"] = hconfig.conf["COINBASE_LOCKTIME"]
    else: txn["locktime"] = 0

    # the public-private key pair for this transaction
    transaction_keys = rcrypt.make_ecc_keys()

    # previous transaction fragments spent by this transaction
    total_spendable = 0

    ########################
    # Build the vin array
    ########################
    txn["vin"] = []

    # genesis block transactions have no prior inputs.
    # coinbase transactions do not have any inputs
    if (blockno > 0) and (is_coinbase != True):
        max_inputs = secrets.randbelow(hconfig.conf["MAX_INPUTS"])
        if max_inputs == 0: max_inputs = hconfig.conf["MAX_INPUTS"] - 1

        # get some random previous unspent transaction
        # fragments to spend
        ind = 0
        ctr = 0
```

```python
while ind < max_inputs:
    # get a random unspent fragment from a previous block
    index = secrets.randbelow(len(unspent_fragments))
    frag_dict = unspent_fragments[index]
    key = [*frag_dict.keys()][0]
    val = [*frag_dict.values()][0]
    if val["blockno"] == blockno:
        ctr += 1
        if ctr == 10000:
            print("failed to get random unspent fragment")
            return False
        continue

    unspent_fragments.pop(index)

    total_spendable += val["value"]
    tmp = hchaindb.get_transaction(key)
    if tmp == False:
        print("cannot get fragment from chainstate: " + key)

    assert tmp != False
    assert tmp["spent"] == False
    assert tmp["value"] > 0

    # create a random vin element
    key_array = key.split("_")

    signed = rcrypt.sign_message(val["privkey"], val["pubkey"])
    ScriptSig = []
    ScriptSig.append(signed)
    ScriptSig.append(val["pubkey"])

    txn["vin"].append({
            "txid": key_array[0],
            "vout_index": int(key_array[1]),
            "ScriptSig": ScriptSig
        })
```

```
            ctr = 0
            ind += 1

####################
# Build Vout list
####################
txn["vout"] = []

# genesis block
if blockno == 0:
    total_spendable = secrets.randbelow(10_000_000) + 50_000

# we need at least one transaction output for non-coinbase
# transactions
if is_coinbase == True: max_outputs = 1
else:
    max_outputs = secrets.randbelow(hconfig.conf["MAX_OUTPUTS"])
    if max_outputs == 0: max_outputs = 6

ind = 0

while ind < max_outputs:
    tmp = rcrypt.make_SHA256_hash(transaction_keys[1])
    tmp = rcrypt.make_RIPEMD160_hash(tmp)

    ScriptPubKey = []
    ScriptPubKey.append("<DUP>")
    ScriptPubKey.append("<HASH-160>")
    ScriptPubKey.append(tmp)
    ScriptPubKey.append("<EQ-VERIFY>")
    ScriptPubKey.append("<CHECK-SIG>")

    if is_coinbase == True:
        value = hmining.mining_reward(blockno)
    else:
        amt = int(total_spendable/max_outputs)
        value = secrets.randbelow(amt)    # helium cents
        if value == 0:
```

```
                pdb.set_trace()
                value = int(amt / 10)
            total_spendable -= value
            assert value > 0
            assert total_spendable >= 0

        txn["vout"].append({
                "value": value,
                "ScriptPubKey": ScriptPubKey
            })

        # save the transaction fragment
        fragid = txn["transactionid"] + "_" + str(ind)
        fragment = {}
        fragment[fragid] = { "value":value,
                             "privkey":transaction_keys[0],
                             "pubkey":transaction_keys[1],
                             "blockno": blockno
                        }
        unspent_fragments.append(fragment)
        print("added to unspent fragments: " + fragid)

        if total_spendable <= 0: break
        ind += 1

    return txn


##############################################################
# Build some random Synthetic Blocks For Testing.
# Makes num_blocks, sequentially linking each
# block to the previous block through the prevblockhash
# attribute.
# Returns an array of synthetic blocks
##############################################################

def make_blocks(num_blocks):

    ctr = 0
    blocks = []
```

```python
    global unspent_fragments
    unspent_fragments.clear()
    hblockchain.blockchain.clear()

    while ctr < num_blocks:
        block = {
                "prevblockhash": "",
                "version": "1",
                "timestamp": int(time.time()),
                "difficulty_bits": 20,
                "nonce": 0,
                "merkle_root": "",
                "height": ctr,
                "tx": []
            }

        # make a random number of transactions for this block
        # genesis block is ctr == 0
        if ctr == 0: num_transactions = 200
        else:
            num_transactions = secrets.randbelow(50)
            if num_transactions == 0: num_transactions = 40
            num_transactions = 2

        txctr = 0
        while txctr < num_transactions:
            if ctr > 0 and txctr == 0: is_coinbase = True
            else: is_coinbase = False

            trx = make_random_transaction(ctr, is_coinbase)
            assert trx != False
            block["tx"].append(trx)
            txctr += 1

        if ctr > 0:
            block["prevblockhash"] = \
                hblockchain.blockheader_hash(hblockchain.blockchain[ctr - 1])
```

```
        ret = hblockchain.merkle_root(block["tx"], True)
        assert ret != False
        block["merkle_root"] = ret

        ret = hblockchain.add_block(block)
        assert ret == True
        blocks.append(block)
        ctr+= 1

    return blocks

####################################################
# make the simulated blockchain
####################################################
startup()
make_blocks(500)
print("finished synthetic blockchain construction")
stop()
```

APPENDIX 8

Helium Data Structures

In this appendix, we summarize the main data structures of the Helium cryptocurrency. Tokens in angle brackets refer to data types. Brackets as well as the token *list* denote a list.

Blockchain Structures

Primary Blockchain

```
list<block>
```

Secondary Blockchain

```
    list<block>
```

Block

```
            {
                "prevblockhash":   <string>
                "version":         <string>
                "timestamp":       <integer>
                "difficulty_bits": <integer>
                "nonce":           <integer>
                "merkle_root":     <string>
                "height":          <integer>
                "tx":              <list>
            }
```

© Karan Singh Garewal 2020
K. S. Garewal, *Practical Blockchains and Cryptocurrencies*, https://doi.org/10.1007/978-1-4842-5893-4

Block Files

Block filename = "block_" + str(block Height) + ".dat"

Block heights start at 0. The genesis block has height 0.

Transaction Data Structures

Transactions

```
{
        "transactionid": <string>
        "version":       <integer>
        "locktime":      <integer>
        "vin":           list<vin>
        "vout":          list<vout>
}
```

VIN

```
{
  "txid":                <string>
  "vout_index":          <integer>
  "ScriptSig":           list<string>
}
```

VOUT

```
{
   "value":  <integer>,
   "ScriptPubKey": list<string>

}
```

ScriptSig

```
["signature", "public key"]
```

ScriptPubkey

```
["<DUP>", "<HASH-160>", PK_HASH, "<EQ_VERIFY>", "<CHECK-SIG>"]
```

Mining

Address List

```
list<remote node address >
```

Mempool

```
list<transactions>
```

Received Blocks

```
list<blocks>
```

Orphan Blocks

```
list<blocks>
```

APPENDIX 9

Helium Database Maintenance

This appendix contains Python files that rebuild the *Chainstate* and the *blk_index* databases from the Helium blockchain files. Before any of these maintenance functions is invoked, ensure that the corresponding database directory is deleted.

Chainstate Maintenance

Save the program code, infra, to the file *build_chainstate.py*.

Rebuild the Chainstate database as follows. Firstly, ensure that you are in your active Helium virtual environment. Traverse to the directory which will contain the database. Remove the chainstate directory, *heliumdb*, if it exists. Execute the Chainstate maintenance file:

```
$(virtual) python build_chainstate.py
```

```
###########################################################################
# build_chainstate.py: Builds the chainstate database from the blockchain files.
# Ensure that the directory containing the Chainstate is deleted.
###########################################################################
import hblockchain
import hchaindb
import pickle
import os.path
import pdb
```

© Karan Singh Garewal 2020
K. S. Garewal, *Practical Blockchains and Cryptocurrencies*, https://doi.org/10.1007/978-1-4842-5893-4

```python
def startup():
    """

    start the chainstate database
    """

    # start the Chainstate Database
    ret = hchaindb.open_hchainstate("heliumdb")
    if ret == False:
        print("error: failed to start Chainstate database")
        return
    else: print("Chainstate Database running")

def stop():
    """

    stop the chainstate database
    """

    hchaindb.close_hchainstate()

def build_chainstate():
    '''

    build the Chainstate database from the blockchain files
    '''

    blockno  = 0
    tx_count = 0

    try:
        while True:
            # test whether the block file exists
            block_file = "block" + "_" + str(blockno) + ".dat"
            if os.path.isfile(block_file)== False: break

            # load the block file into a dictionary object
            f = open(block_file, 'rb')
            block = pickle.load(f)

            # process the vout and vin arrays for each block transaction
            for trx in block["tx"]:
                ret = hchaindb.transaction_update(trx)
                tx_count += 1
```

```
            if ret == False:
                raise(ValueError("failed to rebuild chainstate. block
                no: " \
                    + str(blockno)))

        blockno += 1

    except Exception as err:
        print(str(err))
        return False

    print("transactions processed: " + str(tx_count))
    print("blocks processed: " +  str(blockno))

    return True

################################
# start the chainstate build
################################
print("start build chainstate")
startup()
build_chainstate()
print("chainstate rebuilt")
stop()
```

blk_index Maintenance

Save the program code, infra, to the file *build_blk_index.py*.

Rebuild the *hblk_index* database as follows. Firstly, make sure that you are in your active Helium virtual environment. Traverse to the directory which will contain this database. Remove the *hblk_index* directory, if it exists. Execute the *blk_index* maintenance file:

```
$(virtual) python build_blk_index.py
```

```
#############################################################################
# build_blk_index: rebuilds the blk_index database from the blockchain
# Ensure that the directory containing this database is deleted first.
```

```python
################################################################################
import blk_index
import pickle
import os.path
import pdb

def startup():
    """
    start/create the hblk_index database
    """
    # start the hblk_index Database
    ret = blk_index.open_blk_index("hblk_index")
    if ret == False:
        print("error: failed to start blk_index database")
        return
    else: print("blk_index Database running")
    return True

def stop():
    """
    stop the blk_index database
    """
    blk_index.close_blk_index()

def build_blk_index():
    '''
    build the blk_index database from the blockchain
    '''
    blockno = 0
    tx_count = 0

    try:
        while True:
            # test whether the block file exists
            block_file = "block" + "_" + str(blockno) + ".dat"
            if os.path.isfile(block_file)== False: break

            # load the block file into a dictionary object
```

```
            f = open(block_file, 'rb')
            block = pickle.load(f)

            # process the transactions in the block
            for trx in block["tx"]:
                ret = blk_index.put_index(trx["transactionid"], blockno)
                tx_count += 1
                if ret == False:
                    raise(ValueError("failed to rebuild blk_index. block
                    no: " \
                        + str(blockno)))

            blockno += 1

    except Exception as err:
        print(str(err))
        return False

    print("transactions processed: " + str(tx_count))
    print("blocks processed: " +  str(blockno))

    return True

############################################
# start the hblk_index database rebuild
############################################
print("start build hblk_index")
ret = startup()
if ret == False:
    print("failed to open hblk_index database")
    os._exit(-1)
build_blk_index()
print("hblk_index database rebuilt")
stop()
```

Helium Source Code Listing

This appendix contains all of the source code pertaining to the Helium cryptocurrency.

Helium Configuration Module

```
"""
hconfig.py:  module contains parameters that are used to configure Helium.
"""

conf = {

    # The Helium version no.
    'VERSION_NO': "1",

    # The maximum number of Helium coins that can be mined
    'MAX_HELIUM_COINS': 21000000,

    # The smallest Helium currency unit
    'HELIUM_CENT':  1/100000000,

    # The maximum size of a Helium block in bytes
    'MAX_BLOCK_SIZE': 1000000,

    # The maximum amount of time in seconds that a transaction can be locked
    'MAX_LOCKTIME': 30*1440*60,

    # The maximum number of Inputs in a Helium Transaction
    'MAX_INPUTS': 10,
```

© Karan Singh Garewal 2020

K. S. Garewal, *Practical Blockchains and Cryptocurrencies*, https://doi.org/10.1007/978-1-4842-5893-4

```
    # The maximum number of Outputs in a Helium Transaction
    'MAX_OUTPUTS': 10,

    # The number of new blocks from a reference block that must be mined before
    # coinbase transaction  in the previous reference block can be spent
    'COINBASE_INTERVAL': 100,

    # The number of blocks for which a coinbase transaction is locked
    'COINBASE_LOCKTIME': 36,

    # The starting nonce value for the mining proof of work computations
    'NONCE': 0,

    # Difficulty Number used in mining proof of work computations
    'DIFFICULTY_BITS': 20,
    'DIFFICULTY_NUMBER':  1/ (10 **20),

    # Retargeting interval in blocks in order to adjust the DIFFICULTY_
    NUMBER
    'RETARGET_INTERVAL': 1000,

    #Mining Reward
    'MINING_REWARD': 5_000_000,

    # Mining reward halving interval in blocks
    'REWARD_INTERVAL': 210000

}
```

The rcrypt Module

```
"""
The rcrypt module implements various cryptographic functions that are
required by
the Helium cryptocurrency application
This module requires the pycryptodome package to be installed.
The base58 package encodes strings into base58 format.
This module uses Python's regular expression module re.
This module uses the secrets module in the Python standard library to generate
```

```
cryptographically secure hexadecimal encoded strings.
"""

# import the regular expressions module
import re
# imports from the cryptodome package
from Crypto.Hash import SHA3_256
from Crypto.PublicKey import ECC
from Crypto.PublicKey import DSA
from Crypto.Signature import DSS
from Crypto.Hash import SHA256
from Crypto.Hash import RIPEMD160

import base58
import secrets

# import Python's debugging and logging modules
import pdb
import logging

"""

    log debugging messages to the file debug.log
"""

logging.basicConfig(filename="debug.log",filemode="w", \
        format='%(asctime)s:%(levelname)s:%(message)s', level=logging.
        DEBUG)

def make_SHA256_hash(msg: 'string') -> 'string':
    """

    make_sha256_hash computes the SHA-256 message digest or cryptographic hash
    for a received string argument. The secure hash value that is generated
    is converted
    into a sequence of hexadecimal digits and then returned by the function.
    The hexadecimal format of the message digest is 64 bytes long.
    """

    #convert the received msg string to a sequence of ascii bytes
    message = bytes(msg, 'ascii')
```

```
    # compute the SHA-256 message digest of msg and convert to a
    hexadecimal format
    hash_object = SHA256.new()
    hash_object.update(message)
    return hash_object.hexdigest()

def validate_SHA256_hash(digest: "string") -> bool:
    """

    validate_SHA256_hash: tests whether a string has an encoding conforming
    to a
    SHA-256 message digest in hexadecimal string format (64 bytes).
    """

    # a hexadecimal SHA256 message digest must be 64 bytes long.
    if len(digest) != 64: return False

    # This regular expression tests that the received string contains only
    # hexadecimal characters
    if re.search('[^0-9a-fA-F]', digest) == None: return True
    return False

def make_RIPEMD160_hash(message: 'byte stream') -> 'string':
    """

    RIPEMD-160 is a cryptographic algorithm that emits a 20 byte message digest.
    This function computes the RIPEMD-160 message digest of a message and
    returns
    the hexadecimal string encoded representation of the message digest (40
    bytes).
    """

    # convert message to an ascii byte stream
    bstr = bytes(message, 'ascii')
    # generate the RIPEMD hash of message
    h = RIPEMD160.new()
    h.update(bstr)
    # convert to a hexadecimal encoded string
    hash = h.hexdigest()
    return hash
```

```python
def validate_RIPEMD160_hash(digest: 'string') -> 'bool':
    """

    tests that a received string has an encoding conforming to a RIPE160
    hash in
    hexadecimal format
    """

    if len(digest) != 40: return False

    # This regular expression tests that received string only contains
    # hexadecimal characters
    if re.search('[^0-9a-fA-F]+', digest) == None: return True

    return False


def make_ecc_keys():
    """

    make a private-public key pair using the elliptic curve cryptographic
    functions in the pycryptodome package.
    returns a tuple with the private key and public key in PEM format
    """

    # generate an ecc object
    ecc_key = ECC.generate(curve='P-256')
    # get the public key object
    pk_object = ecc_key.public_key()
    # export the private-public key pair in PEM format
    p = (ecc_key.export_key(format='PEM'), pk_object.export_
key(format='PEM'))

    return p

def sign_message(private_key: 'String', message: 'String') -> 'string':
    """

    digitally signs a message using a private key generated using the
    elliptic cryptography module of the pycryptodome package.
    Receives a private key in PEM format and the message that is to be
    digitally signed.
    returns a hex encoded signature string.
```

```
    """

    # import the PEM format private key
    priv_key = ECC.import_key(private_key)

    # convert the message to a byte stream and
    # compute the SHA-256 message digest of the message
    bstr = bytes(message, 'ascii')

    hash    = SHA256.new(bstr)
    # create a digital signature object from the private key
    signer = DSS.new(priv_key, 'fips-186-3')

    # sign the SHA-256 message digest.
    signature = signer.sign(hash)
    sig = signature.hex()
    return sig
def verify_signature(public_key: 'String', msg: 'String', signature:
'string') -> 'bool':
    """

    tests whether a message is digitally signed by a private key to which a
    public key is paired.
    Receives a ECC public key in PEM format, the message that is to to be
    verified
    and the digital signature of the message.
    Returns True or False
    """

    try:
        # convert the message to a byte stream and compute the SHA-256 hash
        msg = bytes(msg, 'ascii')
        msg_hash = SHA256.new(msg)

        # signature to bytes
        signature = bytes.fromhex(signature)
        # import the PEM formatted public key and create a signature verifier
        # object from the public key
        pub_key  = ECC.import_key(public_key)
        verifier = DSS.new(pub_key, 'fips-186-3')
```

```
        # Verify the authenticity of the signed message
        verifier.verify(msg_hash, signature)
        return True

    except Exception as err:
        logging.debug('verify_signature: exception: ' + str(err))
def make_address(prefix: 'string') -> 'string':
    """

    generates a Helium address from a ECC public key in PEM format.
    prefix is a single numeric character which describes the type of
    the address. This prefix must be '1'
    """

    key = ECC.generate(curve='P-256')
    __private_key = key.export_key(format='PEM')
    public_key = key.public_key().export_key(format='PEM')

    val = make_SHA256_hash(public_key)
    val = make_RIPEMD160_hash(val)
    tmp = prefix + val

    # make a checksum
    checksum = make_SHA256_hash(tmp)
    checksum = checksum[len(checksum) - 4:]

    # add the checksum to the tmp result
    address = tmp + checksum

    # encode addr as a base58 sequence of bytes
    address =  base58.b58encode(address.encode())

    # The decode function converts a byte sequence to a string
    address = address.decode("ascii")

    return address

def validate_address(address: 'string') -> bool:
    """

    validates a Helium address using the four character checksum appended
```

```
    to the address. Receives a base58 encoded address.
    """

    # encode the string address as a sequence of bytes
    addr = address.encode("ascii")
    # reverse the base58 encoding of the address
    addr = base58.b58decode(addr)
    # convert the address into a string
    addr = addr.decode("ascii")

    # length must be RIPEMD-160 hash length + length of checksum + 1
    if (len(addr) != 45): return False
    if (addr[0] != '1'):  return False

    # extract the checksum
    extracted_checksum = addr[len(addr) - 4:]

    # extract the checksum out of addr and compute the
    # SHA-256 hash of the remaining addr string
    tmp = addr[:len(addr)- 4]
    tmp = make_SHA256_hash(tmp)

    # get the computed checksum from tmp
    checksum = tmp[len(tmp) - 4:]

    if extracted_checksum  == checksum: return True


    return False

def make_uuid() -> 'string':
    """
    makes an universally unique 256 bit id encoded as a hexadecimal string
    that is
    used as a transaction identifier. Uses the Python standard library
    secrets module to
    generate a cryptographically strong random 32 byte string encoded as a
    hexadecimal
    string (64 bytes)
```

```
"""

    id = secrets.token_hex(32)

    return id
```

Helium Blockchain Module

```
"""

hbockchain.py: This module creates and maintains the Helium blockchain
"""

import rcrypt
import hconfig
import hchaindb
import tx
import blk_index as blockindex
import json
import pickle
import pdb
import logging
import os
"""
log debugging messages to the file debug.log
"""

logging.basicConfig(filename="debug.log",filemode="w", format='%(asctime)
s:%(levelname)s:%(message)s',
    level=logging.DEBUG)

"""
A block is a Python dictionary that has the following
structure. The type of an attribute is denoted in angle delimiters.

                {
                    "prevblockhash":   <string>
                    "version":         <string>
                    "timestamp":       <integer>
                    "difficulty_bits": <integer>
```

```
                "nonce":              <integer>
                "merkle_root":        <string>
                "height":             <integer>
                "tx":                 <list>
            }

The blockchain is a list where each list element is a block
This is also referred to as the primary blockchain when used
by miners.
"""

blockchain   = []

"""

secondary block used by mining nodes
"""

secondary_blockchain = []

def add_block(block: "dictionary") -> "bool":
    """

    add_block: adds a block to the blockchain. Receives a block.
    The block attributes are checked for validity and each transaction in
    the block is
    tested for validity. If there are no errors, the block is written to a
    file as a
    sequence of raw bytes. Then the block is added to the blockchain.
    The chainstate database and the blk_index databases are updated.
    returns True if the block is added to the blockchain and False otherwise
    """

    try:
        # validate the received block parameters
        if validate_block(block) == False:
            raise(ValueError("block validation error"))

        # validate the transactions in the block
        # update the chainstate database

        for trx in block['tx']:
            # first transaction in the block is a coinbase transaction
```

```
            if block["height"] == 0 or block['tx'][0] == trx: zero_inputs =
            True
            else: zero_inputs = False

            if tx.validate_transaction(trx, zero_inputs) == False:
                raise(ValueError("transaction validation error"))

            if hchaindb.transaction_update(trx) == False:
                raise(ValueError("chainstate update transaction error"))

        # serialize the block to a file
        if (serialize_block(block) == False):
                raise(ValueError("serialize block error"))

        # add the block to the blockchain in memory
        blockchain.append(block)

        #  update the blk_index
        for transaction in block['tx']:
            blockindex.put_index(transaction["transactionid"],
            block["height"])

    except Exception as err:
        print(str(err))
        logging.debug('add_block: exception: ' + str(err))
        return False

    return True


def serialize_block(block: "dictionary") -> "bool":
    """

    serialize_block: serializes a block to a file using pickle.
    Returns True if the block is serialized and False otherwise.
    """

    index = len(blockchain)
    filename = "block_" + str(index) + ".dat"

    # create the block file and serialize the block
    try:
```

```python
        f = open(filename, 'wb')
        pickle.dump(block, f)

    except Exception as error:
        logging.debug("Exception: %s: %s", "serialize_block", error)
        f.close()
        return False

    f.close()

    return True

def read_block(blockno: 'long') -> "dictionary or False":
    """

    read_block: receives an index into the Helium blockchain.
    Returns a block or False if the block does not exist.
    """

    try:
        block = blockchain[blockno]
        return block

    except Exception as error:
        logging.debug("Exception: %s: %s", "read_block", error)
        return False

    return block


def blockheader_hash(block: 'dictionary') -> "False or String":
    """

    blockheader_hash: computes and returns SHA-256 message digest of a
    block header
    as a hexadecimal string.
    Receives a block those blockheader hash is to be computed.
    Returns False if there is an error, otherwise returns a SHA-256
    hexadecimal string.

    The block header consists of the following block fields:
    (1) version, (2)previous block hash, (3) merkle root
    (4) timestamp, (5) difficulty_no, and (6) nonce.
```

```
    """

    try:
        hash = rcrypt.make_SHA256_hash(block['version'] +
block['prevblockhash'] +
                                    block['merkle_root'] +
                                    str(block['timestamp']) +
                                    str(block['difficulty_bits']) +
                                    str(block['nonce']))

    except Exception as error:
        logging.debug("Exception:%s: %s", "blockheader_hash", error)
        return False

    return hash

def validate_block(block: "dictionary") -> "bool":
    """

    validate_block: receives a block and verifies that all its attributes have
    valid values.
    Returns True if the block is valid and False otherwise.
    """

    try:
        if type(block) != dict:
            raise(ValueError("block type error"))

        # validate scalar block attributes
        if type(block["version"]) != str:
            raise(ValueError("block version type error"))

        if block["version"] != hconfig.conf["VERSION_NO"]:
            raise(ValueError("block wrong version"))

        if type(block["timestamp"]) != int:
            raise(ValueError("block timestamp type error"))

        if block["timestamp"] < 0:
            raise(ValueError("block invalid timestamp"))

        if type(block["difficulty_bits"]) != int:
```

```
        raise(ValueError("block difficulty_bits type error"))

    if block["difficulty_bits"] <= 0:
        raise(ValueError("block difficulty_bits <= 0"))

    if type(block["nonce"]) != int:
        raise(ValueError("block nonce type error"))

    if block["nonce"] != hconfig.conf["NONCE"]:
        raise(ValueError("block nonce is invalid"))

    if type(block["height"]) != int:
        raise(ValueError("block height type error"))

    if block["height"] < 0:
        raise(ValueError("block height < 0"))

    if len(blockchain) == 0 and block["height"] != 0:
        raise(ValueError("genesis block invalid height"))

    if len(blockchain) > 0:
        if block["height"] != blockchain[-1]["height"] + 1:
            raise(ValueError("block height is not in order"))

    # The length of the block must be less than the maximum block size that
    # specified in the config module.
    # json.dumps converts the block into a json format string.
    if len(json.dumps(block)) > hconfig.conf["MAX_BLOCK_SIZE"]:
        raise(ValueError("block length error"))

    # validate the previous block by comparing message digests.
    # the genesis block does not have a predecessor block

    if block["merkle_root"] != merkle_root(block["tx"], True):
        raise(ValueError("merkle roots do not match"))

    if block["height"] > 0:
        if block["prevblockhash"] != blockheader_hash(blockchain[-1]):
            raise(ValueError("previous block header hash does not
            match"))
    else:
```

```
        if block["prevblockhash"] != "":
            raise(ValueError("genesis block has prevblockhash"))

    # genesis block does not have any input transactions
    if block["height"] == 0 and block["tx"][0]["vin"] !=[]:
        raise(ValueError("missing coinbase transaction"))

    # a block other than the genesis block must have at least
    # two transactions: the coinbase transaction and at least
    # one more transaction
    if block["height"] > 0 and len(block["tx"]) < 2:
        raise(ValueError("block only has one transaction"))

    except Exception as error:
        logging.error("exception: %s: %s", "validate_block",error)
        return False

    return True


def merkle_root(buffer: "List", start: "bool" = False) -> "bool or string":
    """
    merkle_tree: computes the merkle root for a list of transactions.
    Receives a list of transactions and a boolean flag to indicate whether
    the function has been called for the first time or whether it is a
    recursive call from within the function.
    Returns the root of the merkle tree or False if there is an error.
    """
    try:
        # if start is False then we verify have a list of SHA-256 hashes
        if start == False:
            for value in buffer:
                if rcrypt.validate_SHA256_hash(value) == False:
                    raise(ValueError("tx list SHA-256 validation failure"))
                buflen = len(buffer)
                if buflen != 1 and len(buffer)%2 != 0:
                    buffer.append(buffer[-1])

        # make the merkle leaf nodes if we are entering the function
```

```
            # for the first time
            if start == True:
                tmp = buffer[:]
                tmp = make_leaf_nodes(tmp)
                if tmp == False: return False
                buffer = tmp[:]

            # if buffer has one element, we have the merkle root
            if (len(buffer) == 1):
                return buffer[0]

            # construct the list of parent nodes from the child nodes
            index = 0
            parents = []

            while index < len(buffer):
                tmp = rcrypt.make_SHA256_hash(buffer[index] + buffer[index+1])
                parents.append(tmp)
                index += 2

            # recursively call merkle tree
            ret = merkle_root(parents, False)

        except Exception as error:
            logging.error("exception: %s: %s", "merkle_root",error)
            return False

        return ret


def make_leaf_nodes(tx_list: "list") -> "List or False":
    """

    make_leaf_nodes: makes the leaf nodes of a merkle tree.
    Receives a list of transactions. If the number of transactions is an
    odd number, appends the last transaction to the list again so that we
    can make a balanced tree.
    Computes the hexadecimal string encoded SHA-256 message digest of each
    transaction and appends it to a leaf node list that is initially empty.
    Returns the leaf node list or False if there is an error
```

```
"""
try:
    # cannot have an empty transaction list
    if (len(tx_list) == 0): raise(ValueError("tx list zero length"))

    # verify we have a list type
    if type(tx_list) is not list: raise(ValueError("tx is not a list
    type"))

    # verify the type of each transaction is a dict
    for tx in tx_list:
        if type(tx) is not dict: raise(ValueError("tx is not a dict type"))

    # must have an even number of transactions
    if len(tx_list) % 2 == 1 or len(tx_list) == 1:
        tx_list.append(tx_list[- 1] )

    # copy the transaction list
    trx_list = list(tx_list)

    # convert each transaction into a JSON string
    tx = []

    for transaction in trx_list:
        tx.append(json.dumps(transaction))

    # make the leaf nodes
    sha256_list = []

    for transaction in tx:
        sha256_list.append(rcrypt.make_SHA256_hash(transaction))

except Exception as err:
    logging.debug('make_leaf_nodes: exception: ' + str(err))
    return False

return sha256_list
```

Helium tx Module

```
"""
The tx module defines the structure of Helium transactions and implements
basic
transaction operations.
"""

import hconfig
import hblockchain as hchain
import hchaindb
import json
import rcrypt
import secrets
import pdb
import logging

"""
log debugging messages to the file debug.log
"""
logging.basicConfig(filename="debug.log",filemode="w",\
  format='%(asctime)s:%(levelname)s:%(message)s', level=logging.DEBUG)

"""
Each transaction is modeled as a dictionary:

                {
                    "transactionid": <string>
                    "version":    <integer>
                    "locktime":   <integer>
                    "vin":        <list<dictionary>>
                    "vout":       <list<<dictionary>>
                }

transactionid is the id of the the present transaction.
vin is a list of spendable inputs that are owned by the entity spending
them.
Each spendable input comes from the vout list of a previous transaction.
Each vin is a list and each element is a dictionary object with the
```

following structure:

vin element:

```
{
    "txid":             <string>
    "vout_index":       <int>
    "ScriptSig":        <list<string>>
}
```

txid is the transaction id of a previous transaction. vout_index is an index into this transaction's vout list.

vout is a list and each element in the vout list is a dictionary with the following structure:

vout element:

```
{
    "value": <integer>,
    "ScriptPubKey": <list<string>>

}
```
"""

```python
def create_transaction(transaction: 'dictionary', zero_inputs:
'boolean'=False) \
    -> 'bool':
    """

    creates a transaction. Receives a transaction object and a predicate.
    zero_inputs is True if the transaction is in the genesis block or if
    the transaction
    is a coinbase transaction, otherwise zero_inputs is False.
    Returns False if the transaction parameters are invalid. Otherwise
     returns True
    """

    if validate_transaction(transaction, zero_inputs) == False: return False
    return True
```

```python
def validate_transaction(trans: "dictionary", zero_inputs: "boolean"=False)
-> "bool":
    """

    verifies that a transaction has valid values.
    receives a transaction and a predicate.
    zero_inputs is True if the transaction is in the genesis block or if
    the transaction
    is a coinbase transaction, otherwise zero_inputs is False.


    The following transaction validation tests are performed:
        (1)  The required attributes are present.
        (2)  The locktime is greater than or equal to zero.
        (3)  The version number is greater than zero.
        (4)  The transaction ID has a valid format.
        (5)  The vin list have positive length.
        (6)  The vin list is not greater than the maximum allowable length.
        (7)  The vin list has valid format.
        (8)  The vout list has positive length.
        (9)  The vout list is not greater than the maximum allowable length.
        (8)  The vout list elements have valid format.
        (9)  The The vout list implements a p2pkhash script.
        (10) The reference to a previous transaction ID is valid.
        (11) The total value spent is less than or equal to the total
                spendable value.
        (12) The spent values are greater than zero.
        (13) The index values in the vin array reference valid elements in the
                vout array of the previous transaction.
        (14) The transaction inputs can be spent
        (15) The genesis block does not have any inputs
    """

    try:
        if type(trans) != dict:
            raise(ValueError("not dict type"))

        # Verify that required attributes are present
```

```python
if trans.get("transactionid") == None: return False
if 'version' not in trans: return False
if trans['locktime'] == None: return False
if trans['vin'] == None: return False
if trans['vout'] == None: return False

# validate the format of the transaction id
if rcrypt.validate_SHA256_hash(trans['transactionid']) == False:
    raise(ValueError("not SHA-256 hash error"))

# validate the transaction version and locktime values
if trans['version'] != hconfig.conf["VERSION_NO"]:
    raise(ValueError("improper version no"))

if trans['locktime'] < 0:
    raise(ValueError("invalid locktime"))

# genesis block or a coinbase transaction do not have any inputs
if zero_inputs == True and len(trans["vin"]) > 0:
    raise(ValueError("genesis block cannot have inputs"))

# validate the vin elements
# there are no vin inputs for a genesis block transaction
spendable_fragments = []

for vin_element in trans['vin']:
    if validate_vin(vin_element) == False: return False
    tx_key = vin_element['txid'] + '_' + str(vin_element['vout_
    index'])

    spendable_fragment = prevtx_value(tx_key)

    if spendable_fragment == False:
        raise(ValueError("invalid spendable input for
        transaction"))
    else:
        spendable_fragments.append(spendable_fragment)

# validate the transaction's vout list
```

```
        if len(trans['vout']) > hconfig.conf['MAX_OUTPUTS'] or
        len(trans['vout']) <= 0:
            raise(ValueError("vout list length error"))

        for vout_element in trans['vout']:
            if validate_vout(vout_element) == False: return False

        # validate the transaction fee
        if zero_inputs == False:
            if (transaction_fee(trans, spendable_fragments)) == False:
            return False

        # test that the transaction inputs are unlocked
        ctr = 0
        for vin in trans['vin']:
            if unlock_transaction_fragment(vin, spendable_fragments[ctr])
            == False:
                raise(ValueError("failed to unlock transaction"))
            ctr += 1

    except Exception as err:
        logging.debug('validate_transaction: exception: ' + str(err))
        return False

    return True


def validate_vin(vin_element: 'dictionary') -> bool:
    """

    tests whether a vin element has valid values
    returns True if the vin is valid, False otherwise
    """

    try:
        if vin_element['vout_index'] < 0: return False
        if len(vin_element['ScriptSig']) != 2: return False
        if len(vin_element['ScriptSig'][0]) == 0: return False
        if len(vin_element['ScriptSig'][1]) == 0: return False

        if rcrypt.validate_SHA256_hash(vin_element['txid']) == False:
```

```
            raise(ValueError("txid is invalid"))

    except Exception as err:

        print("validate_vin exception" + str(err))
        logging.debug('validate_vin: exception: ' + str(err))
        return False

    return True

def validate_vout(vout_element: 'dictionary') -> bool:
    """

    tests whether a vout element has valid values
    returns True if the vout is valid, False otherwise
    """

    try:
        if vout_element['value'] <= 0:
            raise(ValueError("value is <= 0"))

        # validate the p2pkhash script
        if len(vout_element["ScriptPubKey"]) != 5:
            raise(ValueError("ScriptPubKey length error"))

        if vout_element["ScriptPubKey"][0] != '<DUP>':
            raise(ValueError("ScriptPubKey <DUP> error"))

        if vout_element["ScriptPubKey"][1] != '<HASH-160>':
            raise(ValueError("ScriptPubKey <HASH-160> error"))

        if vout_element["ScriptPubKey"][3] != '<EQ-VERIFY>':
            raise(ValueError("ScriptPubKey <EQ-VERIFY> error"))

        if vout_element["ScriptPubKey"][4] != '<CHECK-SIG>':
            raise(ValueError("ScriptPubKey <CHECK-SIG> error"))

        if len(vout_element["ScriptPubKey"][2]) == 0:
            raise(ValueError("ScriptPubKey RIPEMD-160 hash error"))

    except Exception as err:
        print("validate_vout exception" + str(err))
```

```python
        logging.debug('validate_vout: exception: ' + str(err))
        return False

    return True

def prevtx_value(txkey: "string") -> 'bool':
    """

    examines the chainstate database and returns the transaction fragment
    corresponding to txkey:
        {
            "pkkhash":  <string>,
            "value":    <int>,
            "spent":    <bool>,
            "tx_chain": <string>
        }

    receives a transaction fragment key:
            "previous txid" + "_" + str(prevtx_vout_index)

    Returns False if the transaction if does not exist, or if the
    value has  been spent or if value is not a positive integer
    otherwise returns the previous transaction fragment data
    """
    try:
        fragment = hchaindb.get_transaction(txkey)
        if fragment == False:
            raise(ValueError("cannot get fragment from chainstate"))

        # return False if the value has been spent or if the value is
        # not positive

        if fragment["spent"] == True:
            raise(ValueError("cannot respend fragment in chainstate: " +
            txkey))

        if fragment["value"] <= 0:
            raise(ValueError("fragment value <= 0"))

    except Exception as err:
```

```python
        logging.debug('prevtx_value: exception: ' + str(err))
        return False

    return fragment

def transaction_fee(trans: 'dictionary', value_list: 'list<dictionary>' ) \
    -> 'integer or bool':
    """
    calculates the transaction fee for a transaction.
    Receives a transaction and a list of chainstate transaction fragments
    Returns the transaction fee (in helium_cents) or False if there is an error.
    There is no transaction fee for the genesis block or coinbase transactions.
    """
    try:
        spendable_value = 0
        spent_value     = 0

        for val in value_list:
            spendable_value += val["value"]

        for vout in trans['vout']:
            spent_value += vout['value']

        if spendable_value <= 0:
            raise(ValueError("spendable value <= 0 "))

        if spent_value <= 0:
            raise(ValueError("spent value <= 0 "))

        if spendable_value < spent_value:
            raise(ValueError("spendable value < spent value"))

    except Exception as err:
        logging.debug('transaction_fee: exception: ' + str(err))
        return False

    return spendable_value - spent_value

def unlock_transaction_fragment(vinel: "dictionary", fragment:
"dictionary") \
```

```python
    -> "boolean":
    """

    unlocks a previous transaction fragment using the p2pkhash script.
    Executes the script and returns False if the transaction is not unlocked
    Receives: the consuming vin and the previous transaction fragment consumed
    by the vin element.
    """

    try:
        execution_stack = []
        result_stack = []

        # make the execution stack for a p2pkhash script
        # since we only have one type of script in Helium
        # we can use hard-coded values
        execution_stack.append('SIG')
        execution_stack.append('PUBKEY')
        execution_stack.append('<DUP>')
        execution_stack.append('<HASH_160>')
        execution_stack.append('HASH-160')
        execution_stack.append('<EQ-VERIFY>')
        execution_stack.append('<CHECK_SIG>')

        # Run the p2pkhash execution stack
        result_stack.insert(0, vinel['ScriptSig'][0])
        result_stack.insert(0, vinel['ScriptSig'][1])
        result_stack.insert(0, vinel['ScriptSig'][1])

        hash_160 = rcrypt.make_SHA256_hash(vinel['ScriptSig'][1])
        hash_160 = rcrypt.make_RIPEMD160_hash(hash_160)

        result_stack.insert(0, hash_160)
        result_stack.insert(0, fragment["pkhash"])

        # do the EQ_VERIFY operation
        tmp1 = result_stack.pop(0)
        tmp2 = result_stack.pop(0)

        # test for RIPEMD-160 hash match
```

```
    if tmp1 != tmp2:
        raise(ValueError("public key match failure"))

    # test for a signature match
    ret = rcrypt.verify_signature(vinel['ScriptSig'][1],
    vinel['ScriptSig'][1],\
        vinel['ScriptSig'][0])
    if ret == False:
        raise(ValueError("signature match failure"))

except Exception as err:
    logging.debug('unlock_transaction_fragment: exception: ' + str(err))
    return False

return True
```

Helium hchaindb Module

```
"""

Implementation of the Helium chainstate key-value store. This store lets us
access information about transaction fragments through a transaction key.
"""

import hconfig
import rcrypt
import plyvel
import logging
import json
import pdb

"""

log debugging messages to the file debug.log
"""

logging.basicConfig(filename="debug.log",filemode="w", \
    format='%(asctime)s:%(levelname)s:%(message)s', level=logging.DEBUG)

# handle to the Helium Chainstate Database
hDB = None
```

```python
def open_hchainstate(filepath: "string") -> "db handle or False":
    """

    opens the Helium Chainstate key-value store and returns a handle to
    it. The database will be created if it does not exist.  All of the
    directories in filepath must exist.
    Returns a handle to the database or False
    """

    try:
        global hDB
        hDB = plyvel.DB(filepath, create_if_missing=True)

    except Exception as err:
        logging.debug('open_hchainstate: exception: ' + str(err))
        return False

    return hDB

def close_hchainstate() -> "bool":
    """

    close the Helium Chainstate store
    Returns True if the database is closed, False otherwise
    """

    global hDB
    try:
        hDB.close()
        if hDB.closed != True: return False

    except Exception as err:
        logging.debug('close_hchainstate: exception: ' + str(err))
        return False

    return True

def put_transaction(txkey: "string", tx_fragment: "dictionary") -> "bool":
    """

    creates a key-value pair in the Chainstate Database
    Receives a transaction key and a transaction_fragment.
    The transaction key is: transactionid + "_" + str(vout_index)
```

The tx_fragment parameter received is:
```
{
            "pkhash":                   <string>
            "value":                    <int
            "spent":                    <bool>
            "tx_chain"                  <string>
}
```

Returns True if the key-value pair is created and False otherwise
"""
```python
    try:
        # if transaction key already exists delete because
        # the transaction fragment is going to be updated
        encoded_key = str.encode(txkey)
        hDB.delete(encoded_key)

        keyvalue = json.dumps(tx_fragment)
        # save the txkey-fragment pair to the store
        hDB.put(encoded_key, str.encode(keyvalue))

    except Exception as err:
        print(str(err))
        logging.debug('put_transaction: exception: ' + str(err))
        return False

    return True

def get_transaction(key: "string") -> "False or dictionary":
    """
```
Receives a transaction key (transactionid + "_" + str(vout_index))
for a transaction fragment
returns False or the key value. The transaction fragment returned has
form:
```
{
            "pkhash":                   <string>
            "value":                    <string>
            "spent":                    <string>
            "tx_chain"                  <string>
```

```
        }
        """

    try:
        # get the transaction fragment corresponding to the transaction
        # key, return False if the key does not exist
        fragment = hDB.get(str.encode(key))
        if fragment == None:
            raise(ValueError("transaction fragment not found"))

        fragment = json.loads(fragment.decode())

    except Exception as err:
        logging.debug('get_transaction: exception: ' + str(err))
        return False

    return fragment

def transaction_update(trx: "transaction")-> "bool":
    """

        receives a transaction. Updates the chainstate database to
        reflect the transaction. Sets previous transaction fragments
        to indicate that they have been spent. Updates these fragments
        to indicate the transaction id of the consuming transaction.
        returns True or False if there is an error
    """

    try:
        # collect all of the outputs of previous transactions and set them
        to spent
        # specify the transaction key consuming the previous transaction
        inputs

        for vin in trx["vin"]:
            # fetch a previous transaction fragment. It must exist
            prev_tx_key = vin["txid"] + "_" + str(vin["vout_index"])

            tx_fragment = get_transaction(prev_tx_key)
            if tx_fragment == False:
```

```
        print("vin fragment not found: " + prev_tx_key)
        raise(ValueError("transaction fragment not found"))

    # double spend error
    # should be detected prior to writing to the Chainstate
    if tx_fragment["spent"] == True:
        print("fragment is double spend error: " + prev_tx_key)
        raise(ValueError("transaction fragment double spend error:
        " + \
            prev_tx_key))

    # set the spent values to True in the previous transaction
    # fragment
    tx_fragment["spent"] = True

    # set the reference to the consuming transaction
    tx_fragment["tx_chain"] = trx["transactionid"] + "_" +
    str(vin["vout_index"])

    # save to HeliumDB
    ret = put_transaction(prev_tx_key, tx_fragment)
    if ret == False:
        raise(ValueError("failed to update spent tx fragment"))
# put the fragments of the consuming transaction into the HeliumDB
ctr = 0
for vout in trx["vout"]:
    tx_fragment = {}
    txkey = trx["transactionid"] + "_" + str(ctr)
    tx_fragment["pkhash"] = vout["ScriptPubKey"][2]
    tx_fragment["value"] = vout["value"]
    tx_fragment["spent"] = False
    tx_fragment["tx_chain"] = ""

    if put_transaction(txkey, tx_fragment) == False:
        raise(ValueError("failed to insert consuming transaction
        fragment"))

    ctr += 1
```

```
    except Exception as err:
        print(str(err))
        logging.debug('transaction_update: exception: ' + str(err))
        return False

    return True
```

Helium blk_index Module

```
"""

Implementation of the Helium block index key-value store
lets us search for the block that contains a transaction
"""

import plyvel
import pdb
import logging
import json
import rcrypt

"""

log debugging messages to the file debug.log
"""

logging.basicConfig(filename="debug.log",filemode="w",\
    format='%(asctime)s:%(levelname)s:%(message)s',level=logging.DEBUG)

# handle to the Helium blk_index key-value store
bDB = None

def open_blk_index(filepath: "string") -> "db handle or False":
    """

    opens the Helium blk_index store and returns a handle to
    the database. Any directories in filepath must exist. The
    database will be created if it does not exist.
    Returns a handle to the database or False
    """
```

```python
    try:
        global bDB
        bDB = plyvel.DB(filepath, create_if_missing=True)
        print("blk_index opened")
    except Exception as err:
        print("open_blk_index: exception: " + str(err))
        logging.debug("open_blk_index: exception: " + str(err))
        return False

    return bDB

def close_blk_index() -> "bool":
    """
    close the Helium block index store
    Returns True if the database is closed, False otherwise
    """
    try:
        bDB.close()
        if bDB.closed != True: return False

    except Exception as err:
        logging.debug("close_blk_index: exception: " + str(err))
        return False

    return True

def get_blockno(txid: "string") -> "False or integer":
    """
    Receives a transaction id (not a transaction fragment id)
    returns the block no. of the block that contains the transaction:
    """

    try:
        # get the block no, return False if the
        # transaction does not exist in the store
        block_no = bDB.get(str.encode(txid))
        if block_no == None:
            raise(ValueError("txid does not have a block no."))
```

```python
            block_no = block_no.decode()
            block_no = int(block_no)

    except Exception as err:
        logging.debug('get_blockno: exception: ' + str(err))
        return False

    return block_no

def put_index(txid: "string", blockno: "integer") -> "bool":
    """
    Returns True if the trainsactionid_block_no key-value pair is created
    and False otherwise
    """
    try:
        if len(txid.strip()) != 64:
            raise(ValueError("txid invalid length"))

        if len(str(blockno).strip()) == 0:
            raise(ValueError("blockno field is empty"))

        if blockno < 0:
            raise(ValueError("negative blockno"))

        # save the transactionid-block no pair in the store
        bDB.put(str.encode(txid), str.encode(str(blockno)))

    except Exception as err:
        logging.debug('put_blockno: exception: ' + str(err))
        return False

    return True

def delete_index(txid: "string"):
    """
    deletes a (txid, blockno) pair from the blk_index store
    """
    try:
        bDB.delete(str.encode(txid))
```

```python
    except Exception as err:
        logging.debug('delete_tx_blockno: exception: ' + str(err))
        return False

    return True
```

Helium Mining Module

```python
"""
    hmining.py: The code in this module implements a Helium mining node.
    The node is listening for transactions propagating over the Helium
    peer-to-peer
    network.
"""

import blk_index
import hconfig
import hblockchain as bchain
import hchaindb
import networknode
import rcrypt
import tx
import asyncio
import json
import math
import sys
import time
import threading
import pdb
import logging

"""
    log debugging messages to the file debug.log
"""
logging.basicConfig(filename="debug.log",filemode="w", \
    format='%(asctime)s:%(levelname)s:%(message)s',
```

```
    level=logging.DEBUG)
"""
address list of nodes on the Helium network
"""
address_list = []

"""
    specify a list container to hold transactions which are received by the
    miner.
"""
mempool        = []

"""
    blocks mined by other miners which are received by this mining node
    and are to intended to be appended to this miner's blockchain.
"""
received_blocks = []

"""
    blocks which are received and cannot be added to the head of the blockchain
    or the parent of the block at the head of the blockchain.
"""
orphan_blocks = []

"""
list of transactions to be removed from memcache because they are part of a
block that has been mined
"""
remove_list = []

semaphore = threading.Semaphore()

def mining_reward(block_height:"integer") -> "non-negative integer":
    """
    The mining_reward function determines the mining reward.
    When a miner successfully mines a block he is entitled to a reward which
    is a number of Helium coins.
```

```python
    The reward depends on the number of blocks that have been mined so far.
    The initial reward  is hconfig.conf["MINING_REWARD"] coins.
    This reward halves every hconfig.conf["REWARD_INTERVAL"] blocks.
    """

    try:
        # there is no reward for the genesis block
        sz = block_height
        sz = sz // hconfig.conf["REWARD_INTERVAL"]
        if sz == 0:   return hconfig.conf["MINING_REWARD"]

        # determine the mining reward
        reward = hconfig.conf["MINING_REWARD"]
        for __ctr in range(0,sz):
            reward = reward/2

        # truncate to an integer
        reward = int(round(reward))

        # the mining reward cannot be less than the lowest denominated
        # currency unit
        if reward < hconfig.conf["HELIUM_CENT"]: return 0

    except Exception as err:
        print(str(err))
        logging.debug('mining reward: exception: ' + str(err))
        return -1

    return reward

def receive_transaction(transaction: "dictionary") -> "bool":
    """

    receives a transaction propagating over the P2P cryptocurrency network
    this function executes in a thread
    """

    # do not add the transaction if:
    #     it already exists in the mempool
    #     it exists in the Chainstate
```

```
    #      it is invalid

    try:
        # if the transaction is in the mempool, return
        for trans in mempool:
            if trans == transaction: return False

        # do not add the transaction if it has been accounted for in
        # the chainstate database.
        tx_fragment_id = transaction["transactionid"] + "_" + "0"

        if hchaindb.get_transaction(tx_fragment_id) != False:
            return True

        # verify that the incoming transaction is valid
        if len(transaction["vin"]) >  0: zero_inputs = False
        else: zero_inputs = True
        if tx.validate_transaction(transaction, zero_inputs) == False:
            raise(ValueError("invalid transaction received"))

        # add the transaction to the mempool
        mempool.append(transaction)

        # place the transaction on the P2P network for further
        # propagation
        propagate_transaction(transaction)

    except Exception as err:
        logging.debug('receive_transaction: exception: ' + str(err))
        return False

    return True

async def make_candidate_block() -> "dictionary || bool":
    """

    makes a candidate block for inclusion in the Helium blockchain.
    A candidate block is created by:
            (i)  fetching transactions from the  mempool and adding them to
                    the candidate blocks transaction list.
            (ii) specifying the block header.
```

returns the candidate block or returns False if there is an error or if
the mempool is empty.
Executes in a Python thread
"""

```
try:
    # if the mempool is empty then no transactions can be put into
    # the candidate block
    if len(mempool) == 0: return False

    # make a public-private key pair that the miner will use to receive
    # the mining reward as well as the transaction fees.
    key_pair = make_miner_keys()

    block = {}

    # create an incomplete candidate block header
    block['version']   = hconfig.conf["VERSION_NO"]
    block['timestamp'] = int(time.time())
    block['difficulty_bits']   = hconfig.conf["DIFFICULTY_BITS"]
    block['nonce']     = hconfig.conf["NONCE"]

    if len(bchain.blockchain) > 0:
        block['height'] = bchain.blockchain[-1]["height"] + 1
    else:
        block['height'] = 0

    block['merkle_root'] = ""

    # get the value of the hash of the previous block's header
    # this induces tamperproofness for the blockchain
    if len(bchain.blockchain) > 0:
        block['prevblockhash'] = bchain.blockheader_hash(bchain.
        blockchain[-1])
    else:
        block['prevblockhash'] = ""

    # calculate the  size (in bytes) of the candidate block header
    # The number 64 is  the byte size of the SHA-256 hexadecimal
    # merkle root. The merkle root is computed after all the
```

```python
    # transactions are included in the candidate block
    # reserve 1000 bytes for the coinbase transaction
    block_size =  sys.getsizeof(block['version'])
    block_size += sys.getsizeof(block['timestamp'])
    block_size += sys.getsizeof(block['difficulty_bits'])
    block_size += sys.getsizeof(block['nonce'])
    block_size += sys.getsizeof(block['height'])
    block_size += sys.getsizeof(block['prevblockhash'])
    block_size += 64
    block_size += sys.getsizeof(block['timestamp'])
    block_size += 1000

    # list of transactions in the block
    block['tx'] = []

    # get the Unix Time now
    now = int(time.time())

    # add transactions from the mempool to the candidate block until
    # the transactions in the mempool are exhausted or the block
    # attains its maximum permissible size
    for memtx in mempool:
            # do not process future transactions
            if memtx['locktime'] > now: continue

            memtx = add_transaction_fee(memtx, key_pair[1])

            # add the transaction to the candidate block
            block_size += sys.getsizeof(memtx)
            if block_size <= hconfig.conf['MAX_BLOCK_SIZE']:
                block['tx'].append(memtx)
                remove_list.append(memtx)
            else:
                break

    # return if there are no transactions in the block
    if len(block["tx"]) == 0: return False

    # add a coinbase transaction
```

```python
        coinbase_tx = make_coinbase_transaction(block['height'], key_
        pair[1])
        block['tx'].insert(0, coinbase_tx)

        # update the length of the block
        block_size += sys.getsizeof(block['tx'])

        # calculate the merkle root of this block
        ret = bchain.merkle_root(block['tx'], True)

        if ret == False:
            logging.debug('mining::make_candidate_block - merkle root
            error')
            return False

        block['merkle_root'] = ret


        ####################################
        # validate the candidate block
        ####################################
        if bchain.validate_block(block) == False:
            logging.debug('mining::make_candidate_block - invalid block
             header')
            return False

    except Exception as err:
        logging.debug('make_candidate_block: exception: ' + str(err))

    # At this stage the candidate block has been created and it can be mined
    return block

def make_miner_keys():
    """

    makes a public-private key pair that the miner will use to receive
    the mining reward and the transaction fee for each transaction.
    This function writes the  keys to a file and returns hash:
    RIPEMD160(SHA256(public key))
    """
```

```
    try:
        keys    = rcrypt.make_ecc_keys()
        privkey = keys[0]
        pubkey  = keys[1]

        pkhash  = rcrypt.make_SHA256_hash(pubkey)
        mdhash  = rcrypt.make_RIPEMD160_hash(pkhash)

        # write the keys to file with the private key as a hexadecimal string
        f = open('coinbase_keys.txt', 'a')
        f.write(privkey)
        f.write('\n')        # newline
        f.write(pubkey)
        f.write('\n')
        f.close()

    except Exception as err:
        logging.debug('make_miner_keys: exception: ' + str(err))

    return mdhash

def add_transaction_fee(trx: 'dictionary', pubkey: 'string') -> 'dictionary':
    """

    add_transaction_fee directs the transaction fee of a transaction to
    the miner.
    receives a transaction and a miner's public key.
    amends and returns the transaction so that it consumes the transaction fee.
    """

    try:
        # get the previous transaction fragments
        prev_fragments = []

        for vin in trx["vin"]:
            fragment_id = vin["txid"] + "_" + str(vin["vout_index"])
            prev_fragments.append(hchaindb.get_transaction(fragment_id))

        #  Calculate the transaction fee
        fee = tx.transaction_fee(trx, prev_fragments)
```

```
        if fee > 0:
            vout = {}
            vout["value"] = fee
            ScriptPubKey = []
            ScriptPubKey.append('SIG')
            ScriptPubKey.append(rcrypt.make_RIPEMD160_hash(rcrypt.make_
            SHA256_hash(pubkey)))
            ScriptPubKey.append('<DUP>')
            ScriptPubKey.append('<HASH_160>')
            ScriptPubKey.append('HASH-160')
            ScriptPubKey.append('<EQ-VERIFY>')
            ScriptPubKey.append('<CHECK_SIG>')
            vout["ScriptPubKey"] = ScriptPubKey

            trx["vout"].append(vout)

    except Exception as err:
        logging.debug('add_transaction_fee: exception: ' + str(err))
        return False

    return trx

def make_coinbase_transaction(block_height: "integer", pubkey: "string") ->
'dict':
    """

    makes a coinbase transaction, this is the miner's reward for mining
    a block. Receives a public key to denote ownership of the reward.
    Since this is a fresh issuance of heliums there are no vin elements.
    locks the transaction for hconfig["COINBASE_INTERVAL"] blocks.
    Returns the coinbase transaction.
    """

    try:
        # calculate the mining reward
        reward = mining_reward(block_height)

        # create a coinbase transaction
        trx = {}
        trx['transactionid'] = rcrypt.make_uuid()
```

```
        trx['version']  = hconfig.conf["VERSION_NO"]
        # the mining reward cannot be claimed until approximately 100
        blocks are mined
        # convert into a time interval
        trx['locktime'] = hconfig.conf["COINBASE_INTERVAL"]*600
        trx['vin']  = []
        trx['vout'] = []

        ScriptPubKey = []
        ScriptPubKey.append('SIG')
        ScriptPubKey.append(rcrypt.make_RIPEMD160_hash(rcrypt.make_SHA256_
        hash(pubkey)))
        ScriptPubKey.append('<DUP>')
        ScriptPubKey.append('<HASH_160>')
        ScriptPubKey.append('HASH-160')
        ScriptPubKey.append('<EQ-VERIFY>')
        ScriptPubKey.append('<CHECK_SIG>')

        # create the vout element with the reward
        trx['vout'].append({
                            'value':  reward,
                            'ScriptPubKey': ScriptPubKey
                    })

    except Exception as err:
        logging.debug('make_coinbase_transaction: exception: ' + str(err))

    return trx

def remove_mempool_transactions(block: 'dictionary') -> "bool":
    """

    removes the transactions in the candidate block from the mempool
    """

    try:
        for transaction in block["tx"]:
            if transaction in mempool:
                mempool.remove(transaction)
```

```python
    except Exception as err:
        logging.debug('remove_mempool_transactions: exception: ' + str(err))
        return False

    return True

async def mine_block(candidate_block: 'dictionary') -> "bool":
    """
    Mines a candidate block.
    Returns the solution nonce as a hexadecimal string if the block is
    mined and False otherwise

    Executes in a Python thread
    """

    try:
        final_nonce = None
        save_block = dict(candidate_block)

        # Loop until block is mined
        while True:
            # compute the SHA-256 hash for the block header of the
            candidate block
            hash = bchain.blockheader_hash(candidate_block)
            # convert the SHA-256 hash string to a Python integer
            mined_value = int(hash, 16)
            mined_value = 1/mined_value

            # test to determine whether the block has been mined
            if mined_value < hconfig.conf["DIFFICULTY_NUMBER"]:
                final_nonce = candidate_block["nonce"]
                break

            with semaphore:
                if len(received_blocks) > 0:
                    if compare_transaction_lists(candidate_block) == False:
                        return False

            # failed to mine the block so increment the
```

```
            # nonce and try again
            candidate_block['nonce'] += 1

        logging.debug('mining.py: block has been mined')

        # add block to the miner's blockchain
        with semaphore:
            ret = bchain.add_block(save_block)
            if ret == False:
                raise(ValueError("failed to add mined block to blockchain"))

        # propagate the block on the Helium network
        propagate_mined_block(candidate_block)

    except Exception as err:
        logging.debug('mine_block: exception: ' + str(err))
        return False

    return hex(final_nonce)

def proof_of_work(block):
    """

    Proves whether a received block has in fact been mined.
    Returns True or False
    """

    try:
        if block['difficulty_bits'] != hconfig.conf["DIFFICULTY_BITS"]:
            raise(ValueError("wrong difficulty bits used"))

        # compute the SHA-256 hash for the block header of the candidate block
        hash = bchain.blockheader_hash(block)
        # convert the SHA-256 hash string to a Python integer to base 10
        mined_value = int(hash, 16)
        mined_value = 1/mined_value

        # test to determine whether the block has been mined
        if mined_value < hconfig.conf["DIFFICULTY_NUMBER"]: return True

    except Exception as err:
```

```python
        logging.debug('proof_of_work: exception: ' + str(err))
        return False

    return False

def receive_block(block):
    """
    Maintains the received_blocks list.
    Receives a block and returns False if:

    (1)  the block is invalid
    (2)  the block height is less than (blockchain height - 2)
    (3)  block height > (blockchain height + 1)
    (4)  the proof of work fails
    (5)  the block does not contain at least two transactions
    (6)  the first block transaction is not a coinbase transaction
    (7)  transactions in the block are invalid
    (8)  block is already in the blockchain
    (9)  the block is already in the received_blocks list

    Otherwise (i)  adds the block to the received_blocks list
              (ii) propagates the block

    Executes in a python thread
    """

    try:
        # test if block is already in the received_blocks list
        with semaphore:
            for blk in received_blocks:
                if blk == block: return False

        # verify the proof of work
        if proof_of_work(block) == False:
            raise(ValueError("block proof of work failed"))

        # reset the nonce to its initial value
        block["nonce"] == hconfig.conf["NONCE"]

        # validate the block
```

461

```
        if bchain.validate_block(block) == False: return False

        if len(bchain.blockchain) > 0:
            # do not add stale blocks to the blockchain
            if block["height"] < bchain.blockchain[-1]["height"] - 2:
                raise(ValueError("block height too old"))

            # do not add blocks that are too distant into the future
            if block["height"] > bchain.blockchain[-1]["height"] + 1:
                raise(ValueError("block height beyond future"))

        # test if block is in the primary or secondary blockchains
        if len(bchain.blockchain) > 0:
            if block == bchain.blockchain[-1]: return False

        if len(bchain.blockchain) > 1:
          if block == bchain.blockchain[-2]: return False

        if len(bchain.secondary_blockchain) > 0:
            if block == bchain.secondary_blockchain[-1]: return False

        if len(bchain.secondary_blockchain) > 1:
            if block == bchain.secondary_blockchain[-2]: return False

        # add the block to the blocks_received list
        received_blocks.append(block)

        process_received_blocks()

    except Exception as err:
        logging.debug('receive_block: exception: ' + str(err))
        return False

    return True


def process_received_blocks() -> 'bool':
    """

    processes mined blocks that are in the in the received_blocks
    list and attempts to add these blocks to a blockchain.
```

Algorithm:
  (1) get a block from the received blocks list.

  (2) if the blockchain is empty and the block has an empty
       prevblockhash field
       then add the block to the blockchain.

  (3) Compute the block header hash of the last block on the blockchain
       (blkhash).

       if blkhash == block["prevblockhash"] then add the block to the
       blockchain.

  (4) if the blockchain has at least two blocks, then if:
           let blk_hash be the hash second-latest block of the
           blockchain, then if

           block["prevblockhash"] == blk_hash

           create a secondary block consisting of all of the blocks of
           the blockchain
           except for the latest. Append the block to the secondary
           blockchain.

  (5) Otherwise move the block to the orphans list.

  (6) If the received block was attached to a blockchain, for each block
       in the orphans
       list, try to attach the orphan block to the primary blockchain or
       the secondary
       blockchain if it exists.

  (7) If the received block was attached to a blockchain and the
       secondary blockchain has
       elements then swap the blockchain and the secondary blockchain if
       the length of the
       secondary blockchain is greater.

```
(8)   if the receive block was attached and the secondary blockchain has
      elements then
      clear the secondary blockchain if its length is more than two
      blocks behind the
      primary blockchain.

  Note: Runs In A Python thread
  """
  while True:
      # process all of the blocks in the received blocks list
      add_flag = False

      # get a received block
      if len(received_blocks) > 0:
          block = received_blocks.pop()
      else:
          return True

      # add it to the primary blockchain
      with semaphore:
          if bchain.add_block(block) == True:
              logging.debug('receive_mined_block: block added to primary
              blockchain')
              add_flag = True

          # test whether the primary blockchain must be forked
          # if the previous block hash is equal to the hash of the parent
          block of the
          # block at the head of the blockchain add the block as a child
          of the parent and
          # create a secondary blockchain. This constitutes a fork of the
          primary
          # blockchain
          elif len(bchain.blockchain) >= 2 and  block['prevblockhash'] ==
          bchain.blockheader_hash(bchain.blockchain[-2]):
              logging.debug('receive_mined_block: forking the blockchain')
              fork_blockchain(block)
```

```
                if bchain.add_block(block) == True:
                    logging.debug('receive_mined_block: block added to
                    blockchain')
                    add_flag = True

            # add it to the secondary blockchain
            elif len(bchain.secondary_blockchain) > 0 and
            block['prevblockhash'] == bchain.blockheader_hash(bchain.
            secondary_blockchain[-1]):
                swap_blockchains()
                if bchain.add_block(block) == True:
                    logging.debug('receive_mined_block: block added to
                    blockchain')
                    add_flag = True

            # cannot attach the block to a blockchain, place it in the
            orphans list
            else:
                orphan_blocks.append(block)

        if add_flag == True:
            if block["height"] % hconfig.conf["RETARGET_INTERVAL"] == 0:
                retarget_difficulty_number(block)
            handle_orphans()
            swap_blockchains()

            # remove any transactions in this block that are also
            # in the the mempool
            with semaphore:
                remove_mempool_transactions(block)

        propagate_mined_block(block)

    return True

def fork_blockchain(block: 'list') -> 'bool':
```

```python
    """

    forks the primary blockchain and creates a secondary blockchain from
    the primary blockchain and then adds the received block to the
    secondary block
    """

    try:
        bchain.secondary_blockchain = list(bchain.blockchain[0:-1])
        bchain.secondary_blockchain.append(block)

        # switch the primary and secondary blockchain if required
        swap_blockchains()

    except Exception as err:
        logging.debug('fork_blockchain: exception: ' + str(err))
        return False

    return True

def swap_blockchains() -> 'bool':
    """

    compares the length of the primary and secondary blockchains.
    The longest blockchain is designated as the primary blockchain and the
    other
    blockchain is designated as the secondary blockchain.
    if the primary blockchain is ahead of the secondary blockchain by at least
    two blocks then clear the secondary blockchain.
    """

    try:
        # if the secondary blockchain is longer than the primary blockchain
        # designate the secondary blockchain as the primary blockchain
        # and the primary blockchain as the secondary blockchain
        if len(bchain.secondary_blockchain) >= len(bchain.blockchain):
            tmp = list(bchain.blockchain)
            bchain.blockchain = list(bchain.secondary_blockchain)
            bchain.secondary_blockchain = list(tmp)

        # if the primary blockchain is ahead of the secondary blockchain by
        # at least two blocks then clear the secondary blockchain
```

```
        if len(bchain.blockchain) - len(bchain.secondary_blockchain) > 2:
            bchain.secondary_blockchain.clear()

    except Exception as err:
        logging.debug('swap_blockchains: exception: ' + str(err))
        return False

    return True

def handle_orphans() -> "bool":
    """

    tries to attach an orphan block to the head of the primary or secondary
    blockchain.
    Sometimes blocks are received out of order and cannot be attached to
    the primary
    or secondary blockchains. These blocks are placed in an orphan_blocks
    list and as
    new blocks are added to the primary or secondary blockchains, an
    attempt is made to
    add orphaned  blocks to the blockchain(s).
    """

    try:
        # iterate through the orphan blocks attempting to append an orphan
        # block to a blockchain
        if len(bchain.blockchain) == 0: return
        # try to append to the primary blockchain
        for block in orphan_blocks:
            if block['prevblockhash'] == bchain.blockheader_hash(bchain.
            blockchain[-1]):
                if block["height"] == bchain.blockchain[-1]["height"] + 1:
                    bchain.blockchain.append(block)
                    orphan_blocks.remove(block)

                    # remove this orphan blocks transactions from the mempool
                    with semaphore:
                        remove_mempool_transactions(block)
```

```python
            # try to append to the secondary blockchain
            if len(bchain.secondary_blockchain) > 0:
                for block in orphan_blocks:
                    if block['prevblockhash'] == bchain.blockheader_
                    hash(bchain.secondary_blockchain[-1]):
                        if block["height"] == bchain.secondary_blockchain[-1]
                        ["height"] + 1:
                            bchain.secondary_blockchain.append(block)
                            orphan_blocks.remove(block)

                            # remove this blocks transactions from the mempool
                            with semaphore:
                                remove_mempool_transactions(block)

            # remove stale orphaned blocks
            for block in orphan_blocks:
                if bchain.blockchain[-1]["height"] >=3:
                    if bchain.blockchain[-1]["height"] - block["height"] >=
                    2: orphan_blocks.remove(block)

        except Exception as err:
            logging.debug('handle_orphans: exception: ' + str(err))
            return False

        return True

    def remove_received_block(block: 'dictionary') -> "bool":
        """
        remove a block from the received blocks list
        """
        try:
            if block in received_blocks:
                    received_blocks.remove(block)

        except Exception as err:
            logging.debug('remove_received_block: exception: ' + str(err))
            return False

        return True
```

```python
def retarget_difficulty_number(block):
    """

    recalibrates the difficulty number every hconfig.conf["RETARGET_
    INTERVAL"] blocks
    """

    if block["height"] == 0: return

    old_diff_no   = hconfig.conf["DIFFICULTY_NUMBER"]
    initial_block = bchain.blockchain[(block["height"] - hconfig.
    conf["RETARGET_INTERVAL"])]
    time_initial  = initial_block["timestamp"]
    time_now      = block["timestamp"]

    elapsed_seconds = time_now - time_initial
    # the average time to mine a block is 600 seconds
    blocks_expected_to_be_mined = int(elapsed_seconds / 600)
    discrepancy = 1000 - blocks_expected_to_be_mined

    hconfig.conf["DIFFICULTY_NUMBER"] =  old_diff_no - \
        old_diff_no * (20/100)*(discrepancy /(1000 + blocks_expected_to_be_
        mined))

    return

def propagate_transaction(txn: "dictionary"):
    """

    propagates a transaction that is received
    """
    if len(address_list) % 20 == 0: get_address_list()
    cmd = {}
    cmd["jsonrpc"] = "2.0"
    cmd["method"]  = "receive_transaction"
    cmd["params"]  = {"trx":txn}
    cmd["id"] = 0

    for addr in address_list:
        rpc = json.dumps(cmd)
        networknode.hclient(addr,rpc)

    return
```

```python
def propagate_mined_block(block):
    """

    sends a block to other mining nodes so that they may add this block
    to their blockchain.
    We refresh the list of known node addresses periodically
    """

    if len(address_list) % 20 == 0: get_address_list()

    cmd = {}
    cmd["jsonrpc"] = "2.0"
    cmd["method"]  = "receive_block"
    cmd["params"]  = {"block":block}
    cmd["id"] = 0

    for addr in address_list:
        rpc = json.dumps(cmd)
        networknode.hclient(addr,rpc)

    return

def get_address_list():
    '''

    update the list of node addresses that are known
    AMEND IP ADDRESS AND PORT AS REQUIRED.
    '''

    ret = networknode.hclient("http://127.0.0.69:8081",
            '{"jsonrpc":"2.0","method":"get_address_
list","params":{},"id":1}')
    if ret.find("error") != -1: return
    retd = json.loads(ret)

    for addr in retd["result"]:
        if address_list.count(addr) == 0:
            address_list.append(addr)

    return
```

```python
def start_mining():
    """

    assemble a candidate block
    then mine this block
    """

    while True:
        candidate_block = make_candidate_block()
        if candidate_block() == False:
            time.sleep(1)
            continue
        # remove transactions in the mined block from the mempool
        if mine_block(candidate_block) != False:
            remove_mempool_transactions(remove_list)
        else: time.sleep(1)

def compare_transaction_lists(block):
    """

    tests whether a transaction in a received block is also in a candidate
    block that is being mined
    """

    for tx1 in block["tx"]:
        for tx2 in remove_list:
            if tx1 == tx2: return False

    return True


########################################
# start mining in a thread:
# $(virtual) python hmining.py
########################################

if __name__ == "__main__":
    #Create the Threads
    t1 = threading.Thread(target=start_mining, args=(), daemon=True)
    t1.start()
    t1.join()
```

Helium Wallet Module

```
###########################################################################
# wallet.rb: a command-line wallet for Helium
###########################################################################
import hblockchain
import hchaindb
import rcrypt
import logging
import pdb
import pickle

logging.basicConfig(filename="debug.log",filemode="w", \
     format='%(asctime)s:%(levelname)s:%(message)s', level=logging.DEBUG)

# the state of the wallet
wallet_state = {
                 "keys": [],          # list of private-public key tuples
                 "received": [],      # values received by the wallet
                                          holder
                 "spent": [],         # values transferred away by the
                                          wallet holder
                 "received_last_block_scanned": 0,
                 "spent_last_block_scanned": 0
               }

def create_keys():
    key_pair = rcrypt.make_ecc_keys()
    wallet_state["keys"].append(key_pair)

def initialize_wallet():
    wallet_state["received"] = []
    wallet_state["spent"] = []
    wallet_state["received_last_block_scanned"] = 0
    wallet_state["spent_last_block_scanned"] = 0

def value_received(blockno:"integer"= 0) -> "list" :
    """
```

obtains all of the helium values received by the wallet-holder by examining
transactions in the blockchain from and including blockno onwards.
Updates the wallet state.
```python
"""

hreceived = []
tmp = {}

try:
# get values received from the blockchain
    for block in hblockchain.blockchain:
        if block["height"] < blockno: continue

        for transaction in block["tx"]:
            ctr = -1
            for vout in transaction["vout"]:
                ctr += 1
                for key_pair in wallet_state["keys"]:
                    if rcrypt.make_RIPEMD160_hash(rcrypt.make_SHA256_
                    hash(key_pair[1])) \
                        == vout["ScriptPubKey"][2]:
                        tmp["value"] = vout["value"]
                        tmp["blockno"] = block["height"]
                        tmp["fragmentid"] =
                        transaction["transactionid"] + "_" + \
                            str(ctr)
                        tmp["public_key"] = key_pair[1]
                        hreceived.append(tmp)
                        break

    # update the wallet state
    last_block = hblockchain.blockchain[-1]
    if last_block["height"] > wallet_state["received_last_block_
    scanned"]:
        wallet_state["received_last_block_scanned"] = last_
        block["height"]
```

```
        for received in hreceived:
            wallet_state["received"].append(received)

    except Exception as err:
        print(str(err))
        logging.debug('value_received exception: ' + str(err))
        return False

    return

def value_spent(blockno:"integer"= 0):
    """

    obtains all of the helium values transferred by the wallet-holder by
    examining transactions in the blockchain from and including blockno.
    onwards. Updates the wallet state.
    """

    hspent = []
    tvalue = {}

    try:
        # get values spent from  blockchain transactions
        for block in hblockchain.blockchain:
            if block["height"] < blockno: continue

            for transaction in block["tx"]:
                for vin in transaction["vin"]:
                    for key_pair in wallet_state["keys"]:
                        \prevtxid =  vin["transactionid"] + "_" +
                        str(vin["vout_index"])
                        fragment = hchaindb.get_transaction(prevtxid)

                        if \
                    rcrypt.make_RIPEMD160_hash(rcrypt.make_SHA256_
                    hash(key_pair[1])) \
                            == fragment["pkhash"] :
                            tvalue["value"] = vin["value"]
                            tvalue["blockno"] = block["height"]
```

```
                        tvalue["fragmentid"] = vin["transactionid"] +
                        "_" \
                            + str(vin["vout_index"])
                        tvalue["public_key"] = key_pair[1]
                        hspent.append(tvalue)
                        break

        last_block = hblockchain.blockchain[-1]
        if last_block["height"] > wallet_state["spent_last_block_scanned"]:
            wallet_state["spent_last_block_scanned"] = last_block["height"]

        for spent in hspent:
            wallet_state["spent"].append(spent)

    except Exception as err:
        print(str(err))
        logging.debug('value_sent: exception: ' + str(err))
        return False

    return

def save_wallet() -> "bool":
    """

    saves the wallet state to a file
    """

    try:
        f = open('wallet.dat', 'wb')
        pickle.dump(wallet_state, f)
        f.close()
        return True

    except Exception as error:
        print(str(error))
        return False

def load_wallet() -> "bool":
    """

    loads the wallet state from a file
    """
```

```
    try:
        f = open('wallet.dat', 'rb')
        global wallet_state
        wallet_state = pickle.load(f)
        f.close()
        return True

    except Exception as error:
        print(str(error))
        return False
```

Helium Directory Server Module

```
'''
start a directory server on 127.0.0.69:8081
'''

import hmining
from tornado import ioloop, web
from jsonrpcserver import method, async_dispatch as dispatch
import ipaddress
import json
import threading
import pdb
import logging

# A Fake list of addresses for testing only
address_list = ["127.0.0.10:8081", "127.0.0.11:8081", "127.0.0.12:8081",
"127.0.0.13:8081", \
            "127.0.0.14:8081", "127.0.0.15:8081", "127.0.0.16:8081",
            "127.0.0.17:8081", \
            "127.0.0.18:8081", "127.0.0.19:8081", "127.0.0.20:8081" ]

logging.basicConfig(filename="debug.log",filemode="w",  \
format='server: %(asctime)s:%(levelname)s:%(message)s', level=logging.
DEBUG)
```

```python
@method
async def get_address_list():
    with hmining.semaphore:
        ret = address_list
    return ret

@method
async def register_address(address: "string"):
    global address_list
    try:
        # validate IP address and port format: addr:port
        if address.find(":") == -1: return "error-invalid address"
        addr_list = address.split(":")
        addr_list[1]=addr_list[1].strip()
        if len(addr_list[0]) == 0 or len(addr_list[1]) == \
            0: return "error-invalid address: " + address
        if int(addr_list[1]) <= 0 or int(addr_list[1]) >= \
            65536: return "error-invalid address: " + address

        _ = ipaddress.ip_address(addr_list[0])
        addr = addr_list[0] + ":" + addr_list[1]
        if addr not in address_list:
            with hmining.semaphore:
                address_list.append(addr)
        return address

    except Exception as err:
        logging.debug('directory server::register address - ' + str(err))
        return "error-register address"

class MainHandler(web.RequestHandler):
    async def post(self):
        request = self.request.body.decode()
        logging.debug('decoded server request =  ' + str(request))
        response = await dispatch(request)
        print(response)
        self.write(str(response))
```

```python
app = web.Application([(r"/", MainHandler)])

# start the network interface for a node on the local loop: 127.0.0.69:8081
if __name__ == "__main__":
    app.listen(address="127.0.0.69", port="8081")
    logging.debug('server running')
    print("directory server started at 127.0.0.69:8081")
    ioloop.IOLoop.current().start()
```

Helium Networknode Module

```python
'''

netnode: implementation of a synchronous RPC-Client node that makes remote
procedure calls to RPC servers using the JSON RPC protocol version 2, and
a JSON-RPC server that responds to requests from RPC client nodes.
'''

import blk_index as blkindex
import hblockchain
import hchaindb
import hmining
import networknode
from    tornado import ioloop, web
from    jsonrpcserver import method, async_dispatch as dispatch
from    jsonrpcclient.clients.http_client import HTTPClient
import ipaddress
import threading
import json
import pdb
import logging
import os
import sys

logging.basicConfig(filename="debug.log",filemode="w",  \
format='server: %(asctime)s:%(levelname)s:%(message)s', level=logging.
DEBUG)
```

```
####################################
# JSON-RPC Client
####################################

def hclient(remote_server, json_rpc):
    '''
    sends a synchronous request to a remote RPC server
    '''
    try:
        client = HTTPClient(remote_server)

        response = client.send(json_rpc)
        valstr = response.text
        val = json.loads(valstr)
        print("result: " + str(val["result"]))
        print("id:   " + str(val["id"]))
        return valstr

    except Exception as err:
        logging.debug("node_client: " + str(err))
        return '{"jsonrpc": "2.0", "result":"error", "id":"error"}'

########################################
# JSON-RPC Server
########################################

address_list = []

@method
async def receive_transaction(trx):
    """
    receives a transaction that is propagating on the Helium network
    """
    try:
        hmining.semaphore.acquire()
        ret = hmining.receive_transaction(trx)
        hmining.semaphore.release()
        if ret == False: return "error: invalid transaction"
        return "ok"
```

```
        except Exception as err:
            return "error: " + err

@method
async def receive_block(block):
    """

    receives a block that is propagating on the Helium network
    """

    try:
        ret = hmining.receive_block(block)
        if ret == False: return "error: invalid block"
        return "ok"
    except Exception as err:
        return "error: " + err

@method
async def get_block(height):
    """

    returns the block with the given height or an error if the block
    does not exist
    """

    with hmining.semaphore:
        if len(hblockchain.blockchain) == 0:
            return ("error: empty blockchain")

        if height < 0 or height > hblockchain.blockchain[-1]["height"]:
            return "error-invalid block height"

    block = json.dumps(hblockchain.blockchain[height])
    return block

@method
async def get_blockchain_height():
    """

    returns the height of the blockchain. Note that the first block has
    height 0
    """

    with hmining.semaphore:
```

```
            if hblockchain.blockchain == []: return -1
            height = hblockchain.blockchain[-1]["height"]

        return height

@method
async def clear_blockchain():
    """

    clears the primary and secondary blockchains.
    """

    with hmining.semaphore:
        hblockchain.blockchain.clear()
        hblockchain.secondary_blockchain.clear()
    return "ok"

class MainHandler(web.RequestHandler):
    async def post(self):
        request = self.request.body.decode()
        logging.debug('decoded server request =  ' + str(request))
        response = await dispatch(request)
        print(response)
        self.write(str(response))

def startup():
    '''

    start node related systems
    '''

    try:
        # remove any locks
        os.system("rm -rf ../data/heliumdb/*")
        os.system("rm -rf ../data/hblk_index/*")
        # start the Chainstate Database
        ret = hchaindb.open_hchainstate("../data/heliumdb")
        if ret == False: return "error: failed to start Chainstate
        database"
        else: print("Chainstate Database running")
        # start the LevelDB Database blk_index
```

```
            ret = blkindex.open_blk_index("../data/hblk_index")
            if ret == False: return "error: failed to start blk_index"
            else: print("blkindex Database running")

    except Exception:
            return "error: failed to start Chainstate database"

    return True

app = web.Application([[(r"/", MainHandler)]])

#######################################################
# start the network interface for the server node on
# the localhost loop: 127.0.0.19:8081
#######################################################
if __name__ == "__main__":
    app.listen(address="127.0.0.51", port="8081")
    logging.debug('server node is running')
    print("network node starting at 127.0.0.51:8081")

    ##############################
    # start this node
    ##############################

    if startup() != True:
        logging.debug('server node resource failure')
        print("stopping")
        sys.exit()

    logging.debug('server node is running')
    print('server node is running')

    ###############################
    # start the event loop
    ###############################
    ioloop.IOLoop.current().start()
```

Index

A

Advanced Encryption Standard (AES), 33
app.listen function, 351
Asymmetric key, 48, 58
Authenticity, 37, 43, 45

B

Basic attention token (BAT), 19, 24
Binance Coin (BNB), 19, 25, 27
Bitcoin, 1, 12–15, 121, 181, 182
Bitcoin Cash (BCH), 19, 21, 22, 27
BitTorrent, 16, 25, 26
blk_index database
    code, 203–205
    interface functions, 202
    Pytests, 206, 207
blk_index database, 328–330
blk_index maintenance, 411–413
Block, 64
Blockchain, 59, 61–63
    attributes, 96
    block fields, 98
    blockheader_hash function, 94
    config module, 99
    crypto packages, 79, 80
    dictionary data structure, 92, 93
    exception error, 100
    hblockchain.py, 93
    module, 207–209
    Pytest primer, 86
    Python logger, 91

rcrypt code, 80–86
read_block function, 94
unit tests, 87–90
validate_block function, 94
Blockchain maintenance
    get_block, 313
    peer-to-peer network, 313
Block checks, 216
Brave browser, 24
Brute-force attack, 31

C

Caesar cipher, 30
Canonical transaction processing, 149
Canonical transaction structure, 116
    execution stack, 126–132
    Heliums, 121
    locktime, 117
    mechanics, 118, 119
    unlocked, 133
    vin list, 117
    vout list, 117
Cassandra, 63
Chainstate database
    code, 185–190
    interface functions, 184, 185
    pk_hash, 184
    public-private key pairs, 183
    Pytests, 191–195, 197–200
    structure, 183
    transaction key, 183